HANSARD SOCIETY SERIES IN POLITICS AND GOVERNMENT

Edited by F.F. Ridley

HANSARD SOCIETY SERIES IN POLITICS AND GOVERNMENT

Edited by F.F. Ridley

The Quango Debate, edited with David Wilson

British Government and Politics since 1945: Changes in Perspectives, edited with Michael Rush

Sleaze: Politicians, Private Interests and Public Reaction, edited with Alan Doig

Women in Politics, edited with Joni Lovenduski and Pippa Norris

Under the Scott-Light: British Government seen Through the Scott Report, edited with Brian Thompson

Britain Votes 1997, edited with Pippa Norris and Neil T. Gavin

Protest Politics: Cause Groups and Campaigns, edited with Grant Jordan

Parliament in the Age of the Internet, edited by Stephen Coleman, John Taylor and Wim van de Donk

Democracy and Cultural Diversity, edited by Michael O'Neill and Dennis Austin

Britain Votes 2001, edited by Pippa Norris

The Hansard Society Series in Politics and Government brings to the wider public the debates and analyses of important issues first discussed in the pages of its journal, Parliamentary Affairs

Britain Votes 2001

Edited by Pippa Norris

OXFORD
UNIVERSITY PRESS

in association with
HANSARD SOCIETY SERIES IN POLITICS
AND GOVERNMENT

OXFORD

UNIVERSITY PRESS

Great Clarendon Street, Oxford OX2 6DP

Oxford University Press is a department of the University of Oxford.
It furthers the University's objective of excellence in research, scholarship,
and education by publishing worldwide in

Oxford New York

Athens Auckland Bangkok Bogota Buenos Aires Calcutta
Cape Town Dar es Salaam Delhi Florence Hong Kong Istanbul
Karachi Kuala Lumpur Madrid Melbourne Mexico City Mumbai
Nairobi Paris São Paulo Shanghai Singapore Taipei Tokyo Toronto Warsaw

and associated companies in
Berlin Ibadan

Oxford is a registered trade mark of Oxford University Press
in the UK and in certain other countries

Published in the United States
by Oxford University Press Inc., New York

The moral rights of the author have been asserted

Database right Oxford University Press (maker)

First published 2001

A catalogue for this book is available from the British Library

Library of Congress Cataloging in Publication Data

ISBN 019 851049 7

Typeset by SetSystems Ltd, Saffron Walden, Essex
Printed in Great Britain by Headley Brothers Limited, The Invicta Press,
Ashford, Kent and London
on acid-free paper

Contents

Contributors

Judith Bara is Research Fellow in the Department of Government, University of Essex

Michael Billig, Professor of Social Science, Department of Social Sciences, Loughborough University

Alice Brown is Pro-Vice Principal and Professor of Politics at the University of Edinburgh

Ian Budge is Professor of Government at the University of Essex

Harold Clarke is Ashbel Smith Distinguished Professor, School of Social Sciences, University of Texas at Dallas and co-director of the 2001 British Election Study

Daniel Collings is a freelance writer, whose work includes *Britain Under Thatcher* (Longman, 1999) and who worked in television news during the 2001 election campaign

Philip Cowley is Lecturer in Politics and Deputy Director of the Centre for Legislative Studies at the University of Hull

Stephen Coleman is Director of the Hansard e-democracy programme and Lecturer in Media and Communication at the London School of Economics and Political Science

Ivor Crewe is Vice Chancellor and Professor of Government at the University of Essex

John Curtice is Deputy Director, ESRC Centre for Research into Elections and Social Trends (CREST) and Professor of Politics, Strathclyde University

David Deacon is Senior Lecturer in Communication and Media Studies, Department of Social Sciences, Loughborough University

David Denver is Professor of Politics at Lancaster University

Geoffrey Evans is Official Fellow in Politics at Nuffield College, Oxford

Justin Fisher is Lecturer in Political Science at Brunel University

Peter Golding, Professor of Sociology, and Head of Department of Social Sciences, Loughborough University

Joni Lovenduski is Professor of Politics at Birkbeck College, University of London

Paul Mitchell is Lecturer in European Politics and Political Methodology, London School of Economics and Political Science

Brendan O'Leary is Professor of Political Science at the London School of Economics and Political Science

Pippa Norris is Associate Director (Research) at the Shorenstein Center, John F. Kennedy School of Government, Harvard University

Shamit Saggar is Reader in Politics at Queen Mary College, University of London

David Sanders is Professor of Government at the University of Essex and co-director of the 2001 British Election Study

Anthony Seldon is Founding Director (with Peter Hennessy) of the Institute of Contemporary British History and Headmaster of Brighton College

Patrick Seyd is Professor of Politics at the University of Sheffield

Marianne Stewart is Professor of Government, Politics and Political Economy, University of Texas at Dallas and co-director of the 2001 British Election Study

Dafydd Trystan is Lecturer in the Department of International Politics at the University of Wales, Aberystwyth

Richard Wyn Jones is Senior Lecturer and Director of the Institute of Welsh Politics in the Department of International Politics at the University of Wales, Aberystwyth

Paul Whiteley is Professor of Government at the University of Essex and co-director of the 2001 British Election Study

PIPPA NORRIS

Apathetic Landslide: The 2001 British General Election

With dawn breaking on the morning of 8 June, Tony Blair flew back to the Millbank celebration knowing that Labour had achieved yet another historic victory. The election saw the return of 413 Labour MPs, almost two-thirds of the Commons. Tony Blair's second administration has an unassailable 167-seat parliamentary majority, more than Mrs Thatcher enjoyed at the apex of her success. Landslides are not uncommon in British politics: understood as a majority of about 100 seats or more, there have been 13 in the 27 general elections since 1900. But back-to-back landslides are far rarer. Given Labour's record-breaking 179-seat majority in 1997, many expected the pendulum in British politics to swing back to normal: every other temporary Labour peak (in 1929, 1945, 1966) saw a substantial fall in the subsequent election. But this time Labour MPs fell by only six. After four years dallying on the hard opposition benches, the number of Tory MPs rose by a grand total of one. Far from Blair's bubble bursting, it was not even deflated.

So what explains the remarkable scale of the second Labour landslide? The fact that the size of Blair's majority had been confidently predicted in opinion polls for months and months does not make the outcome any less puzzling or intriguing. Especially since this was the British Labour Party—characterised in the early 1980s by a shrinking working-class inner-city base, unpopular policies on unilateral disarmament, trade unions, and nationalisation, and deep internal organisational splits and factions—which many commentators had written off on the assumption that the Conservatives were 'the natural party of government'. As discussed throughout this volume, the outcome of the election is open to multiple interpretations. Theories of *political communication* focus on the month of the general election campaign and the strategic decisions taken by party leaders and campaign professionals about the battleground issue agenda, as well as the pattern of news coverage and reports in the opinion polls. Alternative theories of

economic voting suggest that the seeds of the Labour victory could have
been sown long before Tony Blair even went to the Palace, if the
performance of the Labour government, particularly Gordon Brown's
macroeconomic management, was decisive for the outcome. By proving
a safe pair of hands on the basics of inflation, jobs and interest rates,
Labour may have overcame long-standing fears about their economic
competence. Accounts based on *social dealignment* emphasise the way
that Labour has reinvented itself under successive leaders since the early
1980s as a catch-all party, overcoming the limitations of its shrinking
base by appealing across regional divisions and class lines. Lastly,
theories of *policy mood cycles* suggest that the major changes may have
occurred even earlier, based on the underlying dynamics of public
opinion, and the way that parties have or have not responded to these
tides, with Labour moved to capture the centre-ground of British
politics, thereby becoming the least-worse choice of middle England,
while the Liberal Democrats shifted towards the left, and the Conservatives remained with clear blue water on the far right.

The first part of this introduction highlights and summarises the
major features of the election results—with each topic covered in
greater depth in subsequent chapters—including the striking impact of
the British electoral system, the main reasons for the plummeting
turnout, and the significant changes in party fortunes. Subsequent
sections discuss alternative theories explaining the outcome, and the
conclusion considers the implications for the future of British party
politics.

A popular mandate?

As first glance, the day after the election, the frontpage pictures of the
Sunday-best Blair family outside of No. 10 and headlines trumpeting
Labour predominance at Westminster suggest a groundswell of public
support and a renewed mandate for an overwhelmingly popular government at a time of widespread peace and prosperity. But closer examination shows that Labour's success rested on a more fragile popular
mandate.

THE ELECTORAL SYSTEM: First, Labour's landslide of seats was based
on 40.7% of the UK vote, which was slightly lower than the share of
the vote won in successive elections by Mrs Thatcher and John Major
(see Figure 1). It was the workings of the electoral system that generated
Labour's parliamentary success. The British system of first-past-the-post
generally produces a manufactured 'winner's bonus', exaggerating the
proportion of seats won by the party in first place compared with their
proportion of votes. For proponents of plurality elections, this bias is a
virtue since it can guarantee a decisive outcome at Westminster, and a
workable parliamentary majority, even in a close contest in the electorate.[1] One simple way to capture the size of the 'winner's bonus'

Figure 1. UK Seats and Votes, 1900–2001

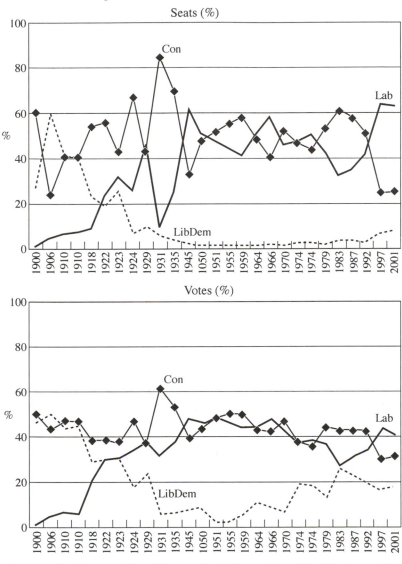

Source: Colin Rallings and Michael Thrasher, *British Electoral Facts 1832–1999*, Ashgate, 2000; British Parliamentary Constituency Database, 1992–2001.

produced by the electoral system is to divide the proportion of votes into the proportion of seats. A ratio of 1:1 would suggest no bias at all. But as Figure 2 shows, the bias in the 'winner's bonus' has fluctuated but also gradually risen since the 1950s. In this election, the winner's bonus was the highest ever recorded in the postwar era. As well as the steady rise, there was also a step-change evident in 1974 due to the growing vote-winning power of the minor parties. This phenomenon is

Figure 2. Government's Ratio of Votes to Seats

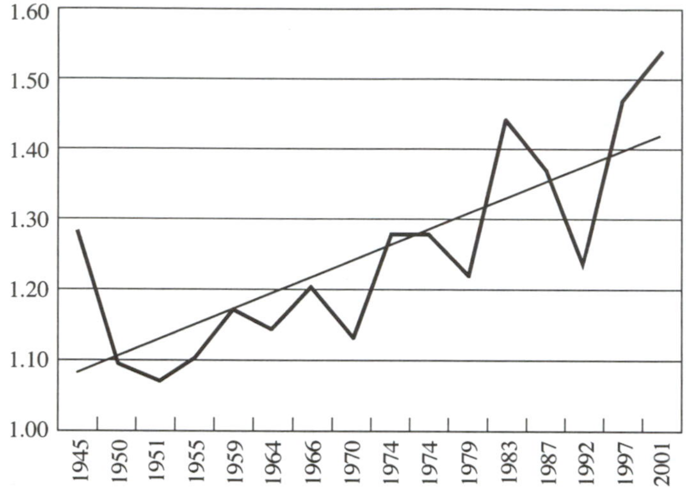

Note: The votes—seats ratio calculated as the proportion of UK votes cast for the government divided into the proportion of UK seats held by the government. Sources: Calculated from Colin Rallings and Michael Thrasher, *British Electoral Facts 1832–1999*, Ashgate, 2000; British Parliamentary Constituency Database, 1992–2001.

the product of three factors, discussed in detail later in this volume by Curtice: the geographical spread of party support, the effects of anti-Conservative tactical voting, and disparities in the size of constituency electorates. The Conservatives remain the one party that is most firmly opposed to any reform of first-past-the-post for Westminster, yet ironically they, more than Labour, might well benefit from such a development.

Even more disheartening for the Conservatives, like rolling a Sisyphean bolder up a hill, given the current electoral system, any subsequent reversal in Tory fortunes almost certainly requires more than one more heave. Depriving Labour of their overall majority in the next election needs a uniform national swing towards the Conservatives of at least 6.5% (see Table 1). A swing of 9% means that the Conservatives become the largest party. But *winning the next election requires a Lab–Con swing of 10.5% for the Conservatives to have an overall majority of one*, a Herculean task twice the size of any swing experienced by the Conservatives in the postwar era. Labour did achieve just such a massive swing in 1997 but only by virtually reinventing itself. If the Conservatives merely draw even in votes with Labour this simply won't do the trick; if both major parties got 36.2% of the vote in the next election, for example, Labour would still have 151 more seats and a comfortable majority. The bias of the electoral system is such that the Conservatives need a 13% vote lead over Labour to form the next government.

1. Projections of Seat Change By Uniform Vote Swing in the Next General Election

Swing	% UK vote			Number of seats				Govnt	Parl. maj.
	Con	Lab	LibDem	Con	Lab	LibDem	Other		
−1.0	30.7	41.7	18.3	159	416	54	28	Lab	175
0.0	31.7	40.7	18.3	166	413	52	28	Lab	167
1.0	32.7	39.7	18.3	177	406	48	28	Lab	153
2.0	33.7	38.7	18.3	184	400	47	28	Lab	141
3.0	34.7	37.7	18.3	198	388	44	29	Lab	117
4.0	35.7	36.7	18.3	208	379	43	29	Lab	99
5.0	36.7	35.7	18.3	232	357	41	29	Lab	55
6.0	37.7	34.7	18.3	249	341	40	29	Lab	23
6.5	38.2	34.2	18.3	263	328	39	29	–	–
7.0	38.7	33.7	18.3	274	317	39	29	–	–
8.0	39.7	32.7	18.3	287	306	38	28	–	–
9.0	40.7	31.7	18.3	300	293	38	28	–	–
10.0	41.7	30.7	18.3	315	279	37	28	–	–
10.5	42.2	30.2	18.3	330	268	35	26	Con	1
11.0	42.7	29.7	18.3	337	262	34	26	Con	15
12.0	43.7	28.7	18.3	352	247	33	27	Con	45

Note: The estimates assume a Con–Lab uniform national swing across the UK with no change in the share of the vote for the other parties. Source: British Parliamentary Constituency Database, 1992–2001.

TURNOUT: Moreover, turnout plummeted, from 71.5% to 59.4%, the lowest since the khaki election of 1918 (see Figure 3). Four out of ten voters stayed home so that any electoral mandate was grudging and tepid, vitiating the sense that the public had given the government a fresh popular mandate and that Labour has won the electorate's 'hearts and minds' for the reform of public services, for entry of Britain into the Euro, or for other aspects of the Blair project. Voting tumbled most sharply in safe Labour seats — places like Liverpool Wavertree, Stockport, Bootle — while falling far less in marginal Conservative seats such

Figure 3. UK Turnout, 1900–2001 (%)

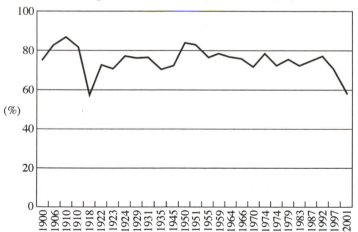

Note: UK Turnout is based on the number of votes cast as a proportion of the eligible electorate.
Sources: Colin Rallings and Michael Thrasher, *British Electoral Facts 1832–1999*, Ashgate, 2000; British Parliamentary Constituency Database, 1992–2001.

as Norfolk North and Hexham, where parties had greater motivation
to mobilise support and voters had more incentive to feel that casting a
ballot could make a difference to the outcome. One consequence was a
reduction in the North-South divide in party support. Turnout was also
stronger in Northern Ireland, with highly competitive parties offering
alternative visions of the peace process. Attempts to boost participation
by devices such as easier access to postal ballots failed to reverse the
tide. The most plausible reason for the fall in turnout was less a
dramatic crisis of British democracy, as some suggest, nor even widespread public cynicism, nor even a uniform cross-national trend, but
probably the more prosaic fact that the Labour victory had been
predicted in the polls and popular commentary for so long that few
people felt that participating could make much difference to the outcome. Ever since 1997, poll-after-poll by the major national companies
reported a 15–20 point Labour lead, with the Conservatives trailing at
about 30%, and the Liberal Democrats becalmed before the campaign
at about 13%. Before the polling stations had closed, one bookmaker
even started paying out to punters who had placed a flutter on a Labour
victory. In 1997 the country, gripped by the scale of the Conservative
defeat, had stayed up on election night for Portillo. At its peak, 12.7
million people tuned into the election night specials in 1997, or about
one third of the electorate.[2] In 2001, the country barely stayed up for
the first declaration in Sunderland South: at most, the BBC and ITV
drew 7.3 million viewers. Comparative evidence around the world
suggests that turnout is closely associated with the pattern of party
competition. Compared with more competitive contests, voting participation is usually about 10% lower in elections where the leading
party has 50% or more of the popular vote in an election and others
trail far behind, as the pre-election and campaign polls suggested was
the case in Britain.[3]

Labour's victory was also tempered and cautious because, at least on
the more impressionistic basis of the campaign polls, the overwhelming
public mood suggested a prevalent sense of tepid ennui, a potent mix of
disaffection and impatience. Rather than displaying an enthusiastic
endorsement of the Labour Party, the public seemed resigned to giving
the government another chance to get it right this time and to fix basic
public services like schools, hospitals and trains. While Blair attracted
lukewarm support, there was unwillingness to forgive the Conservatives
for their 18-year rule, fractious squabbling, unpopular policies and
ineffective leadership. The pervasive sentiment, perfectly encapsulated
in Sharon Storrer's televised harangue of Tony Blair about health
services, was that Labour had been given a massive parliamentary
majority in 1997, which the government squandered by overcaution
and lack of courage, and by too much positive spin surrounding
promises about the radical changes they were going to produce in stark
contrast to the mouse that they had actually achieved. There was strong

2. The Share of the Vote, 1997–2001

| | Percentage UK vote | | | Percentage GB |
	1997	2001	Change	2001
Labour	43.3	40.7	−2.6	42.0
Conservative	30.7	31.7	+1.0	32.7
Liberal Democrat	16.8	18.3	+1.5	18.8
SNP	2.0	1.8	−0.2	1.8
Plaid Cymru	0.5	0.7	+0.2	0.8
Other	6.8	6.8	0.0	3.9
Turnout	71.5	59.4	−12.1	
Lab to Con swing			1.8	

Source: British Parliamentary Constituency Database, 1992–2001.

criticism from the centre-left that Labour had adopted Conservative limits on public spending during their first two years, when the public preferred better services, even at the cost of some tax increases. Sensing this mood, the mantra of Labour's campaign became roll-up-the-sleeves delivery, delivery, delivery on schools and hospitals, hospitals and schools. Blair's speeches emphasised how much had to be done before the railways ran on time, the NHS had more nurses and doctors, and schools more teachers and higher standards. Even after the Blair family re-entered No. 10, there was a sense of post-electoral triste rather than flag-waving enthusiasm.

Nevertheless, the outcome remains a solid victory for Blair (see Tables 2 and 3). Labour lost eight seats and gained two (Dorset South from the Conservatives and Ynys Mon from Plaid Cymru). They did particularly well by advancing in swathes of southern England, notably in Greater London, as well as in many middle-class suburbs and prosperous retirement areas. The electoral map has been transformed as Blair consolidated his grip over large areas of England that had seemed beyond Labour's grasp throughout the 1980s and early 1990s, increasing the Labour vote against the national trend in place like Dorset and Sussex, Wiltshire and Kent. The Conservatives gained nine seats but

3. Share of UK Seats, 1997–2001

	At election 1 May 1997	At dissolution 14 May 2001	Gains	Losses	Net change	New Parliament after 7 June 2001	Percentage of seats
Labour	418	419	2	8	−6	413	62.7
Conservative	165	161	9	8	+1	166	25.2
LibDem	46	47	8	2	+6	52	7.9
SNP	6	6	0	1	−1	15	0.8
PC	4	4	1	1	0	4	0.6
N. Ireland	19	19	6	6	0	19	2.9
Independent	1	1	1	1	0	1	0.2
Labour maj.	179	179				167	
Total	659	659				659	100

Note: Including the Speaker and Deputy Speaker. Source: British Parliamentary Constituency Database, 1992–2001.

lost eight in the process. William Hague promptly resigned; he had set himself a minimal target of thirty net gains to continue as Conservative leader. With only 166 seats, except for the 1997 election, the result represents the lowest number of Conservative MPs since 1906. More-over, with the exception of a solitary gain in Scotland (Galloway and Upper Nithsdale, from the SNP), the Conservatives remain confined to rural and suburban England, and wiped out of the rest of Scotland and Wales. Parallels are commonly drawn between the current result and Michael Foot's disastrous defeat in 1983 but, in fact, the Conservatives have far fewer MPs today than Labour had at the depths of *their* slough of despond. In 2001 the Conservatives won just 31.7% of the UK vote, their second worst result since the Great Reform Act of 1832. The elections saw a Lab–Con swing of 1.8 percentage points, but this was nowhere near the 11.6% swing required in the last election to bring the removal trucks back to No. 10.

THE FORTUNES OF THE MINOR AND FRINGE PARTIES: The Liberal Democrats remained firmly in third place in this election, but Charles Kennedy had good cause to break out the champagne since his parlia-mentary party swelled from 47 to 52 MPs, the highest number since the old Liberals in 1929. The Liberal Democrat share of the vote rose by only 1.5%, but the party deployed their limited resources strategically, consolidating Liberal Democrat support by far more than average with tactical voting in their own marginals like Kingston and Surbiton (+23.5%) and Torbay (+10.9%). The Liberal Democrats won seven Conservative seats, probably due to effective grassroots canvassing, leafleting, and get-out-the-vote drives. There is also evidence that, despite all the speculation in the press, new tactical voting had little impact in securing further seat gains: in the dozen Con–LibDem ultra-marginals (with a majority of 5% or less), the fall in the Labour vote and the rise in the Liberal Democrat vote was roughly similar to the national swing. The Liberal Democrats boosted their support in true-blue Guildford (where their share of the vote went up by 8.4%), Ludlow (+13.5%), and post-by-election Romsey (+17.5%). In contrast, the Conservatives only exacted revenge by winning the Liberal Demo-crats seats of the Isle of Wight and Taunton. As discussed in detail in subsequent chapters, in Scotland, the SNP lost 2% of their vote, returning only five MPs (losing one). In Wales, Plaid Cymru boosted their share of the vote by 4%, although making no net advance on their four MPs. In Northern Ireland hard-line nationalists and hard-line unionists gained seats and votes, although on a moderated platform, with the consequences for the future of the province currently remaining unclear.

The fringe parties provided minor skirmishes in the battleground: the Greens fought 145 seats but got on average only 1,135 votes per seat, with their best performances in Brighton Pavilion (with 9% of the vote) as well as Bradford West and Hornsey Wood Green, and their greatest regional strength in Greater London and the South West. The better-funded UK Independence Party ran 423 candidates but failed to get more than 1,000 votes on average per seat, including in Dover, despite all the press coverage of the asylum issue there, proving strongest in the south-west of England. On the far right, the British National Party contested only 34 seats but they attracted considerable publicity by their results in Oldham West and Royton (6,552 votes) and Oldham East and Saddleworth (5,091), touched by heated racial conflagration during the campaign. Overall 3,294 candidates stood, or on average five per seat, slightly down on the 1997 election.

Explaining the Labour landslide

THE ELECTION CAMPAIGN: Did the campaign matter? There are many reasons why it could potentially have made an important difference to the outcome. Theories of dealignment suggest that today the British electorate has become far more detached from their partisan and social roots.[4] If tribal loyalties have withered, this suggests that many voters have become more willing to switch party based on the appeal of particular issues and leaders, the messages and images communicated via the mass media, and short-term events occurring during the month-long campaign. The recent literature in political communications, which once stressed 'minimal effects', has similarly come to recognise that campaigns do have the *potential* capacity to matter both for civic engagement and for political persuasion.[5] These general assumptions also permeate accounts provided by many journalists and popular commentators who emphasise that the heart of the problem facing the Conservatives was bound up in the campaign, including the unpopularity of William Hague as a leader, unable to connect with the British public. The strategy of using resolutely old-fashioned soap-box oratory and gut instincts in the days of professionalised political marketing, and the fact that the Tory campaign fought aggressively, and perhaps even successfully in achieving media headlines early in the campaign, but on the wrong agenda. The Conservatives banged on about the Euro, asylum seekers, tax cuts, and crime, in a dialogue of the deaf, while the public remained more concerned about schools and hospitals. The Conservative Party machine showed evidence of organisational disarray at the grass roots, eroding activism, and reduced revenues, all of which meant that Smith Square was probably out-spun, out-organised and out-spent by Labour's Millbank machine. Conservative Party membership has plummeted from an estimated 756,000 in 1992 down to 400,000 in 1997, then to about 330,000 today. The Conservatives also faced an uphill task in getting their message across in this election because most of the press had turned against them, with *The Times* and the *Economist* endorsing Labour for the first time in their histories (see Deacon, Golding and Billig this volume), and the opinion polls had predicted their wipe-out for four years (see Crewe). In this perspective, the campaign was principally to blame for the defeat, but the Conservative Party retains the capacity to spring back to life as 'the natural party of government' with the prospect of solid gains under new leadership. The party has been radically reconstructed before: under Benjamin Disraeli after 1846, Winston Churchill a century later, and Margaret Thatcher in the mid-1970s.

But in practice did the month-long campaign change any hearts and minds, or merely function to reinforce long-standing preferences and consolidate partisan dispositions? The British Election Study (BES) campaign tracking 'rolling' thunder survey, with daily samples conducted by Gallup, suggests minimal shifts registered during the campaign from 14 May until 6 June in leadership popularity, likelihood of voting, and issue preferences. There was evidence of flagging interest during the middle of the campaign but this recovered again by polling day. The survey evidence, from the published campaign polls by MORI, ICM, Gallup and NOP, suggests that Conservative support, like an ER patient, essentially flat-lined. Electoral flux may have occurred, as people vacillated, but this did not result in a strong tidal flow in Conservatives fortunes. At the same time, there was a perceptible improvement in support for the Liberal Democrats at the expense of Labour, as shown by Figure 4 summarising trends in voting intentions throughout the campaign where Liberal Democrat support rises from about 13% at the start to 18% at the end. Yet as Denver discusses later, the exact reasons for this improvement are not clear. It may be the result of their greater media exposure during elections, due to the rules of party balance governing television news and current

Figure 4. Campaign Opinion Polls, 2001

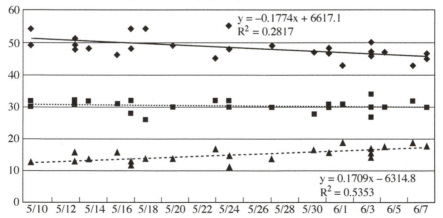

Note: The figure includes data from all published national opinion polls by the major companies (MORI, NOP, ICM, Gallup) from 8 May until 6 June 2001 and the regression line representing the best fit of the trends.

affairs during elections. Or the gain could be attributed to the systematic bias of positive news coverage in their favour, as documented in content analysis of newspapers by Echo Research.[6] Or the explanation may rest on their high-energy, low-budget, no-frills campaign headed by Charles Kennedy. What is clear, however, is that no matter how much the Conservatives managed to set the news agenda in the early stages by focusing aggressively on their 'keep the pound', anti-asylum seekers, and tax-cutting campaign, no matter the Labour flubs and flurries of the St Saviour's and St Olave's one-spin-too-many launch, the Prescott Punch and the Storrer harangue, the Conservatives failed to gain momentum with the public. This does not imply that alternative campaign strategies, issue agendas, and leadership images during the general election campaign could not have improved Conservative fortunes. The initial results of experimental research suggests that different patterns of news coverage and party election broadcasts could have a significant impact on what the public learnt about the major issues during the election, as well as levels of party support.[7] But in practice, given the strategies adopted by parties and the news media, this potential was never realised. There is a growing body of evidence that campaigns *can* make an important difference; whether they *do* is another matter.

OR THE ECONOMY, STUPID: Econometric models provide an alternative tack. In this view, elections are rarely won or lost in the space of a month-long campaign. Instead government popularity is a predictable function of the 'pocket-book' economy and how well most people feel that they have been doing in the run up to polling day.[8] Commentators on the centre-left commonly criticised the constraints on the public purse under Gordon's Brown's 'Iron Chancellorship', and the fact that spending on services like health and education dipped below the levels set by the previous Major government. Nevertheless, leaving aside for one moment the issue of public spending, the 'dog that didn't bark' during the election was Labour's macroeconomic performance. The standard bread-and-butter indicators on the economy tell the story. Inflation as measured by the retail price index was 2.1% in May, falling slightly over the previous 12-months and lower that the European Union average. Mortgage bills fell in May with a cut in interest rates. Jobs continued to grow in Britain with the ILO unemployment rate standing at 5% in spring 2001, down 0.7 on a year earlier, and the number of people claiming unemployment-related benefits also fell.[9] With the combined 'misery index' in single digits, the performance of the pocket-book economy looked reasonably rosy. Retail sales in May 2001 were up, showing their highest annual growth for four years. The United States experienced a slump in November 2000, triggered in large part by the bursting of the 'dot.com' high-tech bubble, as well as the Bush administration's use of the 'r' word (recession) to justify a $1.35

4. The Issue Agenda in the British Campaign, 2001

Issue	Public opinion	Labour	Rank Conservative	Liberal Democrat
Healthcare	1	1	4	3
Education	2	3	5	2
Law and order	3	7	6	9
Pensions	4	15	11	6
Taxation	5	4	2	1
Public transport	6	10	14	11
The economy	7	5	7	8
Unemployment	8	18	27	29
Immigration/asylum	9	12	3	10
Europe	10	2	1	5

Note: see Table 1. The figures give the rank for the 'most important problem' in the MORI poll of public opinion published in *The Times* on 7 June and the rank in how much issue coverage of parties was devoted to each issue in the daily newspapers. Source: Echo Research, www.echoresearch.com.

trillion tax cut, and this American slow-down did depress sectors of the British economy like telecoms. Nevertheless overall, compared with the US or EU, Britain's economy remained buoyant.

Not surprisingly the issue of macroeconomic *performance* (as distinct from levels of public spending and taxation) did not feature as a major concern among the public; in MORI polls published on 7 June, when the public was asked about the most important problem facing the country, the economy was ranked seventh and unemployment eighth, with inflation not even included in the top ten issues (see Table 4). In the news media's agenda, as well, economic performance issues rarely played a prominent role. Echo Research's content analysis of the press revealed that taxation and spending were heavily featured in the news, but unemployment was hardly mentioned at all. The analysis in this volume by Sanders takes a closer look at this issue and the extent that the 'pocket book' economy influenced patterns of party support. But according to the standard view presented in economic theories of voting, at a time of widespread peace and prosperity, it would have been difficult, if not impossible, for any Conservative leader, no matter how determined, charismatic and popular, to mount an effective challenge to the Labour government. In this sense, oppositions do not 'win' elections, but governments can certainly lose them.

THE IMPACT OF SOCIAL DEALIGNMENT: But by itself a strong economic performance, while facilitating a Labour victory, fails adequately to explain the scale of the Conservative defeat and their failure to advance in previous areas of the country where they were strong throughout the 1980s. One popular explanation lies in theories of social dealignment — that Labour was able to reach beyond its core base to maximise support from all sectors of society. Catch all parties appeal beyond particular areas of the country or their class base to form an electoral coalition attracting widespread backing.

The geography of the vote, and in particular the closure of the

5. The North–South Divide

Year	Conservative vote (%)			Labour vote (%)		
	North	South		North	South	
1992	30.7	69.2	100%	50.6	49.4	100%
1997	29.0	70.9	100%	46.5	53.4	100%
2001	28.3	71.6	100%	45.0	54.9	100%

Note: The figures measure the proportion of Conservative and Labour votes from the South and the North. The South equals Greater London, the South East, South West, East Anglia and Midlands. The North equals the remainder of Britain. Source: British Parliamentary Constituency Database, 1992–2001.

North-South divide for Labour, was critical to the outcome. Closer analysis revealed that vote gains for the Conservatives were wastefully distributed, so that in most of their target seats the Conservatives fell back rather than advancing. By appealing to their hard-core base of elderly true believers in the English countryside, the Conservatives failed to attract many waverers by an anti-Euro, pro-tax cut platform. The Tory vote rose by 2.6% in Conservative-held seats, but by only 0.17% in Labour-held seats, and it actually fell (by −0.15%) in Liberal Democrat-held constituencies. The North-South divide can be summarised most simply by measuring the proportion of votes that Labour and the Conservatives each get from the South and the North (see Table 5). Since 1992 Labour has strengthened support in the South, as they have gathered votes outside of their city bastions like Liverpool, Glasgow and Newcastle. In 2001, Labour got almost six million votes in the South and almost five million in the North. In contrast, the Conservatives remain confined to middle-England: they won almost six million votes in the South but only 2.4 million in the North (see Figure 5).

Not only did geography become less important in predicting Labour support, social class eroded as the classic-defining cleavage in twentieth-century British politics. Blair made further inroads into the leafy suburbs of Brent North, Enfield Southgate, Wimbledon and Bristol West. At the same time Labour support drained away most where it did not matter, in safe Labour seats, like Birmingham Perry Bar, South Shields, and Leicester East where, rather than defecting, Labour voters stayed home in massive numbers. Social dealignment is shown by comparing party support against the socio-economic profile of constituencies provided in the 1991 Census. The correlations in Table 6 confirm that as usual the Labour vote remained strongest in the last general election in bedrock working-class seats. Nevertheless, the change in the share of the vote from 1997 to 2001 reveals that, in contrast to the national swing, Labour support swelled in middle-class constituencies with many professional, managerial and skilled white-collar residents, as well as in suburban areas of homeowners. In contrast the Labour vote eroded consistently in working-class neighbourhoods, especially urban areas with many poorer residents living in council estates. The aggregate MORI campaign poll confirms these patterns at individual level, with

Figure 5. The UK Electoral Map, 2001

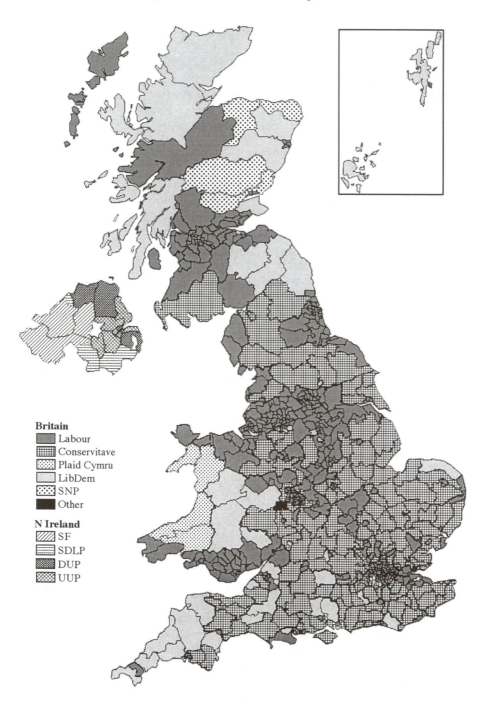

Britain
- Labour
- Conservitave
- Plaid Cymru
- LibDem
- SNP
- Other

N Ireland
- SF
- SDLP
- DUP
- UUP

6. Vote by Type of Seat

% Of each socio-economic group	2001			Change 1997–2001		
	Con	Lab	LibDem	Con	Lab	LibDem
I: Professional	.441	−.436	.339	−.259	.164	
II: Managerial and technical	.661	−.676	.384		.230	−.090
IIIN: Skilled non-manual	−.308			−.379	.126	.136
IIIM: Skilled manual	−.181	.429	−.309	.287	−.204	−.086
IV: Partly skilled	−.530	.499	−.295	.093	−.235	
V: Unskilled	−.716	.480	−.241	−.085	−.231	.123

Note: The figures represent the correlation between the 2001 share of the vote (and the change in the share of the vote 1997–2001) and the demographic characteristics of the seat derived from the 1991 Census. Only significant correlations (with probabilities greater than .05) are reported. Source: British Parliamentary Constituency Database, 1992–2001.

class voting falling further from 1997 to 2001 (see Table 7). The middle-class professionals and managers split 39:30 in favour of the Conservatives, but Labour enjoyed a slight edge with the C1's and a substantial lead among the working-class, although the Labour vote fell most (−4%) among unskilled manual workers. It remains to be seen whether this pattern is confirmed in the BES but the poll strongly suggests that class voting is withering away in British politics. As Evans suggested in the 1997 election,[10] the most plausible reason is Blair's strategy of straddling the centre-ground, promising improved public services but no rise in income tax, a safe pair of hands handling the economy but better heath and education. By this careful ideological balancing act, Labour has succeeded in creating a catch-all party, losing some traditional support, but gaining substantially in middle-England.

Parties can try to broaden their appeal through many different strategies including crafting specific policies designed to be popular with particular groups like pensioners or parents with young children, framing their campaign messages and images to make the party appear socially diverse, such as in their manifesto document, and selecting parliamentary candidates drawn from all sectors of society. In this latter regard, Labour and the Liberal Democrats remain far more socially inclusive than the Conservative Party. The social profile of the new Parliament continues to remain, as ever, predominately white, male, and middle-class. The 99 new members reflect the professionalisation of the political-class, drawn largely from backgrounds in local government and party staffers, as well as the usual sprinkling of lawyers, journalists and teachers. That being said, more ethnic minority candi-

7. Vote by Class

	2001			Change 1997–2001		
	Con	Lab	LibDem	Con	Lab	LibDem
Middle-class (AB)	39	30	25	−2	−1	3
Lower middle-class (C1)	36	38	20	−1	1	12
Skilled working-class (C2)	29	49	15	2	−1	−1
Unskilled working-class (DE)	24	55	13	3	−4	0

Source: MORI Aggregate Campaign Polls (N. 18,657).

8. Profile of Parliamentary Candidates for the Major Parties, 2001

	Con N	Lab N	LibDem N	Total N	Con %	Lab %	LibDem %	Total %
Non-incumbents	501	260	596	1357	78.5	40.7	93.6	61.2
Woman	92	146	135	373	14.4	22.8	21.1	16.8
Ethnic minority	16	20	28	64	2.5	3.1	4.4	2.9
ALL	639	640	637	2216				

Source: British Parliamentary Constituency Database, 1992–2001.

dates (64) stood for the major parties than ever before, although most faced hopeless contests (see Tables 8 and 9). As analysed in detail later by Saggar, a dozen Asian and black MPs were returned to Westminster, up three from 1997. Ethnic minority MPs now constitute 1.8% of the House of Commons, compared with about 5.5% of the electorate. In general, Asian and black candidates in all three major parties did slightly less well in vote swings than the national average, suggesting that they may face an additional electoral hurdle, although this may also be attributable to the type of seat they fought. As discussed further by Lovenduski, 644 women candidates stood for Parliament, constituting about one in five candidates (19.3%). Overall 118 women were returned to Westminster, or 17.9, slightly fewer than the record 120 elected in 1997. The swing in the vote experienced by women candidates in the major parties was similar to the national average. The lack of progress in women's representation was due to low levels of incumbency turnover; only 78 MPs retired and only 20 seats changed hands, producing only 99 new MPs (the lowest standardised annual turnover in the postwar era). Moreover, where Labour MPs did stand down, few women inherited these seats, because Labour had abandoned the use of all-women shortlists in its target constituencies. Recognising this problem, the Labour manifesto and the Queen's speech for the new Parliament promised to introduce legislation allowing parties to adopt positive strategies to increase the representation of women in future. In addition, Labour women MPs have been gaining in experience, seniority and reputation; seven entered Cabinet, the highest proportion ever, including heading heavy-weight spending ministries. 'Blair's babes', these women are not. The selection of candidates from every walk of life can only help to make Parliament more socially representative but in this regard, as in many others, the Conservative Party needs to re-examine its selection process so that it widens its appeal to all sectors

9. Profile of Elected MPs for the Major Parties, 2001

	Con N	Lab N	LibDem N	Total N	Con %	Lab %	LibDem %	Total %
New MPs	34	40	14	88	20.5	9.7	26.9	13.9
Woman MPs	14	94	5	113	8.4	22.8	9.6	17.9
Ethnic minority MPs	0	12	0	12	0.0	2.9	0.0	1.9
ALL	166	413	52	631				

Source: British Parliamentary Constituency Database, 1992–2001.

of the electorate, rather than picking the typical public school, Oxbridge-educated men who fail to connect with the concerns of the ordinary public.

PARTY COMPETITION AND THE PUBLIC MOOD?:   Yet as ever answers to one question raise more puzzles. In particular, if Labour was able to take advantage of social dealignment by broadening their base and widening their appeal, and this strategy clearly worked so successfully in the 1997 election, why did the Conservatives fail to learn these lessons and follow in the same path? Theories of party competition suggest that if something works to one party's electoral advantage (negative advertising, telephone canvassing, professional political marketing), after a natural lag, others ambitious for office should adopt the same tactics, producing a level playing-field in subsequent elections. The unpopularity of the strategies followed by William Hague's Conservatives could hardly have been a surprise: every monthly poll had carried the same message for four years. The answer to this conundrum may rest with the dynamics of public opinion and the way that Labour learnt to connect with the public mood from their long years on the opposition benches so that they now straddle the centre-ground of British politics, flanked by Liberal Democrats to the left and the Conservatives to the right (see Bara and Budge this volume).

Recent studies have attempted to make sense of whether changes in mass opinion are relatively meaningless, random or incoherent, or whether there are consistent patterns behind the day-to-day fluctuations monitored in a half-century of public opinion polls. One of the most persuasive theories has been developed by James Stimson who suggests that there are some powerful tides rippling and surging through the body politic that can lead national sentiment in a consistent direction.[11] In this account, like seismic tremors, surveys often detect a series of small shifts in public opinion. Some may represent nothing more than capricious fluctuations caused by particular events. Some shifts, however, may cumulatively gradually transform the *policy mood*, or the common bundling of policy preferences over time. Policy moods become evident as a consistent aggregate pattern-linking attitudes towards issues so that, for example, the public gradually comes to favour a more isolationist role for Britain that links together critical attitudes towards the European Union, anti-globalisation, and support for stricter controls over asylum seekers.

The idea of a policy mood is not particularly novel. But Stimson's theory goes one step further in claiming that changes over time in these policy moods may display three distinct patterns: they may be the product of meandering *fluctuations* back and forth, like a drunken walk, or they may *consistent trends* flowing in one direction over time, or alternatively they may be the result of *systemic cycles* in response to government actions. Stimson suggests that in democratic societies most policy-makers are fairly sensitive to policy moods, since they wish to maintain electoral support by remaining within the 'zone of acquiescence' where the public is in accord with policy proposals, rather than moving too far across the ideological spectrum to the left or right. Most politicians therefore implement changes step by step broadly in terms of their *perceptions* of what the public wants. The distribution of policy preferences at mass level, however, is not stable since, although there is some time lag, public opinion also moves relative to the actions of policy-makers. The public gains experience of the impact of policy changes gradually, as they become aware of the costs and other trade-offs produced by particular government actions. If the British public initially supported the sale of British Rail, for example, in anticipation of greater investment and more efficient services, and they subsequently experienced rail crashes, unaccountable endless delays, and widespread ticket shock, then the policy mood can be expected to switch towards restoring government regulation, public investment, or even state ownership. At a certain stage, the theory suggests, public preferences shift in a contrary direction, although policy changes continue to overshoot the new public consensus, until politicians become aware of the shift and move back in line with the zone of acquiescence.

If this theory can be applied more widely to understanding the outcome of the British election it suggests that the underlying public mood can be expected to reflect what government actually does. Where the public becomes dissatisfied with the state of public services, disillusioned with the power of public sector unions, and angry about levels of taxes, then, as in the late 1970s and early 1980s, they can be expected to support Thatcherite initiatives designed to 'shrink the state'. After successive governments responded to the perceived public mood by introducing a series of substantial tax cuts but also dramatic reductions in public services like health, education, and social protection. After experiencing the trade-offs involved in this process, over time the public mood eventually swung towards supporting greater public expenditure, even at the price of tax rises.

The available evidence testing this thesis in the context of the British election remains limited at this stage. Nevertheless, four important indicators provide support for the theory. First, analysis by Bara and Budge later in this volume demonstrates party competition among the three major British parties, established by content analysis of their official manifestos. The pattern shows that in from 1997 to 2001 *Labour and the Conservatives did shift slightly towards the left in their official policy platforms*, notably by policies stressing the delivery of better public services. As a result, by the last election all major parties were positioned relatively close together in the centre-right of the political spectrum, with the smallest gap between Labour and the Conservatives since the Butskellite fifties.

Evidence from the 2001 British Representation Study helps explain why this shift occurred. The survey conducted just prior to the election asked more than 1,000 parliamentary candidates and MPs in all British parties to place themselves on six 10-point scales ranging from left (0) to right (10). A similar survey was conducted in 1997. The results in Table 10 show that by the time of the 2001 election most Conservative politicians placed themselves slightly centre-left compared with where most Conservative politicians placed themselves in 1997. That is to say, *the overall policy mood within the parliamentary party moved modestly leftwards*, in line with the shift in their official manifesto policies. This pattern was found consistently across five different issue scales, such as privatisation vs. nationalisation, tax cuts vs. public spending, and jobs vs. prices, with the party only moving rightwards on the question of greater unification or independence from the European Union.

Moreover, the evidence from the BRS surveys suggests that one reason why Conservatives politicians moved may have been their *perception that Conservative voters had also shifted left during these years*. The surveys also asked politicians to estimate where their voters were located on the same issues scales. Tables 10a and 10b shows that Conservative politicians believed that they were usually to the right of their own voters on most issues, especially economic ones, although they believed that they were more egalitarian on the issue of women's equality. But the pattern also confirms that in 2001 Conservative politicians placed their supporters slightly to the left of where they placed them in 1997 on four out of six issues, particularly giving greater priority to public services rather than to tax cuts. The only issue where Conservative politicians believed that their supporters had shifted rightwards was the EU. Hopeful candidates and MPs thought that they were moving in step with the mood of their voters. It is not clear whether the Conservative shift towards the left, found in the parliamentary party

10a. Changes in How Conservative Politicians see Themselves and Their Voters, 1997 and 2001

| | Own position on scales | | | Perceptions of Conservative voters | | |
	1997	2001	Change 1997–2000	1997	2001	Change 1997–2000
Jobs vs. prices	6.37	6.10	−0.27	5.89	6.02	+0.13
Nationalisation vs. privatisation	8.88	8.13	−0.75	7.44	7.19	−0.25
Public spending vs. tax cuts	7.87	6.66	−1.21	7.10	6.09	−1.01
EU unite fully vs. independence	8.22	8.64	+0.42	8.30	8.57	+0.27
Women's rights	3.14	1.87	−1.27	4.33	3.48	−0.85
Left-right scale	7.34	7.10	−0.24	7.19	7.15	−0.04

Note: The figures represent the mean scores where Conservatives candidates and MPs placed themselves on the issue scales, and where they perceived Conservative voters were located on the same scales, immediately prior to the 1997 and 2001 campaigns. The 10-point scales ranged from 0 (left) to 10 (right). A negative coefficient indicates a shift towards the left while a positive coefficient indicates a shift towards the right. Number of Conservative candidates and MPs in the surveys: 285 in 1997 and 351 in 2001. Full details of the questions and survey can be found at www.pippanorris.com/data. Source: Joni Lovenduski and Pippa Norris, *The British Representation Study, 1997 and 2001.*

10b. Perceived Differences Between Conservative Politicians and Conservative Voters, 1997–2001

	1997			2001		
	Con politicians	Perceived voters	Con Diff.	Con politicians	Perceived voters	Con Diff.
Women's rights	3.14	4.33	−1.19	1.87	3.48	−1.61
Left-right scale	7.34	7.19	+0.15	7.10	7.15	−0.05
EU unite fully vs. independence	8.22	8.30	−0.08	8.64	8.57	+0.07
Jobs vs. prices	6.37	5.89	+0.48	6.10	6.02	+0.08
Public spending vs. tax cuts	7.87	7.10	+0.77	6.66	6.09	+0.57
Nationalisation vs. privatisation	8.88	7.44	+1.44	8.13	7.19	+0.94

Notes and Sources: See Table 10a.

and in official party policy, was actually reflected in the Conservative message and leadership speeches during the campaign, still less whether it was evident to most observers of the party. Nevertheless, at a more subtle and deeper level, a modest ideological drift back towards the centre of British party politics was evident.

Yet the question remains whether the Conservative Party had moved sufficiently far back towards the centre-ground in the 2001 election to recapture support, particularly if they were chasing a public mood that has continued to move further leftwards. Full analysis about public opinion will only be possible once comparable issue scale data is available from the British Election Study. But initial evidence from a series of published opinion polls, such as the BBC/ICM election survey, suggests that compared with the Thatcherite ethos of the late 1970s and early 1980s, *today the public mood in Britain has swung quite far back towards the left on the economic and social agenda.*[12]

The conventional wisdom suggests that British voters would punish politicians that envisaged tax increases, and in the last election the major parties provided the electorate with an exceptionally clear-cut choice that allows us to test this proposition in a 'natural' experiment. The Conservative manifesto promised to introduce £8 billion pounds worth of tax cuts, and indeed this was their major election theme, repeated throughout their campaign, alongside being anti-Euro and seeking a clamp-down on asylum seekers. In contrast, Labour pledged to maintain the status quo with no increases in income tax (although Gordon Brown and Tony Blair maintained a fuzzy stance about other taxes). The Liberal Democrat platform highlighted a proposed 1p in the pound tax rise to pay for increased spending on education and social services. The BBC/ICM election poll tested the popularity of the Liberal Democrat hypothecated tax proposal and found that the majority of the public (58%) expressed approval for the idea of tax rises with money spent on schools. And majority support was found across all social groups by gender, age and class, with about three-quarters of Liberal Democrat and Labour voters approving, along with even 41% of Conservatives (see Table 11).

More evidence of attitudes towards public spending is available in Gallup polls that have regularly used the trade-off question asking:

11. Public Support for Left-Right Policy Issues

	Should	Should not	Diff.	% should		
				Con	Lab	LD
Increase taxes and spend the money on schools	58	35	+23	41	71	79
Bring the railways back into public ownership	65	21	+44	56	70	74
Get private companies to run NHS hospitals	26	65	-39	43	25	13
Get private companies to run more state schools	30	58	-28	42	26	20

Note: Q. 'Would you say that the government should or should not . . .'. Source: BBC/ICM Research Election Poll, 30 May–4 June 2001 (N. 2000).

People have different views about whether it is more important to reduce taxes or keep up government spending. How about you? Which of these statements comes closest to your own views:

— Taxes being cut, even if it means some reduction in government services such as health, education and welfare.

— Things should be left as they are.

— Government services such as health, education and welfare should be extended, even if it means some increases in taxes.

The trends in Gallup polls during the last twenty years show that in 1979, when Mrs Thatcher first came to power, about half the British public favoured maintaining public services even at the expense of tax rises, while the remainder were fairly evenly divided between maintaining the status quo and enjoying tax cuts.[13] During the rest of Mrs Thatcher's term of office, however, the proportion that preferred maintaining public services steadily rose, until the peak in 1995 when almost three-quarters opted for better public services even with tax rises. The policy mood appears to have reacted against the direction of government's policies, by demanding today that investment in education, health and welfare should be prioritised now over the pocket book economy. In the June 2001 general election, when the BBC/ICM poll repeated this question, *only 4% of the British electorate (and only 6% of Conservative voters) favoured tax cuts and less spending on health and education*, while 56% preferred increased taxes and spending. Moreover, among the major parties, it has already been established that it was the Liberal Democrats who registered the most consistent rise in support during the campaign. If tax rises were once thought anathema to electoral popularity, it appears that the public mood has swung so far in Britain that this is no longer so. Yet the campaign run by both Conservative *and* Labour politicians, recalling the apparent popularity of Thatcherism in the 1980s, may be out of touch with the new zone of acquiescence.

What of the Labour proposals to bring private companies into the running of state schools and into the National Health Service? An expansion of private–public finance initiatives was announced in Labour press conferences and leadership speeches during the campaign, as a way to attract private investment while maintaining into public services free at the point of delivery, as well as being mentioned briefly in the manifesto. The Queen's speech has reiterated some of these ideas and although attracting considerable debate, and opposition from public sector unions, the way that this proposal is going to be implemented in schools and hospitals remain to be worked out. Nevertheless, there is evidence in the BBC/ICM election poll that the initial response of the public has been extremely hostile towards these proposals. People were asked whether they approved of the idea that the government should or should not get private companies to run NHS hospitals and to run more state schools. The results in Table 10 show that the majority of the public opposed these policies, with the greatest opposition (65%) towards private companies running NHS hospitals. Disapproval was widespread throughout all sectors of the public, including in the case of health care, half of all Conservative voters and 80% of all Liberal Democrats. If the Blair government does go ahead with the proposals to expand private–public finance initiatives in schools and hospitals, for pragmatic reasons because this will raise public sector investment in the short-term, it appears that Labour face an uphill battle in persuading the British public of the merits of this case, especially among their own supporters. There is convincing evidence that in the late 1970s and early 1980s nationalisation was one of the main millstones hanging around Labour's neck, and subsequently ditched in the modernisation process. Yet, at least in the case of railways, at the time of the last election the BBC/ICM poll shows that dispirited by broken down trains, fatal crashes and unreliable services, almost two-thirds of the public favoured bringing the railways back into public ownership. Most remarkably, even a majority of Tories agreed. At the same time we cannot assume that the public mood is fixed on these issues, anymore than it was fixed in the past, and if the government goes ahead with proposals for private–public partnership agreements, and if (and this is a big 'if') the health, education and transport services are seen to work better as a result of these initiatives, then by the time of the next election opinion may shift in its favour. But the size of the challenge facing the government should not be underestimated.

Conclusion

What are the implications of this analysis for the future of British party politics? The theory of policy moods and cycles suggests that where parties are sensitive to public opinion, once they *perceive* the switch in national sentiment, then they will eventually move in a tango tandem on the policy agenda, to maintain popular support. But politicians may move only sluggishly, misjudging the extent of the shift in the public mood, for a variety of possible reasons; Conservatives may have reasoned that public opinion polls are often unreliable, so it is better to trust gut instincts that scientific mumbo-jumbo. In interpreting the public mood, politicians may follow many different cues such as communications with activists, conversations with local constituents, and debates in the news media, as much as more scientific techniques like opinion polls and focus groups. After all Conservatives recall that Mrs Thatcher had been returned to power throughout the 1980s on a platform of tax cuts, and it is not wholly irrational to assume that the public continue to support these initiatives, that they may simply lie by reporting socially-acceptable attitudes in surveys. Politicians may feel that if they ditch basic principles and established brand images in get-votes-quick schemes, like the disastrous launch of New Coke, they are in danger of losing all public trust. As in a complex tango, leaders may feel that their job is to lead, not follow. Ageing Tory Party activists, in particular, as true believers, may act as an anchor-dragging ideological revisions, particularly if parties are failing to attract new blood at grass-root levels. By picking other like-minded souls as Tory candidates, the parliamentary party may drift rightwards, even if the public mood moves centre-left. If the Conservative Party proves unable to reinvent itself, unable to grasp that they have gradually moved out-of-step with the public's zone of acquiescence, then politicians face the sanction of (repeated) electoral defeat, like shock therapy. The link between public preferences and electoral outcomes inevitably remains crude and imperfect, since left-wing or right-wing parties may be returned to power on successive occasions for many reasons like the workings of the electoral system, even when the policy mood is moving against them. Nevertheless, in the longer term, any growing disjunction between public preferences and the actions of policy-makers can be expected to produce an electoral response favouring others more in tune with the national mood.

The theory of policy moods and cycles provide important insights into the strategies adopted by both the Conservatives, *and* to a lesser extent the Labour Party, even in the face of the survey evidence that the public zone of acquiescence has shifted to opt for higher public spending even if it means tax increases. More research is required to flesh this theory out fully, in particular, at elite-level we still need to understand why ambitious politicians, seeking office, so often fail to read the policy mood correctly, and how the mechanism of 'selective perception' and ideological blinkers lead policy-makers to misinterpret public opinion.[14] But, if this account is true, it suggests that one major reason for the failure of the Conservatives in the last election is the broad cycles in the policy mood, with the public responding to changed circumstances and what government actually does to alter the balance between the public and private sectors. In particular, if in a series of steps parties tilt too far in the direction of either markets or the state, then given the complex trade-offs involved, public opinion can be expected gradually to shift the balance of policy preferences back towards the centre-ground. But until Conservatives perceive this shift, in a lagged process they may continue to follow what they believe to be public preferences, even though in fact the policy mood may have changed more radically. Despite their massive landslide of seats, or indeed because of it, Labour may fall into a similar trap by promising privatisation of public services. The apathetic landslide does not mean that the public was persuaded of many core aspects of Labour's platform; merely that they mistrusted the Tories more because they were even further away from the contemporary national sentiment, stranded unreconstructed in their glory days of the 1980s, uncomprehending that the tide has rapidly flowed past them, becoming as unfashionable as power shoulder-pads, Jane Fonda's legwarmers, and Geeko's 'greed is good'. In many ways this theory does help to explain what has happened in the tide of public opinion in Britain in recent decades, and the way that the Conservatives, and so some extent Labour too, have lagged behind the national sentiment. The British public spoke in the last election: it remains to be seen how far politicians listened and learnt the right lessons.

Pippa Norris

* Notes: I am most grateful to all who provided comments especially Ron Johnston, Ivor Crewe, Phil Cowley and Shamit Saggar; to Nick Sparrow for providing data from the BBC/ICM Election Poll 30 May– 4 June 2001. Details at www.icmresearch.co.uk; to Martin Rosenbaum and Bob Worcester for providing the MORI aggregate campaign data; and to Peter Christophersen for data from the content analysis of all national newspapers during the campaign from 18 May until 7 June conducted by Echo Research. Further information can be found at www.echoresearch.com. The British Representation Study 2001 was funded by the Center for Public Leadership at the John F. Kennedy School of Government in conjunction with Birkbeck College, London and directed by J. Lovenduski and P. Norris, with the help of David Baker, Robert Hanna and Andrea Stephanos. The data used in the electoral analysis from the British Parliamentary Constituency Database, 1992–2001 is available for downloading at www.pippanorris.com.

1   For a discussion see P. Norris, 'The Twilight of Westminster?', *Political Studies*, 2001.
2   P. Norris, J. Curtice, D. Sanders, M. Scammell and H.A. Semetko, *On Message: Communicating the Campaign*, Sage, 1999, p. 88.
3   P. Norris, *Count Every Voice: Political Participation Worldwide*, Cambridge University Press, 2002.
4   See I. Crewe and K. Thomson, 'Party Loyalties: Dealignment or Realignment?' in G. Evans and P. Norris (eds), *Critical Elections: British Parties and Voters in Long-Term Perspective*, Sage 1999; and also G. Evans, A. Heath and C. Payne, 'Class: Labour as a Catch-All Party? in G. Evans and P. Norris (eds), *Critical Elections: British Parties and Voters in Long-Term Perspective*, Sage, 1999.
5   For a discussion see J. Bartle and D. Griffiths (eds), *Political Communication Transformed: From Morrison to Mandelson*, Palgrave, 2001.
6   More details can be found at P. Norris, 'All Spin and No Substance? The 2001 British Election Campaign, 6 *Harvard International Journal of Press/Politics*, 4, 2001.
7   See P. Norris and D. Sanders, 'Knows Nothing, Learns Less? An Experimental Study of the Impact of Television, Newspapers and the Internet on Cognitive Learning during the 2001 British General Election Campaign', Paper presented at the annual meeting of the American Political Science Association, San Francisco, August 2001.
8   M. Lewis-Beck, *Economics and Elections: The Major Western Democracies*, Michigan, 1990.
9   *Labour Market Statistics June 2001, Consumer Price Indices May 2001, and Retail Sales Briefing for May 2001*. All published by National Statistics, 12–13 June 2001, www.statistics.gov.uk.
10   G. Evans, 'Class: Labour as a Catch-all Party?' in G. Evans and P. Norris (eds), *Critical Elections: British Parties and Voters in Long-Term Perspective*, Sage, 1999.
11   J. Stimson, *Public Opinion in America: Moods, Cycles and Swings*, Westview, 1991.
12   For more details about recent trends leading up to the election see A. Heath, R. Jowell and J. Curtice, *The Rise of New Labour*, Oxford University Press, 2001.
13   See A. King (ed.), *British Political Opinion 1937–2000*, Politico's, 2001.

14 For evidence of this pattern in the 1997 election see P. Norris, 'New Politicians? Changes in Party Competition at Westminster' in G. Evans and P. Norris (eds), *Critical Elections: British Parties and Voters in Long-Term Perspective*, Sage, 1999. Also P. Norris, and J. Lovenduski, 'The Iceberg and the Titanic: Electoral Defeat, Policy Moods, and Party Change', Paper presented at the annual EPOP conference, September 2001.

JUDITH BARA AND IAN BUDGE

Party Policy and Ideology: Still New Labour?

The results of the 2001 election were discounted long in advance. Labour's lead in the polls continued through the unanticipated domestic upheavals of 2000–2001. The outbreak of foot and mouth disease forced a postponement of the election but this was merely a hiccup in the long-term Labour strategy of going to the country in the fourth year of their term while the government was still at a high tide of support and the Conservatives divided and demoralised.

In these circumstances the main policy question is whether Labour consolidated its centrist stance, which produced such a landslide in 1997, or felt liberated by the almost certain prospect of electoral victory to edge back towards its natural home on the left. In our assessment of their 1997 strategy[1] we saw parallels between Labour in the 1990s and the Conservatives in the 1950s. Just as the Conservatives swung massively leftwards in the 1950s but then returned rightwards when they had retrieved their electoral position, so one could see Labour possibly reverting to more interventionist and communitarian positions once they felt free to do so. Several arguments supported the idea that a leftward shift might occur. The massive ideological weight of party traditions is likely to compromise the efforts of a reformist leadership to create a new image. The experience of being in government and having to confront problems creates its own momentum towards intervention. Policy concessions which MPs and activists might be prepared to make to reverse a tide of electoral defeats are less easy to extract when victory is confidently expected.

This last consideration has been the subject of theoretical treatment by Robertson[2] in one of the most successful neo-Downsian theories of party competition. Robertson reasons that parties generally operate on the basis of rational expectations about the next election result. Where this is perceived to be highly competitive, with every vote vital, parties will move to the centre in search of extra support. This idea seems to apply to Labour in 1997. When parties expect to win anyway, there is no incentive to gather extra votes from policy concessions, so the party stand could revert to the one naturally favoured by its ideology, in the

Labour case back to the left. Robertson extends this inference not just to the winning but also to the losing party. Granted that by the time of the election the Conservatives must have expected to lose in 2001, given the relentless message in the opinion polls, there was no pressure on the leadership to moderate policy. On the contrary, the best way for the leadership to survive after the election was to stick to basic ideology. It was better to confront the inevitable post-mortem as men of principles rather than temporising moderates who lost the election anyway. The logic of this approach was to hold the right-wing positions held under Mrs Thatcher and maintained with little change up to 1997. This seemed in fact to be the tactic of the Conservative leader, William Hague, during the campaign. Of course, the eternal optimism of politicians, often mistaken, might push them towards the centre anyway. As we shall see, the manifesto was more centrist than the Hague campaign.

The parties' actual records between 1997 and 2001 support the expectation that they might have retreated to their ideological homes. The Labour government made great efforts to appear business-friendly and financially orthodox. Nevertheless, Gordon Brown imposed a levy on recently privatised industries and in 1998 increased allocations for social spending quite markedly. Measures like the 'right to roam' over most of the countryside carried through traditional radical projects. Meanwhile William Hague and his team, after flirting with 'Caring Conservatism' in the first two years after electoral defeat, turned to a series of traditional stances on immigration, law and order, and 'little England' nationalism. These did not improve his standing in the polls but neither had 'Caring Conservatism'. The Liberal Democrats' best hope was to benefit from these moves by sticking to the centre-left ground they have held from the 1960s. They could thus attract votes by appealing to those disillusioned with Thatcherism and at the same time provide an attractive option for strategic Labour voters in the constituencies where they could win.

Examining the three major party manifestos and comparing them to previous ones can check how far these expectations actually materialised. The importance of the manifesto is twofold. It is the only official statement of policy made by the parties. In contrast, leaders' speeches are to considerable extent expressions of opinion, which are not necessarily binding in government. Second, although not read directly by many electors, the manifesto is designed to pre-empt and direct media discussion. It thus helps set the agenda to an extent not equalled by any other document or pronouncement. A comparison with party policy emphases during the actual campaign as reflected in newspaper coverage (see Table 4 in the Introduction to this issue) shows how far the main contenders were seen to carry through these emphases into the final stages of the election.

Analysing and comparing manifestos

Manifestos, of course, are long and complex documents open to various interpretations — the only Five Year Plans for comprehensive social development issued by any organisation in democratic societies. On the other hand they do aim at getting a series of fairly simple priorities through to a mass audience and thus rely heavily on emphasis and repetition of their main points. This makes them ideal for a content analysis aimed at tracing such shifts of emphasis over time and comparing them among countries.

The British party manifestos, along with others from over fifty other democracies, have been coded into a form that makes long time-series more manageable by subjecting them to statistical analysis. The procedure codes party policy emphasis from 1945 to 2001. The Manifesto Research Group of the European Consortium for Political Research developed categories from reading party documents in each country and grouping references into major themes and policy areas. This comprehensive listing of politically relevant policy areas is given in Appendix Table A1. For the analysis, each sentence of each document was counted under one, and only one, of these categories. The resulting numerical distribution of sentences was then percentaged out of the total number of sentences to standardise for the varying lengths of documents.[3]

This set of simple and directly interpretable percentages thus gives us the opportunity to compare each of the 2001 manifestos with the others and with their predecessors in earlier elections as well. We can also track the parties' policy movements, in terms of topics they endorse, in a graphical form (Figure 1). And we can see in detail what particular

Figure 1. British Parties' Ideological Movements on a Left-Right Scale, 1945–2001

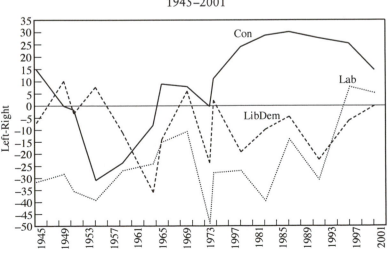

policy shifts have brought about general convergence or divergence in left-right terms. Quantitative analysis of these key texts, therefore, gives us an enormously powerful tool to judge precisely whether there is anything new in Labour policy positions: and if so, what it is. It thus provides direct evidence, at least in terms of leadership appeals, for evaluating whether the last election duplicated the policy positions of 1997, or deviated from them in the ways anticipated above.[4]

Left-right movement of the parties

Tony Blair and his followers were commonly credited with 'seizing the centre-ground' in their pursuit of 'Middle England' in 1997. Moving to the centre implies that there actually is a centre, differentiated from the extremes of 'left' and 'right' along a one-dimensional policy continuum (Figure 1). Though this is a bold assumption there are good grounds for making it. Media and party debates often simplify policy alternatives into one overriding choice between 'left' and 'right'. In 1997, for example, 'more of the same' under Major and the Conservatives — privatisation, centralisation, social conservatism, sound economic management — was contrasted with the constitutional and legal reforms, social concern (and sound economic management) promised by Blair and New Labour.

This kind of left-right contrast is not new; it has dominated party confrontation throughout the postwar — and even pre-war — eras. Because of this it can also be traced throughout the earlier manifestos. The only question is how to measure it. Previous research across a number of countries has identified a number of policy stands and emphases as classically 'left-wing' and another set as characteristically 'right-wing'.[5] By adding all the percentages of sentences in 'left' categories and subtracting the total from the sum of percentages in 'right' categories, we can create a unified scale going from +100% (all sentences in a manifesto are 'right-wing') to −100% (all sentences in a manifesto are 'left-wing') (Appendix Table A2). More details about the creation of this scale are given in the Appendix at the end of the chapter. It should be noted here, however, that it is a simple additive measure which sums and subtracts percentages of sentences devoted to certain policies, and it is *not* based on factor scores.

Of course, no manifesto makes exclusively 'left-' and 'right-' wing references, many sentences do not fall under either type, and both 'left' and 'right' references generally occur in any specific manifesto. There are also important issues like 'Europe' that do not fall easily into this classification scheme. However, we can trace the relative leanings of manifestos towards 'left' and 'right', and hence of the party which published them in a particular election year, by estimating the combined final score. This is generally in the range −40 to +30, reflecting the general ideological moderation of British parties.

On the basis of these calculations we can examine the movement of all British parties, in 'left-right' terms, over the whole postwar period (Figure 1). What the graph reveals overall is the initial sharp separation of Labour from Conservatives and Liberal Democrats in 1945: movements first by Conservatives towards the Labour position in the 1950s, then by Labour towards Conservative positions (but much less so) in the 1960s. Labour headed leftwards again in the 1970s up to 1983, then rightwards in 1987 and leftwards in 1992. Meanwhile the Conservatives moved fairly consistently rightwards from 1959 onwards. From 1964 the Liberals took up a centre position between the two major parties, however, much closer to Labour from 1974 onwards.

These ideological tendencies have been recognised by historians and political commentators. In particular the emergence of the 'Social Democratic Consensus' in the 1950s chimes in with Conservative acceptance of the 1945–51 restructuring. The figure also reflects the generally acknowledged fracturing of the consensus in the late 1960s and early 1970s. The predominance of the 'New Right' among Conservatives is well-attested in the 1980s. The graph helps to fill in details of the parties' ideological progression. But its broad conformity to accepted historical interpretations helps confirm its general validity.

Our faith in the representation is also strengthened by what it shows from 1992 to 1997 in terms of 'left-right' movement. Here there is a marked change. Labour moved sharply rightwards and, *for the first time in postwar history, in 1997 Labour shows a preponderance of right-wing positions over left-wing ones* (+8). The Liberal Democrats shadowed Labour's move but their stance remained more consistent with their positions of the 1970s and 1980s, producing a left-leaning balance of –6. The Conservatives remained broadly where they were throughout the 1980s at +30, relatively far from Labour in a rightward direction.

Labour's move to the centre-right in the mid-1990s confirms the overwhelming perception that it had moderated its traditional policies by the time of the 1997 election. Indeed the evidence may have a certain value in correcting the more exaggerated depictions of this move. In particular, Labour was far from whole-heartedly endorsing Thatcherite positions. A fair amount of 'clear blue water' still separated the Conservative position from Labour. Nevertheless, compared with the Liberal Democrats, by 1997 Labour moved rightwards and 'leapfrogged' over them for only the second time in the postwar period. In relative terms, *Labour became the most centrist party*.

Looking now to the party positions of 2001 in Figure 1, how do the overall policy stances compare with the expectations summarised earlier? The first finding is indeed that Labour moved left, but only very slightly (from +8 in 1997 to +6 in 2001), still on the right-wing side of the scale. The Liberal Democrats changed from a left-wing position of –6 to a centre-right one of +0.3. This is accounted for in part by their increased manifesto emphasis on policy areas traditionally associated

1. 'Top Ten' Issues for Major British Parties, 2001

Policy areas	Labour Rank	Labour Emphasis (%)	Liberal Democrat Rank	Liberal Democrat Emphasis (%)	Conservative Rank	Conservative Emphasis (%)
			Sentences in manifesto (%)			
Government effectiveness and authority	1	14.0	1	11.4	1	17.3
Social services expansion	2	10.2	3	7.3	2	9.0
Law and order	3	8.7	4	6.9	4	6.4
Education expansion	4	7.2	5	5.7	8	3.3
Non-economic groups	5	6.1	7	5.6	3	7.0
Technology and infrastructure	6	5.9	6	5.7		
Internationalism: positive	7	3.6	8	4.2		
Environmental protection	7	3.6	2	7.4		
Decentralisation: positive	9	3.0			5	4.6
Economic goals	10	2.8				
European Union: positive			8	4.2		
Government efficiency			10	4.1	10	2.8
European Union: negative					6	4.0
Art, sport, leisure, media					7	3.6
Agriculture					10	2.8
Incentives					9	3.0

Note: The entries in the Table are percentages of sentences in each party manifesto for 2001 devoted to the policy areas listed down the side, together with the rank order position of each area for each party. Percentages are given only for the leading ten issues in each manifesto. Where these do not coincide, no entry is given for the party(ies) for which they do not come in the top ten. Source: Comparative Manifestos Project, Wissenschaftzentrum, Berlin, 2001.

with the right, such as law and order and, especially, government effectiveness which had not been among their 'top ten' priorities in 1997 (see Tables 1 and 2). These changes clearly outweighed the emphasis on traditional left-wing issues, such as the renationalisation of Railtrack. The Conservatives still remained at a distinctively right-wing position (+15) but made a substantial move to the centre compared with 1997 (+26).

2. 'Top Ten' Issues for Major British Parties, 1997

Policy areas	Labour Rank	Labour Emphasis (%)	Liberal Democrat Rank	Liberal Democrat Emphasis (%)	Conservative Rank	Conservative Emphasis (%)
			Sentences in manifesto (%)			
Government effectiveness and authority	1	13.4			1	11.3
Law and order	2	9.9	4	5.8	2	6.9
Economic goals	3	8.0	5	5.5	5	5.8
Regulation of capitalism	4	5.4				
Technology and infrastructure	5	5.1	7	4.5	3	6.5
Incentives	6	4.7				
Non-economic groups	7	4.0	6	4.8	8	4.0
Decentralisation: positive	7	4.0	7	4.5	6	5.4
European Union: negative	9	3.9				
European Union: positive			7	4.5	10	3.4
Social services expansion			1	9.5	4	6.4
Social justice			3	6.5	6	5.4
Education expansion	10	3.4	4	5.8	9	3.9
Environmental protection			2	8.0		

Note: The entries in the Table are percentages of sentences in each party manifesto for 1997 devoted to the policy areas listed down the side, together with the rank order position of each area for each party. Percentages are given only for the leading ten issues in each manifesto. Where these do not coincide no entry is given for the party(ies) for which they do not come in the top ten. Source: Budge et al., *Mapping Policy Preferences*, Oxford University Press 2001.

How do these moves compare with initial expectations? Apart from the Liberal Democrat attempt to regain the centre-ground, important for their ability to attract waverers from the main parties, Labour's relative lack of movement and the Conservatives' centrist move both go against what was anticipated from Robertson's theory. Labour strategists obviously feel they are in a vote-winning position at the median, which they did not wish to abandon, and the Conservatives do seem to have felt the need to finally moderate Thatcherite positions. What is very noticeable about the 2001 positions of all three parties on the left-right scale is that they are closer to each other than at any time during the postwar period, and, in general ideological terms, the competitive arena has shrunk. The median position for the range of left-right scores for the three parties is now about +0.7, which is a massive change from the late 1950s when it was about −0.17. Indeed if we omit the Liberal Democrats and look just at Labour and the Conservatives in these terms, these figures become about +0.11 and −0.25 respectively.

2001 in comparative perspective

It is interesting to see how Labour's tenacity in the centre looks in comparative perspective. The most obvious comparison is with the 1996 US Presidential Election when Bill Clinton also held on to the middle-ground in making his bid for a second term. Labour's own move to the middle in 1997 was attributed by commentators in part to Clinton's influence over New Labour and his success in attracting votes with a centrist stand in 1996. Gore's campaign of 2000 offers an interesting example of how a moderate party of the left does react after eight years in government — does it *have* to revert left to renew its ideological bases? Figure 2 illustrates Clinton's quite dramatic move to the centre-right in 1992 and its continuance, albeit with a slight lurch

Figure 2. USA Parties' Ideological Movements on a Left-Right Scale, 1948–2000

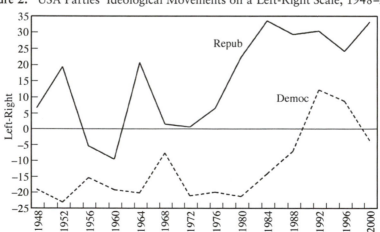

to the left, in 1996. The figure also illustrates Gore's equally dramatic shift leftwards in 2000. This may prefigure Labour's future strategy in 2005/6.

Specific party positions in the general election

General conclusions about party positions can usefully be fleshed out by asking how the parties stood on particular issues in the election, such as Europe or delivery of social services, which assumed a prominent place in campaign exchanges. Looking at specific issues allows us to ask what particular policy changes affected the Labour position, and how these corresponded to, or contrasted with, other party positions. This is all the more relevant as some important policy areas such as Europe do not enter into the calculation of 'left-right' differences. As party attitudes towards the EU were an important topic of debate in the election, this could alter our judgments both of where Labour stood and of its tendency to change in the future. Table 1 lists the 'top ten' issues in the 2001 manifestos, in terms of sentences counted into the separate categories specified in the Appendix.

The most striking feature of the table is the emphasis — direct and indirect — by all of the parties on government effectiveness in delivering services. This is accompanied by a strong common focus on the expansion of education and social services and pensions, and for law and order. Such emphasis on effective and efficient government is especially striking for the Liberal Democrats who largely ignored it in 1997. It is also a major component in the rightward orientation of the parties in general and helps explain the rightward shift by the Liberal Democrats.[6] Government effectiveness and authority is classified as right-wing as it is a recurrent claim of parties of the right to deal with government and bureaucracy better than the left. This has its importance in the campaign of 2001, as a major part of the public debate was about efficient delivery of public services. Non-economic groups were more emphasised by everyone and Labour joined the Liberal Democrats in putting more stress on the environment. As in 1997 the Conservatives were distinguished by their negative attitude towards the European Union, clearly magnified during the campaign. Their leftward shift is due above all to their joining other parties in their stress on social services expansion. This component of the Labour manifesto is the major traditional left-wing element in it.

Manifestos compared with campaign handling of policy issues

As noted, manifesto emphases set the initial cues for the election campaign, which nevertheless takes on a momentum of its own as the days go by. Newspaper emphases on the various policy areas reflects to some extent how parties actually handled issues, so it is interesting to compare manifesto issue rankings with Table 4 in the Introduction to this volume, which ranks issues for each party in terms of newspaper coverage. Of course the coding into issue areas differs in detail between the two, but we can still draw some general conclusions. It is hardly surprising to discover social services and law and order ranking high both in manifestos and the press. Government effectiveness and efficiency is subsumed in these categories so far as the press was concerned as their main emphasis was on *government's* delivery of public services.

In general, we can say that the most obvious discrepancies between the manifestos and campaigns show with the Conservatives. Europe is promoted from eighth ranking issue in the manifesto to number one with the 'Save the Pound' campaign. 'Taxation' is not matched by any manifesto topic in Table 2, although illegal immigration and 'bogus asylum seekers' reflect an emphasis on law and order. The comparison does support interpretations of an initial Conservative emphasis on service delivery ('You've paid for them, where are they?') becoming lost under the leader's concerns, especially with Europe. This inconsistency suggests that the Conservatives, more than other parties, found it more difficult to remain 'on message'.

Manifesto emphases compared with public opinion

All the parties were aiming their issue appeals at the electorate with the hope of attracting more votes. How far did the manifestos anticipate popular concerns? Again, looking back to Table 4 in the Introduction we can compare manifesto emphases with public nominations of the most important issues for them in response to MORI polls.

Generally, there seems to be a fair correspondence, particularly on public service questions. No manifesto talked much about taxation, but public nominations of that topic as important reflect more of a concern to raise money for spending on social services, rather than tax cutting. This is probably caught in the manifesto concern for social services' expansion. Transport is covered under technology and infrastructure, and the parties also discussed economic goals, including employment, thus anticipating popular concern with this question. Our overall judgment has to be that election programmes did either shape or anticipate public concerns in this election. If any gap opened up it was between campaign emphases and public opinion, rather than between the latter and manifesto priorities as such. This corroborates our impression that manifesto emphases are getting to grips with issues of concern raised by the public.[7]

Change in manifesto coverage of major issues

To give some historical background to the issues highlighted in 2001, and the changes in emphasis that have occurred over the postwar period, we can examine graphically how party stances have changed across the period. Below we trace changes by combining some of the categories listed in Appendix Table A1. These indicators are designed

Figure 3. Party Programmatic Emphasis on Market Economy, 1945–2001

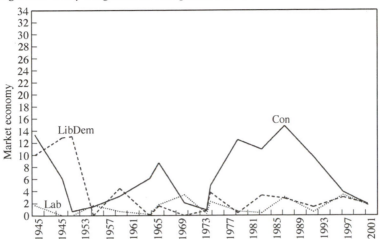

to illustrate changes in certain key policy areas of the postwar period at a more specific level than the left-right scale. Their construction is described in Appendix Table A3.

A central division between Labour and the Conservatives has traditionally been whether to run the economy through free markets or government planning. Figures 3 and 4 show how this division, so important in the past as a component of left-right differences, has totally disappeared in 2001. Not only have overall emphases dropped but also there are hardly any differences between the parties. The main traditional difference—greater Conservative acceptance of spending on public services notwithstanding—remains in the area of welfare (see

Figure 4. Party Programmatic Emphasis on Planned Economy, 1945–2001

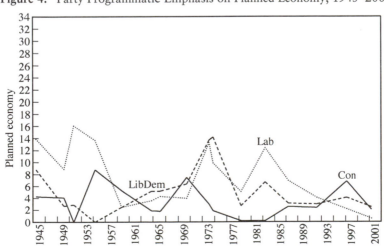

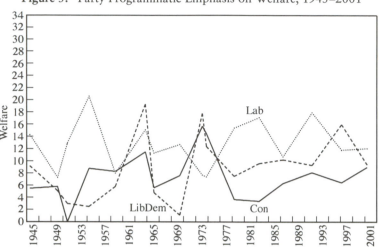

Figure 5. Party Programmatic Emphasis on Welfare, 1945–2001

Figure 5). Here Labour continues to manifest its traditional support for this area and there is clear differentiation between Labour and the other two parties.

Some distinctions also remain in terms of social conservatism (see Figure 6). This is mainly because it incorporates law and order — a topic that the Conservatives continue to prioritise heavily. Both Labour and the Liberal Democrats, however, have markedly increased their emphasis on this area in the last two elections to an extent that helps to account for their overall rightwards moves demonstrated in Figure 1.

Quality of life, incorporating concern for the environment, remains

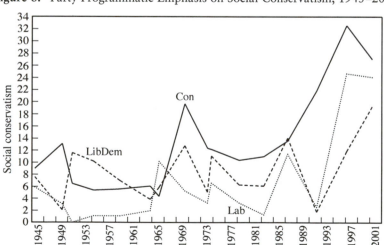

Figure 6. Party Programmatic Emphasis on Social Conservatism, 1945–2001

Figure 7. Party Programmatic Emphasis on Quality of Life, 1945–2001

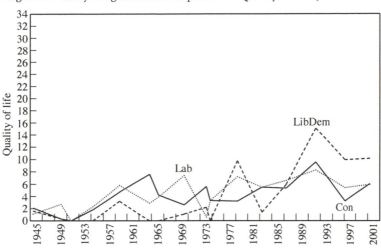

the Liberal Democrats' most distinctive issue (see Figure 7). Here a major gap has opened up between them and the two other parties that has continued over the last three elections. The Liberal Democrat stand here does not find much resonance in contemporary public opinion (see Table 4 in the Introduction to this issue) but may well anticipate future concerns, given the increase in problems related to the area.

Another distinctive Liberal Democrat position has been its support for greater European integration, as demonstrated in Figures 8 and 9. This remains true of 2001, where the party's support for the project is still greater than that of the other two parties, though Labour is closing

Figure 8. Party Programmatic Emphasis on 'Europe': Positive, 1945–2001

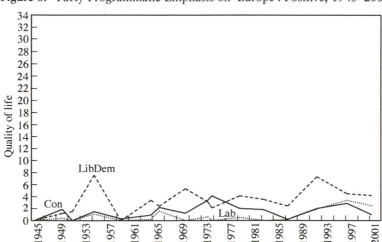

Figure 9. Party Programmatic Emphasis on 'Europe': Negative, 1945–2001

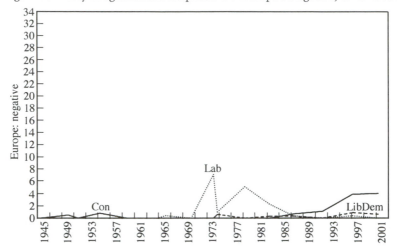

the gap. The Conservatives distinctiveness occurs in their opposition to the European Union, which has grown consistently throughout the nineties. In light of the issue's centrality to their election campaign it is hardly surprising that their hostility reaches a high in their 2001 manifesto.

Overall the figures discussed above confirm general impressions about the development of party policy in recent years. A 'neo-liberal' or Thatcherite consensus has emerged on the economy, centred on a reduced role for government and acceptance of the market. All three parties' convergence on these matters, as on social conservatism, has removed these issues from the hub of party debate that now focuses on the question of who can deliver services most effectively. Differences on welfare remain to some extent, but the major point of party contention is Europe. The environment and quality of life remain potential sources for differentiation in the future, from which the Liberal Democrats are well-placed to profit.

Conclusion

Most assessments of elections base themselves on only half the evidence — on how voters reacted to parties rather than what the parties themselves were doing. The proper analytic question to ask is how electors reacted to the cues parties were sending out, rather than trying to infer indirectly, from electors' responses, what these cues were in the first place.

This imbalance results in large part from a bias in the evidence about elections that is usually examined. Analysts base themselves on survey evidence from the typical large-scale election study, or from polls and macroeconomic data put together to form a time series. From such a perspective, political influences usually enter to fill the gaps left by a purely economic explanation. We have a 'Blair' or 'New Labour' effect, for example, because the improving economy does not produce the expected Conservative revival from 1994 onwards.

Analysing the written texts by which leaders try to appeal to voters through the media provides direct information on what parties attempt to do. This gives independent evidence on what the party appeal actually was. With regard to voting reactions it enables us to ask the more interesting question of how voters responded to a particular campaign strategy, rather than trying to infer from their responses what the nature of the strategy was in the first place.

What our direct textual analysis of manifestos demonstrates is that 2001 was largely a holding or 'maintaining' election. In left-right terms Labour remained in the middle but was challenged for the centre-ground by the Liberal Democrats. The Conservative shift towards the centre probably prefigures a more marked change in the next election. Labour's slight shift leftwards may indicate a propensity to move more sharply in that direction next time, following the American example. But if 'normal' ideological tendencies may reassert themselves in the future, they have not yet done so in this election.

In these terms we can certainly see the 'Old Conservatives' and 'Old Liberals' in control of their respective parties and 'New' Labour has certainly not moved far enough leftwards to discard its soubriquet of 'New'. It will be interesting to see whether increased pressure for more government intervention on transport, social reform and delivery of improved public services will prompt a further move to the left in 2005/6.

We may expect the main policy changes to come from the Conservatives. Having experienced electoral bankruptcy by maintaining their pure Rightist position if they wish to expand their popular base they have nowhere to go in policy terms but centre-left — seeking to propagate 'Caring Conservatism' on a more sustained and extended basis. As Labour found from 1985–97, a return to the centre may not bring immediate results, but it is in the end the only road to take to achieve electoral success. We may see a 'New Conservatism' emerging yet.

Judith Bara and Ian Budge

1   I. Budge, 'Party Policy and Ideology: Reversing the 1950s?' in G. Evans and P. Norris (eds), *Critical Elections: British Parties and Voters in Long-Term Perspective*, Sage, 1999.
2   D. Robertson, *A Theory of Party Competition*, Wiley, 1976.
3   A comprehensive description of these procedures is given in I. Budge, H.-D. Klingemann, A. Volkens, J. Bara and E. Tanenbaum, *Mapping Policy Preferences*, Oxford University Press, 2001.
4   For more on this general approach to the analysis of elections through texts, see Robertson 1976, op. cit.; I. Budge and D.J. Farlie, *Explaining and Predicting Elections*, Allen and Unwin, 1983; I. Budge, D. Robertson and D.J. Hearl (eds), *Ideology, Strategy and Party Change*, Cambridge University Press, 1987; Budge et al. 2001, op. cit., especially Introduction.

5　H.-D. Klingemann, R.I. Hofferbert and I. Budge, *Parties, Politics and Democracy*, Westview, 1994, pp. 38–41.
6　For detail of components of the left-right scale see Appendix Tables A1 and A2. For more extensive description of the individual categories see Budge et al. 2001, op. cit., Ch. 4 and Appendix III.
7　J. Bara, 'Tracking Estimates of Public Opinion and Party Policy Intentions in Britain and the USA' in M. Laver (ed.), *Estimating the Policy Position of Political Actors*, Routledge, 2001.
8　S. Bartolini and P. Mair, *Identity, Competition and Electoral Availability: The Stabilization in European Electorates, 1885–1985*, Cambridge University Press, 1990.
9　M.J. Laver and I. Budge (eds), *Party Policy and Government Coalitions*, Macmillan, 1992.

APPENDIX

The creation of a left-right scale from manifesto emphases

In their analysis of European voting behaviour over the last century, Bartolini and Mair[8] pointed out that the only universal political division between parties is the left-right one. This conclusion receives support from the factor analyses of election programmes in 20 postwar democracies reported in Budge et al. where the leading dimension in practically all of them was left-right. The factor solutions for each country produced three or four other less important dimensions, usually peculiar to that country. A complete specification of national politics thus has to take several dimensions into account. To locate national politics in their general setting however, a one-dimensional, left-right analysis is not only sufficient but necessary — in the sense that it is the only dimension not bounded by national idiosyncrasies.

Building on these results a later comparative investigation of election programmes (manifestos) constructed the simple additive scale whose construction is summarised in Table 2.[9] Essentially the method there was to group the emphases on government intervention, welfare and peace, which left-right parties put together to make the basis of their appeal, and to contrast these with the emphases on freedom, traditional morality and military alliances which right-wing parties put together. Other issues were examined comparatively to see whether they consistently loaded on the resulting scale. Any that did were added to it. Factor analysis of the programmatic data was also done to see if any second dimension emerged consistently across all countries. None did, leaving the left-right scale used in this article as the only dimension which is able to be generalised and which enables positions estimated for British parties to be compared across time and across countries — as is demonstrated here.

Although validated by factor analysis as well as its fit to accepted historical interpretations of British and other national politics, the left-right scale used here is not based on factor scores that vary sharply with the cases taken into analysis. Instead it is based on simple addition and subtraction of percentages, as described in Table 1 and the text.

A1. Major Policy Areas in Election Manifestos, 1945–2001

101	Foreign special relationships: positive	410	Productivity
102	Foreign special relationships: negative	411	Technology and infrastructure
103	Decolonisation	412	Controlled economy
104	Military: positive	413	Nationalisation
105	Military: negative	414	Economic orthodoxy
106	Peace	415	Marxist analysis
107	Internationalism: positive	416	Anti-growth economy
108	European Community: positive	501	Environmental protection
109	Internationalism: negative	502	Arts, sports, leisure, media
110	European Community: negative	503	Social justice
201	Freedom and domestic human rights	504	Social services expansion
202	Democracy	505	Social services limitation
203	Constitutionalism: positive	506	Education expansion
204	Constitutionalism: negative	507	Education limitation
301	Decentralisation	601	National way of life: positive
302	Centralisation	602	National way of life: negative
303	Government efficiency	603	Traditional morality: positive
304	Government corruption	604	Traditional morality: negative
305	Government effectiveness and authority	605	Law and order
401	Free enterprise	606	National effort and social harmony
402	Incentives	607	Multiculturalism: positive
403	Regulation of capitalism	608	Multiculturalism: negative
404	Economic planning	701	Labour groups: positive
405	Corporatism	702	Labour groups: negative
406	Protectionism: positive	703	Agriculture
407	Protectionism: negative	705	Minority groups
408	Economic goals	706	Non-economic demographic groups
409	Keynesian demand management		

Source: Comparative Manifestos Project, Wissenschaftzentrum, Berlin, 2001.

A2. The Left-Right Scale

Right emphases (%)		**Left emphases (%)**
Pro-military (104)		Decolonisation (103)
Freedom, human rights (201)		Anti-military (105)
Constitutionalism (203)		Peace (106)
Effective authority (305)		Internationalism (107)
Free enterprise (401)		Democracy (202)
Economic incentives (402)		Regulate capitalism (403)
Anti-protectionism (407)	Minus	Economic planning (404)
Economic orthodoxy (414)		Pro-protectionism (406)
Social services limitation (505)		Controlled economy (412)
National way of life (601)		Nationalisation (413)
Traditional morality (603)		Social services expansion (504)
Law and order (605)		Education expansion (506)
Social harmony (606)		Pro-labour (701)

Source: I. Budge et al., *Mapping Policy Preferences: Estimates for Parties, Electorates and Governments 1945–98*, Oxford University Press, 2001, p. 22.

A3. Combination of Full Policy-Coding Categories into Relevant Groupings

New category		Old categories
Planned economy	403	Regulation of capitalism
	404	Economic planning
	412	Controlled economy
Quality of life	501	Environmental protection
	502	Art, sport, leisure and media
Market economy	401	Enterprise
	414	Economic orthodoxy
Welfare	503	Social justice
	504	Social services expansion
European Union: positive	108	European Union: positive
European Union: negative	110	European Union: negative
Social conservatism	203	Constitutionalism: positive
	305	Government effectiveness and authority
	601	National way of life: positive
	603	Traditional morality: positive
	605	Law and order
	606	National effort, social harmony

Note: We would like to thank Carol Ward for her help in coding the documents with speed and accuracy.

PATRICK SEYD

The Labour Campaign

The Labour Party's campaigning efforts to win a second, consecutive general election in 2001 can be distinguished along both temporal and spatial dimensions. During the four-year period of Labour government various phases of campaigning occurred involving long, medium and short time-frames. Over the long period the party's overall strategic aims and objectives were established. They were firstly, to establish a governing reputation for economic competence and the improvement of public services, secondly, to maintain an electoral strategy of appealing to 'middle England' voters and, thirdly, to manage a single-minded and united party. These objectives were then more immediately operationalised during the medium and short campaigns. A spatial dimension to the campaign is also apparent with the party campaigning both at the centre and in the constituencies and, as far as constituency campaigning is concerned, a further distinction can be made between activity coordinated from the centre and that emerging from purely local initiatives (see Table 1).

The long campaign

It is often suggested that contemporary parties are in permanent campaigning mode. There is evidence to confirm Labour's permanent, professional, opinion assessment and management. The government constantly sampled and managed public opinion. A 'People's Panel' was created to monitor attitudes towards a range of government services, a large public consultation exercise on the health services took place, and innumerable focus groups were initiated by government departments to assess public support. The government published annual reports itemising progress on every one of its 1997 manifesto promises. And, finally, from the first moment that the Labour government took office it used every opportunity to manage news in as favourable a manner as possible.

However, the realities of government also intruded. Senior politicians became increasingly absorbed in their day-to-day tasks of government and, consequently, gave little thought or time to the more immediate demands of opinion management. The party's large parliamentary majority, and a demoralised and divided Conservative opposition,

1. Labour's Election Campaign 2001

Spatial	Temporal		
	Long (May 1997–March 2000)	**Medium** (March 2000–February 2001)	**Short** (February 2001–June 2001)
Central	Government policies	HQ organisational structures established	Ministerial policy initiatives
	Government annual reports	Preparation of election manifesto	Publication of election manifesto
	Government news management	Advertising agency employed	News conferences
	Government sampling of public opinion	Priority constituencies selected	Speeches and interviews
	Party management	National telephone bank established	Party election broadcasts
	Fighting elections	Training of full-time organisers	Party advertising
			Party opinion polling
Centrally-coordinated local	Reselection or selection of MPs/candidates	Agreement of priority constituency targets	Production and distribution of candidates' election addresses
		Commencement of voter identification	Registration of postal voters
		First direct mailings to targeted voters	Direct mailings and leaflet distributions
			Candidates' news releases, meetings and interviews
Local	Selection of candidates		Production and distribution of candidates' election addresses
			Registration of postal voters
			Leaflet distributions
			Candidates' news releases, meetings and interviews

encouraged a sense of complacency at all levels of the party during the early years of government. Furthermore, immediately after the election the campaign team at party headquarters in Millbank was disbanded and the professional staff that remained devoted their energies to other matters. In addition to these factors which question the idea of a permanent election campaign, there was another difficulty for the party. The party's pre-1997 campaign professionalism had been an electoral bonus but the government's attempts to control the news agenda made it renowned more for its 'spin' than for its policy performance, and this became something of an electoral handicap. In the years following Labour's general election triumph the apparently sophisticated assessors of public opinion often turned out to be incompetent managers of news. Examples abound, of which the most prominent would be the government's inability to counteract the critical media treatment of the Millennium Dome. The government's difficulties in communicating its political messages were also compounded by the emergence of unforeseen events, such as floods, rail disasters, fuel shortages and, finally, foot and mouth disease among farm animals, from which it was often unable to distance itself.

Notwithstanding these day-to-day difficulties of governing, Blair's clear objective was to ensure that the twenty-first century would be the Labour century in the way that the twentieth had been the Conservative century. For Labour to achieve this and become the permanent governing party he believed that it had to adopt two guiding principles. Firstly, the party should not repeat its previous practice in government of introducing unrealistic policies followed by retreats a year or two later to a chorus of criticism and subsequent premature loss of office. Even before the 1997 general election, Blair had engaged in a process of deliberately lowering public expectations of what a Labour government might deliver, and he maintained this process once in office. Any idea that New Labour was no more than a short-term electoral tactic to reassure voters of the party's moderation before the 1997 general election was soon revealed to be incorrect by the actions of the new government. Blair's first Labour government set out to demonstrate its competence rather than its impractical idealism.

The second guiding principle was that the party's electoral appeal should be broad enough to include all progressive, non-Conservative voters. In Blair's opinion, Labour and Liberal Democrats were natural partners divided only by the accident of history. Liberal Democrats might not have become members of the Labour Cabinet as he and Paddy Ashdown had planned before the 1997 general election, but they remained important political partners, even if not in formal alliance. Writing in the *Guardian* (20.5.00), Blair stated that 'the truth of the matter is that people like myself in the Labour Party today and people like Charles Kennedy and the Liberal Democrats . . . are driven by the same value systems . . . So I think it's important that we move together'.

What linked both parties were progressive, anti-Conservative values. Speaking at the party's 1999 annual conference, Blair made clear his rejection of old, class-war ideology. He claimed that 'the twenty-first century will not be about the battle between capitalism and socialism but between the forces of progress and the forces of conservatism'. The party's 'historic mission' was 'to liberate Britain from the old class divisions, old structures, old prejudices, old ways of working and of doing things, that will not do in this world of change'. Labour offered a third way which 'is progressive politics distinguishing itself from conservatism of left or right'.[1]

Labour's 1997 general election manifesto contained 177 specific commitments and, in addition to these, the party made five specific pre-election pledges. It is impossible here to examine the government's record in its entirety but we can concentrate upon those areas on which it placed considerable emphasis in its 2001 election campaign, namely the economy, public services in general, and schools and hospitals in particular.

Labour in government: the economy

Gordon Brown's last budget speech before the general election claimed the lowest inflation for 30 years, the lowest long-term interest rates for 35 years, lower mortgage payments, more people in work than ever before, and the lowest unemployment since 1975. His claims contrast strikingly with the records of previous Labour Chancellors of the Exchequer during the governments of the 1960s and 1970s when economic management was the party's Achilles' heel. Previous Labour governments' economic goals were undermined by a combination of balance of payments problems, currency crises, interventions by external economic agencies, and public expenditure cuts, so the party's reputation for economic incompetence grew (see Sanders this volume).

During his first three years as Chancellor, Brown revelled in the title of the 'iron chancellor' as he balanced the current budget, brought public debt down towards 40% of GDP, and made low inflation his key objective. With the exception of boosts to educational and health spending in 1999, he refused to sanction any significant increases in public expenditure until 2000. Brown reduced public expenditure as a proportion of GDP from 41% in 1996/97 to 38% in 1999/2000, and only planned to return it to its 1997 share of GDP in 2003/4. In addition, Brown also maintained the party's pre-election commitment not to raise the level of personal, direct income tax. In April 2000 he reduced the basic rate of income tax to 22% and introduced a new starting rate of 10% on the first £1,500 of personal income. Notwithstanding these lower rates of personal tax, in 2000 the Treasury publicly acknowledged that the overall level of taxes had increased since Labour came to office. Tax levels had risen by stealth as indirect taxes, in particular value added tax, excise duties and national insurance contributions, had been modified and more money had flowed into Treasury funds from more people being in work.

In order to reassure the financial markets that management of the economy would not be subordinated to political pressures, upon becoming Chancellor, Brown immediately passed the powers to manage interest rates over to the Bank of England. This measure, combined with his financial orthodoxy, so reassured the financial community that his announcement of plans to raise public expenditure by £74 billion between 2000/1 and 2003/4 prompted no collapse of financial confidence as had occurred in the mid-1960s and 1970s under previous Labour Chancellors.

So with justification, Labour could campaign in 2001 as competent managers of the economy. The party's problem, however, was in convincing the voters that the planned growth in public expenditure, first promised in 2000, was not just an exercise in political spin and that they would experience an improvement in frontline public services.

Labour in government: the public services

Public service priorities since 1997 had been to target and improve the incomes of the most deserving groups in society, to provide more cash to schools and hospitals, and to create safer communities. The key aspect of the government's welfare policy was to provide work for people so that they would no longer rely upon state payments. The financial savings arising from a decline in the numbers of welfare claimants would then be concentrated on the worse-off, particularly poor families and pensioners. The centrepiece of the government's welfare programme was its 'New Deal' scheme which promised that 250,000 young unemployed would be found jobs in the government's first term by using £5bn from the tax levied on the 'windfall' profits of the privatised utilities. By 2001 the government claimed that 280,000 young unemployed had been found jobs on this programme.

A second feature of the government's welfare programme was the targeting of low pay. So the working families tax credit scheme, which involved combining taxes and personal allowances, benefited families in households with low-income earners. In addition, the government introduced a new childcare allowance, raised child benefit, created a new minimum income guarantee for pensioners, and introduced a statutory minimum wage of £3.60 per hour in April 1999. On the other hand, it attacked what it regarded as the 'something for nothing' culture and proposed that benefits to single parents and to the disabled should taper off very rapidly once the recipients obtained other, relatively low, forms of income such as a private pension. The overriding objective was to ensure that state benefits would only go to those in most need.

Welfare provision was the area in which the government faced its most persistent critics. The sacking of two health ministers—Harriet Harman and Frank Field—reflected the dilemmas and difficulties the government faced as it tried to resolve the demands for improved welfare services. The government's critics argued that the welfare measures it had introduced merely redistributed resources among the very needy rather than from rich to poor, which would only be achieved by taxing the better off and using such money to increase overall levels of public expenditure. Yet an Institute for Fiscal Studies examination of the impact of the government's first four budgets suggested that the changes to taxes and benefits had been redistributory by helping the poorest fifth, more than the richest fifth, of the population (*Economist*, 12.5.01). The electoral dilemma for the party, however, was that among this poorest 20% were many least likely to vote. As we will see later, the Labour Party therefore made very particular campaign efforts to target this group and ensure that they voted.

In addition to its welfare record, the government constantly stressed its improvements to hospitals, schools and communities. The government's main priority had been to cut hospital waiting lists and raise spending on the NHS in real terms. While it claimed to have succeeded in the former the problem it faced with the latter was that little of the proposed rise in real terms in aggregate health spending of 35% between 2000 and 2005 would be felt by voters at the time of the general election.

Blair's oft-repeated claim before the 1997 election was that his government's first priority would be to 'education, education, education'. The government promised to raise educational standards in schools, by extending the system of testing pupil performance and the inspection of schools by OFSTED previously introduced by the Conservatives, and by employing more teachers. By 2001 pupils' standards had improved, as measured by reading and numeracy skills at the age of 11, and GCSE passes at the age of 16. Furthermore, additional teachers employed in primary schools meant that class sizes had been reduced. However, critics pointed out that education expenditure as a percentage of GDP had not reached 5%. In addition, they argued that educational opportunity for all had been undermined by encouraging parental choice of schools. They complained that the commitment made by David Blunkett prior to the 1997 election to end selection of pupils at the age of 11 had been abandoned, and that the procedures which allowed parents to challenge the existence of local grammar schools and replace them with comprehensive schools had been rigged in favour of the former. However, Blair's hostility to comprehensive schools was all too apparent when he claimed that 'too often . . . (they) adopted a one-size-fits-all mentality — no setting, uniform provision for all, hostile to the notion of specialisation and centres of excellence within areas of the curriculum' (*Guardian*, 9.10.00). Blair's press spokesman, Alastair Campbell, further angered opponents of selective secondary education by pointedly referring to 'bog-standard comprehensives'.

In the election campaign the government's appeal to the party's traditional working-class constituency was based upon its creation of almost full employment and its introduction of a minimum wage and a working families tax credit scheme, both of which boosted the incomes of low-paid families. Its other claim for working-class voters' support was based around its creation of safer communities. The government's tougher attitude toward criminal behaviour and the introduction of child protection, child safety and anti-social behaviour orders had helped communities plagued by crime. Jack Straw, as Home Secretary, consistently argued that the critics of his tough policing and sentencing policies were middle-class, 'Hampstead liberals', out of touch with the concerns and fears of the working-class.

Labour in government: public support

A cursory glance at the opinion polls between 1997 and 2001 suggests that Labour's task of winning the general election was easy because public support remained consistently high. However, well-publicised cases of public service failures in the early months of 2000 contributed to a decline in public support for the government. By June 2000 a MORI poll revealed that between December 1999 and June 2000 Blair's public approval rating had dropped by 35 points and Labour's lead over the Conservatives had fallen by 12 points (*The Times*, 30.6.00). In June Blair suffered the ignominy of being barracked and silenced when he addressed the annual meeting of the Womens' Institutes. Further evidence of Labour's waning public popularity was seen by a sharp dip in the polls during the protests over the fuel price rises in September and October 2000, the one occasion when the Conservatives managed to close the gap.

To make matters worse this drop in the party's opinion poll support seemed to confirm what the voters had been saying over a twelve-month period in the Scottish, Welsh, European and London Assembly elections (see Table 2). The erosion in the party's opinion poll-ratings and the poor election results prompted a wave of public criticism from people who previously had been fully signed up members of the New Labour project, and leaks of information from the very heart of government. One such leak, from Philip Gould, Blair's key public opinion adviser, described the party's predicament as 'serious' and

2. Labour's Electoral Performance, 1997 and 2000

Vote (%)	UK general election June 1997	Scottish Parliament May 1999	Welsh Assembly May 1999	European Parliament June 1999	London Assembly May 2000
Labour	43	39	38	28	30
Conservative	31	16	16	35	29
Liberal Democrat	17	14	14	12	15
Nationalists	3	29	28	–	–
Others	7	3	5	24	26

Source: G. Evans and P. Norris, *Critical Elections*, Sage 1999; *Representation* 1999 and 2000.

suggested that 'Labour's majority will fall dramatically' (*Guardian*, 20.7.00). At the very heart of government a nervousness and insecurity existed engendered by fear that a Labour government would only be a temporary phenomenon in conservative Britain. Blair was concerned that popular support was fragile and the government needed to reassure the readers of the *Daily Mail* and the *Sun* that it was responding to their views. Hence his response to Gould's gloomy memo was to assert that on 'the touchstone issues' of the family, asylum and crime, and the nation the government was seen as 'insufficiently assertive' (*The Times*, 17.7.00) and needed a strategy of tough measures on these issues with some eye-catching proposals to reassure public opinion. Soon after came his specific proposal for on-street fines of people engaged in rowdy, drunken street behaviour.

The poor election results also prompted argument within the party regarding political strategy and, in particular, whether it should be directing its appeal primarily to 'core' or 'non-core' voters. Critics of New Labour claimed that the party's 'core' voters — defined in socio-economic terms as the working class and in spatial terms as those living in industrial areas — were abstaining from voting because the government was failing to deliver improved public services. Such criticisms were publicly rejected by Blair, by John Prescott who was seen as the guardian of the 'Old', working-class Labour Party and, perhaps surprisingly, by Claire Short who had publicly criticised aspects of the party's media management prior to the 1997 general election. Blair argued that 'the whole country is our core constituency', and continued, 'I was never able to do anything for the unemployed or the poor in my constituency until we were capable of winning in the south as well as the north. So don't let us ever be pushed back into the position of saying "there is one part of the country we represent and some parts we don't represent". We represent all of Britain' (*Guardian*, 2.2.00).[2]

Labour in government: party management[3]

All previous, postwar Labour Prime Ministers experienced considerable difficulties in managing their party while in government. Their parliamentary colleagues were often divided and the number of persistent rebels in the PLP was high, and in the extra-parliamentary party both the NEC and the annual conferences were a focal point for critical party activists. On occasions open warfare between party and government had seemed to be the norm. Blair and his colleagues believed that Labour disunity was a powerful explanation of the party's previous poor electoral record and set out to make sure this did not occur after 1997. Their task was made more difficult, however, because they had two contradictory aims concerning the party. The first was to create 'a modern, disciplined party with a strong centre' (Blair, *Independent*, 20.11.98), and the second was 'to give the party back to its membership, to empower members'.[4]

New policy-making institutions and procedures were introduced in 1997 which replaced the century-long traditions of NEC policy documents and annual conference resolutions. An attempt was made to introduce a new form of consensual management and to encourage a broader sense of stakeholding within the party. A joint policy committee, a national policy forum, and eight policy commissions were created to discuss the proposals which would form the party's future political programme. Although there were possibilities for members to play a prominent role in policy making in this new system, in fact the procedures made it easier for the leadership to dominate the discussions. Meanwhile, although the party rules stipulated that the annual conference remained the sovereign policy-making body, in practice it now played a subordinate role and became more of a tightly-controlled showcase for the leadership. A problem with these new procedures and institutions was that the majority of members felt little sense of ownership of their party's policies and therefore were less likely to act as ambassadors or election campaigners.

What also concerned the leadership was that the calibre of the party's elected representatives was often not good enough, in its opinion, for them to act as effective political communicators. As a consequence, the procedures for selecting candidates, whether European, national or devolved parliamentary or assembly elections, were completely overhauled. Although the procedures varied slightly according to the institution, the principles remained similar throughout. A two-stage sifting process of personal applications was established, based upon a range of criteria and conducted by members of the central political elite, prior to the successful ones being included on an approved panel of candidates. The practice of the various selection panels varied, nevertheless the leadership now had the powers to devise a candidates' panel made up of people more likely to be 'on message'.[5]

There is no doubt that by 2001 the party was a more singular body than at any previous time in its history, making the leadership's task of political communication so much easier. By a combination of control and leadership patronage and persuasion the various wings of the party — parliamentary and extra-parliamentary, central and local, professional and voluntary — were all talking a very similar language.

The post-1997 practice of party management often seemed incompetent and inefficient compared with the years 1994–97 when it had been highly effective. No doubt this is partly explained by the fact that many of the key actors were now more concerned with government than party affairs and, therefore, left it to others less skilled in these matters. Two serious mistakes were for the leadership to interfere in selecting a party leader in Wales and a mayoral candidate in London which resulted in choices contrary to the wishes of the majority of individual members in those regions. Neither episode enhanced Blair's reputation among members and reduced the likelihood of their fulfilling their role as ambassadors.

After 1997 the number of members declined by over 100,000 to 255,000.[6] Decline was partly inevitable now that there was no longer a Conservative government to oppose and to act as an incentive to join Labour. Particular Labour government policies and the treatment of members in Wales and London also contributed to falling numbers. Apart from an exit strategy there was also some voice by New Labour's critics, but nothing like the organised opposition from within the party that previous Labour governments had experienced. The election of a number of 'grassroots alliance' candidates to the NEC was no more than a minor irritant although it did demonstrate that among the diminishing number of party members, not all were fans of New Labour.

If exit and voice were apparent among the membership after 1997 so also was loyalty. In 1999 62% of members approved of the government's record.[7] However, a problem for the leadership was that these loyal members were now less active than previously. Whereas in 1990 51% of the members devoted no time to party activities by 1999 this had risen to 65%. Some of the activities which members were no longer engaging in were election related, such as leafleting, contacting voters and working for the party on election days. As we will see when examining the spatial dimension, the Labour Party could not manage all its election campaigning from the centre and it still required local activists.

The medium campaign

The medium campaign commenced in spring 2000 with the approval at the centre of the main campaign themes and the establishment of the organisational structures in anticipation of a possible general election twelve months later. An all-day meeting of Cabinet ministers in March discussed a paper prepared by Brown which highlighted five key themes for the party's campaign—employment opportunities for all, tackling child poverty through help for families, strong public services, security in retirement and support for business. Following this meeting, the essential features of the party's organisational structures were established. The party headquarters staff based at Millbank were organised into 11 task forces,[8] the party's advertising agency was employed and detailed planning of the campaign was initiated. General election planning and strategy groups were created, the former chaired by Mandelson (replaced by Prescott when he resigned as a minister), and the latter by Brown. For a period of six months the details of every aspect of the campaign were meticulously prepared.

Even though in the Millbank party headquarters this phase was more one of preparing for the short campaign by selecting key personnel and establishing essential structures, in the constituencies which had been selected for special attention the campaigning commenced. Activists' first priority in the summer months was to make direct contact with the voters and ascertain their political loyalties. These up-to-date records were then checked against similar voter identification exercises in 1997, and any similar material obtained in subsequent European or local elections, to identify Labour voters whose political commitments might have slipped. These were the people upon whom the local parties concentrated most of their efforts over the next twelve months. In addition, by the autumn activists were identifying and contacting particular voters, in particular those having a vote for the first time and those Labour sympathisers with a tendency not to vote.

The short campaign

Blair fired the starting gun for the immediate race in February 2001 with a keynote speech promising a 'radical second-term agenda'. This was followed one week later by, what party headquarters grandly titled, a party 'spring conference' in Glasgow, to enable all senior Cabinet ministers to make speeches and launch new policy initiatives. The question of whether the election would be called in late April or in May had still been left open, but all the planning was derailed by the outbreak of foot and mouth disease. The postponement of the general election until 7 June caused all sorts of complications, particularly since there were now strict financial accounting regulations for both party donations and national campaign expenditure. Furthermore, many of the party's full-time organisers had been appointed on short-term contracts that terminated at the end of May. For a few weeks at the end of April and the beginning of May a phoney election war prevailed and the party's constituency campaigning went on hold until after the Easter holiday. A major feature of a party's short campaign is the publication of its election manifesto. We have previously referred to the party's institutional reforms and new processes for developing its long-term programme. Since 1997 local and national policy forums and policy commissions had spent many hours producing and discussing proposals covering a wide range of policy options. The immediate responsibility for producing the first draft of the election manifesto was given to Ed Richards, appointed in autumn 1999 to the Prime Minister's policy unit. Over the following fifteen months he was involved in detailed discussions with ministers, civil servants, backbenchers, think tank personnel, academics, and trade union leaders on the future programme. The most influential input to this exercise came from ministerial advisers. By contrast, the input from the entire national policy forum exercise was limited. The final detailed drafting of the manifesto was the responsibility of Blair, Brown, and a few senior members of the Cabinet, including Blunkett and Straw, aided by senior personnel from the Prime Minister's office.

Formal approval of the manifesto by a joint meeting of the members of the Cabinet and NEC is required by the party constitution. On the last occasion in 1979 when a Labour government had devised a manifesto for a second term this meeting had been confrontational and ill tempered. By contrast, nothing similar occurred this time reflecting either the harmony, accord and support for New Labour within the party or the limited opportunities within the new party structures for dissent.

The manifesto was entitled 'Ambitions for Britain', suggesting that the party's tasks were not yet completed. In his introduction, Blair made clear that only the foundations of the new Britain had been laid and the election now gave the party the opportunity to build on this for the future. The manifesto contained two fundamental commitments — 'renewal of our public services' and 'spreading power, wealth and opportunity more widely'. In pursuit of both it offered 'ten-year goals', 'next steps' and, as in 1997, 'five pledges for the next five years'. Not surprisingly the themes were very similar to those contained in the 1997 manifesto. The only significant difference was that the stress placed upon the need for reform of state institutions in 1997 was not repeated in 2001.

Labour's 1997 and 2001 campaigns

Labour's 'Operation Victory' in 1997 had clear targets. Firstly, its efforts were directed specifically at Conservative voters and, in particular, at the 'aspirational working-class in manual occupations' and 'the increasingly insecure white-collar workers with middle-to-low incomes'.[9] Secondly, it concentrated all its campaigning efforts in ninety target constituencies. In 1997 central direction of the party from top to bottom was clear and the language of the war room, battle plan, generals and troops was appropriate. By contrast, the organisation of the campaign in 2001 was different and the language and metaphors used to describe it need to be modified.

In 2001 'Operation Turnout' targeted weak Labour supporters defined as first-time Labour voters in 1997, as well as Labour voters in 1997 whose support for the party was now less firm or who had not voted in local or European elections in the intervening years, and Labour supporters in low turnout areas. The party believed that the problem with these weak Labour voters would not be that they might switch to other parties but that they might not vote and then 'if just one in five voters who voted at the last general election stays at home this time, and nobody switches their support back to the Tories, we stand to lose 60 seats'.[10] In 1997 all the party's campaigning resources had been strictly concentrated within the 90 target seats, but in 2001 'there are no key seats, only key voters'.[11] It would have been very difficult for party headquarters to abandon any of the 146 seats gained in the 1997 election. So resources were concentrated on 148 'priority' seats and members were encouraged, not instructed, to work in them.[12]

The central campaign

We have already referred to the structures established to oversee the campaign, namely the general election planning and strategy groups and the eleven Millbank task forces. Some of the key features of the central campaign during the thirty days following the formal announcement of the election date were the publication of five manifestos,[13] the 26 national news conferences, the five party election broadcasts, and the national advertising campaigns. Blair made 29 formal speeches in total, six of which were keynote speeches, engaged in four open question or studio debates, and gave four lengthy one-to-one media interviews. John Prescott's travels over 6,000 miles on his 'express-bus' took him to 120 'priority', 'battleground' and 'heartland' constituencies. This part of the agenda-setting campaign was conducted almost entirely through the media. The party's main targets were the nightly national and regional TV news bulletins. As far as national newspapers were concerned, the party's view was that they had their own political agendas and therefore unmediated communication was almost impossible; it was better, therefore, to target local newspapers which contained less opinion and more news.

Throughout these thirty days the campaign remain centred upon its pre-planned grid of themes; firstly, the strong economy then, secondly the commitment to public services and then, in the final days of campaigning, to schools and hospitals. Every aspect of the party's communications via the press conferences, leadership speeches, election broadcasts, advertisements, and website pages[14] were integrated into these themes. So, for example, the first two of the party election broadcasts emphasised Labour's economic performance and contrasted this with a likely Conservative 'economic disaster'. The third concentrated on Blair as leader, and then the final two stressed ordinary people's dedication to the public services, and the need to vote to maintain these services. At no time was the party drawn into a detailed debate on the issue of Europe. At this level of campaigning the language of the battle zone remains appropriate in that Labour strategists set out immediately to destabilise the Conservative campaign, which they succeeded in doing by concentrating upon the 'hidden Conservative agenda' of public expenditure cuts and ruthlessly exploiting Oliver Letwin's off-the-record suggestion in the *Financial Times* of a figure of £20m. It was also noticeable that at the centre Labour made no public attacks upon the Liberal Democrats. But within the priority seats, Liberal Democrat voters and sympathisers were specifically targeted to switch to Labour.

Throughout the campaign opinion polls confirmed that voters were overwhelmingly concerned with public services and thus Labour's campaign was well directed. Nevertheless its campaign was publicly wrong footed on three occasions when leadership nervousness over the question of taxation was apparent. The first occurred immediately after the election date had been announced when an Institute for Fiscal Studies' report stated that the government's expenditure plans could not be sustained solely by economic growth from 2003 onwards and would therefore either have to be cut or be funded by additional taxes. Secondly, in the eight-day gap between the announcement of the election date and the publication of the election manifesto no one was willing to state, in response to questioning, whether or not personal taxes would rise if Labour were re-elected. Thirdly, the leadership was slow in responding to the question of whether or not Labour would raise the ceiling on national insurance contributions as a means of increasing revenue. In addition, the emphasis the leadership gave to the possible private delivery of public services created some apprehension among its supporters.

By contrast with 1997, the media was more critical of Labour's 2001 campaign. The manifesto launch seemed to confirm its view that the party was over reliant upon spin. Furthermore, journalists gleefully emphasised the occasions when the party's attempts to choreograph the campaign were undermined by the Prescott punch, by Jack Straw being barracked at a police federation conference, and by Blair being unexpectedly confronted outside a Birmingham hospital by an angry voter.

The centrally-coordinated local campaign

All the centrally coordinated campaigning initiatives coming from party headquarters in Millbank were organised around the priority seats. These constituency parties were eligible for central technological support, namely the leasing of computers and election software, full-time, organising support,[15] access to both the national telephone call centre in North Shields (set up in January 2001 with 60 staff) and the regional call centres, and the receipt of centrally-produced literature, including leaflets, the 'Labour Rose' newspaper and personal letters, targeted at particular groups of voters, from Blair and Brown. In addition, 63 of the priority seats received 5,000 copies of specially produced videos highlighting the achievements of the local Labour MP to be distributed among Labour-supporting households with less likelihood of voting. Finally, the priority seats received a centrally planned stream of senior politicians and other prominent personalities to help generate material for the local media.

In return for this central support, local parties were set distinct targets. By June 2000, they had to have contacted half of all voters, and identified all first-time voters and all those who had voted Labour in the 1997 general election but not since. Then by October 2000 local parties were expected to have telephoned all first-time voters, written to all general election only voters, and 'blitzed'[16] all low turnout areas twice. And, finally, by December 2000 they had to have communicated twice with all first-time voters and organised a programme of events in low turnout areas.

What the local parties provided in this centrally coordinated part of the campaign were human and financial resources. Active members were required to carry out the 'voter identification' and 'building relationships' exercises by using local telephone banks; the national telephone bank would then supplement their efforts. Once the targeted group of voters had been identified the direct mailings had to be delivered by hand since postal charges would have been too expensive. Beyond these two key activities, local members were needed to resource the street stalls (important for general voter contact and for the registration of postal votes) and for the 'blitzing' of areas of strong Labour support.

The local campaign

Campaigning — voter identification, leafleting and communicating with voters — in the non-priority seats varied considerably depending upon the numbers and commitments of members. These safe ('heartland') or hopeless constituencies received none of the centrally-provided technology, trained staff or literature and videos, but electronic mail, used extensively for the first time by headquarters, gave them direct access to material — daily briefings, campaign arguments and publicity opportunities — which helped their campaigns. Whereas in 1997 local parties had been instructed by headquarters to send their members to work in the target seats, in 2001, in both safe and hopeless constituencies, they were left to work out for themselves whether to assist in the priority seats.

Conclusion

The Labour campaigns of 1997 and 2001 can be analysed along both temporal and spatial dimensions, however within such a framework there are important differences between the two campaigns which need to be stressed. The most obvious is that in 2001 Labour was the incumbent government and therefore both the long and the short campaigns were of a different nature. As far as the centrally coordinated local campaign in 2001 is concerned, there are also differences. Firstly, by 2001 telephone canvassing had almost completely replaced any face-to-face canvassing. Campaigners believed it to be more efficient in the numbers contacted and the information acquired. It enabled direct mail to be more accurately targeted. As one party professional commented to the author, 'carpet bombing has been replaced by cruise missile accuracy'. Secondly, the 2001 campaign was less about commands and instructions from Millbank and more about facilitating and assisting local, trained personnel. Beyond Millbank there are now highly trained, albeit smaller, teams of party activists. These groups are aware that there are fewer committed partisans among the voters, whether in

3. General Election Results, 2001

Vote (%)	Great Britain	Labour's priority seats	Labour's battleground seats	Labour's heartland seats*
Number of seats	–	148	62	319
Labour	43.8	47.9	46.8	56.8
Conservative	31.0	35.0	35.1	21.6
Liberal Democrat	18.1	12.8	13.5	21.6

Note: * Heartland seats are defined as those with a Labour majority in 2001 of 15% or over. Source: British Parliamentary Constituency Database, 1992–2001.

priority or heartland seats, so that there needs to be more regular voter contact over a long campaign.

The fact that Labour was returned again to government with as large a parliamentary majority must be counted as a campaign success. Its four-year strategy of governing competence, 'broad-tent' electoral appeal, and efficient party management reaped electoral dividends. The party's strict planning of its indirect forms of communication meant that for much of the short, official campaign its agenda was more relevant to voters' concerns than the Conservative's agenda. Furthermore, it avoided any elephant traps set by its opponents. It should be noted, however, that the trends in all the national opinion polls suggest that during the official campaign Labour's support showed a modest but steady erosion, while the Liberal Democrats gained.

There were also successes in the party's direct forms of campaigning. Among its 'priority' seats the party lost only five, and gained one. Furthermore, the campaigning in the 'priority' and 'battleground' seats paid dividends; in the former, the drop in the Labour vote was less than the drop in Labour's vote overall, and in the latter Labour's share of the vote marginally increased (see Tables 3 and 4). Over the past three general elections the Labour Party has created a formidable campaign machine which, in relation to the overall shares of the vote, succeeded in restricting the Conservative's parliamentary majority in 1992 and then in strengthening Labour's parliamentary majorities in 1997 and 2001. Labour's successful campaigning in 2001 makes the Conservative Party's recovery all that more difficult.

The one significant campaign failure, as discussed further by Whiteley in this volume, was that 40% of the electorate did not vote. Party strategists had long recognised turnout to be a potential problem,

4. Change in General Election Results, 1997–2001

Change 1997–2001 (%)	Great Britain	Labour's priority seats	Labour's battleground seats	Labour's heartland seats*
Number of seats	–	148	62	319
Labour	−2.0	−0.3	+0.6	−3.7
Conservative	+0.8	−0.3	−1.0	+0.2
Liberal Democrat	+1.5	+0.6	+0.6	+2.7
Turnout	−12.5	−12.6	−12.0	−13.5

Note: * Heartland seats are defined as those with a Labour majority in 2001 of 15% or over. Source: British Parliamentary Constituency Database, 1992–2001.

especially in Labour-held seats. But larger falls in turnout overall, and in Labour's share of the vote, in its heartland seats pose problems which might necessitate a shift in campaign strategies for the next general election.

Patrick Seyd

* I am grateful to the Labour MPs and candidates, election agents, national and regional full-time staff, and party advisers who gave time to discuss the campaign with me.

1   Speech at the Annual Conference of the Labour Party, 1999.
2   For Prescott, see *Guardian* (31.5.00) and for Short, see *Tribune* (7.4.00). See also, P. Diamond et al, 'Must Labour Choose?', *Progress*, 2000.
3   For a more detailed analysis of this topic see P. Seyd, 'Labour Government-Party Relationships: Maturity or Marginalisation?' in A. King (ed.), *Britain at the Polls, 2001*, Chatham House, 2001.
4   *Twenty-First Century Party*, Labour Party, 1999.
5   See E. Shaw, 'New Labour: New Pathways to Parliament', *Parliamentary Affairs*, 2001.
6   Accurate membership figures are difficult to obtain. The party's latest available official figures record a decline of 44,000 between 1997 and 1999. *Tribune* (29.6.01) suggests a figure of 254,000 in 2001.
7   The figures are taken from surveys of the Labour Party membership conducted in 1990, 1997 and 1999. For further details see P. Seyd and P. Whiteley, *Labour's New Grassroots: The Transformation of the Party Membership*, Palgrave, 2002.
8   The task forces were: attack and rebuttal, coordination, external projection, field operations, fundraising and endorsements, leader's tour, legal, media, membership, operations and policy briefing.
9   P. Gould, *The Unfinished Revolution*, Little Brown, 1998, p. 396.
10 *Operation Turnout Explained*, Labour Party, 2000.
11 Ibid.
12 In addition to the 146 seats Labour won in 1997 two seats were added to the list — Dorset South and Boston and Skegness. Within this group of 148 'priority' seats, however, there was a smaller group of 'battleground' seats, which were regarded as the most electorally vulnerable. The Millbank staff operated with some degree of flexibility in choosing the 'battleground' seats. They included the 56 seats which Labour had not targeted in 1997 and had won unexpectedly plus some others believed to be particularly vulnerable. The number therefore varied between 60 and 70. These 'battleground' seats received more central help (for example, more access to the national telephone bank) than the 'priority' seats. In addition, a few other Labour-held seats (Carmarthen East and Dinefwr, Cardiff Central and Chesterfield), were believed to be possible losses and were therefore accorded some central assistance.
13 In addition to the national manifesto, separate Scottish, Welsh, business and small business manifestos were produced.
14 See Coleman, this volume.
15 80 full-timers were recruited on short-term contracts in 1999 and then intensively trained in election campaigning over the next 12 months before being sent in Autumn 2000 to particular regions to take responsibility for a group of priority seats.
16 'Blitzing' involved the MP and a group of members knocking on doors in a strong Labour neighbourhood and inviting people to meet and raise issues with the MP. The belief was that this more direct, face-to-face contact would reinforce people's likelihood of voting in such areas.

Conservatives in Opposition

From 1997 to 2001 the Conservatives experienced their most futile period in Opposition in the last one hundred years. It was an utterly bleak period that could have been largely avoided with a steadier hand and a clearer strategic direction.

The debacle of the 1997 general election

The 1997 general election saw the worst performance for the party in votes since 1832 and in seats since 1906. In 1992 14.1 million had voted Conservative compared with 9.6 million in 1997 with the party's share of the popular vote falling from 41.9% to 30.7%.[1] The swing from Conservative to Labour of 10% was below that of 1945 (12%). But the party trailed in every age and occupational group, except the over 65s and the AB professional classes.[2] The party was left without any seats in Scotland and Wales and was largely denuded of seats in the large cities and metropolitan areas of England. The parliamentary party was halved in size, losing 178 seats and retaining just 165. A record number of Cabinet ministers lost their seats, while a third of the successful MPs won with majorities of fewer than 5,000. The greatest losses, both in share of votes and in seats, came in Greater London and the South East of England.[3] The Conservatives were left requiring a swing of 11.6% to win an overall majority in the 2001 general election.

Changes in leadership, June 1997

The defeated Prime Minister John Major announced his resignation as party leader on 2 May, the day after the election. He was criticised rather than admired for this swift action. The former Deputy Prime Minister and principal contender for the succession, Michael Heseltine, ruled himself out following heart problems. Five candidates were nominated for the election: Kenneth Clarke, William Hague, Michael Howard, Peter Lilley and John Redwood. Michael Portillo and Malcolm Rifkind, Defence Secretary and Foreign Secretary until the election defeat, were ruled out as they had lost their seats. Howard, Lilley and Redwood were knocked out in the initial rounds, Howard and Lilley supporting Hague and Redwood eventually deciding to support Clarke in a bizarre dual ticket designed to unite left and right.[4] Seven weeks elapsed between Major's resignation and the eventual defeat of Clarke by Hague on 19 June by a margin of 92 to 70 votes. Gillian Peele suggests that had the party members voted in the 1997 leadership contest, then Clarke would probably have won, due to his popularity in the country.[5] As it was, his pro-Europe stance counted against him among the electorate of the 165 MPs, while Hague was able to portray himself as presenting a clean break from the Majorite past, and being blessed with the mantle of Lady Thatcher. At 36 he became the youngest leader of the Conservative Party since 1783.

Changes to the Shadow Cabinet

Until Hague's election on 19 June 1997, those members of Major's last Cabinet who survived election defeat held the Shadow Cabinet posts. Hague had five Shadow Cabinets in the space of four years, a rapid rate of change, although his final reshuffle was only minor.[6] His first Shadow Cabinet had a broad-base and involved all his fellow leadership contenders, except Ken Clarke, who made it clear that he wanted to return to the backbenches, from where he pursued an active business career. Hague's first Shadow Cabinet also contained ten members of Major's last Cabinet, including himself. Howard was Shadow Foreign Secretary, Lilley Shadow Chancellor, Mawhinney Shadow Home Secretary, Gillian Shephard Shadow Leader of the Commons, Lord Cranborne Shadow Leader of the Lords, whilst John Redwood (*hors de combat* since the 1995 leadership election) was brought back to the top table as Shadow Secretary for Trade and Industry. Lord Parkinson, architect of the 1983 general election victory, was appointed as Party Chairman, whilst Iain Duncan Smith from the right wing was appointed Shadow Social Security Secretary and John Maples on the left became Shadow Health Secretary.

The first reshuffle on 1 June 1998 saw the rehabilitation of some former senior Conservatives including Ann Widdecombe, who became Shadow Health Secretary and David Willetts, Shadow Secretary for the DfEE, while space was also found for newcomers including Liam Fox (constitutional affairs) and Gary Streeter (international development). The next reshuffle on 15 June 1999 saw a large clear-out of Major's team with the departures of Lilley (most recently Deputy Leader in charge of policy renewal), Howard, Fowler and Shephard. The balance shifted to the right with promotions into the Shadow Cabinet of Bernard Jenkin, Angela Browning and Teresa May. While Ann Widdecombe became Shadow Home Secretary and Iain Duncan Smith, Shadow Defence Secretary. The next reshuffle of 1 February 2000 saw the departure of John Redwood and John Maples and the promotion of Michael Portillo, who had re-entered Parliament in a by-election as the Member for Kensington and Chelsea, to Shadow Chancellor. Hague's final reshuffle came on 26 September and saw the young Oliver Letwin becoming Shadow Chief Secretary to the Treasury.

Changes in structure, organisation and personnel at Conservative Central Office

Hague needed to find a replacement for Brian Mawhinney, who had been Major's Party Chairman during the 1997 election campaign. His choice fell on Lord Parkinson, chosen for his experience, popular appeal, as well as his closeness to Lady Thatcher. Parkinson presided over some internal party reforms, but no longer possessed the same acumen and flair for the job, least of all at such an unpropitious point in the party's history. Michael Ancram, a Tory grandee with support across the party, a former Northern Ireland minister and since 1997, Deputy Chairman, succeeded Parkinson in October 1998. Ancram worked closely with Archie Norman, former Chief Executive of Asda, in overhauling the internal structure of Conservative Central Office, which must qualify as one of the most regularly overhauled organisations in Europe. Conscious attempts were made to learn from New Labour's 'Millbank model', by establishing a campaign war-room and an open-plan office integrating press, policy and research. The key policy figure was Danny Finkelstein, appointed director of the research department in 1995 under Major and who had become head of the new policy unit in January 1999. Finklestein was an excellent strategist, but the leadership did not listen carefully to his advice. Amanda Platell was brought in as head of media in 1999. Highly experienced in Fleet Street, and a former editor of the *Sunday Express*, she played a part in raising the profile of the party in the press and in matching Labour's highly sophisticated media management. Former Major policy wonks Tim Collins and Andrew Lansley advised on strategy, whilst Sebastian Coe, former Olympic runner and Tory MP played a ubiquitous role as Hague's chief of staff. 'Yellow M', the little known Edinburgh advertising agency, replaced the party's long-standing usage of M&C Saatchi. They were responsible for the hard-hitting 2001 poster campaigns: 'You paid the taxes, so where are the . . . nurses, teachers, police' etc.

Changes to the party constitution, constituency associations and membership

Hague made a wide-ranging review of party organisation an early priority. In a keynote speech in July 1997 he set out his themes — unity, decentralisation, democracy, integrity, and openness.[7] He also acknowledged the need for much tighter control over MPs following the allegations of sleaze, which had mired the last years of Major's premiership. He established a single-governing board of the Conservative Party, overseeing organisation and management, and uniting the professional and voluntary wings of the party. Little was achieved, though, in arresting the long-term erosion of party membership, which had been 756,000 in 1992, 400,000 in 1997 and by 2001 just over 300,000.[8]

A more decisive change came in 1998 with the adoption of a new procedure for the election of party leader. Annual elections were abandoned, but a contest could be triggered either by the leader's voluntary resignation or formal notification to the 1922 Committee by 15% of the parliamentary party.[9] A series of elimination ballots by Conservative MPs would reduce the number of candidates to just two before the final stage, where their fate would be decided by a postal ballot of the whole party membership. Hague hoped that the new model would encourage more active grass roots participation. In the same vein, he introduced membership ballots to endorse or reject major policy proposals, as occurred in 1998 with policy towards the Euro. An ethics and integrity committee was set up to combat sleaze but it did not save the party from Lord Archer entering the mayoral campaign in November 1999, nor Hague's humiliating endorsement of Archer, who withdrew his candidature under a cloud. 'Conservative Future' replaced the Young Conservatives in 1997, while 'Conservative Network' was set up as a national organisation aimed at professionals. A new 'Cultural Unit' was set up to promote ethnic minority membership and external links and participation within the party, whilst 'Renewing One Nation' sought to revive relations with charities and religious groups. The 'Conservative Political Forum' was introduced in 1998 to galvanise constituency discussion groups. Despite all these initiatives, the scale of constituency association involvement, activity, and the numbers of volunteers were all on the wane.

Party funding

Over £20 million was spent on the 1997 election campaign, which left the party four million pounds in debt.[10] Large corporate donations, which dwindled when the party was still in power, dried-up further. Business saw little need to give to the Tories, with the party in opposition and no prospect of returning to power in the foreseeable future, and with Labour under Blair and Brown no longer such a serious threat to their interests.[11] As discussed by Fisher in this volume, the Political Parties, Elections and Referendums Act, which came into effect in February in 2001, required parties to name their donors and specify the size of their gifts. For the first time there were caps on election campaign expenditure and foreign donations were banned. Michael Ashcroft and Graham Kirkham, party treasurers, worked hard to raise revenue with the new guidelines looming. By 2000, the party's financial position had partly recovered from the post-1997 slump. The outlook was also transformed by a number of individual donations including a donation of several million pounds from businessman Stuart Wheeler, in the run up to the election. Finance had been a constant worry during four years from 1997 to 2001. Few individuals and corporations appeared keen to give their money to a stumbling party so far off the lead.

Changes in policy and ideological direction

The Conservatives' biggest failure between 1997 and 2001 was in policy direction and clarity. Rather than holding a deep and sustained rethink, as the party had done between 1945–50, 1965–70 and 1975–79, the party let policy go in far too many directions, with little clear grasp of overall strategy. Hague may have been a brilliant tactician, but he was a poor strategist. In his Shadow Cabinet team he had thinkers like Peter Lilley and David Willetts, and in Central Office, Danny Finkelstein and Andrew Cooper, but he did not use them to best effect. Instead of calling for a three to four-year policy rethink, Hague let policy bob around like a buoy in a choppy sea. Policy went through a number of manifestations: 'caring, compassionate Conservatism' combined with social liberalism from 1997 to 1998, followed by 'kitchen table Conservatism', designed to shift Tory thinking towards issues of concern to 'ordinary voters'. Then came Lilley's 1999 speech calling for more focus on health and education, reform of the public services, and a distancing from Thatcherism. This led to Lilley's departure, a great loss to the party. Success in the European elections in June 1999 on a Euro-sceptic ticket, and the arrival into the press office that summer of Amanda Platell and Nick Wood, combined to drive the party in a more right-wing and populist direction. 'Popularism' then held sway until the 2001 general election, with leadership support for Tony Martin, the Norfolk farmer who shot dead an intruder, and the fuel protestors ('fine upstanding citizens'). 'Bogus' asylum seekers were disparaged, with anti-Europeanism to the fore.[12] Rather than defining and then preaching core Conservative values, Tory policy seemed designed to gain the approval of David Yelland, Editor of the *Sun*. The fact that the 2001 Conservative Manifesto, written by David Willetts, Danny Finkelstein and Greg Clark, contained some deep thinking, was largely ignored by both press and electorate.

Party divisions

The party remained deeply divided between 1997 and 2001. There were two defections to Labour, Peter Temple-Morris in June 1998 over the party's Euro-sceptic line and the more high profile defection of former communications supremo, Shaun Woodward, in December 1999 over leadership policy on 'Section 28' and the alleged abandonment of 'middle-of-the-road' Conservatism. The deepest bloodletting was over Britain's future role and participation in the European Union.[13] A minority of the parliamentary party, championed by Kenneth Clarke, wanted the options on the euro to remain open. Hague, however, announced in 1998 that he would rule out membership of the single currency during the following parliament, regardless of a referendum.

Europhiles Ian Taylor and David Curry both resigned from the front-bench and it became clear that open enthusiasm for the EU would not result in preferment. Allied to this central divide was the debate over whether Thatcherism should be continued until all last vestiges of state ownership and public provision were removed, or whether Conservatives should advocate a more pragmatic role for the state as a provider of services. A further divide came between the 'social liberals', such as Michael Portillo and Peter Lilley, and the authoritarians, above all Ann Widdecombe. This debate came to a head at the 2000 Party Conference, when her proposals for spot checks for soft drugs resulted in ridicule and the admission by nearly half the Shadow Cabinet that they had dabbled with soft drugs (no doubt without inhaling). Both right and left had seen the divisions within the party in the mid-1990s as the fault of John Major's weak leadership. This explanation came to be seen as a shallow scapegoat. In reality, the party had lost its sense of direction.

Mid-term elections, 1997–2001

If the story of the 1997 and 2001 general elections was one of unremitting gloom for the Tory Party, some comfort was drawn from the elections that took place between those depressing bookends. The party did well in local government elections, especially in 1999 and 2000, although it was recovering from very low bases in the mid-1990s.[14] In 1999 the party polled 33% of votes cast compared to Labour's 36%: the Tories gained 1,200 seats, supplanting the Liberal Democrats as the second party of local government in England. Compared to the period before 1990 though, the party was still in a trough: it had just 5,000 councillors in 1999 compared to 12,000 in 1979. In the London Mayoral election of May 2000, eventual Tory candidate Steve Norris won 27% of the vote compared to Livingstone's 38%, and the Tories won as many seats as Labour (nine) on the Greater London Authority. In the newly devolved Scottish Parliament and Welsh Assembly, the Conservatives polled 15% and 16% respectively, with representation only ensured by the 'list seats' in the hybrid proportional representation electoral systems. All these results should be treated with caution due to the low turnout in the mid-term elections, which was only 24% in the European contests of June 1999. The Conservatives, nevertheless, won 36% of the votes cast in these elections, producing 36 MEP seats, seven ahead of Labour.

The four years saw less excitement than usual in by-elections. Most came in safe Labour constituencies. The most surprising moment for the party came with the loss of the safe seat of Romsey to the Liberal Democrats, following the death in a fire of sitting Tory MP, Michael Colvin. The brightest moment came in the Kensington and Chelsea by-election in November 1999, when Michael Portillo held the seat vacated by the death of Alan Clark with an increased share of the vote. The bleakest moment probably came in Winchester in November 1997, when the formerly safe Conservative seat was lost to the Liberal Democrats, who increased their majority by over 20,000.[15]

The 2001 manifesto

The delay of the expected election date of 3 May to 7 June, on account of the 'foot and mouth' epidemic, might have led to more thinking than it did. Hague launched the 2001 manifesto, 'Time for Common Sense', a week before Labour, hailing it as the 'most ambitious for a generation'. It showed some signs of innovative thinking. The 2001 manifesto promised to retain and even extend Labour's initiative of an independent Bank of England.[16] It was more specific about tax cuts (£8 billion) and on reducing the role of the state in education and health. It did not advocate reversing devolution, but wanted non-English MPs restricted from voting on issues that only effect England. Whereas the 1997 manifesto kept the option open of entering the single currency, 2001 ruled out entry during the next parliament and also promised to renegotiate the Nice Treaty expanding EU member states. The 2001 manifesto pledged two and a half thousand extra police in England and Wales, as well as introducing secure reception centres for asylum seekers.

Conservative election campaign, May–June 2001

Many commentators were quick to write off the Conservative campaign of 2001 as a complete failure. It has been portrayed as flawed from the outset by the narrow focus on issues of little importance to voters. To critics such as Kenneth Clarke, the campaign was the culmination of four wasted years for the Tory Party.[17] In this account, the leadership chose to campaign obsessively around right-wing themes, with Europe being particularly prominent as William Hague declared the election the 'last chance to save the pound'. However, the Conservatives failed adequately to address the crisis in schools and hospitals, the issues that topped the list of voters' priorities. In essence therefore, despite the efforts of William Hague to energise the voters around his themes, the campaign missed the point. The hard core of increasingly elderly committed Tory voters no doubt felt their spines tingle as they marched to the polling booths, honoured to play their part in the epic struggle for the pound's survival. But back in the real world, the critical mass of moderate voters, disillusioned with the perceived failures of the government, desperately looked around for a credible alternative. They saw William Hague. And they voted Labour.

Powerful as the above critique seems, careful dissection of the Conservative campaign suggests a more subtle approach is needed. Indeed, buried within the Tory campaign lies a paradox that few commentators have touched upon. For in basic strategic terms the campaign enjoyed some success. We shall see how, on occasion, the Tories succeeded in setting the media agenda, winning many arguments they advanced and critically managing to raise the importance of the issues they campaigned about in the eyes of the whole electorate, not just their own supporters. Nevertheless, the key distinction to be drawn is between this tactical success and the success that matters, that of increasing the party's share of the vote, which the Tory campaign consistently failed to do. The critical focus therefore shifts to why strategic success did not translate into increased support and to find the answer to this it is necessary to focus back on the credibility of the opposition team, and the image and policy direction of the Conservative Party since 1997.

We can look at the campaign through four main themes, allowing us to consider both the issues as well the style and method of communication deployed by Central Office. These themes are tax, crime and asylum, Europe, and the 'final wobbles' as the campaign drew to a close. Finally, we shall draw common threads together to provide a final evaluation of the Conservative campaign.

Tax

From the relentless tax cutting of the Thatcher governments to the legendary 1992 'tax bombshell' campaign that has been widely credited with playing a key role in helping John Major secure a fourth Conservative term, tax has traditionally been a favourite battleground for Tory election strategists. It was, therefore, perhaps unsurprising that the Tories chose to seize the initiative in the first week of the campaign with their early manifesto launch stressing their plans to cut tax.

At the launch on 10 May, the Tories built on a pre-election poster campaign, which claimed that Labour had raised 'stealth taxes' during their time in office, but failed to deliver improvements in public services. William Hague drew a contrast between a Labour government that would mean more stealth taxes, and a Conservative government that he pledged would deliver a total of £8 billion carefully costed tax cuts, including a headline-grabbing 27p off a gallon of petrol. Hague's argument was bolstered by a report by the respected Institute of Fiscal Studies that suggested that to meet Labour's spending commitments, taxes would have to rise by £5 billion in the last two years of a second term. Gordon Brown's refusal to pledge not to increase taxes at all under a second Labour government added weight to the Tory claims and, by the weekend, the *Sunday Times* noted that: 'senior Labour insiders are already admitting that the Tories have won the first week of the campaign' (*Sunday Times*, 13.5.01).

But then it all went wrong. On BBC's *Newsnight* on 11 May, the Shadow Social Security Spokesman David Willetts seemed to suggest that the proposed tax cuts could amount to only £7 billion rather than £8 billion. More serious though was the 'Oliver Letwin Affair' that broke on Monday 14 May. Letwin, it emerged, had briefed *Financial Times* journalists that, in fact, the Tories would cut taxes by £20 billion. The slick Millbank machine pounced at once on the £12 billion shortfall, using it as evidence of a secret Tory tax-cutting agenda that Letwin had unwittingly exposed: more tax cuts could only mean painful and wide-ranging public service cuts. Hague and Portillo were quick to deny the £20 billion figure and Letwin 'disappeared' for a week, evading countless requests for interviews. However, the damage was done and the spectre of potentially damaging public service cuts hovered in the background for the rest of the campaign.

Shortly after Letwin's gaffe, the Tories moved away from the tax issue, but returned to it with potentially devastating consequences when they fell upon Gordon Brown's refusal specifically to rule out any increase in the maximum national insurance contribution. Here, they argued, was a classic plan for a stealth tax that would be the equivalent to raising the top rate of tax to 50 pence. Neither Brown nor Blair would deny it would happen, the press sensed blood and the *Daily Mail* ran the 'ticking National Insurance timebomb' story on the frontpage (*Daily Mail*, 22.5.01). The Tory strategists rejoiced. It was 1992 'tax bombshell' all over again, Labour's tax plans would once again be their downfall. But it was not to be.

Strategically, despite the Letwin gaffe, tax looked like a Tory success story. Lagging behind at the fifth most important major issue to voters when the campaign began,[18] by the third week it had jumped to third place.[19] Polls repeatedly showed that people believed taxes had gone up under Labour, and identified the Tories as the party most likely to cut them. But the critical point is that 2001 was not 1992. Politics had moved on, but Tory strategy had not. Over half the electorate now accepted that Tory tax reductions would lead to 'drastic cuts in spending on schools and hospitals',[20] and what were the two most important issues to voters throughout the campaign? Schools and hospitals. Tax cuts played well, but just not well enough.

Crime and asylum

Traditionally the issue of crime and criminals has always been another Tory favourite. And sure enough, at the beginning of the second week, just as the success of tax was beginning to unravel with the Letwin affair, Central Office seized the agenda with a bold crime initiative, introduced by their first Party Election Broadcast (PEB) on 15 May. In strategy terms it was the oldest trick in the book: deliberately shocking, the PEB showed prisoners being released only to commit more crime. The claim was that Labour's early release scheme had led to more criminal offences, including two rapes.

With the media abuzz with the controversy the PEB had generated, at the morning news conference the next day William Hague continued the attack. Flanked by the shadow Home Secretary, Ann Widdecombe, he accused Labour of being soft on crime and pledged that a future Conservative government would increase police numbers and end Labour's early release scheme. Questioned on the use of shock tactics,

Hague refused to apologise. Later, when asked whether the Tories blamed Labour for the two rapes that had taken place, the Tory vice-chairman, Tim Collins, refused to back down noting simply that the PEB had presented the facts and added: 'I leave the question of blame to others' (*Sunday Times*, 20.5.01).

As with their early tax attack, the Tories seemed to have struck a chord. But their success was cut short as the Prescott punch of 16 May obliterated election coverage. Once the dust began to settle, instead of pushing on with the crime offensive, the Tories jumped issues. On 18 May William Hague plunged headfirst into controversy once again, as he headed to Dover to talk about asylum seekers. At Dover, we saw a classic exposition of the Hague campaign style. Old fashioned, and in contrast to the slick photo opportunities with teachers and nurses favoured by Blair, Hague seemed happiest with a loudspeaker out on the streets fighting his corner. Flanked as ever by his silent wife, Ffion, he relentlessly pressed his views, unperturbed by the abuse and cries of 'racist' from the surrounding crowd. These strong images may have actually distracted television viewers from the verbal message Hague was seeking to get across. But on the streets Hague felt confident. Using the slogan: 'a safe haven, not a soft touch' he focused his attacks on Labour's failure to stem growing abuse of the system by those immigrants whose claims to persecution in their own country would not stand up to scrutiny. The most controversial policy was to introduce secure 'reception centres', where all those claiming asylum would be held until their claim was processed.

Once again the Tories has seized the news agenda, but was this issue really helping them? They certainly established themselves as the party most likely to get tough with illegal immigrants, but as polls repeatedly showed immigration was simply not a very important issue to the majority of the electorate (see Saggar in this volume). Amongst the Tory core voters it struck a slightly more resonant chord, but even after the Dover initiative, schools, hospitals and taxes remained far more important to the most committed Tories.[21] In the event, after this first outing the Tories seemed happy to let asylum fade into the background as tax and Europe became the main issues once again.

More surprisingly, crime too was allowed to fall by the wayside. Although there were periodic references to it after the two-day blitz discussed above, such as the second PEB on 24 May that showed truant school children turning to crime, it was never again pushed as the critical issue of the campaign. Given the fact that, at the start of the campaign, not only were the Conservatives considered by far the party most likely to be 'tough on criminals' but the issue was also the third most important to the electorate, just behind schools and hospitals,[22] failure to engage more on this issue may have been the Conservatives' biggest missed opportunity.

Europe

Although, as we have already seen, the Conservatives did address a range of issues in their campaign, it was Europe to which the most effort and passion were directed. The legendary 'save the pound' banners appeared on the very first day of the campaign and at the last Prime Minister's Questions, on 9 May, Hague made saving the pound the centrepiece of his final onslaught. Having raised the issue early on, the plan was to let it rest until around 26 May when the strategists aimed to unleash their potentially election-winning issue.

In the event, Europe and the single currency were propelled into the media spotlight a little earlier than planned when on the evening of 22 May, Margaret Thatcher departed from an agreed speech to the party faithful by declaring that Britain should 'never' surrender to the single currency. While the publicity may have been welcome to the Tory leadership, the message was not. The official party line was that the single currency would be ruled out only for the next parliament. Although this led to inevitable charges of splits within the party, Hague managed to keep momentum, presenting a leaked EU commission document on 23 May, that, it was claimed, showed Brussels was planning to harmonise taxes across the EU. In fact, the document was deeply ambiguous and the row soon died down. But the fight was just beginning. For the very next day, in an interview with the *Financial Times*, Tony Blair declared for the very first time that he believed he could persuade the British people to give up the pound.

The reaction in Central Office was ecstatic. The received wisdom had been that Blair would never engage on Europe, but here he was playing into their hands. The Tory strategists moved in for the kill: Blair would dump the pound and only Hague could save it. On 25 May, William Hague assumed the role of defender of Britain's sacred currency: there were now only 'two weeks left to save the pound'. He stepped up the campaign the next day, unveiling a digital clock counting down to the end of the campaign: the time left to save the pound. By elevating the single currency as the new central campaign issue, Hague sought to make the election a referendum on the Euro and win by appealing to British patriotism. Anyone who pointed out that Labour was committed to a proper referendum before going into a single currency was dismissed on the grounds that Labour would be unlikely to present a 'fair' question to the electorate.

To Tory strategists, the dominance of the European issue from 22 May onwards could only be a winner. Writing after the campaign, two of them, Andrew Lansley and Tim Collins, pointed out that saving the pound struck a real chord with the electorate ('there were not many other policies we had which were supported by over 70% of the public'). This may be true, but the critical point is that the issue lacked sufficient importance amongst voters to make a real difference. In fact, by the end of May saving the pound had jumped up the issue importance table to third place following the Tory campaign.[23] Another 'victory' for Tory strategists in the ivory towers of Central Office maybe, but out in the country the pound was simply not changing people's votes.

Final wobbles

As the campaign entered its final week and the polls continued to predict a massive Labour landslide, signs of panic in Tory high command began to show. According to Amanda Platell, there was even evidence of senior Tories such as Francis Maude beginning to criticise and dissociate themselves from the campaign in private briefings to journalists.[24] Meanwhile, back at the frontline old themes continued to run but the overall message became highly muddled, as new campaign themes were launched one after another. First, on 31 May, Hague declared on BBC television that another landslide for Tony Blair would be 'very dangerous'. Lady Thatcher, by now playing a prominent role in the campaign, followed up the attack with an article suggesting that another Blair government would lead to the 'progressive extinction of Britain as a nation state' (*Daily Telegraph*, 1.6.01). While on 3 June Hague again railed against the possibility of another Labour landslide warning that it would lead to 'the most arrogant, aggressive and intimidatory government in modern history' (*The Times*, 4.6.01). In effect an admission of a Labour victory, the new Tory-rallying cry thus appeared to be 'don't let them win by too much'.

But if this was one theme, a discernible policy shift was also in evidence as Hague the moderate was suddenly unleashed. 'Hague turns left' was the *The Times* headline (2.6.01) after he focused on health and One Nation Tory themes in a speech in Bradford on 1 June. Over the weekend Hague even talked about public services before returning to the Euro. And just to thoroughly muddy the waters, on 4 June he declared that under Labour there was the real possibility of another major cull of animals to counter foot and mouth disease. So many issues and so little clarity. Thus ended the Tory campaign on a curious mishmash of themes shot through by an increasingly risible battle cry to 'save the pound'. It fooled no one.

Conclusion

It is difficult to categorise the Tory campaign as a success. It is true that some lines of attack adopted by William Hague struck a chord with certain sections of the electorate and enjoyed some tactical success, as the core Conservative issues, notably crime and Europe, rose in importance amongst the electorate. However, in the final analysis, the Tory campaign missed the point and the boat. Campaign 2001 was there for the taking as an election about the standard and renewal of public services. Many were disappointed with Labour's record since 1997. Many were desperate for an alternative approach. Most found this singularly lacking in the Conservative campaign. The real problem lay deeper than the mere four weeks of the campaign. Indeed, the lack of strategic clarity was the inevitable concomitant of a similar lack of clarity in the previous four years. From 19 June 1997, when Hague was elected as leader, the party threw itself into a desperate ferment in seeking a 'fresh start' with which to rebuild the party's fortunes. Although Peter Lilley's rethink showed signs of promise for a new direction, the leadership quickly ditched this in favour of a 'clear blue water' approach falsely animated with populist initiatives. The party faithful might have loved Hague's rallying cry, but from the moment he turned his back on the moderate agenda, the prospect of a 2001 victory was not only politically unobtainable but was a cruel mirage. Ultimately, had the party reconnected with the electorate's most pressing concerns earlier in the Parliament and ran the campaign correspondingly, would this have been enough to deliver William Hague to Downing Street? Though at times convincing and resolute, Hague was never able to lift himself into the stature of an impressive and agenda-changing leader. Such was the party's low-esteem in the country and poor morale internally, and the lack of nous and political courage in realising that a deep and lasting rethink was necessary, his task of presenting a credible alternative government was doomed.

So what of the future? The next Tory leader should spend the next four years saying 'Labour will not deliver its promises on health, education and transport'. While doing this he should send the ablest twenty minds he can cajole (women as well as men) off for three years to a Hebridean island (at least it would give the Tories a further presence in Scotland) to think deeply about Tory principles and policies in the information and global age. But, without telling anyone, the leader should also be planning for another eight years in opposition. Whether the party improves its fortunes in 2005 will have little or nothing to do with what goes on in the Tory Party, and almost everything to do with whether New Labour can hold together or whether it will implode. But that is another story.

Daniel Collings and Anthony Seldon

---

* Additional research by Peter Snowdon, postgraduate at the Government Department, London School of Economics and Political Science.

1   For a breakdown and analysis of the 1997 election results see D. Butler and D. Kavanagh, *The British General Election of 1997*, Macmillan, 1997.
2   Ibid., pp. 244–6.
3   The Conservative share of the vote fell by 14.1% (30 seat losses) in Greater London and 13.2% (39 losses) in South East England, ibid., p. 256.
4   For an interesting assessment of the events of June 1997, see K. Alderman, 'The Conservative Party Leadership Election of 1997', *Parliamentary Affairs*, April 1999.
5   See G. Peele, 'Towards "New Conservatives"? Organisational Reform and the Conservative Party, *Political Quarterly*, 69, 1998.

6   See *Vachers Parliamentary Companion*, Numbers 1086 to 1110, Vacher Dod, 1997–2000, for complete listings of successive shadow cabinets and frontbench spokesmen.

7   See G. Peele, 'Towards "New Conservatives"?' Organisational Reform and the Conservative Party, *Political Quarterly*, 69, 1998.

8   See P. Whiteley, P. Seyd and J. Parry, *Labour and Conservative Party Members 1990–92: Social Characteristics, Political Attitudes and Activities*, Dartmouth, 1996, p. 25. Also see W.F. Deedes, 'How the Tories Lost their Precious Volunteer Army', *Daily Telegraph*, 8.6.01.

9   For a detailed account of the reforms to the leadership election process see K. Alderman, 'Revision of Leadership Procedures in the Conservative Party', *Parliamentary Affairs*, April 1999.

10 D. Wastell, 'Tory U-turn on Party Funding, *Sunday Telegraph*, 1.3.98.

11 T. Baldwin and R. Watson, 'Unwanted Publicity Turns Rich Off Party Donations', *The Times*, 2.1.01.

12 See A. Gamble and T. Wright, 'A New Narrative for the Tories?', *Political Quarterly*, 71, October–December 2000, pp. 383–5.

13 See M. Holmes, 'The Conservative Party and Europe: From Major to Hague', *Political Quarterly*, 69, 1998.

14 See C. Rawlings and M. Thrasher, *British Electoral Facts, 1832–1999*, 2000 for all figures in this section.

15 For a superb analysis of the by-elections in the 1997–2001 Parliament see, S. Henig and L. Baston, *Politico's Guide to the General Election*, Politico's, 2000.

16 See the 1997 and 2001 *Conservative Party Manifestos*, Conservative Central Office, 1997 and 2001 and *Sunday Times Election Guide*, 13.5.01.

17 'Question Time' programme, BBC Television, 5.7.01.

18 ICM Channel Four News Message Poll, 3.5.01 — all polling data in this chapter is taken from research carried out by ICM for Channel Four. This highly detailed poll provides all the insights of traditional polls, but looks deeper at issues of language and political messages, particularly amongst key sections of the electorate. Several polls were conducted throughout the campaign and provide a rich resource for political scientists.

19 ICM Channel Four News Message Poll, 22.5.01.

20 ICM Channel Four News Message Poll, 22.5.01.

21 ICM Channel Four News Message Poll, 22.5.01.

22 ICM Channel Four News Message Poll, 3.5.01.

23 ICM Channel Four News Message Poll, 31.5.01. Most polls showed a similar story. Indeed two weeks after the campaign (21–26 June) MORI suggested that the EU had become the second most important issue facing Britain today.

24 'Unspun: Amanda Platell's Secret Diary', Channel Four Television, 2001.

DAVID DENVER

The Liberal Democrat Campaign

General election campaigning by the Liberal Democrats — as with the Liberals before them — is affected by three persistent problems. The first is a chronic lack of money. Unlike the Conservatives and Labour, the Liberal Democrats have few institutional sources of finance upon which the party can rely and they are almost entirely dependent upon money raised from individual supporters. As a consequence, they have much less to spend on campaigning. In 1996 and 1997, for example, the Liberal Democrats at national level spent £3.5 million on campaigning as compared with £25.7 million spent by Labour and £28.3 million by the Conservatives. At constituency level, expenditure on behalf of Liberal Democrat candidates in the 1997 election was about half that of the other parties (£1.9 million compared with £3.8 million spent by Labour and £3.9 million by the Conservatives). The Liberal Democrats simply cannot afford to undertake extensive polling, buy reams of advertising space in national newspapers or rent large numbers of advertising hoardings across the country. Despite the fact that national expenditure was capped for the first time in 2001, thus making for a slightly more level playing-field, the Liberal Democrats remained at a serious disadvantage in this respect.

Second, there is an inevitable tension between local and national campaigning. The latter is generally intended to increase the popularity of a party across the country as a whole but such an increase — unless it were very dramatic — would not result in the Liberal Democrats gaining many seats. What is required for victory is a good performance in specific seats where there is a reasonable chance of winning — which is achieved by targeted local campaigning — rather than an across-the-board improvement that might pay few dividends. This was clearly appreciated in the 1997 election. Largely as a result of strongly targeted local campaigning, the number of seats won by the Liberal Democrats more than doubled from 20 in 1992 to 46, even though their overall share of the vote declined.

Finally, as the party traditionally seen as being 'in the middle', the Liberal Democrats have to campaign on two fronts. In most places where they are strong, their main competitors are the Conservatives, with Labour being largely out of the running. In some areas, however — mainly in the north of England and including cities such as Liverpool and Sheffield — the Liberal Democrats are in contention with Labour and relations between the two parties are characterised by mutual hostility. Initially the solution to this difficulty was to maintain a stance of 'equidistance' between the other two parties — refusing to indicate a preference for one or the other or to rule out cooperating with either. Between 1992 and 1997, however, the Liberal Democrats significantly redefined their position.

The abandonment of 'equidistance'

Almost immediately after the 1992 general election the party leader, Paddy Ashdown, announced that the Liberal Democrats should 'work with others to assemble the idea around which a non-socialist alternative to the Conservatives can be constructed'.[1] A major step towards the realisation of this goal occurred in July 1994 when Tony Blair became Labour leader. Blair was receptive to the idea of cooperation, appeared in tune with many Liberal Democrat values and within a relatively short time had virtually turned the Labour Party into just the sort of 'non-socialist alternative' to which Ashdown aspired. In September 1995 the Liberal Democrat conference adopted a statement saying that their primary aim was now to defeat the Conservatives and that Liberal Democrat MPs would not sustain a Conservative government in office. Equidistance had been abandoned.

In the months that followed, relations between the two parties in public became closer and this process culminated in the autumn of 1996 when they agreed to hold joint talks with a view to future collaboration on constitutional reform. It emerged later that relations between the two party leaders had been much closer than anyone suspected at the time. They began to have informal meetings shortly after Blair became Labour leader and, according to reports, discussions went as far as to include the possibility of a coalition government with the Liberal Democrats having two seats in the Cabinet. The price of Liberal Democrat support would be a commitment to a referendum on electoral reform on Blair's part.[2]

The 1997 election and constructive opposition

The new approach of the Liberal Democrats apparently paid dividends in the 1997 election, as Table 1 shows. As noted, the share of the vote that they gained in 1997 fell by just over one percent but the number of seats won more than doubled from 20 to 46. In the 1950s it used to be said, with only slight exaggeration, that all Liberal MPs could go to the House of Commons in a single taxi; after 1997 the Liberal Democrats would have required a coach. The improvement in 1997 resulted from two developments. The first was an increase in tactical voting in

1. Liberal Democrat Performance in the 1992 and 1997 General Elections

	1992	1997
Share of votes (%)	18.3	17.2
Seats won	20	46
Second place	153	104
(to Conservative)	(144)	(73)
(to Labour)	(8)	(31)
(to other)	(1)	–
Third place or lower	461	490

favour of the Liberal Democrats in seats where Labour had no chance of winning. Secondly, they successfully targeted their constituency campaign effort on a relatively small number of seats. The data in the Table also illustrate the electoral logic underlying the Liberal Democrats' change of tack in 1995, in that in the 1992 election they were second to the Conservatives in 144 constituencies but to Labour in only eight. Moreover, of the 20 seats that they won in 1992, the Conservatives were second in 16.

Yet the achievement of the Liberal Democrats was overshadowed by that of New Labour. As it happened, the strongest Liberal Democrat showing in many years coincided with a Labour landslide. With an overall majority of 179 Labour had little need of support from Paddy Ashdown and his sizeable band of MPs. Nonetheless, on the day after the election Ashdown announced that his party would be a voice of 'constructive opposition' in the new Parliament. He elaborated shortly afterwards in the debate on the Queen's Speech in the House of Commons saying:

If a generation of progressive change, founded on constitutional and electoral reform, is what the Government intend, the Prime Minister can count on the Liberal Democrats to be critical but firm supporters of every step that he takes along the way ... (We will) provide a constructive opposition, and if that breaks the outmoded convention that Oppositions must always oppose, whatever the merits of the case, we make no apologies for it.[3]

The fruits of cooperation with Labour were not long in appearing. The government almost immediately began the process that would lead to (successful) referendums on devolution in Scotland and Wales in September 1997 – a long-held Liberal aspiration. In July, Tony Blair, in an unprecedented and unexpected move, announced the creation of a Joint Cabinet Committee (JCC) comprising himself and senior members of the government together with Ashdown and four leading Liberal Democrats. Initially the JCC was to discuss constitutional reform but it was to meet every two months and was expected to go on to other matters. Repaying his part of the bargain, Blair also established an independent commission on the electoral system in December 1997, to be headed by Lord Jenkins who, as Roy Jenkins, had been one of the original 'Gang of Four' which split off from the Labour Party to form the SDP in 1981.

The Blair–Ashdown strategy of cooperation was not without critics in their respective parties. Several Labour heavyweights and many on the backbenches (not to mention party activists) simply saw no need for it while many in the Liberal Democrats feared that their independence and integrity would be threatened. Nonetheless, in November 1998 Blair and Ashdown renewed their commitment to cooperation by issuing a joint statement announcing that the role of the JCC would be extended to include issues such as health, education and the modernisation of the welfare state. They stated that their long-term aim was 'to ensure the ascendancy of progressive politics in Britain' (*Guardian*, 12.11.98).

Later in the Parliament, cooperation took an even more concrete form in Scotland and Wales. Following the first elections (under a form of PR) to the new Scottish Parliament in May 1999 the Liberal Democrats were in a position to hold the balance of power. Negotiations between Labour and the Liberal Democrats began almost immediately and shortly afterwards a coalition government was formed, giving the Liberal Democrats their first-ever taste of government above local level. The Welsh Assembly elections also resulted in no party having an overall majority but Labour initially decided to go it alone as a minority administration. In October 2000, however, there was an almost exact rerun of earlier events in Scotland and the two parties agreed a programme for a 'partnership government'.

Kennedy replaces Ashdown

In July 1998 Paddy Ashdown celebrated ten years as leader of the Liberal Democrats. Addressing speculation about his possible retirement, he responded, 'You must be joking. This is where the fun begins. Let me make my intention absolutely clear—I intend to lead this party through this parliament, through the next election and into the next government' (*Guardian*, 23.7.98). In the following January, however, Ashdown announced that he would retire in June.[4] The absence of an obvious heir-apparent made for a rather crowded field in the leadership election which followed—within days 13 possible contenders had been named in the press (almost 30% of the parliamentary party)—and this threatened to turn the election into something of a farce. In the end, however, Charles Kennedy was elected from a field of five in August 1999, comfortably defeating his nearest challenger, Simon Hughes. By this time Kennedy, formerly critical of 'cosying up' to Labour, was the candidate of the party establishment and pledged to continue the constructive opposition strategy.

During 2000, however, relations between the government and the Liberal Democrats became distinctly cooler, mainly because of the apparent unwillingness of the government to do anything about electoral reform or the Jenkins report. A referendum before the next election was now clearly off the agenda and the issue became whether

Labour would commit itself to a referendum in the next parliament. On the eve of the Liberal Democrats' spring conference in March, Kennedy declared that without a firm Labour manifesto commitment to holding a referendum on reforming the Westminster electoral system he could not see 'much basis for further meaningful cooperation' between the two parties (*Guardian*, 20.3.00). The JCC met for the last time in July 2000 and in January 2001 Kennedy declared that 'the project' was 'in a coma'. He saw little point in maintaining the committee if Labour would not shift its stance on proportional representation and so it was mothballed until after the general election. Future cooperation would depend on the contents of the Labour election manifesto (*Guardian*, 4.1.01).

Trends in popularity 1997–2001

The changing relationship between the Liberal Democrats and Labour and the emergence of a new leader had little effect on the party's popularity. Under previous Conservative governments the Liberal Democrats had made notable electoral advances, especially in parliamentary by-elections and local elections. Between 1997 and 2001 there was little to match these performances and there were some clear setbacks. Only one seat in the House of Commons (Romsey) was gained from the 16 by-elections that took place in Britain. In part this was a result of simple bad luck in that Romsey was the only Conservative-held seat falling vacant in which the Liberal Democrats were the clear challengers to the incumbent — precisely the type of seat in which the party would hope to make significant advances. In the by-election, in May 2000, there was clear evidence of tactical voting as the Labour vote collapsed and there was a 12.6% swing from the Conservatives to the Liberal Democrats. The result perfectly illustrated the potential electoral pay-off from enhanced cooperation between Labour and the Liberal Democrats. On the other hand, the party suffered a net loss of council seats in each round of local elections (1998, 1999, 2000). In 1996 they had 5,078 councillors across the country but by 2000 this had fallen to 4,450.

Four other sets of elections produced mixed results. In the first elections for the Scottish Parliament and Welsh Assembly in May 1999 the Liberal Democrats increased their share of constituency votes[5] by a modest 1.2% in each case, as compared with the general election. In the European Parliament election of June 1999, however, the Liberal Democrat vote share declined by 4.5%. On the other hand, their share of London votes increased by 4.3% in the Assembly election in May 2000. In each of these elections a proportional electoral system was used which gave the party four seats (out of 25) in the London Assembly, a record number of members of the European Parliament (10) and the opportunity to participate in government above local level in Scotland and, eventually, Wales.

A regular record of trends in Liberal Democrat support is provided

2. Trends in Liberal Democrat Support, 1997–2001 (%)

	1997	1998	1999	2000	2001
January	–	14	14	15	14
February	–	15	14	16	15
March	–	15	13	14	14
April	–	15	14	14	13
May	17 (GE)	14	15	15	13
June	14	15	16	15	–
July	14	16	14	14	–
August	13	14	15	15	–
September	14	16	15	18	–
October	12	16	14	18	–
November	14	14	14	15	–
December	15	14	15	15	–

Note: The figures shown are means for all published polls in the relevant month. That for May 2001 is derived from four polls undertaken before the date of the election was announced. Source: MORI website.

by the monthly opinion polls and Table 2 shows the party's mean monthly share of voting intentions from the 1997 general election to April 2001. After the general election, as is customary, support declined somewhat, reaching a low of 12% in October 1997. Thereafter, it is difficult to imagine a clearer case of a party's support 'flatlining' — the Liberal Democrat share of voting intentions strayed outside a very narrow band of 13% to 16% in only two months. In the autumn of 2000, at the time of the fuel tax protests, the government became unpopular and the Liberal Democrats benefited, scoring 18% in successive months. Indeed, eight individual polls in late September put them at 20% or more. This surge created a sense of euphoria at the party conference, leading Lord Razzall, campaign chair, to declare 'Order the champagne for the day after the election. We will be celebrating winning more seats and more votes than in 1997' (*Guardian*, 20.9.00). The autumn 2000 surge in support for the Liberal Democrats proved temporary, however, and from November until the election was called poll-ratings were around the level that had been sustained from late 1997.

Expectations, plans and the campaign

The Liberal Democrats could enter the 2001 general election campaign in reasonable heart. Relations with Labour remained difficult and controversial within both parties but, despite the loss of a popular leader, they appeared to have a solid core of support of about 15% the electorate. Although this slipped a little in the last three months before the election was called, it was still at about the same level as they had when the 1997 campaign began. On the basis of the 1997 experience an improvement in their position as the campaign progressed could reasonably be anticipated and the party would also expect to benefit from a 'first-time incumbency effect' in the seats that were won in 1997. However, it was not clear that the party would benefit from tactical voting to the extent that it had in 1997. Then, Labour voters had a clear incentive to vote tactically in seats where the Liberal Democrats were in second place—to remove the Conservative government. Now, however, with Labour in office and expected to win the election comfortably, the need to vote tactically against the Conservatives was less pressing. In addition, Charles Kennedy was as yet untested as party leader in a general election. His 'satisfaction ratings' among the electorate were consistently positive—more people were satisfied with his leadership than dissatisfied—but not as strong as Ashdown's had been in 1997. Moreover, Ashdown had had a higher profile. An average of 30% had no opinion on Ashdown's leadership from January to April 1997 but the figure for Kennedy in April 2001 was 45%. It could be anticipated, however, that the campaign itself would enable Kennedy to enhance his profile among the voters.

The general campaign strategy adopted by the Liberal Democrats was a combination of targeting resources and effort on specific seats while at the same time attempting to increase the share of the vote nationally. The latter was believed to be necessary since the results in 1997—while in some ways very gratifying—had also revealed the limitations of ruthless targeting. Although 46 seats were won, the party was now in second place in only 104 constituencies, which left relatively little scope for future advances. As well as making a big push in targets, therefore, the party also sought to raise its vote in order to gain more second places.

Two main features of the Liberal Democrat national campaign in 2001 stand out. It was almost entirely focussed on Charles Kennedy the party leader; and it attempted to differentiate the party from Labour and the Conservatives in terms both of policy and style. The 'flying start' to the campaign involved Kennedy undertaking a lightening tour (by jet) of 11 British cities. He was seen in every TV region and gave 105 media interviews in the first three days. The rather old-fashioned looking first party election broadcast was entirely devoted to Kennedy —his origins, family, affability and so on—with the leader himself providing the voice-over. The second election broadcast concentrated on Kennedy's approachability and ability to relate to various sorts of people. This focus on the leader continued throughout, with other leading Liberal Democrat politicians rarely being mentioned in the media. Initially there were fears that Kennedy's relaxed and informal style would not stand up to the rigours of the campaign. Senior colleagues were reported as thinking that he lacked the heart for the fight (*Daily Telegraph*, 14.5.01) and it was suggested that the daily party press conference was switched from 7.15am in 1997 to 8am this time because the leader did not want to get up so early (*Telegraph*, 15.5.01). These criticisms quickly disappeared, however, as Kennedy kept up a relentless pace, fulfilling a demanding schedule with his characteristic humour, approachability and affability. Kennedy came across as simply a likeable man and opinion polls suggested that his popularity increased as the campaign progressed. According to MORI, the proportion of voters regarding him as likely to be the most capable Prime Minister rose steadily from 9% when the campaign started to 14% in the last week. ICM figures for who would be the best Prime Minister showed Kennedy increasing from 9% in the first week to 13% in the last. These ratings are not startling and, of course, placed Kennedy well behind Tony Blair. Nonetheless, on MORI's figures he had drawn level with William Hague as polling day approached while on ICM's he had narrowed the gap from eight points to four. Given that he stood no chance of actually becoming Prime Minister, the figures indicate a marked improvement in Kennedy's personal standing during the campaign. More direct evidence of his personal impact comes from the rolling series of polls conducted by Gallup on behalf of the British Election Study (BES). Respondents were asked to rate each of the party leaders on a scale running from 0 (Strongly dislike) to 10 (Strongly like). When the series began on 14 May Hague's mean score was 3.9, Blair's 5.6 and Kennedy's 4.9. By the end of the campaign Hague was still on 3.9 and Blair had increased to 5.9 but Kennedy had made the biggest advance, scoring 5.4.

The Liberal Democrat manifesto was launched (by the leader) on 16 May. It was innovatively produced in the form of a tabloid newspaper and entitled *Freedom, Justice, Honesty*. Despite the commendable vagueness of the title (who could be against any of these?) the manifesto contained a large number of detailed policy commitments. For a party with no hope of forming the government this seemed rather superfluous and attracted some derision, notably in a *Newsnight* interview by Jeremy Paxman and in an article in the *Daily Telegraph* (16.5.01) which argued that the Liberal Democrats' 'big idea' was to screen *Eurotrash* later — a reference to a manifesto commitment to move the television watershed for more adult programmes from 9pm to 11pm. Nonetheless, the manifesto made a clear attempt to promote the party's green credentials and emphasised the party's policy of increasing income tax in order to increase public spending.

During the campaign the latter became clearly the dominant theme. Kennedy sought to position himself and the party to the left of Labour, calling for increased spending on public services to be paid for by increases in direct taxation — a penny on the standard rate of income tax, to be devoted to education, and a increase from 40% to 50% in the rate paid by those earning more than £100,000 per year — and talked of little else. He continually attacked Labour as being too timid and the Conservatives for their tax-cutting proposals. Some doubted whether this was a wise strategy given the Liberal Democrats' need to defend seats or make progress in traditional Conservative areas. By contrast, Liberal Democrat policy on Britain's entering the European monetary system — in favour, and thus likely to be a vote loser in key areas — was buried deep in the manifesto and rarely raised by Kennedy.

Overall, it would be fair to say that the Liberal Democrat manifesto and campaign emphasised the 'opposition' aspect of 'constructive opposition'. They had, of course, been sniping at the Labour government from a radical perspective throughout the 1997–2001 Parliament, but the election gave the Liberal Democrats the opportunity to alert the wider public to their left-of-centre stance. This, of course, would make it easier to attract tactical votes from Labour supporters.

Perhaps more important than the stress on a tax-to-spend policy was the attempt of the Liberal Democrat campaign to convey an image of honesty and straight talking. Campaign strategists calculated correctly that voters were fed up with endless 'spin' from the other parties, with evasive answers given by politicians to questions and with being bamboozled with statistics. Kennedy and his team made a virtue of giving straight answers, of being honest in saying that tax increases were required if services were to improve and of shunning (or at least *saying* that they were shunning) 'negative' campaigning.

Quite apart from the evidence of the election results themselves, there is little doubt that this strategy paid off. Towards the end of the campaign MORI asked respondents which party had impressed them most during the campaign and most (30%) chose the Liberal Democrats. Labour was chosen by 20% and the Conservatives by 11% with the remainder saying that none had impressed then (28%) or that they didn't know (9%). Many commentators shared the judgment of the electorate on the performance of Charles Kennedy and the Liberal Democrats during the campaign. In the *Daily Telegraph* (6.6.01) for example, Peter Osborne began what turned out to be a critical article by saying:

There is no doubt which party leader has enjoyed the best campaign in 2001. Charles Kennedy for the Liberal Democrats has made many friends. He has come across as open, affable and decent. He has cleverly positioned the Liberal Democrats as a constructive alternative for voters sickened by the negativism, hypocrisy and cynicism of the two main parties.

The outcome

In line with the data already quoted on Charles Kennedy's personal popularity and voters' reactions to the parties' campaigns, support for the Liberal Democrats increased steadily during the campaign — giving the lie to the impression conveyed repeatedly by the media that the campaign made no difference to the eventual outcome. In the early part of May, before the election was called, the party averaged 12.8% of voting intentions in four opinion polls. In subsequent weeks this rose to 13.8%, 15.0%, 14.3% (including a MORI poll that was clearly out of line), 16.7% and 18.8%. The last figure refers to the last week of the campaign and was exactly the share of the vote that the Liberal

Democrats gained in Great Britain — a six-point rise in the space of a month.

Why did this happen? Although minor parties gain more exposure during general election campaigns there is no 'iron law' that this will result in increased support. The Liberal Democrats also improved their position during the 1997 campaign (by about five points), although this was achieved over a lengthier period, but in 1992 any increase in support was very slight and in 1987 there was actually a decrease in support for the Alliance partners (Liberals and SDP) as the campaign progressed. Simple exposure is not enough. The electorate must also warm to what it is that they are being exposed to. In 2001 they appear to have increasingly liked the general policy stance of the Liberal Democrats, their campaign style and Charles Kennedy himself. The rise in Liberal Democrat support during the campaign was, then, not extraordinary but it was, nonetheless, a significant achievement.

The outcome of the election for the Liberal Democrats over Britain as a whole is shown in Table 3. Although the party's hopes and expectations fluctuated during the campaign — with Kennedy initially saying that to lose only a few seats would be a major success and later coming close to suggesting that the Liberal Democrats could form the Opposition — their major objectives were largely achieved. Firstly, their overall share of the vote increased to a level above that obtained in 1992. This improvement was widespread — of the 637 seats contested in both 1997 and 2001 the Liberal Democrat share increased in 448 and declined in 189. Secondly, they held on to all but two (Isle of Wight and Taunton) of the thirty seats that they had gained in 1997, as well as the by-election gain of Romsey, while adding seven further constituencies. Thirdly, the number of seats in which they are now in second place, and thus in a position to challenge the incumbent next time round, increased slightly and, perhaps more significantly, they are now second to Labour in almost as many seats as they are to the Conservatives.

There was some regional variation in the change in the Liberal Democrat share of the vote and the pattern suggests that they experienced something of a 'ceiling' effect. In their previously strongest region, the South West, their vote share actually declined slightly (−0.1%)

3. Liberal Democrat Performance in the 2001 General Election

	2001	Change from 1997
Share of votes (%)	18.8	+1.6
Seats won	52	+6
Second place	110	+6
(to Conservative)	(58)	(−15)
(to Labour)	(51)	(+20)
(to other)	(1)	(+1)
Third place or lower	477	−13

Note: Of the 641 British seats, the Liberal Democrats did not contest Glasgow Springburn (the Speaker's seat) or Wyre Forest.

while in their next strongest, South East, the increase was minimal (+0.2%). On the other hand, they obtained their largest increase (+3.8%) in North, previously their weakest English region. There was also an above-average increase for the Liberal Democrats in Scotland (+3.3%) which suggests that participation in the coalition with Labour to form the Scottish executive did them no harm — and may have helped. There was also possibly a 'coat-tails' effect here — Charles Kennedy is a Scot representing a Scottish constituency (and his own vote share in his constituency leapt up by a massive +15.4%). In Wales, however, where the Labour-Liberal Democrat coalition is of much more recent vintage, the change (+2.0%) was close to the national average.

There is little doubt that the Liberal Democrats benefited from a 'first-time incumbency' effect. Although this did not happen in all cases, the average increase in the Liberal Democrat share of the vote in the 26 seats that the party had gained in 1997 and where the same candidate stood again was 4.6%. This seems to have been at least partly a result of tactical voting by former Labour supporters as the Labour share in these seats declined by an average of 2.1%. Tactical voting also appears to have influenced the outcome in the seven seats gained from the Conservatives. Here, while the Conservative share changed little (−0.5% on average) the mean change in Labour's share was −5.8% while the Liberal Democrats increased by 8.7%. Further, with a few exceptions (notably the Westmorland and Lonsdale constituency) there is little evidence of Labour voters voting tactically to help the Liberal Democrats in the sixteen seats where the latter needed less than a five per cent swing to take the seat from the Conservatives and which were not won. The failure to get enough former Labour supporters to make a tactical switch in these seats is something of a mystery. It may be that local campaigning was not as effective here or that the Labour had already been squeezed to the limit in 1997 such that remaining Labour supporters constituted a solid core who could not be persuaded to switch in any circumstances.

The Liberal Democrats' policy of ending student tuition fees — much-trumpeted as their major achievements in Scotland — may have had some specific appeal in that in the 43 seats with the largest proportions of students their vote share increased by slightly more than average (+2.5%). The data on numbers of students are very out of date, however, deriving from the 1991 Census) and other factors would have to be taken into account before any firm conclusion on this point could be agreed.

Conclusion

There is no doubt that the 2001 general election was widely seen as a success story for the Liberal Democrats and for Charles Kennedy in particular. It remains the case, however, that in the great majority of seats they still trail well behind the other parties. A straight uniform national swing of 5% to the Liberal Democrats from the Conservatives, on top of the 2001 result, would net them only 15 additional seats. A similar swing from Labour would result in only three seats changing hands. And it should remembered that even the good performance in this election resulted in swings to the Liberal Democrats of only 0.25% and 2.0% from the Conservatives and Labour respectively.

Although the total of 52 seats won in 2001 is far from negligible, it still represented a relatively poor return in seats (8.1% of the British total) for almost 19% of the votes. As ever, some form of proportional representation remains the key to a genuine breakthrough for the Liberal Democrats and the size of Labour's majority in the new Parliament means that even with 52 seats the party will have little leverage on government policy in this respect. Hopes that a referendum on PR for Westminster would be held in the first term of Blair's government were ultimately dashed and if any progress is to be made in the lifetime of the new Parliament Charles Kennedy and his colleagues will have to demonstrate that they possess not only abundant campaigning skills but also more general political skills.

David Denver

1 Quoted in D. Butler and D. Kavanagh, *The British General Election of 1997*, Macmillan, 1997, p. 68.
2 For an account of developing relations between the parties in this period see A. Leaman, 'Ending Equidistance', *Political Quarterly*, 1998.
3 *Hansard*, 14 May 1997, col. 71.
4 A full account of Ashdown's resignation and the subsequent leadership contest can be found in K. Alderman and N. Carter, 'The LibDem Leadership Election', *Parliamentary Affairs*, 2000.
5 In these elections, as in the election of the London Assembly, electors voted for both a constituency member and a party list.

IVOR CREWE

The Opinion Polls: Still Biased to Labour

The significance of opinion polls for an election, and their prominence in campaigns, have ebbed and flowed over the years. In the 1950s and 1960s they were minor commentators on the electoral game, with little impact on how it was played. From the 1970s they moved onto the pitch influencing the election timing, campaign strategies, media coverage and, arguably, outcome. Campaign poll results came to dominate newspaper frontpages and party press conferences. Arcane aspects of polling methods became issues in their own right. Pollsters and polling commentators became minor media celebrities.

Yet in 1997 the opinion polls departed centre stage; and in 2001 they withdrew further into the wings. There were fewer of them, they figured less conspicuously in the media and they appeared to exert less influence on the campaign. Despite their lower profile, however, they made a significant contribution to the ambience of the election. An unchanging backdrop to the contest, the campaign polls influenced the assumptions of politicians and public alike; but the backdrop was deceptive, and had the polls been more accurate the character and consequences of the election might have been a little different.

From catastrophe to complacency: 1992, 1997 and 2001

The influence of opinion polls depends on their credibility. Until 1992 their forecasting record on election eve had been impressive, with an average error of only 1.3% per party and of 3.1% on the winning party's majority. Only once before 1992 had they called a clear result wrongly, in 1970, when the Conservatives under Edward Heath won by 3% and 30 seats, even though three of the four final polls forecast a clear Labour victory. But in that election the polls completed their interviewing three days before polling day and thus failed to detect a late swing to the Conservatives. After 1970 the polling organisations closed off this source of error by interviewing up to the day before the election for their final forecast poll.

In 1992 the polls met their Waterloo. Throughout the campaign they showed the Conservative and Labour parties level-pegging. The four

final polls produced an average gap, in Labour's favour, of a mere
0.9%. Everything pointed to a hung parliament and a coalition government. In the event, the Conservatives won with an overall majority of
21 seats, 7.6% ahead of Labour in the popular vote. In their forecast of
the lead, the polls were out by over eight points, having underestimated
Conservative support and overestimated Labour support each by four
percentage points.

The post-mortem conducted by the Market Research Society attributed the debacle to three causes: a small, late swing to the Conservatives
on the eve and day of election; a 'spiral of silence' in which closet
Conservatives, sensing a hostile climate of opinion, hid their true voting
intentions; and faulty sample design, specifically unsuitable and misde-
fined 'quotas' by which interviewers selected respondents.[1] After 1992
the four main polling organisations experimented with various techniques and refinements to overcome these errors. By 1997 all had
changed their methods, although each in slightly different ways. All
interviewed until as late as possible on the eve of polling, although
some relied on last-minute telephone call-backs to a sample of respondents interviewed earlier in the week. They tried to address the problem
of 'shy Tories' by allocating non-disclosers (the 'don't knows', 'won't
votes' and 'won't says') according to telltale signs of their real intentions, such as their preferred party leader, the party they identified with,
the party they recalled supporting in 1992, or the party they thought
the more competent at running the economy. They dealt with biased
samples by drawing up more elaborate quotas, incorporating characteristics that were politically more sensitive (e.g. housing tenure and car
ownership), and updating and cross-checking their estimates of the
proportion of the electorate falling into each quota. More controversially, three of them (MORI being the exception) weighted the answer
to their vote intention question so that recalled vote in 1992 came into
line with the actual result in 1992, although they differed in their
application of the weighting.[2]

In 1997 the opinion polls avoided the disaster of 1992. In their relief
the pollsters swanked:

. . . through this election campaign, the publication of nearly every poll was
accompanied by carping that the polls could not possibly be right, that they
had again under estimated the Conservative share, and it was 'inconceivable'
that Labour could win by the margins indicated.

Not in the 1997 general election.

Yesterday the five polling organisations got the average share of the vote for
each party within the usually accepted plus or minus 3% sampling tolerance.[3]

The media largely accepted this claim, not least because all the polls
had forecast the substantial victory that Labour achieved. In reality,
however, their performance in 1997 was mediocre. Their mean error in

forecasting the parties' vote shares was the third largest since the war. Five of the seven final polls and both exit polls underestimated the Conservative vote, albeit by smaller margins and within accepted sampling error. Contrary to their boast, they had not finally cracked the problem of 'closet Conservatives'. More significantly, eight of the nine final/exit polls overestimated the Labour vote, in four cases by more than the accepted 3% sampling error, and in three further cases by close to it. The probability that sampling error was responsible for overestimates of such consistency and magnitude was extremely remote. Evidently the polling organisations had not licked the other half of the problem in 1992 — the 'lost Labour voters'. They exaggerated Labour's lead by an average of 4%; seven of Britain's sixteen postwar elections have been won by smaller margins. What should have given the polling organisations most pause for thought was the difficulty of identifying which of the refinements they had adopted since 1992 had made a clear contribution to greater accuracy.

Satisfied with their patchy performance in 1997, the polling organisations engaged in much less self-analysis and development than they had after 1992. There was no self-consciousness about the fact that for the third election in succession they had exaggerated the Labour vote and understated the Conservative vote.[4] Yet there were warning signs after 1997 that at least some of the polling organisations were consistently inaccurate and, in particular, that most were continuing to inflate Labour's true support to a marked degree. Three of the main polling organisations conducted monthly polls for newspapers: Gallup for the *Daily Telegraph*, ICM for the *Guardian* and MORI for *The Times*. Throughout the 1997–2001 Parliament, except for the two months of the petrol tax protest and its aftermath in September/October 2000, the polls continuously reported double-digit leads for Labour. But ICM consistently reported a smaller Labour lead, by 6 percentage points, than Gallup or MORI did (see Table 1). Compared with Gallup and MORI, whose figures were very similar, ICM attributed four points less support to Labour, and two points more support to both the Conservative and Liberal Democrat Parties. The explanation was that ICM adjusted its results so as to bring the recalled 1997 vote of its respondents in line with the actual 1997 result, whereas MORI and Gallup did not. In this way ICM could compensate for the possibility raised in the 1992 and 1997 elections that opinion poll samples were for various reasons systematically biased in favour of Labour supporters.

1. Monthly Polls by Gallup, MORI and ICM, May 1997–April 2001

Polling organisation	Number of polls	Labour lead	Cons	Labour	LibDem	Other
Gallup	48	23.7	28.4	52.1	13.7	5.6
MORI	47	24.0	28.2	52.2	14.3	5.3
ICM	47	17.5	30.6	48.0	16.0	5.5

Source: Author's database of opinion polls.

The discrepancy between ICM, and the Gallup and MORI polls during 1997–2001 did not, of course, prove that one or other was the more accurate; the ICM and Gallup final forecast polls had shared the honours in 1997 (ICM for the parties' vote shares, Gallup for the percentage majority). But the consistency of the divergence over four years did suggest that either ICM or MORI and Gallup were applying faulty methods.

Warning lights that the true Labour lead was closer to ICM's estimates than those of MORI and Gallup were indicated by the failure of the polls in the Scottish Parliamentary election of May 1999, the Euro-election of June 1999, and the London mayoral election of 2000. For example, a MORI/*Sunday Herald* poll, completed a week before the election to the Scottish Parliament (and thus not a forecast poll) reported Labour's level of support at 48% in the constituency ballot and at 44% in the party list ballot; in the election the actual figures were 39 and 34% respectively. Conservative support was understated by 8 and 6 percentage points in the two ballots.[5] A Gallup/*Daily Telegraph* poll, whose fieldwork was completed a week before the European elections, reported that 33% would 'definitely' vote and that among those intending to vote, Labour enjoyed a 48% to 26% lead over the Conservatives. In the event only 23% turned out to vote and Labour trailed 28% to the Conservatives' 35% — a huge 29 percentage point discrepancy.[6] This was not a forecast poll: a late swing to the Conservatives and, more likely, the exceptionally low turnout, can explain part of the discrepancy, but its size should have alerted the polling community to the possibility that poll samples were biased in favour of Labour voters.

In the May 2000 elections for London's mayor and Assembly, MORI's final forecast poll for Carlton TV proved seriously inaccurate, again in Labour's favour. It reported a 44–29 Labour-to-Conservative lead in the first (constituency) ballot for the Assembly, when the actual result was a narrow Conservative lead of 33–32: the forecast of the gap was 16 percentage points awry. In its forecast of the second (party list) ballot, the MORI poll was 15 points awry. In both cases it seriously underestimated support for the Greens. In the mayoral election MORI forecast a 46% to 23% margin for Ken Livingstone over Steve Norris; in reality the margin was 39% to 27%. The low turnout (a mere 31%) explains part of the inaccuracy, but only part. The forecast for the mayoral election was based only on respondents claiming they were 'certain to vote'.[7] Although low turnout does make the polling organisations' task more difficult, it cannot always be cited as the explanation for inaccuracy. Turnout in the Scottish parliamentary elections, for example, was a respectable 58%. Moreover, the polling organisations had coped with low turnout in the past, notably the Euro-elections of 1994, when turnout was 37%, and 'super-adjusted' polls by Gallup and MORI came very close to the result.[8] A dispassionate analyst of the pollsters' record during the 1997–2001 Parliament would conclude that some of the polling organisations were systematically overestimating the Labour vote and underestimating the Conservative vote, even allowing for the distorting effects of turnout, and that an exploration of techniques to address the problem might be wise; but it did not transpire.

Opinion polls in the 2001 campaign

Five polling organisations conducted regular national polls in the 2001 campaign: Gallup for the *Daily Telegraph*, ICM for the *Guardian* and the *Observer*, MORI for *The Times*, *Sunday Telegraph* and the *Economist*, NOP for the *Sunday Times* and Rasmussen Research, an American company new to political polling in the UK, for the *Independent*.[9] Each adopted slightly different approaches, in particular to the potential problems of pro-Labour samples and low turnout, and one changed its methods in mid-campaign.

Rasmussen Research adopted the most radical approach, a computer-based telephone poll. It replaced human interviewers with a computer that randomly dialled telephone owners and used an embedded voice recording to ask questions. Respondents answered by pressing the number corresponding to their answer on their telephone keypad. Weighting was applied to bring the social profile of respondents in line with that of the electorate. To general scepticism in the polling community Rasmussen claimed that the disembodied anonymity of the process would encourage respondents conscious of their minority views, such as 'shy Tories', to cooperate, and would discourage their giving politically 'correct' answers.[10]

ICM, NOP and Gallup conducted telephone surveys of the conventional kind and only MORI stuck to traditional face-to-face interviewing for *The Times*.[11] ICM continued with the methods that made it the most accurate of the pollsters in 1997. To overcome the problem of a pro-Labour bias in its samples (whether arising from Conservatives refusing to cooperate or from Labour supporters being more accessible by telephone) it weighted its sample according to respondents' recall of their 1997 vote, bringing it into line with the actual 1997 result. In addition, ICM included the main party names in its vote intention question. The combined effect was to report higher support than other polls for the Conservatives and, more noticeably, the Liberal Democrats, at the expense of Labour. NOP did not prompt by party but during the campaign did weight by recalled 1997 vote.

Gallup changed its methods specifically for the election. Conscious that turnout was likely to fall, it adopted the tried and tested 'likelihood-to-vote' model of its sister organisation in the United States, where low turnout has always been a challenge to accurate polling. Based on a battery of questions about past voting, party identification, interest in politics and so forth, the model estimates and rank orders the probability of a respondent turning out to vote. Gallup reported the vote intentions only of those respondents identified as likely to vote for the level of turnout that Gallup predicted (by means not revealed) would occur. It also used the party prompt in its vote intention question, to catch tactical voters.[12] Finally, it allocated non-disclosers to a party if they gave a consistently partisan answer to the questions of which party leader they would prefer as prime minister and which party would manage the economy more competently.

MORI made the most startling change of approach, at least in terms of outcome. Among all the polling organisations, MORI has been the least inclined to adopt what it regards as the unproven techniques of its competitors, such as weighting by recalled vote, the allocation of non-disclosers, and adjustments for turnout. In its penultimate poll for *The Times*, however, MORI incorporated the names of parties and constituency candidates in the vote intention question. The result was dramatic: the reported Labour lead of 25% the previous week fell to 18%. This was because, while Conservative support was unchanged, at 30%, Labour support fell from 55% to 48% (and Liberal Democrat support increased from 11% to 16%).[13] MORI claimed that it was merely repeating what it had done in 1997, providing the names of candidates once nominations of candidates had closed. But in 1997 it made the change for its final forecast poll only (and the change made almost no difference). The probable explanation is that MORI became concerned that it was reporting much larger Labour leads—always above 20%—than its competitors were, and had a failure of nerve.[14] It was, wrote one commentator, 'as though the scoreboard at a football match shows one side three-nil up until the 89th minute when the referee suddenly announces that he has made a mistake and it is only two-nil'.[15] Whether failure of nerve or wise judgment, it saved MORI and *The Times* from being embarrassingly adrift on election day.

Opinion polls, the media and the 2001 campaign

Opinion polls retreated from the spotlight in 2001. The overall amount of polling, which had slowly grown from 1959 to 1979, and then accelerated from 1983 to 1992, fell back in 1997 and again in 2001 (see Table 2). Fewer agencies conducted polls and fewer newspapers or television programmes commissioned them; as a result the total number of national polls conducted and published during the campaign shrunk to its lowest level since 1979.[16] The four main daily broadsheets published weekly polls, but only two of the Sunday broadsheets (*Sunday Times* and *Observer*) did so. The tabloids largely confined themselves to two-sentence summary reports of the broadsheets' polls; and some of the middlebrow tabloids reported the views of 'focus groups', typically in marginal constituencies, a cheap and reader-friendly way of describing public opinion, but in no sense an opinion poll. Most broadsheets also featured similar focus groups. As in 1997, television

2. Growth and Decline of National Opinion Polls in General Election Campaigns, 1945–2001

Year	Number of national polls in campaign	Number of different agencies conducting polls	Number of different newspaper/TV programmes commissioning polls
1945	1	1	1
1950	11	2	2
1951	n/a	3	3
1955	n/a	2	2
1959	20	2	4
1964	23	4	4
1966	26	4	8
1970	25	5	6
Feb 74	25	6	9
Oct 74	27	6	11
1979	26	5	8
1983	46	6	14
1987	54	7	15
1992	57	7	18
1997	44	5	13
2001	32	5	11

Note: The number of polls excludes election-day surveys and private polling by the parties, as well as regional and local surveys.

steered away from commissioning polls, with the exception of Channel 4 for which NOP polled weekly but did not publish vote intention figures. Notably rare were special polls of regions, marginal seats, single constituencies, or special groups such as ethnic minorities, first-time voters or particular occupations, which had been such a feature of the 'saturation polling' in 1983, 1987 and 1992. Instead the media resorted to unstructured interviews with small panels of students, first-time voters and people living in marginal seats.

Media attention to the polls also declined. Television news never led on a poll and limited itself to brief factual reports well down the bulletin running order. The BBC and ITN did a weekly wrap-up of the polls, with Peter Snow for the BBC doing his best to breathe life into them through ingenious graphics. Newspapers rarely devoted their lead story to a poll, even when reporting their own; more often the frontpage carried a capsule summary while the main report was confined to an inside page. About a fifth of all frontpage lead stories in the national press were devoted to the polls in 1987 (20%) and 1992 (18%); in 1997 the proportion dropped to 4% and in 2001 to 3%.

The decline in the media's demand for polls is all the more striking in the light of Deacon et al.'s content analysis of the media for this volume, which shows that stories about the election process absorbed almost half the campaign coverage by television and the press. The paucity of poll stories reflected commercial realities and media values. The polls had pointed to Labour's comfortable re-election throughout the 1997–2001 Parliament. The only exception was the six-week period in September/October 2001, after the petrol tax protest, when the Conservatives briefly captured the lead. Immediately a flurry of additional polls appeared: instead of the usual four there were fifteen. But

3. Opinion Polls and the 2001 Election

Date of fieldwork	Number of polls	Polling organisation/outlet	Lab maj. (%)	Con (%)	Lab (%)	LibDem (%)	Other (%)
Pre-campaign polls							
Jan 2001	7		−16.3	32.3	48.6	13.7	5.4
Feb 2001	6		−19.3	30.5	49.8	14.2	5.6
March 2001	7		−18.1	31.7	49.9	13.6	4.9
April 2001	6		−20.7	30.0	50.7	13.3	6.0
Campaign polls							
30 Apr–13 May	11		−18.4	31.2	49.6	13.5	5.8
14–20 May	5		−17.0	31.0	48.0	14.4	7.0
21–27 May	5		−18.2	30.4	48.6	14.8	6.2
28 May–3 June	7		−16.4	30.4	46.9	16.7	6.0
Final forecast polls							
June 1–3		NOP/*Sunday Times*	−17	30	47	16	7
June 2–3		Rasmussen/*Independent*	−11	33	44	16	7
June 2–4		ICM/*Guardian*	−11	32	43	19	6
June 5–6		MORI/*The Times*	−15	30	45	18	7
June 6		Gallup/*Daily Telegraph*	−16	30	47	18	5
Exit polls		NOP/BBC	−12	32	44	17	7
Exit polls		MORI/ITN	−13	31	44	19	7
Final poll mean	5		−14.0	31.0	45.2	17.4	6.4
Forecast poll mean	3		−14.0	30.7	45.0	18.3	6.0
Exit poll mean	2		−12.5	31.5	44.0	18.0	7.0
Actual result (GB)			−9.3	32.7	42.0	18.8	6.5

Note: Excludes the YouGov internet poll for *Sunday Business*.

4. Comparison of Vote Intention Figures between Different Polling Organisations

Polling organisation	Number of polls	Labour lead	Con (%)	Lab (%)	LibDem (%)	Other (%)
MORI	7	–22.7	28.7	51.4	14.4	5.4
NOP	5	–18.4	30.6	49.0	14.0	6.4
Gallup	5	–16.2	31.4	47.8	15.0	5.8
ICM	9	–14.6	31.3	45.9	16.7	6.2
Rasmussen	4	–12.0	32.5	44.5	15.5	7.8
Actual result (GB)		–9.3	32.7	42.0	18.8	6.5

Note: All national polls published by these companies during the campaign (1 May–6 June 2001).

editors noticed how quickly Labour recovered. By January 2001, Labour had restored its percentage lead to 16 points and by February to 19 points. Thereon the chartlines for party support were unremittingly flat. In these circumstances it was hardly surprising that editors were reluctant to go to the considerable expense of commissioning additional polls: they were unlikely to make a splash.

In the campaign the polls pointed with tedious persistence to another runaway Labour win (see Figure 4 in the book's Introduction). Apart from the small increase of about one percentage point a week in the Liberal Democrats' support, at Labour's expense, change from week to week was glacial, as Table 4 shows: the Labour lead drifted down from (apparently) 18% to 16%. Conservative support appeared to be firmly stuck at about 30%, presumably its core: 26 of the 32 campaign polls placed the Conservatives in the 28%–32% range and 30 out of 32 in the 27% to 33% range. Labour support varied more, but the variation was between different polling companies, reflecting their fieldwork methods, rather than within the same polling organisation, reflecting real changes during the campaign. As Table 4 shows, Rasmussen for the *Independent* typically put Labour ahead of the Conservatives by 44.5% to 32.5% whereas NOP for the *Sunday Times* typically put Labour ahead by the much wider margin of 49% to 31%. But in the four Rasmussen polls Conservative support fluctuated between 32 ad 33% and Labour support between 44 and 46%. In the four NOP polls for the *Sunday Times* the variation was almost as narrow: Conservative support varied between 30 and 32% and Labour support between 47 and 49%.[17]

Had the gap between the two major parties been in single figures, sampling error and rogue polls might have occasionally suggested a hung parliament, or narrow Conservative victory, or at the very least some momentum in the Conservatives' favour. As it turned out, the only rogue polls pointed to a Labour avalanche rather than landslide: MORI, which was consistently reporting larger Labour leads than the other polling organisations, put Labour 28% ahead in a poll for the *Economist* in mid-May and 26% and 25% ahead in consecutive polls for *The Times* in the second and third weeks of May. Unlike 1997 (and in 1987 when party fortunes were reversed) not a single poll fell foul of sampling error in the other direction to suggest that the losing party was catching up. Moreover, Labour's perpetually big leads were reinforced by superiority on almost every other measure of party support. Blair's advantage over Hague as a prospective prime minister was even larger than his party's lead over the Conservatives. Labour was the preferred party, typically by double-figure margins, on almost all issues, the main exception being asylum seekers on which the Conservatives were narrowly ahead. Polls in London and Scotland confirmed the picture. From the very beginning of the campaign, therefore, the media could do little more than report the near certainty of a comfortable Labour victory and the possibility of similar or even greater humiliation for the Conservatives than in 1997.

The following headlines to poll stories in the press, listed in chronological order, convey the unremitting message that a large Labour win was a foregone conclusion:

'BLAIR BY 250' (frontpage, *Daily Express*, 9.5.01)

'HAGUE HASN'T GOT A PRAYER' (frontpage, *Sun*, 9.5.01)

'LABOUR LEAD HOLDS AS HAGUE FAILS TO LIFT OFF' (*Sunday Telegraph*, 13.5.01)

'LABOUR TO HOLD ALL 56 SCOTS SEATS' (frontpage, *Scotsman*, 15.5.01)

'RECORD LEAD FOR LABOUR: MORI POLL POINTS TO HUGE VICTORY' (frontpage, *The Times*, 24.5.01)

'TORIES FACE EXTINCTION: POLL PREDICTS A LABOUR MAJORITY OF 355' (*Sun*, 23.5.01)

'TORIES FACE POLL MELTDOWN' (frontpage, *Guardian*, 30.5.01)

'LANDSLIDE: POLL SHOWS BLAIR WILL WIN BY 197 SEATS' (*News of the World*, 3.6.01)

'VOTERS SIGNAL A POLITICAL EARTHQUAKE' (*Observer*, 3.6.01)

'TORIES: WE KNOW WE'RE BEATEN' (frontpage, *Sunday Times*, 3.6.01)

'BLAIR HEADS FOR SECOND LANDSLIDE' (frontpage, *The Times*, 7.6.01)

'BLAIR STILL ON FOR A LANDSLIDE, SAY POLLS' (frontpage, *Daily Mail*, 7.6.01)

Barely a single poll story gave readers any reason to believe that the Conservatives were closing the gap, let alone within striking distance of victory. A cruelly headlined story in the *Independent* (29.5.01) 'AT LAST A POLL THAT BRINGS SOME CHEER TO HAGUE', referred to a finding that William Hague was not quite as unpopular as Michael Foot in 1983. A few stories towards the end of the campaign underlined the gradual growth in support for the Liberal Democrats which may have boosted morale among the party's workers and encouraged its more hesitant supporters.

The polls signalled a Labour landslide. They also forecast a decline in turnout, which fed the themes of public apathy and alienation that threaded together a wide variety of stories in the broadsheets. The main polls reported that the proportion of respondents claiming to be 'definite' or '(very) certain' voters had fallen since the 1997 campaign, typically by 5 to 9 percentage points, and was well below 1997's actual turnout of 71%.[18] The evidence about the impact of a lower turnout on party fortunes was mixed but generally pointed to a slight disadvantage to Labour. Assuming that the 'definite'/'certain to' voters would indeed cast a ballot, the consensus among the poll commentators was that the percentage turnout would fall to the mid-60s. In the event it plummeted much further than expected, to 59%, and may have contributed to the polls' overestimate of the Labour vote.

The performance of the polls

Measuring the performance of the polls is more difficult in 2001 than in previous elections. The standard test is to compare the final forecast polls of the main polling organisations with the four parties' percentage shares of the actual vote. Typically the commissioning media publish their final poll on the day of the election, based on interviews conducted, in the main, on the Tuesday and Wednesday before election day. In 1997 six polls fell into this category but in 2001 only two did, MORI for *The Times* and Gallup for the *Daily Telegraph*. The ICM poll for the *Guardian* was published on the Wednesday and based on interviews conducted over the weekend and Monday. The Rasmussen poll for the *Independent* was published on the Tuesday and based on fieldwork conducted over the weekend. The NOP poll for the *Sunday Times* was published on the Sunday and based on fieldwork conducted the previous week. These were the final polls of the five main polling organisations but the latter two, in particular, were not *forecast* polls by the conventional understanding of the term because fieldwork ended at least four days before the election.[19] This, after all, was the source of the polls' failure in 1970. The fact that in 2001 they did not interview right up to the wire was a sign of the media's and polling organisations' confidence that they had the result reasonably right.

In this election, as in 1997, there was no repeat of the debacle of 1992. The five final polls all indicated a substantial Labour victory and in that crude sense got the result right. But, again as in 1997, the Labour lead they reported varied from ICM/*Guardian*'s and Rasmussen/ *Independent*'s 11-point lead to the 17-point leads of NOP/*Sunday Times* and Gallup/*Daily Telegraph* (see Table 3.) The forecasts of the two exit polls, NOP for the BBC and MORI for ITN, were at the lower end of the range, at 12 and 13 percentage points respectively.

The true test of a poll's accuracy is the mean of the difference between each party's percentage share of the vote (counting 'other' parties as a single party) and the poll's forecast of that share. By that yardstick, the ICM/*Guardian* poll was the runaway winner for the second successive election, with a mean score of 0.75, followed by the Rasmussen/*Independent* poll with a mean score of 1.25, MORI/*The Times* (1.75) and Gallup/*Daily Telegraph* and NOP/*Sunday Times* taking up the rear with 2.75 each. MORI and NOP could at least comfort themselves that their exit polls were well within sampling error with scores of 1.25 and 1.0 respectively, although of course much greater accuracy should be expected of exit polls than conventional polls, because the former do not have to address the problem of turnout.[20]

According to APOPO the performance of the polls was a triumph. The day after the election it bragged:

The opinion polls conducted in the last week of the campaign proved the most accurate since 1987 . . . this level of accuracy in the polls was achieved despite the record low level of turnout, which made forecasting far more difficult.[21]

This self-promotion was predictable but disingenuous, being based on a partial selection of polls.[22] In reality, the performance of the polls was disappointing, both by historical and statistical standards, in a number of ways:

1   As Table 5 shows, the mean error in the five final polls (and the three 'forecast polls) was 1.8, the fifth largest out of the sixteen elections since 1945, although slightly lower than in 1997. By

5. Accuracy of the Final Forecast Polls in General Elections, 1945–2001

Year	Outgoing government	Number of forecast polls	Deviation of mean from share of the vote				Mean error per party	Mean error on gap between first and second party
			Con	Lab	LibDem	Others		
1945	Coalition	1	2	−2	1	−1	1.5	−4
1950	Labour	2	1	−2	2	0	1.3	−3
1951	Labour	3	2	−4	1	1	2.3	−6
1955	Conservative	2	1	1	−1	−1	1.0	0
1959	Conservative	3	0	−1	0	0	0.3	1
1964	Conservative	4	1	1	−1	0	1.0	0
1966	Labour	3	−1	3	−1	0	1.3	4
1970	Labour	5	−2	4	−1	−1	2.0	−6
Feb 74	Conservative	6	0	−2	2	0	1.0	2
Oct 74	Labour	5	−2	3	0	−1	1.5	5
1979	Labour	5	0	1	0	0	0.3	−1
1983	Conservative	7	3	−2	0	−1	1.5	5
1987	Conservative	7	−1	2	−2	0	1.3	−3
1992	Conservative	4	−4	4	1	−1	3.0	−9
1997	Conservative	6	−1	3	−1	−1	2.0	4
2001(a)	Labour	5	−2	3	−2	0	1.8	5
2001(b)	Labour	3	−2	3	−1	−1	1.8	5

Note: A 'final forecast' poll is defined for 1959–97 as any published on polling day and for earlier elections as any described as such. From February 1974 onwards interviews were generally conducted on the Tuesday and Wednesday immediately before election day. The definition for 2001 distinguishing between (a) final polls and (b) forecast polls is explained in the text.

historical standards, 2001 was a small improvement on 1997, but still a relatively poor year.

2   All five final polls, and the two exit polls, overestimated the Labour vote. The phenomenon cannot be attributed plausibly to a very late swing to the Conservatives, since no such trend was reported from the Wednesday polling and the two polls whose interviewers stayed in the field longest (MORI/*The Times* and Gallup/*Daily Telegraph*) showed no signs of Conservative recovery (if anything, the reverse). Nor can it be attributed to last minute tactical switching from Labour to Liberal Democrat: the MORI and Gallup estimates of Liberal Democrat support were accurate. Moreover, both exit polls, which are immune to late swing, also overestimated the Labour vote, albeit by a smaller margin.

3   Indeed every single poll during the campaign estimated Labour support at more than the 42.0% of the vote it actually received. This universal exaggeration of Labour support suggests that sample bias, not random sampling error or late swing, is the key explanation. The polls did not crack the problem that caused them so much grief in the much closer election of 1992 and that persisted, if less conspicuously, in 1997.

4   Four of the five final polls underestimated the Conservative vote (Rasmussen for The Independent being the honourable exception), as did both exit polls. Of the 32 campaign polls only four put support for the Conservatives at or above the 33% vote they actually obtained. The near-universality with which the polls understated Conservative support, as they did in both 1997 and 1992, reinforces the conclusion that the main polling organisations systematically obtained samples with a pro-Labour and anti-Conservative bias and, except for ICM, failed to address it.

5   By consistently overestimating the Labour vote and underestimating the Conservative vote, the five final polls (and the two exit polls) all exaggerated Labour's lead. Labour's actual margin of victory was 9.3%, but the average lead attributed to Labour in the 32 campaign polls was almost double — 17.1% — and not a single poll throughout the campaign gave Labour a lead of under 10%. The mean difference between the forecast and actual gap was 5 percentage points, the (equal) fourth worst performance of the polls by that criterion since the war. Seven of the sixteen postwar elections have been won by smaller margins.

Credibility confirmed or complacency continued?

In a parallel analysis of the opinion polls in 1997, I concluded:

The widespread overestimate of the Labour vote, repeating a pattern found in 1992 and 1987, pinpoints a problem for the polling organisations to address with as much energy as they addressed the issue of 'closet Conservatives'. Lost Labour voters may matter more next time, if the contest is closer . . .[23]

Buoyed by their restored credibility in 1997, the polling organisations chose to ignore or deny the problem, despite strong evidence from the Scottish Parliamentary, European and London elections that they were constantly exaggerating Labour's support. This systematic defect in the opinion polls was masked by the size of the Blair victory. In a landslide they are bound to pick the winner.[24]

It is now evident that most of the established pollsters have been inflating Labour support (with ICM again the exception) and that this is a systematic feature of their sampling design. Roger Mortimore has recently argued that the overestimate of Labour support in 2001 was a function of the exceptionally low turnout.[25] But this claim fails to account for the even greater exaggeration of Labour support in 1992, when turnout, at 78%, was unusually high; or for the more accurate estimates of Labour support by Rasmussen and ICM, neither of which sought to adjust for turnout; or for the fact that in 2001 turnout fell almost as sharply in the Conservative heartlands (by 11.6 percentage points) as in Labour's (by 13.1 percentage points). To establish low turnout as the explanation, one needs to show that Labour-supporting respondents abstained in significantly greater numbers than their Conservative counterparts. Whether or not they did awaits careful re-analysis of the polling data. So far it has not been demonstrated that they did.

What is much easier to establish is that, judging by respondents' recall of their vote at the previous election, most opinion poll samples contained too many Labour voters. One element of this is false recall: some respondents, such as anti-Conservative tactical voters for the Liberal Democrats, will mis-recall voting Labour. But a substantial part must be due to opinion polls disproportionately selecting Labour voters either because they are less reluctant than Conservatives to cooperate, or because they are more immediately accessible. The possible explanations for this phenomenon are numerous and need serious exploration. In this context the polling organisations should acknowledge that interviews of samples of 1,000 or more conducted over a one or two-day period are subject to low response rates because the polling company does not have the time for multiple follow-ups of refusers. Low and progressively declining response rates (which are never divulged, and sometimes not recorded) inevitably introduce bias into the sample. In reality opinion poll samples are representative not of the whole electorate but of that minority within it willing to answer political questions at short notice. Polling organisations should also acknowledge that weighting by the standard demographic characteristics of age, sex and social class is increasingly irrelevant for polls because nowadays each of these characteristics is only weakly associated with party preference.[26]

How much does it really matter if the opinion polls inflate Labour's support and understate the Conservatives' by a few percentage points? Is it not carping to criticise? The answer can be given by imagining what the 2001 campaign and its aftermath might have been like if the opinion polls had been consistently accurate. Assuming that the true Labour lead over the Conservatives was about 10 percentage points throughout the campaign, well-designed polls based on random samples of about 1,000 respondents would have reported Labour leads of between 7 and 13%; a probable Labour victory, but not an inevitable one; a clear Labour majority, but not a landslide; an election to play for, not a foregone conclusion. Labour supporters would have been less complacent, Conservatives less despondent. Conservative Party morale would have been higher and the desperate gamble of staking all on the issue of the Euro might have seemed less attractive. And, after the election, the grotesque disproportionality of a 165-seat overall majority based on a 9-percentage point majority would be more obvious. Turnout and other forms of participation would almost certainly have been higher and the sense that the government won a landslide, but not a mandate, less prevalent. Accuracy in polls matters even when the outcome is clear-cut and inevitable. In 2005/6 when the outcome might be less certain, accuracy in polls will matter even more but, given the prevalent mood of complacency in the polling industry, may be no nearer achievement.

Ivor Crewe

1   See Market Research Society, *The Opinion Polls and the 1992 General Election*, July 1994.
2   See I. Crewe, 'The Opinion Polls: Confidence Restored?', *Parliamentary Affairs*, 50, October 1997, p. 572.
3   APOPO (Association of Professional Opinion Polling Organisations) 'General Election '97 Result', press release, 2.5.97.
4   In 1987 the seven forecast polls averaged at 1% under for the Conservatives and 2% over for Labour. See I. Crewe, ibid., p. 581.
5   See *Sunday Herald* (Scotland), 2.5.99 and the MORI website: http://www.mori.com/polls/1999/sh990409.shtml.
6   See The Gallup Organisation, *Gallup Political Index*, Report No. 466, June 1999, p. 8.
7   See Market & Opinion Research International, *British Public Opinion*, Vol. XXIII, No. 4, May 2000, p. 7.
8   See I. Crewe, ibid., p. 573. Gallup forecast: Con 28, Lab 44, LD 19.5 and MORI forecast Con 27, Lab 47, LD 20. The result was: Con 28, Lab 44, LD 16.5. Both Gallup and MORI re-allocated their non-disclosers and in addition Gallup weighted their data by recall of vote in 1992. In 1999 neither organisation made adjustments of this kind.
9   Gallup also conducted a cumulative daily 'rolling thunder' survey for the British Election Study at the University of Essex, the full results of which were available on the BES website. It indicated very large Labour leads, often exceeding 30%, but it was not claimed to be a predictive poll: no weighting or any other adjustments were made to the raw data. NOP also conducted regular online polls for Channel 4 but the voting figures from these were not published. YouGov, the online partner of the British Election Study, organised an internet poll based on 7,885 web-users for the *Sunday Business* of 3 June (see p. 1). It reported the parties' standing as Lab 45%, Con 34%, LibDem 14%.

10 'A new kind of polling', *Independent*, 25.5.01, p. 6.

11 It interviewed by telephone for the *Sunday Telegraph* and the *Economist* and telephoned a subsample on the Wednesday before polling day, to check for last-minute swing, for its forecast poll in *The Times*.

12 'Experience suggests that if people are asked in a general way how they intend to vote, they respond in terms of which party they want to win the election, rather than in terms of how they themselves will actually vote in their own constituency.' See 'How our campaign Gallups work', *Daily Telegraph*, 17.5.01, p. 8.

13 Not all of the change can necessarily be attributed to the change in question wording. MORI probably happened to select a less pro-Labour sample for this poll. See John Curtice, 'LibDems climb the wobbly poll', *Scotsman*, 1.6.01, p. 10.

14 The Labour lead reported by MORI in its polls before the change of question wording was 24% in *The Times* of 8 May, 20% in the *Sunday Telegraph* of 13 May, 26% in *The Times* of 17 May, 28% in the *Economist* of 18 May and 25% in *The Times* of 24 May.

15 Alan Travis, *Guardian*, 1.6.01, p. 18.

16 However, if the length of the campaign is taken into account the number in 2001 (1.0 per campaign day) was identical to the number in 1997 (also 1.0).

17 NOP also conducted a poll for the *Daily Express*, early in the campaign, putting parties' standing at Con 31%, Lab 51%, LibDem 13%.

18 See, for example, 'Voters plan boycott', *Daily Mail*, 12 May; Anthony King, 'Lowest turnout since 1874 forecast', *Daily Telegraph*, 17 May. One commentator who noticed that the proportion of 'certain/very likely' voters was running at 11 to 12 percentage points below the level of four years previously and thus pointed to the possibility of turnout falling to 60% or worse was Dr Roger Mortimore of MORI. See his 'Turnout: how low might it go?', *MORI Poll Digest*, 27.4.01, MORI website: http://www.mori.com/digest.

19 NOP's unpublished poll for Channel 4 based on interviews conducted over the weekend before the election gave Labour a 27 point lead over the Conservatives (52% to 27%). If broadcast, the public record of the final forecast polls would have appeared considerably worse. ICM also conducted a poll for the *Evening Standard* on Monday 4 June, based on weekend interviews, which gave Labour a 47% to 30% lead and MORI conducted a poll for the *Economist*, based on interviews on the Monday and Tuesday, which gave Labour a 43% to 31% lead. The latter is described as published on election day but it would be more realistic to give Friday 8 June as the date, this being the publication date of the *Economist* both in hardcopy and on the web. These two polls are excluded from the list both of final and forecast polls because the polling organisations concerned published other polls based on later fieldwork dates.

20 Strictly speaking even exit polls have to adjust for the impact of postal voting, which increased under more lenient regulations in 2001; but they do not have to estimate which respondents will turn up at the polling stations. The sources of error in exit polls are biases in the sample of polling stations, or in the sample of voters exiting them, and the partisan unrepresentativeness of respondents who refused to say how they voted.

21 Association of Professional Opinion Polling Organisations, 'Polls confound sceptics', 8.6.01.

22 The estimate included two ICM polls and two MORI polls, including the MORI poll for the *Economist* which was effectively not published until the day after the election. Moreover, it is unusual for APOPO to base its claims on all polls conducted in the final week since in the past it has argued that polls completing their fieldwork by or before the weekend should not be judged against the election result.

23 Ivor Crewe, op. cit., pp. 569–85 (p. 583).

24 As discussed by Curtice, in this volume, Labour also benefited slightly, as they did in 1997, from the pattern of constituency swings.

25 'What shy Tories?', *MORI Poll Digest*, 6.7.01, MORI website: www.mori.com/digest.

26 Weighting by a characteristic more strongly associated with party preferences, such as newspaper readership, would be a more effective way of reducing biases in the sample.

DAVID DEACON, PETER GOLDING AND MICHAEL BILLIG

Press and Broadcasting: 'Real Issues' and Real Coverage

The 2001 election campaign really began, not when Mr Blair went to the Palace, but the previous week when a stream of national press editors and managers was to be seen flowing up and down Downing Street, culminating in Rupert Murdoch's emergence from No. 11. Business was back to normal when, the week after the election, Chancellor Gordon Brown welcomed one of Downing Street's first corporate visitors, the same Mr Murdoch, whose four national newspapers had all endorsed New Labour. The sacked Minister for Culture, Chris Smith, warned swiftly and sharply of the dangers of 'falling in hock' to Mr Murdoch, as the returned government deferred the development of new cross-media ownership rules and an inquiry into BskyB.

The interest shown in the media election, if not intense among voters, was fierce enough among politicians to have Mr Blair declaring in anguish by the third week that the media were 'ignoring the real issues', i.e. those that he wished to campaign on. At the same time Labour Party General Secretary, Margaret McDonagh, accused the broadcasters of contriving camera friendly bust-ups between politicians and protesters. In an exchange with the Prime Minister at the climax of the TV campaign, BBC interviewer Jeremy Paxman, irritated by Blair's insistence that they move onto another topic, interjected 'I assume you want to be Prime Minister, I just want to be an interviewer, so can we stick to that arrangement?'.

Predictions of a low turnout also anticipated voter antipathy to the campaign. Newspaper sales and viewing figures were indeed down, though nothing like as dramatically as in 1997, remembered as an eventful campaign, but in reality only becoming so in its last few days. In 2001 many newspaper sales dipped through the campaign, the *Express* group dropped by 2.8% in the month, the *Sun* by 1.3%, the *Mirror* by 1.1% and *The Times* by 0.7%. A few dailies even reported slight increases in sales (e.g. the *Guardian* by 0.4% and *Financial Times* by 1%). Whether these increases were despite the election only further analysis could tell. While the weekly soap operas continued to attract viewing figures of about 13 million, the BBC's 6.00pm news dropped from a peak of 5.4 million in the first week of the campaign to 4.8 million in the fourth week, while the ITN News at Ten moved from a peak of 5.9 million to 5.4 million in the same period.

The most dramatic media aspect of the 2001 campaign was the increased level of Labour support in the press, consolidating the switch in newspaper partisanship in the 1997 general election. The last Royal Commission on the Press, in 1977, suggested 'There is no doubt that over most of this century the labour movement has had less newspaper support than its right-wing opponents and that its beliefs and activities have been unfavourably reported by the majority of the press'.[1] In 1997 the Murdoch *Sun*'s switch to support Labour was a watershed.[2] In 2001 the support for New Labour by almost all the national press was stunning, not just for its volume but also for the limited comment it evoked. As we discuss below, this may be because old-style partisanship has gone, to be replaced by a qualified and contingent support, in which a sceptical distance from all parties is the common tone rather than ecstatic endorsement of any. The media have become not just reporters but quizzical commentators, more moderators than mediators in the modern campaign.

To assess the role played by the media, the Communications Research Centre at Loughborough University, conducted a weekly analysis of reporting of the campaign in the national press and broadcasting, as it did in 1992 and 1997.[3] In this article we present several measures of media participation in the campaign. These include: the extent of media attention to the campaign, the distribution of party coverage, the range of issues coverage and the evaluative dimensions of media commentary.

The intensity of campaign coverage

We promise not to bore you, so here's how we'll be different. We'll be dispatching our special correspondent — the man in the white suit — also known as the biggest pain in politics. On behalf of 5 News viewers he'll expose what's really going on (Channel 5 News, 9.5.01).

This was to be the 'post-spin' election, in which voters and commentators alike were so battle-hardened and wised-up, that the worst efforts of what we had all learned to call 'spin' in the previous two elections, would fail in the face of stolid and knowing scepticism. But in the end the biggest concern of journalists and politicians was the loss of audiences. As the media were wary of turning us off, how sustained was news attention to a campaign that had long been anticipated and was widely seen as a one-horse race?

The amount of election related news coverage assessed on a calendar week basis varied across media sectors (see Table 1). Broadcast news and current affairs coverage remained fairly constant throughout the

1. Amount of Election News

Dates	Campaign week	Broadcast news (seconds)	Broadsheet press (cm2)	Mid-market tabloids (cm2)	Other tabloids (cm2)
9–11 May 2001	(Week 1)	5842	3237	2481	2326
14–18 May 2001	(Week 2)	6165	3852	2659	1921
21–25 May 2001	(Week 3)	5569	3679	2395	1207
28 May–1 June	(Week 4)	5692	3669	2006	1129
4–6 June 2001	(Week 5)	6276	3887	2185	2164

Notes: Average Amount of Daily Election-Related Coverage By Media Sector. Broadcast news sample: BBC1 10pm news, ITV News at Ten, C4 News, Sky News, BBC2 Newsnight. Broadsheet sample: *Guardian, Telegraph, The Times, Financial Times, Independent, Scotsman.* Mid-market tabloid sample: *Express, Mail.* Other Tabloid sample: *Mirror, Daily Record, Star, Sun.* Averages are calculated by taking the total amount of coverage for the sample periods and dividing them by the number of media in each category and number of days. Source: Loughborough University Content Analysis Study 7 May–6 June 2001.

campaign, aside from a peak in week 2, and overall the total amount was only marginally down on 1997.[4] The distribution in the broadsheet press also followed a similar pattern, rising slightly in week 2, falling slightly through weeks 3 and 4, and then rising again in the last few days of the campaign. In contrast, in the mid-market tabloids (*Express* and *Mail*) cumulative coverage fell more significantly after week 2, but mustered in the last week. But even this reduction pales by comparison with the collapse of attention in the other tabloid newspapers between weeks 1 and 4 (*Mirror, Sun, Daily Record* and *Star*). In the first three days of the formal campaign, average levels of election-related coverage in these papers nearly matched those in the mid-market tabloids, but by the fourth calendar week, levels of coverage were down by half. In the last few days the average figure increased, as some of the 'red tops' engineered their own gimmicks to liven things up. The *Sun* resorted to gratuitous sexism, running a 'get em out . . . to vote' campaign, which involved driving three finalists from the *Sun*'s National Cleavage Week around the country encouraging people to vote on 7 June. Following revelations of the Prime Minister's predilection for expensive designer underwear, the *Mirror* ran a series of simulated photo images speculating on the underpant preferences of other leading politicians. On election day, the *Daily Star* was leading with topless telephoto shots of actress Amanda Holden, and this typified a general trend in this sector.

In the *Sun, Mirror* and *Star*, only one-third (32%) of available frontpage leads during the campaign related to the election, compared with 78% of frontpage leads in the broadsheet press, and 87% of available lead items in TV news programmes. Yet it would be wrong to see these patterns as a unique product of the predictability of this contest. Coverage of the 1997 campaign traced a similar path, with broadcast and broadsheet media stoically sticking to the task while the tabloids looked elsewhere for diversion.[5]

The consistency of the amount of coverage in broadcast and broadsheet coverage was largely due to an 'inertia effect'. Plans for covering the election in these sectors were laid well in advance, and levels of coverage were in many respects independent of events. (Although not completely: as we see later, the slight bulge in coverage in week 2 can be explained by general media fascination with the fallout of the Deputy Prime Minister's fight with a protestor on 16 May.) Evidently, strong vestiges remain in these sectors of what Blumler and Gurevitch have labelled a 'sacerdotal orientation' to the electoral process, i.e. a tendency to see it as 'deserving consideration beyond that prescribed by the application of news values alone'.[6] In contrast, the popular press once again inclined to a more 'pragmatic' approach, in which the treatment of politicians' activities were 'based on journalists' assessments of their intrinsic newsworthiness'.[7]

Who featured in the campaign?

During any election there are predictable concerns about the parity of media exposure between the parties. Indeed, the need for balance has long been inscribed in electoral law in Britain. In 2001, these perennial concerns assumed additional significance. Firstly, recent changes in the Representation of the People Act shifted the emphasis towards self-regulation in the way that broadcasters ensured that 'over a reasonable period of time, a proper balance of different points of view is achieved'.[8] Secondly, given the apparently dramatic *volte-face* in the party affiliations of many newspapers over the recent period, and the fact that newspapers are not bound by the legislation, it is interesting to assess what impact this political realignment has had on the distribution of the amount of party coverage.

Table 2 shows that Labour achieved a marginal cumulative advantage in the *amount* of broadcast coverage received, whether measured by the number of appearances or direct quotation. This differential is mainly due to the intense interest in the implications of the John Prescott punch-up. In newspapers, however, a substantial difference remains in the amount of space given to the two main parties, even controlling for

2. Balance of Party Coverage

| | Appearances (%) | | Amount of direct quotation | |
	Press	Broadcast	Press	Broadcast
Tony Blair	18	16	22	12
William Hague	12	15	13	12
Charles Kennedy	4	11	4	6
All other Labour sources	33	22	29	29
All other Conservative sources	22	20	21	24
All other Liberal Democrat	3	8	3	11
All other parties	8	8	9	6
	100%	100%	100%	100%
	4445	1194	141036	55412
(Total N)	appearances	appearances	quoted words	quoted seconds

Notes: Up to five actors could be coded per news item. The total amount of direct quotation in an item was measured for each actor's appearance (measured in seconds of direct speaking time for broadcast and number of directly quoted words for press). Source: Loughborough University Content Analysis Study, 7 May–6 June 2001.

the Prescott factor. Press realignment may not have delivered plaudits to Labour, but it delivered prominence.

The Liberal Democrats were conspicuously disadvantaged, accounting for less than 7% of all politicians' appearances and quotation space in newspapers, although in broadcasting, the two-party squeeze was far less evident. Overall, the distribution of party coverage in broadcast media suggests that old habits die hard, and that the traditional 'stop watch culture' in British electoral reporting, although no longer a legal obligation,[9] remains tacitly observed.

More generally, these results confirm that British election reporting was highly 'presidentialised'. In the 2001 campaign, the three main party leaders accounted for 41% and 34% of all political sources reported in broadcast and newspaper coverage, respectively.

'Real issues' and real coverage

Tony Blair's complaint about the media's failure to cover the 'real issues' in the campaign, developed an earlier objection raised by his press secretary, Alistair Campbell. Responding to widespread media derision for the 'Blair at Prayer' election launch, Campbell argued that that the problem lay not with the tastefulness of the photo opportunity, but rather the media's obsession with 'process rather than policy'.[10]

Of course, journalists were quick to highlight the hypocrisy of Labour's position, immediately invoking the party's personalised attacks on Hague in one of their poster campaigns as a case in point. Nevertheless, our research confirms that the media campaign dealt with a narrow range of issues (see Table 3). Certainly, the broadsheets and broadcasting duly acted out their civic duties as media of record, delivering extensive analysis, data, and policy dissections. But at centre stage, on the main frontpages and in bulletin leads, it was hard to detect the country which had recently emerged from or was still suffering rail chaos, devastating floods, the foot and mouth epidemic, or major controversies over welfare benefit cuts and the effectiveness of anti-poverty policies. For all the dramatic coverage these matters may have attracted in the pre-election period, the issues underlying them (transport policy, climate change, the conduct and viability of the agri-industry, social and economic exclusion, etc) were swept to the margins of media attention in the campaign itself.

The dominant news theme in all media sectors was the process and conduct of the campaign, followed far behind by 'Europe', 'Health service', and 'Taxation'. As with 'presidentialisation', this emphasis on process rather than policy represents an established rather than emerging trend, being a dominant feature of at least the last two general elections.[11] In contrast, issues such as 'Transport', 'the Environment', 'Food Safety', 'Northern Ireland' and 'Defence' were all marginalised in the news agenda. Even 'Agriculture' failed to play to any significant

3: Issues in Election Coverage

Top issues	Issues coded (%)
1. Election process	45
2. Europe	9
3. Health Service	6
4. Taxation	5
5. Crime	4
6. Education	4
7. Public services	3
8. Social Security	3
9. Economy	2
10. Constitutional issues	2
11. Immigration/race	2
12. Transport	2
13. Farming	2
14. Northern Ireland	1
15. Business	1
16. Employment	1
17. Environment	1
18. Defence	1
19. Other issues (local government, health issues, arts/culture, housing, information technology)	1

Notes: Up to three themes could be coded per item. Percentages are calculated on a total of 5543 themes coded across all media content analysed). Source: Loughborough University Content Analysis Study, 7 May–6 June 2001.

extent (representing 2% of themes covered), despite confident predictions that 2001 would long be remembered as 'the foot and mouth election'.

If anything, it is more likely to go down in the annals as the 'fist in mouth' election, following the vast coverage sparked by John Prescott's fight with an egg-throwing protestor on 16 May. The footage of the Deputy Prime Minister rolling around a flowerbed with a man half his age was lovingly replayed in slow motion on all major news bulletins over the following days, and the tabloid headline writers had a field-day. Alluding to Prescott's earlier nickname of 'two jags' (earned by his penchant for expensive limousines), the *Sun* immediately rechristened him 'Two Jabs'. The *Mirror* headline simply used one word: 'ManiFISTo'

With hindsight the event was a storm in a teacup. For all the media's interest in the wider political consequences of Prescott's recklessness, Labour's support was not affected and, if anything, the Deputy Prime Minister's stock rose with the public. The fracas also conveniently distracted attention from two other unscripted events that had ruffled Labour's feathers on the same day, the booing of the Home Secretary's speech at the Police Federation, and the collaring of the Prime Minister on a hospital walkabout by an irate woman, Sharon Storrer, incensed by the general squalor and shortage of beds at the hospital. But 16 May 2001 also marked the launch of Labour's manifesto — the mission statement of the party that by common consent was virtually certain to govern Britain over the next five years. Even this highly significant event was sidelined by Prescott's fist. The following day, coverage of the

'Manifisto' in the mid-market tabloids exceeded 'Manifesto' coverage by a ratio of 4.6 to 1. Predictably, this imbalance was even more evident in the red top tabloids (5.5 to 1). In the broadsheets, the ratio was 2.2 to 1 and in TV news 2.6 to 1.

The rise of the mediators

Our research also demonstrates that sound-bite politics is growing. Comparing recent elections shows a consistent decline since the 1992 general election in the average time a politician is seen speaking in television news items. In 1992 the average time on ITV was 22.3 seconds, whereas in 2001 this had shortened to 17.6 seconds. The same trend could be found on BBC1. Here the figures were 26.5 in 1992 and 20.3 in 2001. The same story is to be found if we merely take the political leaders. In 1992 the figures on BBC1 and ITV were 37.3 and 32.0 seconds respectively. In 2001 the time was down to 24.8 seconds on BBC1 and 21.2 on ITV. In all these comparisons, the figures for 1997 fell between those of 1992 and 2001.[12] So, a clear trend emerges. The televised quotes from the politicians are getting shorter by the election.

The causes of the shrinking sound bite are not immediately obvious. Certainly, the shrinkage is not due to the actions of the politicians themselves, who continue to speak at length and strive to have their speeches reproduced on the news. Nor, as we have seen, can this be due to any dramatic decline in the attention given to general elections on television. Consequently, the suspicion must be that the producers of news programmes have been cutting down on the words of politicians and filling the space with something else.

The data suggest that the news and current affairs programmes have been giving more airtime to their own correspondents and experts. If we take all the broadcast coverage that we sampled, it emerges that the average speaking time of the media's own journalists was nearly twice as great as the average speaking time of politicians (a hundred seconds as against sixty-one seconds). Moreover, interviewers are not discreet and deferential figures who ask their questions as if seeking information, and then retreat into the background while the politicians deliver their answers. The interviewers are regarded as grand figures in their own right. When Jeremy Paxman interviewed the political leaders, he occupied 30% of the total talking time. Interviewers like Paxman typically challenge politicians by outlining the counter-position. They are like hunters of embarrassment, pursuing lines of questioning that might discomfort the politician.

On news bulletins, the sound bites of the politicians are usually topped and tailed by the correspondents. The sound bites are typically preceded by an introduction and followed by an explanation which can last much longer than the intervening quotations, as if the words of the politicians cannot be transmitted unmediated. On the day the election was announced, on Channel 4 News Jon Snow declared that throughout the campaign his news would be 'cutting through the spin to bring you the facts'. On all channels there are repeated examples of journalists 'writing themselves into the story'[13] and in doing so telling us what the 'real' strategy was behind all the politicians' talk. The paradox is that these specialists are often true enthusiasts of the political process. The more they claimed to decode the strategies and straighten the spins, however, and the more they moved centre stage on the news bulletins, the more the politicians appeared as diminished figures, whose words cannot be trusted.

Press evaluations

But what of occasions when journalists consciously sought to exert political influence? It is frequently remarked that Britain has a highly partisan national press.[14] Yet comments of this kind tend to obscure what are in fact more complex historical shifts in press alignment. The decades after the Second World War saw a decline in 'deliberate partisanship' in the national press.[15] This trend reversed in the late 1970s and 1980s as the press de-camped (unequally) to various sides of the ideological divisions between the Conservative Party of the Thatcher era, the centre alliance parties and the new realists and old socialists of Labour. In this more polarised political environment, the Conservative gained a considerable advantage over their opponents. Whereas in 1974 the circulation gap between papers endorsing Conservative and Labour was merely 18%, by the 1987 general election the Tories' advantage had grown to 48%, falling back slightly to 43% in 1992.[16]

Against this context, the realignment of the majority of press support in 1997 behind Tony Blair and New Labour apparently marked a dramatic reversal of an established political trend. Eleven out of the 19 national newspapers supported Labour, delivering the party a 30% advantage in circulation terms. But even this 'sharp reversal of fortune'[17] pales in significance when compared with the editorial distributions in 2001, where 14 national newspapers endorsed Labour, delivering them a phenomenal circulation lead over the Tories of 64%.[18]

Construing partisanship simply in these aggregated and dichotomous terms, however, tells a potentially misleading story, in which it is assumed the propagandistic instincts of the recent past have remained intact. In our view, this is not the case. The last two campaigns have marked a significant qualitative change in press partisanship in Britain. In 2001 the papers that declared for Labour were: *Guardian*, *The Times*, *Sun*, *Star*, *Mirror*, *Express*, *Observer*, *Financial Times*, *News of the World*, *Sunday People*, *Sunday Mirror*, *Sunday Express* and the *Sunday Times*. The Conservatives were endorsed by only three titles: *Telegraph*, *Sunday Telegraph* and *Mail on Sunday*. Three other newspapers did not align explicitly with any party, but they were prepared to make suggestions as to how their readers should vote to avoid worst-case scenarios. The *Independent* remarked 'we do not presume to recommend to our readers a vote for a particular party. But ... we conclude with regret that the Conservative Party on this occasion "does not deserve to be elected"' ('Why Britain Should Reject This Conservative Party', *Independent*, 6.6.01, p. 3). In contrast, the election editorial in the *Independent on Sunday* recommended that its readers vote tactically 'with sizeable votes for: Greens, Lib Dems — even for the sane wing of the Tory Party' as a means of averting a Labour landslide, promoting environment issues and puncturing 'the unattractive self-esteem which the government seems to carry' ('The Downside of a Landslide', *Independent on Sunday*, 3.6.01). Most remarkable of all was the *Daily Mail's* conspicuous failure to convert its consistently coruscating critiques of New Labour into an explicit endorsement of the Conservatives. In its words: 'Too often the [Conservative] Party as a whole seems timid, incoherent, lacking in the vision and confidence that once made Margaret Thatcher seem unstoppable' ('Use your Vote for Democracy', *Mail*, 6.7.01, p. 10). As with the *Independent on Sunday*, it recommended tactical voting to prevent a Labour landslide.

It is tempting to see these three non-declarations as a case apart, but when one examines the tone and content of many of the other editorials in which a party affiliation was stated, a similar tone of reticence, and even disillusionment, about the political options available is evident. For example, the *News of the World's* editorial emphasised the government's underachievement in delivering improvements in education and the health service, and its failure to heed 'issues that are the heart of every family in the land' ('Delivery, Delivery, Delivery', *News of the World*, 3.6.01, p. 8). Similarly, *The Times* unprecedented decision to back Labour amounted to a 'cautious' endorsement, and was mentioned only in the penultimate paragraph of a nostalgic discussion about Thatcherism's legacy ('In our Time', *The Times*, 5.6.01). The *Sunday Express* editorial was accompanied by a picture of caricatures of the three main party leaders wearing dunces' hats under the headline 'Blair wins our vote but has yet to win our trust' (*Sunday Express*, 3.6.01, p. 38). In the *Sunday Times* judgment, Labour represented 'the Least Worst Party ... It deserves to win with a reduced majority. Intelligent voters will cast their votes accordingly' (*Sunday Times*, 3.6.01, p. 16). And if the *Sun* managed to muster a modicum of more editorial enthusiasm for Blair than in 1997, its final editorial still acknowledged the legitimacy of voting Conservative and the personal qualities of the Tory leader ('A Conservative vote is not a wasted vote ... If Hague resigns tomorrow then we say this: A good man has fallen', *Don't Let Us Down Tony*, *Sun*, 7.6.01, p. 1).

Not all papers were so equivocal in assessing the parties' respective credentials. The *Mirror*, *Sunday Mirror* and the *People* rallied more enthusiastically to Labour's cause, just as the *Sunday Telegraph*, *Daily Telegraph* and *Mail on Sunday* declared a definite preference for the

Conservatives. The *Guardian* and *Observer* also declared firmly for Labour, if more conditionally than in 1997, as did the *Express* and *Star*. In the case of the *Express* this marked a considerable shift from its position in 1997 when it endorsed the Conservatives.

Just as commentators have identified the need to think of votes cast 'as though they are somewhere along a continuum from having definitely decided to vote for a particular party to having decided not to vote for a party at all',[19] so press commitment to a party can range from staunch advocacy to the most tepid of endorsements. Furthermore, the more conditional a paper's support, the more attention needs to be paid to that scepticism rather than any political affiliation eventually conceded. If this is done, a different picture emerges of the shift in press alignment over recent elections than is suggested by global figures about party affiliation. In the 1992 campaign, most national papers expressed their party preferences in an explicit and unconditional way.[20] Only three titles (representing 12% of total circulation[21]) displayed any significant degree of equivocation or scepticism in their stated political preferences. By 1997, this 'sceptic's circle' had widened, with many more national papers clouding their editorial declarations in caveats and qualifications. On this occasion seven papers (representing more than 40% of total circulation[22]) seemed to founder between, on the one hand, a fear of Labour and, on the other, a loathing for the incumbent Conservative administration.[23] The 2001 campaign witnessed a further gravitation in national press opinion towards more ambivalent positions, with nine national papers (representing more than 50% of circulation[24]) either identifying significant failings in their party of choice or choosing not to state a preference. When viewed in this way, the main shift in national press affiliation since 1992 is not a dramatic inversion of an established partisan trend, or realignment, but rather a growing press *dealignment*, expressed as diffuse disenchantment with two major parties of uncertain and increasingly indistinguishable ideological hue.

These observations are primarily focused upon the final editorial declarations of the newspapers, and there are several reasons why these announcements deserve such an emphasis. Firstly, they represent an important indication of political power plays within specific media organisations. Apart from the obvious questions they raise about proprietorial control, they are traditionally the subject of considerable and protracted discussion among senior editorial staff. Secondly, editorial declarations often stimulate considerable media comment in other media sectors, particularly where a change in political allegiance occurs (witness the intense media discussion of the *Sun*'s declaration for Labour in 1997), which, in turn, offers yet another illustration of the growing significance of the media's role as arbiters of the political process. Finally, no journalist works in a political vacuum, and the formation and elaboration of an editorial line often has a subtle but significant framing effect on other areas of editorial practice.

Yet for all these points, it is obvious that these editorial declarations represent just a drop in the ocean of press commentary that accompanies any modern election. Moreover, a lot of the contributions made by regular high-profile star columnists frequently advance arguments that contrast, even conflict, with the official editorial line. For example, whilst the *Mirror*'s full-page editorial on polling day unreservedly allied itself to Blair's cause ('His ideals are the ideals of *Mirror* readers. His aims are our aims', *Mirror*, 7.6.01, p. 6), the following two pages were covered by a far more reserved assessment of Labour's performance by their political editor, Paul Routledge. On the same day the *Sun*'s editorial ran alongside a lengthy piece by columnist Richard Littlejohn in which he suggested his readers vote Labour 'if you're happy with the sleaze, the lies, the stealth taxes, transport, the health service, asylum and really want another four years or more of it'. Alternatively, they should 'hold [their] nose and vote for the Tories' (*Sun*, 7.6.01, p. 8).

On at least one occasion, differences in political preferences among senior commentators erupted into open conflict among colleagues employed on the same paper. The day after Hugo Young wrote in the *Guardian* that the Liberal Democrats were the only party with 'moral authority', and Ros Coward announced her intention to vote for the Greens, Polly Toynbee openly attacked their stances as symptomatic of:

a kind of decadence about the middle-class conscience that puts punishing the government for its moral failings above the reality of improvements in the real, hard lives of people struggling to get by . . . This Labour government has also done great good, with more to come. That is something worth voting for (*Guardian*, 6.6.01).

But the fact that the growing cacophony of comment in the national press drowned out the papers' official editorial line strengthens the argument about the increased dealignment of the press in party political terms. These sorts of high-profile interventions add to the mixed messages already evident in many of the leader columns.

Conclusion

How much does all this matter? Preliminary evidence suggests few voters either made up or changed their minds during the campaign,[25] and the evidence that any did so because of media coverage will be pored over by psephologists for some time to come. Preliminary survey evidence from MORI indicates a swing of 2% overall from Conservative to Labour during the campaign. This rises to 5.5% among *Daily Mail* readers and 6.5% among *Guardian* readers, though it is less dramatic elsewhere. However, whether this relates to the *Mail*'s lukewarm endorsement of the Tories encouraging its Labour voting readers to keep their nerve, or whether *Guardian* Labour voters who were harbouring large doubts about the ideological shifts of Blair's New Labour nonetheless 'came back home' at the crunch, would require more analysis than the polling data reveals.

Campaigns are short and recurring interludes in the life of the body politic. They display intensified features of political communications in the longer term whose more enduring and persistent aspects almost certainly have a greater impact on political culture. Campaigns lasting a few weeks were originally designed to offer candidates an opportunity to declare their convictions and debate their intentions with a major part of their local electorates. But in the age of mass communication they may have become redundant; audiences have instant and extensive access to political offerings without awaiting their local community hall rally or doorstep encounter.

In the UK, the periods between elections foster a continuing definition by the media of issues, ideas, convictions, and solutions of greater moment than those fomented during the campaign. This may create a narrowing of available comment and analysis in which the predilections of the national press, in particular, support a range of opinions less radical than the switch of party allegiances since 1992 implies. As the *Mirror* Group's political editor suggests, 'In New Labour, Britain has a government which has followed the education, home affairs, and European policies of the *Daily Mail* and *Sun*', which he describes as an 'agenda set by a few right-wing newspapers'.[26] Analytical focus on the campaign alone may not reveal all we need to know about the potency of the media in defining the civic culture of politics.

Nonetheless, the ritual of the election campaign has becomes its own justification, and its translation into popular culture by the media is our most recurrent indicator of the state of politics as a form of public discourse. The evidence we have presented speaks of a politics reduced to a few elemental issues, focused on a very limited range of key dominant personalities, and mediated as performance rather than policy. In his predictable complaint, Mr Blair may just have a point.

David Deacon, Peter Golding and Michael Billig

1   House of Commons, *Royal Commission on the Press: Final Report*, Cm 6810, HMSO, 1977, pp. 98–9.
2   D. Deacon, P. Golding and M. Billig, 'Between Fear and Loathing: National Press Coverage of the 1997 British General Election' in D. Denver, J. Fisher, P. Cowley and C. Pattie (eds), *British Elections and Parties Review*, 8, Frank Cass, 1998.
3   The research was commissioned by the *Guardian* newspaper. The newspapers coded were the: *Sun, Mirror, Star, Mail, Daily Record, Express, Scotsman, Financial Times, The Times, Guardian, Daily Telegraph* and *Independent*. The broadcast news coded comprised: the BBC1 10pm news, ITN News at Ten, BBC2 Newsnight, Channel 4's 7pm news, Channel 5's 5.30 News, Sky News 9pm, BBC Radio 4's 'Today' programme (7.30am–8.30am). The analysis began on 7 May and ended on 6 June. Research findings were published every Monday in the Guardian, and to meet the copy deadlines coding was restricted to weekday election coverage. For the newspapers, analysis was restricted to all hard news items and leader editorials found on the frontpages, designated home news sections, designated election segments or pages carrying leader editorials. Feature items or commentary pieces

were not coded. An item was deemed to be 'election related' if there was any manifest reference made to the campaign. Our coding team were Katie MacMillan, Liz Sutton, Sue Becker, Mike Fitchett, Jackie Goode, Dianne Poppleton-Brown and Kate Radley.

4 Levels of coverage in Channel 4 News were identical for 1997 and 2001. For BBC2 Newsnight, the amount of coverage was 18% down, for ITV News at Ten there was a 9% reduction, and BBC1 10pm news, a 29% reduction. The large decrease in BBC news coverage is mainly explained by the Corporation's decision not to extend its main bulletin from 30 to 50 minutes, as it had in 1997.
5 D. Deacon et al., op. cit.
6 J. Blumler and M. Gurevitch, *The Crisis in Public Communication*, Routledge, 1995, p. 89.
7 Ibid.
8 Home office Guidelines on Procedures at a General Election, 2001. (http://www.homeoffice.gov.uk/elections/electionbriefing.htm#broadcasting).
9 See the BBC producer guidelines (http://www.bbc.co.uk/info/genelection/index.shtml) and ITC Programme codes (http://www.itc.org.uk/regulating/prog_reg/prog_code/section_4.asp).
10 'Labour May Rethink Blair's Backdrops', *Guardian*, 10.5.01, p. 7.
11 See, M. Billig, D. Deacon and S. Middleton, 'In the Hands of Spin Doctors: Television, Politics and the 1992 General Election' in N. Miller and R. Allen (eds), *It's Live But Is It Real?*, John Libbey, 1993; Deacon et al., op. cit.
12 In 1992 the founding aspects of the modern publicity process were already clearly evident (a 'presidentialised' campaign, an emphasis on spin and impression management, etc). Therefore, although the reductions between 1992 and 1997 may not seem large, they represent a significant additional compression in what was already a highly pressurised process. Furthermore, the averages presented here cannot be compared directly with averages outlined in US studies (e.g. T. Patterson, *Out of Order*, Vintage, 1994, pp. 74–6). This is because our figures represent the total amount of speaking time a specific political source had in an individual news item. As such, these figures are in many cases based on an aggregation of sound-bite time, rather than the timing of individual speech acts.
13 M.R. Kerbel, *Remote and Controlled: Media Politics in a Cynical Age*, 2e, Westview, 1999, p. 89.
14 K. Newton and M. Brynin, 'The National Press and Party Voting in the UK', *Political Studies*, 49, 2001, p. 267.
15 C. Seymour-Ure, *The British Press and Broadcasting Since 1945*, Blackwell, 1991, p. 199.
16 M. Linton, 'Press Ganged at the Polls' in M. Linton (ed.), *The Guide to the House of Commons*, Fourth Estate, 1992, p. 27.
17 P. Norris, 'Political Communications' in P. Dunleavy, A. Gamble, I. Holliday and G. Peele (eds), *Developments in British Politics 5*, Macmillan, 1997, p. 82.
18 See also D. Wring, 'The "Tony" Press: Media Coverage of the Election Campaign' in A. Geddes and J. Tonge (eds), *Labour's Second Landslide*, Manchester University Press, 2001.
19 P. Norris, J. Curtice, D. Sanders, M. Scammell and H. Semetko, *On Message*, Sage, 1999, p. 160.
20 M. Semetko, M. Scammell and T. Nossiter, 'The Media's Coverage of the Campaign' in A. Heath, R. Jowell, and J. Curtice (eds), *Labour's Last Chance? The 1992 Election and Beyond*, Dartmouth, 1992.
21 The *Financial Times, Star* and *Independent*.
22 The *Sun, News of the World, Financial Times, The Times, Sunday Times, Mail on Sunday*.
23 D. Deacon et al., op. cit.
24 The *Sun, News of the World, Mail, Financial Times, The Times, Sunday Times, Sunday Express, Independent, Independent on Sunday*.
25 See the British Election Survey http://www.essex.ac.uk/bes/.
26 D. Seymour, 'Trembling Before the Right-Wing Press', 12 *British Journalism Review* 2, 2001, pp. 14–15.

STEPHEN COLEMAN

Online Campaigning

Portentously heralded as the UK's 'first internet election', the online campaign of 2001 inspired heady expectations and resulted in prevalent disappointment. In fact, even the claim to be first was somewhat hyperbolic: though in 1992 the UK had a general election with no websites, viral email campaigns, or text messages, the 1997 election had been labelled as 'the first internet election', even though only 2% of the UK population then had home access to the internet. In fact, the two great innovations of 1997 were the Labour Party's rapid rebuttal capacity, thanks to its £250,000 Excalibur computer programme, and the emergence of telephone canvassing. The internet had little impact on the 1997 campaign, when it was still thought by many to be an ephemeral fad.

By 2001 the internet had come of age. Most major businesses in the UK were online; over one-third of the public had internet access at home, with millions more online through workplaces, schools or libraries; the government had set an ambitious target of delivering all of its services online by 2005; the e-prefix had become ubiquitous and it was inconceivable that an election could take place without an online dimension.

But what was the online dimension to be? 2001 witnessed a new medium in search of a purpose, not unlike television in the UK election of 1959. This search for a pivotal electoral role for the internet resulted in the emergence of four rather different types of online activity. Firstly, there was e-marketing of party policies and candidates, essentially little more than e-commerce applied to politics. Secondly, there were new online resources available for voters, including websites for vote swapping, poking fun at politicians, and debating the issues. Thirdly, some of the traditional news media moved online to provide a range of accessible, personalised information that had not been available to voters in previous elections. And fourthly—though this approach was mainly conspicuous by its absence—there were those who regarded the interactivity of the internet as a setting for a new, more participatory style of politics. Each of these activities and aspirations need to be evaluated separately if sense is to be made of the impact and potential of the internet in 2001 and beyond.

The internet as a channel for marketing

The value of the internet to political parties lies in its scope for unmediated communication with the electorate. The parties have grown to distrust the opportunities offered to them via the selective and interpretive filter of television, radio and the press. In an age of marketing, broadcasting represents a crude instrument for the targeted dissemination of messages. The capacity of the web and email to address voters directly with personalised messages is attractive.

How well did the parties use the web? All major parties had websites with a range of features, many of which offered voters access to information that could not have been freely or conveniently found in previous elections. For example, the party manifestos were free to download, as were policy statements, speech transcripts and archives of party election broadcasts.

Party websites fulfilled several different functions during the campaign: to organise the efforts of their members; to turn casual supporters into active campaigners or members; and to turn casual browsers into supporters.

Members were targeted via the password-protected extranets that existed within the party sites; these were spaces for virtual organisation and morale boosting. The Labour Party extranet allowed activists to email campaign experiences for others to share; the Conservative extranet provided graphics for candidates to download on to their own sites. The parties also used text messaging and mobile telephony as a means of instant internal organisation.

Inventive efforts were made to pull in casual supporters. The parties still have relatively small email databases (nothing like the million addresses now owned by the US Republicans) and are wary of sending unsolicited emails (known as spams) to hostile recipients. Labour was most ambitious in its emailing, sending out 32 daily e-bulletins, 12 emails to people who signed up on specific policy issues such as health or education, weekly emails to younger voters and an email message from Tony Blair to all of the 35,000 addresses on its records. The parties also sent text messages to mobile phones and PDA bulletins. Labour sent four mass-text messages, including one to an estimated 100,000 young voters, transmitted at 10.45pm on the Friday before polling day, urging them to vote Labour to extend the licensing hours.

The parties appealed to undecided voters via the web, offering a number of creative ways to connect with them. The Liberal Democrats' database of candidates' biographies, linking to each of their individual websites, pointed to the decentralised nature of their campaign, in contradistinction to Labour's bare-boned alphabetical list of candidates with no links to their sites. The Conservatives' *My Manifesto* feature enabled visitors to their website to fill in an online form and then see a personalised version of the Conservative manifesto; although hardly rocket science in its application, this was a sure sign of things to come in future e-campaigning. Labour's interactive *Mortage Calculator* offered similarly personalised information, though the site was rather hazy about the basis for the calculations. Another Labour web feature, involving the creation of a massive database, enabled visitors to state their constituency to find out about a range of benefits gained thanks to the Labour government. Labour also targeted the youth vote via its *ruup4it* website: a venture that smacked more of condescension than connection.

Overall, the parties failed to exploit the interactivity of the internet: online meeting places they were not. This was understandable: letting potential opponents loose on online bulletin boards is a high-risk activity and political marketing is about winning votes not chatting with the enemy. All the major party websites invited visitors to send in email questions, but not all were answered; questions that were in line with party policy were more likely to receive a response than those that were not.[1]

Turning to the candidates' websites, some had them, few knew what to do with them, and most added little to the campaigns. Candidates and local parties have little time or money to spend on web strategies. The Labour Party provided its candidates with an off-the-shelf web template, the web-in-a-box, which met with much criticism. A study by the Hansard Society's e-democracy programme found that candidates were more likely to state their marital status than their views on the Euro and more likely to state their age than their views on hunting with hounds. Jackie Ballard in Taunton used her site to express her opposition to blood sports and this may have helped to cost her the election — so, perhaps sticking to bland biographical details makes more sense. A few candidate sites were broad and inventive, notably those in marginal constituencies, such as Ed Davey in Kingston and Surbiton (www.eddavey.org.uk) and Howard Dawber in Cheadle (www. cheadlelabour.org.uk). Few candidates' sites made use of interactive features; they were essentially electronic brochures. Some candidates moved from pull to push technology and ran email campaigns; these were effective — localised, personalised, and more economical than delivering leaflets.

There was no single database of candidates' sites, so it is not easy to be sure how many had them; one in five would be a generous estimate. Gibson and Ward's research suggests that the more marginal a constituency, the more likely it was for the incumbent and main challenger to have websites.[2] Smaller parties saw their websites as a way of levelling the campaign playing-field, including the Green Party (www.vote green.org.uk), the UK Independence Party (www.ukip.org), and the Socialist Alliance (www.socialistalliance.net). There is an interesting debate about whether online campaigning offers new opportunities for smaller, less resourced groups to mobilise support or whether the web will inevitably become normalised as part of the traditional media-party hegemony.[3] Evidence from this election does not suggest that much new mobilisation was taking place — although worrying stories about the use of the internet by the extreme right in Oldham and Burnley should give pause for thought.

Although there were no real signs of smaller parties gaining significantly from their web presence, a number of sectional interest groups used the internet in ways that suggest interesting opportunities for the future. Sites ranging from the Asian zindagee.co.uk to the Muslim votesmart.org.uk, the Christian makethecrosscount.com and the gay-vote.co.uk were attempts to customise the campaign for specific groups of voters. Other sites sought to raise campaign issues up the agenda; these included the National Union of Teachers' education-election.com, vAdvocacy Online's Age Concern site (www.advocacyonline.net. learn_say.jsp) and oneworldnet's *Vote For Me* site, which sought to raise the profile of international development issues in the election.

New resources for voters

The most inventive use of the web during the 2001 campaign were not the party or candidates' sites, but the sites presenting cartoons, lampoons, games and jests. These were irreverent manifestations of voter disenchantment with politicians and their styles. Many of them were genuinely funny; even those that were not were widely distributed and commented upon, particularly by young internet users. As soon as a new one appeared vast numbers of messages circulated via an email bush network. The most frequent theme of the humour sites was the 'Prescott punch': there were sites where one could punch a politician, be punched, make politicians dance, put politicians in a blender and create anagrams of their names. On the face of it, none of this had much to do with electoral politics — or, at least, it might not have done had over 40% of the electorate decided not to vote. As it was, these sites were the best clue to the look and feel of apathy and disaffection, especially among younger voters. They were primarily anti-Tory, but not pro-Labour; unsophisticated but decidedly not gullible; frustrated by party politics but not apolitical. In *post mortems* of the 2001 turnout disaster these websites should not be overlooked.

Tactical voting websites sprang up in 2001 as a do-it-yourself version of proportional representation. These sites offered voters a chance to swap their votes (in fact, they could only swap their voting intentions), so that a Labour supporter in a Lib–Con constituency could agree to vote Liberal Democrat, as long as a Liberal Democrat supporter in a Lab–Con constituency agreed to vote Labour. In reality, their aim was to unite the centre-left vote to defeat the Tories. Tactical voting has long existed in British elections, but only via the web has it become convenient for voters in different parts of the country to negotiate vote swaps. The tacticalvoter.net website claimed to receive 200,000 visits and 8,153 vote-swap pledges during the course of the campaign. In two seats, Cheadle and Dorset South, the number of pledges exceeded the winning majority, suggesting that, if those making pledges voted as they said they would, the site may have had an impact on the results.

New routes to information

Over the past forty years people have come to expect most of their encounters with politicians to be mediated by television and the press. The internet offers a possibility of providing more direct public access to information. In the 1997 election an independent company, Online Magic, set up the GE97 website which became the leading online provider of election news. An independent body, UK Citizens Online Democracy (UKCOD) attempted to generate non-partisan online debate. In 2001, online election information and communication was dominated by media organisations with existing offline reputations. Interestingly, the tabloid press refrained from making much of a splash online. The most impressive efforts were made by BBC News Online, the *Guardian* and Channel Four's 'alternative' election site. The *Daily Telegraph, Financial Times, The Times* and *Independent* all produced information-rich sites, but provided few interactive opportunities.

BBC News Online put enormous effort into creating a website that was rich in content, easy to navigate and distinctly a BBC product. There were half-a-million total page views per day throughout the campaign for BBC News Online's *Vote 2001* site, with 10.76 million page views on 7 and 8 June, exceeding the previous record set by the 2000 US presidential election. People go to the web for breaking news (such as election results) and personalised information (such as their constituency results). The *Guardian's Election 2001* saw a similar surge in traffic on election night and the day after.

But online information is about more than headline news. The web can also provide depth and a variety of perspectives, making it a richer information source than others. BBC News Online provided detailed accounts of the main policy issues and the parties' perspectives on them; a guide to marginal constituencies; analyses of opinion polls as they were released; an 'online 1000' panel who were surveyed on various issues throughout the campaign; a 'persuade me to vote' feature in which the public tried to urge intended non-voters to participate in the election; a 'virtual vote' feature, allowing users to play with their own online swingometer; an archive of BBC election coverage since 1945; guides to the electoral system and the local elections; a link to the *Newsround* site and an 'If U were Prime Minister' feature in which several thousand pre-voters stated their political policies; regular webcasts with leading politicians; and several online discussion fora. Moreover, all the main news and current affairs programmes from radio and television were available live or recorded via RealAudio. Nothing in the

US election of 2000 came close to BBC News Online's range and depth of information provision.

The *Guardian's Election 2001* site, launched just in time for an expected 3 May election, included a cutting edge 'Aristotle' search engine that could answer a range of questions, such as the names of all candidates who were Oxbridge educated, married, or from Scotland; a daily email newsletter which was sent to 3,000 people; downloadable election posters from past and present; a fictional candidate's campaign diary; and a multi-topic discussion forum. The Channel 4 website targeted the young and disaffected.

As well as the sites run by established offline media, a few wholly online projects made their impact on the 2001 campaign. Yougov.com ran impressive online polls, under the direction of Peter Kellner, and claimed the prize for being more accurate in its prediction of the election result than any other pollster. The size of Yougov's samples and its capacity to conduct serial polls makes it an important player in the polling world. Epolitix.net sent out thrice-daily emails with latest election news, allowing lay political geeks almost the same access to the news wire as professional journalists. Voxpolitics.com was set up by a group of e-enthusiasts who provided a valuable running commentary on the role of the internet in the election. Having learned the lesson of the ignominious failure of the highly capitalised 'political portal' sites in the 2000 US election, there were no signs in the UK election of investors seeking to make fortunes out of online information provision. The lesson for the UK seemed to be that people wanted direct access to information, but not the disintermediation that was much heralded by early internet enthusiasts; the guidance and interpretation of trusted mediators is still needed in the world of online information.

The feedback path inherent to digital media breaks down traditional divisions between information and communication. The election-news websites not only provided information bonuses for those who wanted them, but also opened up new channels for public discussion. Study of more than two thousand messages to online election discussions suggests that far from facilitating an inclusive, deliberative public dialogue, these online discussions were dominated by a small minority of regular participants who were overwhelmingly male, and who rarely contributed fact-based information or experiential testimonies.[4]

The internet as politics

Commentators were remarkably judgmental about the role of the internet in the 2001 election, criticising it both for promising too much and changing too little. It was almost as if the critics really believed that the internet possessed some kind of mysterious power to transform the communication of politics, but had teased them with its understated performance. In fact, there is only so much that can ever be expected of an information-communication medium; after all, even the mighty medium of television failed to make a dull election lively or to push up ratings. The internet, as a medium, could not reasonably be expected to affect very much, so could not justifiably be blamed for failing.

But there is another way of seeing the internet's relationship to democratic politics. One could argue that the interactivity of the net offers hope for a new kind of politics that is more inclusive, discursive and representative. One could go beyond the idea of the internet as a communicator of old politics to that of the internet as a symbol of a different kind of democratic representation. Given the rhetorical heat that surrounds the internet, it was surprising that no major party addressed the democratic potential of the internet at a policy level — except for the Liberal Democrats, whose manifesto had a passing reference to electronic consultations. Given Labour's stated interest in reconnecting with citizens, and the prevalent fear of voter apathy throughout the campaign, there was surely scope for exploring ways of using e-democracy as an instrument within democratic governance. Instead, the main policy concern about the internet came to the fore in week two of the campaign, when the Home Secretary announced stronger legislation to deal with child pornography on the internet. Policy debates about the internet have tended to emphasise its negative and threatening aspects, which is hardly likely to inspire public confidence in the new medium as a democratising force.

The public reaction

Only a minority of the UK public currently have home access to the internet. This minority is predominantly richer, better educated and younger than the majority who are not yet online.

A MORI poll, conducted for the Hansard Society, conducted between 21–26 June 2001, based on a representative sample of 1,999 British adults, found that one-third of respondents used the internet and email at home; 69% had mobile phones; 32% used text messaging; and 13% used digital TV to access interactive services. Of those respondents with access to the internet and email, 18% used the technology for some purpose connected with the election campaign. This rose to one-quarter among under 35-year-olds.

One in ten of those with access to the internet and/or email visited a media website, such as BBC Online, to read about the election. Men were twice as likely as women to do this. One in twenty sent or received emails about the election, with more women doing this than men. About 4% of respondents with internet access visited websites or exchanged emails to share jokes or play games relating to the election. Interestingly, online humour sites, which one might have expected to attract the wholly disaffected, attracted mainly voters (6%) rather than non-voters (1%.)

What information was the online public seeking? More than one in ten of respondents with internet/email access went online to find out more about the parties' policies, a figure which rose to one in five (21%) for 18–24-year-olds. For the younger generation, who are the most turned off by politics, the internet is already becoming *the* trusted source for political information. Almost one in ten went online to find out about the candidates in their constituency, suggesting that candidates without a web presence could be negatively affected. Three per cent said that they went online to find out how to vote tactically. Most interestingly, those who went to tactical voting sites were distributed equally across the three main parties, rather than being concentrated among Liberal Democrat and Labour voters.

Did the internet or email influence how people voted? This is a notoriously difficult question to answer, because voters are motivated by many information sources, and do not necessarily know what they are. We await further analysis based on the British Election Study survey and related experimental research. Overall, only 1% of respondents with internet/email access in the MORI survey claimed that it was a 'very' important influence. Nevertheless, 6% said that it was 'very or fairly' important, this proportion rising to 17% among 18–24-year-olds. The remainder of the public (77%) said it was 'not very/not at all' important.

The main message from the MORI poll is that the internet's role was probably peripheral, but much more significant within the youngest generation; these, of course, are the trendsetters for the future. It would have been useful to compare these poll findings with actual weblogs for the main party and candidates' sites, but the party webmasters have been insistent about the confidentiality of their user statistics, partly to keep them from their political rivals and partly because they are worried that too few people went to their sites. Tim Collins, the Conservative Party vice-chairman, said after the election that he considered his party's web campaign to have been too costly and not worth the money in comparison with other campaign activities.

Where to next?

2001 was for the internet what 1959 had been for television: both were elections in which a new medium found its way on to the political stage and was tested. Just as in 1959 television producers were not sure what would work, and by 1964 both the parties and the broadcasters began to understand the potential of televised politics, so the 2001 online campaign can be seen as something of a dress rehearsal for bigger things to come. Three kinds of development will shape the future role of the internet in UK politics: technological, political and cultural.

As internet and broadband connections increase, online activity will become less rooted in personal computers and will move to other digital platforms. Digital TV has the potential to bring internet access into poorer households and into the traditional domestic setting for information consumption. If, as the government has stated, the next general election is going to be the last one before analogue switch-off, the election after that (2009/10) will be the first election in which digital interactivity is virtually universal. This leaves less than a decade for the parties and information-providers to work out how political communication will look in a post-analogue, post-broadcast age.

The internet will be tested politically before it develops as a technology. If there is a referendum about the Euro within the next two or three years the information battle will be fought out partly online, especially for the younger generation who look to the web for trusted information. The 2001 election was not a tight race; a referendum on the Euro could be the vigorous test of online information provision and discussion facilitation that could make the internet's political reputation.

But perhaps the most important factor to shape the future of online politics will be political culture. Traditionally amorphous and slow-changing, political culture in the UK is ripe for radical change. The gap between citizens' interest in political issues and their distaste for party politics calls for sophisticated analysis. At least part of the explanation will be found to lie in the anachronistic nature of political communication. Channel 4 has succeeded, against all odds, in rebranding cricket as an exciting sport, but still viewers find the broadcasting of Parliament dull, impenetrable and formulaic; millions of young people vote on who should be in the *Big Brother* house, but not on who should be in the House of Commons. Citizens increasingly shop, bank, learn and chat by email and the web, but still less than a fifth of MPs in the 1997–2001 Parliament had a website, and only half had publicly available email addresses.[5] The project of adapting British democracy so that it relates to the public in the information age could mark the real political coming of age for the internet.

As a simple tool for political marketing, the internet is unlikely to have a significant influence on British politics, although it will continue to be a resource for parties to make unmediated appeals to target voters. As an integral part of the reinvention of democratic representation, linked to agendas for e-government, online parliamentary committee hearings, and trusted spaces for public deliberation (a civic commons in cyberspace),[6] the internet might be the instrument of reconnection and engagement that could bring new vigour to the atrophying British democratic process.

Stephen Coleman

1   See S. Coleman (ed.), *2001: A Cyberspace Odyssey*, Hansard Society, London, 2001, p. 18.
2   R.K. Gibson and S.J. Ward, 'Open All Hours? Political Parties and Online Technologies', unpublished paper for IPPR conference, 20 June 2001, pp. 39–45.
3   For an introduction to this debate, see R.K. Gibson and S.J. Ward, 'UK Political Parties and the Internet: Politics as Usual in the New Media', 3 *Harvard International Journal of Press/Politics* 3, 14–38 and J.

Roper, 'New Zealand Political Parties On Line: The World Wide Web as a Tool for Democracy or for Political Marketing?' in C. Toulouse and C. Luke, *The Politics of Cyberspace*, Routledge, 1999.

4 S. Coleman, 'Was There an Online Public Dialogue?', *2001: A Cyberspace Odyssey*, Hansard Society, London, 2001, pp. 39–45.

5 D. Walker, 'Why the General Election of 2001 is Not Going to be Held Online', *Business*, May 2001, pp. 24–9.

6 J.G. Blumler and S. Coleman, *Realising Democracy Online: A Civic Commons in Cyberspace*, IPPR/ Citizens Online, 2001.

JUSTIN FISHER

Campaign Finance: Elections Under New Rules

The financial rules under which the 2001 election was held represent a new era in British elections. Within six months of Labour's 1997 victory, Tony Blair had extended the remit of the Committee on Standards in Public Life to examine the vexed question of party finance. On past evidence, expectations of widespread change were not great. Previous examinations had led to virtually no change in regulations rooted in the late nineteenth-century and the reaction to earlier reports by the Committee suggested that sweeping reform was an unlikely outcome.[1] Yet just one year later, these preconceptions were shown to be false. The Committee produced perhaps its most radical report yet, promising widespread reform in party finance. Within two years, the report was law (Political Parties, Elections and Referendums Act 2000 —hereafter PPER) with only minor modifications from the original. The electoral battlefield in 2001 was substantially altered from that prevailing four years earlier. With the notable omission of comprehensive state funding, this meant that Britain was now much more akin to other democracies in the regulation of its party finance. Hitherto, Britain was notable for the remarkable lack of legislation in this area. Yet the impact of the new legislation appears to have been slightly different than had been envisaged. On the one hand, it did mean that parties were more disciplined in evaluating their spending. However, equity in spending levels has only really been employed with regard to the main two parties. The playing-field has become slightly more even for the Liberal Democrats and the smaller parties, but the spending gap between them and the main two parties remains large.

Income and expenditure

Until the PPER Act came into force, gaining information about party finance could be a thankless task. Parties were not obliged to provide details regarding their income and expenditure, and the Conservatives did not even publish accounts until the late 1960s. Moreover, the financial accounting year of parties differed: Labour and the Liberal Democrats took their year-end to be December but the Conservatives

Figure 1. Central Party Income and Expenditure, 1989–99

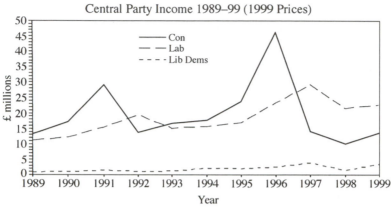

Central Party Income 1989–99 (1999 Prices)

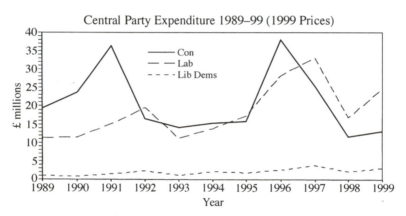

Central Party Expenditure 1989–99 (1999 Prices)

used March. The effect was to make comparisons between the Conservatives and others potentially complex. Finally, unlike at local level, there was no predefined campaign period at national level. Thus, difficulties arose as to when spending on an election campaign actually started.

Notwithstanding, the available data do allow us to establish whether there has been a major shift in parties' financial situations over the last decade (see Figure 1). The evidence shows that Labour's financial resources and spending power has grown, and that of the Conservatives has diminished, while the Liberal Democrats have remained relatively poor cousins.[2] Since the 1997 election, Labour has become the wealthy party; it both generated more income than the Conservatives and spent more. Not only that, Labour's spending did not generally exceed its income. In contrast, Conservative spending, in common with previous trends, was less prudent.[3] The Liberal Democrats, too, have struggled to control electoral spending relative to income.

The Political Parties, Elections and Referendums Act

The election of the Labour government in 1997 meant that some reform of party finance was on the agenda as the party had promised to re-examine the issue of party finance in its manifesto. The Prime Minister instructed the Committee on Standards in Public Life (the Neill Committee) to examine the whole issue in late 1997. The Committee reported in October 1998[4] with proposals for the most fundamental reform in British party finance since the Corrupt and Illegal Practices Act 1883. Critically, the report was supported by all parties and was accepted almost in its entirety when the government published its response in July 1999.[5] The proposals became law on 30 November 2000.

The new Act established a series of key provisions with respect to election campaigns. First, an Electoral Commission was established to oversee the implementation of the law relevant to party finance, as well as for other electoral matters.[6] Its remit is wide. The commission is charged with overseeing electoral boundaries, the registration of parties and designated organisations, the regulations pertaining to elections, and the use of advertising in elections. It provides advice on electoral matters and promotes public awareness of the electoral process. Major parties will now be required to submit audited accounts to the Commission based upon identical time periods in a standard format. Such accounts will be required within three months of the accounting year-end, and will be made available for public inspection. In addition, parties must make regular declarations regarding donations and election expenditure.

Second, the Act covers political donations. It specifies that gifts to parties in excess of £5,000 nationally and £1,000 locally are now publicly declared. Importantly, this includes 'in kind' payments. Declaration is quarterly during non-election periods and weekly during general elections. Anonymous donations to parties in excess of £200 are now prohibited, as are 'blind trusts' and foreign donations. Contributions are only permitted from permissible sources.[7]

Third, one of Act's most radical clauses was to limit campaign spending at national level in general elections. Hitherto, only constituency campaign expenditure had been regulated. One problem with a national limit is the definition of when a campaign begins. For the purposes of the Act, the campaign was defined officially as the 365 days preceding polling day in a general election. The ceiling was set at £30,000 per contested constituency. Thus, if a party contested all 641 seats in Britain, the ceiling would be £19,230,000. In the light of the Bowman case,[8] the Act also increased the sums permitted for 'third party' expenditure at constituency level. The spending cap was a surprise move, given that of all the regulations this was most likely to attract attempts to find loopholes, but the Neill Committee's justification was one similar to that imposed at constituency level. The analogy was with speed limits. A 30mph speed-limit will not prevent drivers travelling at 35mph, but it is likely to prevent speeds of 50mph. In the case of the 2001 election, however, the spending cap was set at approximately £16.3 million per party, since the Act came into force on 16 February 2001 and the definition of the campaign period (365 days) could not be applied retrospectively.

Despite the new Act, the period preceding the election was still characterised by controversy over party finance. In January 2001, Labour revealed that it had received three separate donations of £2 million each.[9] Soon after, the Conservatives noted that they were in receipt of a gift of £5 million.[10] Technically, the parties were not obliged to reveal the identities of the donors nor the sums involved, since the donations had been made prior to the new Act coming into force. Yet conscious of the potentially bad publicity arising from trying to maintain anonymity, the parties did reveal details. There was disquiet at the size of these donations, prompting the chair of the new Electoral Commission, Sam Younger, to suggest that the question of donations caps might be re-examined in future.

Further controversy surrounded the Conservatives' decision to divert some of its income from 'Short' money into the party's day-to-day activities. Short money is intended to assist opposition parties with their work in Parliament, rather than contributing to party infrastructure and campaigning. Labour referred the matter to the Electoral Commission and at the time of writing, it remains unresolved. Finally, Labour was heavily criticised for embarking on an intensive period of government advertising in the period leading up to the election. In the first three months of the year, the government spent over £60 million on advertising, compared with around £103 million for the whole of 2000. This made the government Britain's biggest advertiser during this period. Labour claimed this advertising was necessary to alert people to policy changes in tax credit and pensions. Other parties suggested that the government was using public money to promote Labour's pre-election campaign.[11]

The campaign

DONATIONS: The new legislation has generated previously unavailable data on party income that allows us to examine where parties raised the bulk of their funds as well as the origins of these donations. The data in Tables 1 and 2 show some striking findings. First, in terms of direct cash donations, the Conservatives received most during the campaign and the immediate pre-campaign period. That should be qualified, however, since the party received a single donation of £5m from Paul Getty in early June. Without his generosity (accounting for 77% of Conservative declared donations), Conservative declared income fell short of Labour's. Indeed, Labour's wealth was enhanced by the £163,059 received by the Cooperative Party over the whole

1. Declared Cash Donations

£s	Conservatives	Labour	Liberal Democrats
February–May	555,202	2,397,979	175,655
Week 1	609,001	316,000	30,000
Week 2	146,055	792,000	–
Week 3	25,001	6,000	–
Week 4	100,000	304,000	15,100
Week 5	5,022,250	210,000	–
Total	6,457,509	4,025,979	220,755

Note: From 16 February–7 June 2001. Source: Electoral Commission Register of Donation Returns, http://www.electoralcommission.gov.uk.

period. Though registered as a separate party, the party fields joint candidates with Labour in some constituencies. Second, the relative poverty of the Liberal Democrats is well-illustrated. Labour received almost as much in declared donations in the last three days of the campaign as the Liberal Democrats did over four months. Third, income over the course of the campaign was generally skewed towards the beginning. If we discount Getty's last-gasp donation, the majority of donations were made in the first two weeks. But, more seriously for the Conservatives, while the bulk of their income came early, some may have come too late to spend effectively on the campaign. Whilst a sum like Getty's would of course be welcome, its impact on the campaign would be virtually nil. Parties need to raise seed-money early to have well-funded and well-planned campaigns. The Conservatives raised more in the first week of the campaign than in the three months preceding it, whilst Labour built up a large number of donations in the pre-campaign period.

As regards other parties, the SNP received £27,000 in declared cash donations over the whole period (February to June), PC £12,700, UKIP £11,000, the Progressive Democratic Party £4,000 and the Liberal Party £3,000. All of which emphasises that a spending cap can only perform a limited role in levelling the playing-field between smaller and larger parties.

Examining the sources confirms that individual donations[12] have become more significant to both main parties' finances, an emerging trend originally identified in the 1990s.[13] Even without the £5,000,000 donation, the Conservatives still received more from individuals than

2. Sources of Declared Cash Donations

£s	Conservatives	Labour	Liberal Democrats
Individuals	5,947,354	814,983	168,209
Companies	429,655	114,900	36,212
Unincorporated Associations	80,500	18,700	16,333
Trade Unions	–	3,047,680	–
Friendly Societies	–	2,000	–
Registered Parties	–	27,715	–

Note: From 16 February–7 June 2001. Source: Electoral Commission Register of Donation Return, http://www.electoralcommission.gov.uk.

3. Declared Non-Cash Donations

Value (£s)	February–May	Campaign	Total
Conservative	78,621	396,478	475,099
Labour	17,897	–	17,897
Liberal Democrat	1,125	22,096	23,221
UKIP	–	554,234	554,234

Note: From 16 February–7 June 2001. Source: Electoral Commission Register of Donation Returns, http://www.electoralcommission.gov.uk.

companies. Labour, too, received a significant sum from individuals, but nevertheless received most from trade unions. Coupled with that, the Labour Party also received over half-a-million pounds in affiliation fees during the campaign, which underlines the continuing importance of trade unions to their coffers. The unions may provide a lower proportion of Labour income than they once did, but the loss of this money would still be significant. Finally, it is worth noting that while the Conservatives still received the bulk of corporate donations, Labour attracted some business money, continuing another trend first apparent in the late 1990s.[14]

The wisdom of the PPER Act to include payments in kind to generate a more accurate picture of party finance is well-demonstrated. In addition to cash donations, the Conservatives were in additional receipt of nearly £400,000 of non-cash donations during the campaign, whilst the UK Independence Party received over half-a-million pounds from just one company. Labour, by way of contrast, received few significant 'non-cash' donations (see Table 3).

SPENDING: Spending data for the 12-months preceding the 1997 election revealed that the Conservatives had spent £28.3m and Labour £25.7m, well over the subsequent limits set by the PPER Act. Consequently, both needed to review and reduce their overall budgets. The only impact for the Liberal Democrats in this respect was to narrow the gap between them and the other parties (see Table 4). At the time of writing, parties have yet to declare their total expenditure to the

4. Campaign Expenditure for the 1997 General Election

	Conservative		Labour		Lib Dem	
	£m	%	£m	%	£m	%
Newspaper advertising	3.2	11.3	0.9	3.5	–	–
Outdoor advertising	11.1	39.2	4.8	18.7	0.1	2.9
Other advertising	0.1	0.4	0.1	0.4	–	–
Publications	1.0	3.5	1.5	5.8	0.5	14.3
Direct mail	2.2	7.8	1.8	7.0	0.2	5.7
Telemarketing	–	–	0.5	1.9	0.3	8.6
PEBs and videos	0.5	1.8	0.6	2.3	0.3	8.6
Other	10.2	36.0	15.5	60.3	2.0	57.1
Total	28.3	100.0	25.7	100.0	3.5	100.0

Source: The Committee on Standards in Public Life, The Funding of Political Parties in the United Kingdom pp. 36–8.

Electoral Commission. Nevertheless, broad comparisons can be made with spending in 1997 regarding the principal areas of campaign expenditure.

CONSERVATIVE STRATEGY: The Conservatives re-examined their campaign strategy. They concluded that they had defended the wrong seats in 1997 and decided to make 2001 a highly-targeted campaign, which had important implications for party spending. A sea-change was that the party was determined to emerge from the election in credit. This contrasted with their position in the 1987 election, when the Conservatives knowingly spent more than had been raised in the view that it was better to go into deficit than risk losing the election.[15] Nevertheless, in 2001 the party still spent up the permitted limit.

The targeted campaign manifested itself in a number of ways. Telephone canvassing, staffed mainly by volunteers, focussed on key seats and was based at Conservative Central Office. Posters were placed in and around target seats. But outdoor advertising was limited due to changes in the outdoor advertising industry. Up until 1997, this was dominated by the tobacco industry, which held sites for the Conservatives, thereby ensuring availability. Since the 1997 election, however, the industry has diversified considerably, making it more difficult for the party to acquire poster sites, especially if campaign income arrived late since poster advertising requires a long lead-time. The effect of this policy was neatly demonstrated in the final week of the campaign. The poster, featuring Tony Blair, urging voters to 'Go on. Burst his bubble' appeared on only twenty sites. However, the party gave the impression of it being a national campaign by distributing television and newspapers with an electronic version of the poster, which then appeared as front-page news. There was also a shift in newspaper advertising. The party concluded that advertising in the national press was ineffective but it decided to focus on local and regional newspapers — the view being that more people read these papers and, as a bonus, advertising rates are, of course, cheaper.

Overall, Conservative campaign expenditure focused less on outdoor and newspaper advertising and more on direct mail and direct voter contact. Viral marketing[16] via email was explored, but it was not exploited to a large degree. Experience from the US suggested that the returns were not huge, especially in a campaign that was portrayed, at least, as being held during a period of apathy. Not only that, the Conservative Party concluded that to be effective, viral marketing needed to be of 'questionable taste', which the party wished to avoid. Further changes occurred in the party's opinion research. The Conservatives concluded that national surveys provided poor value for money, since so many were published in the press. Consequently, it decided to spend much less than in 1997 by using two distinct methodologies. First, ICM conducted weekly quantitative surveys across battleground seats. Second, two focus groups were held each night. These consisted of voters who had not supported the Conservatives in 1997, but were possible Conservative supporters this time. On the basis of the groups' findings, the party decided to campaign on the dangers of a landslide during the final week, with the 'bubble' campaign.

The party also spent less on its party election broadcasts (PEBs) than in 1997. This was in part because the party took the shortest possible slot (two minutes and forty seconds) for its broadcasts. This was not a financial decision. Rather, the party wished to make the PEBs more like television advertisements. The party had four 'adverts' — on tax, crime, Europe and education. The view was that this format was more effective that standard PEBs.

LABOUR STRATEGY: As in 1997, Labour concentrated most campaign expenditure on posters after the party's research suggested that this was the most effective available medium. Around £1 million was spent on each poster campaign, costing around £4.5–£5m in total. The party ran a humorous poster campaign to counteract perceived voter apathy. This approach, such as the 'wiggy' poster (featuring William Hague sporting a Margaret Thatcher wig) gained much 'offspin' in the national media, thus strengthening their impact. Like the Conservatives, press advertising was very limited at national level. The party's view was that posters were more effective, and that extensive newspaper advertising was neither cost effective nor necessary, since the bulk of the press was supporting Labour anyway. This was an important change from elections prior to 1997. Nevertheless, the party did engage in some advertising in local and regional newspapers targeted in regions with vulnerable seats.

Telephone canvassing was a bigger priority than in 1997, again partly in response to perceived voter apathy. Labour was particularly concerned to contact its own supporters who did not vote regularly. As discussed by Seyd in this volume, around 200 people were employed at a national call centre in North Shields from mid-January onwards. Direct mail was of a similar magnitude proportionally to 1997. As far as PEBs were concerned, less was spent on the broadcasts due to the spending constraints imposed by the PPER Act. Moreover, all but one of the PEBs was of the minimum time allowed.

For all the broad similarities with 1997, Labour's campaign was innovative in two particular aspects: more use was made of electronic campaigning, though the budget in relative terms was limited. In addition to the party's main website, as Coleman discusses in this volume, Labour attempted to extend voter contact electronically. Election games were emailed to 30,000 activists. Moreover, text messaging to mobile phones was employed. Like the Conservatives, Labour was conscious that such techniques should avoid campaigns of questionable taste, but took the view that they could at least be 'cheeky'. Nevertheless, the primary motive for these campaigns was less voter contact and more the 'offspin' that they generated. In addition, 300,000 videos were distributed to 60 of the 148 'priority' constituencies. The video featured a common section from NEC member Tony Robinson, together with a section featuring the local Labour candidate. Costs were shared equally between the centre and the constituency. Videos were sent on the last weekend of the campaign and were targeted at large households (for multiple viewers), weak Labour supporters, and areas where turnout was predicted to be low.

Overall, despite Labour entering the campaign in good financial shape, it spent less than the limit permitted. The party deliberately set low budgets for its various campaigns, building in the possibility of errors. Since it was a Labour government that had brought in the new regulations, the party was determined that it should not contravene them, even though, by common consent, the new rules would take one election to 'bed in'. In addition, the party wanted to avoid ending in the red (financially). After 1997, some economies had been necessary and despite its relative financial security, the party was keen to avoid deficits where possible.

LIBERAL DEMOCRAT STRATEGY: The Liberal Democrats spent less on this campaign than in 1997. This was due to an accumulated deficit of £500,000, which left the party in a worse financial position than in 1997. These problems further emphasised the major difference between the Liberal Democrats and the other main parties. Overall campaign expenditure was around £2.5 million. The biggest single item was Charles Kennedy's extensive tour, which cost around £500,000. Beyond this, the types of expenditure changes were similar to those made by the Conservatives. The Liberal Democrats changed their poster strategy. In 1997, the party had one fixed site in central London. This time, 'poster vans' were used, driving around the country, generating local and regional news. Like the other parties, the Liberal Democrats concentrated most attention on local media, seen as giving better and less dispassionate coverage than the national media. Unlike the others, however, the Liberal Democrats did not advertise even in local newspapers other than to promote party rallies. Liberal Democrat PEBs were, like the others, of the minimum time permitted.

Unlike Labour and the Conservatives, the Liberal Democrats could not afford any systematic telephone canvassing. Any that did occur, other than a very small amount on the eve of the election, was the result of local initiatives. Direct mail was sent exclusively to members and supporters, rather than voters, and concentrated upon raising funds. If targeted mail was produced, it was delivered by hand due to costs, and this was further complicated by access difficulties in some constituencies due to the foot and mouth disease outbreak.

IMPACT OF REGULATIONS: Whether or not disparities in the levels of spending made a decisive difference to party fortunes is a debatable point. The Neill Committee proposed the capping of national expenditure limits at general elections partly to level the playing-field — especially with the retention of the ban on commercial TV advertising. Yet, the evidence for the putative electoral pay-offs of any spending remains mixed. Johnston and Pattie have consistently shown a link between spending at constituency level and electoral success. Yet Fisher has demonstrated that at national level the relationship between spending and electoral pay-offs is anything but conclusive.[17] A possible reason for these different findings is that whereas the types of expenditure in each election are fairly routine at constituency level, at national level these may change significantly from year to year. Since money may be used with differing degrees of skill, the impact of spending more money will not be so likely to lead to electoral pay-offs. As a consequence, the principal impact of the new spending regulations is likely to have been one of changing the proportions spent on campaign items, and increasing transparency, rather than levelling the electoral playing-field.

The new rules did generate some problems. Before the campaign even began, the new regulations on spending almost cost the parties dearly. To attribute spending correctly, the PPER Act stated that posters and leaflets should carry an imprint with the name and address of the person on whose behalf the material was being issued. As officials from all the main parties failed to spot this new regulation, large quantities of material had already been printed which did not comply with the new regulations. Parties were faced with the prospect of having to destroy this material. However, emergency legislation (Election Publications Act 2001) was passed on 10 April postponing the introduction of these regulations until after the election, thereby saving all parties considerable sums.

Another problem was the delay of the election. All parties had been working towards a 3 May poll and had been focussing their spending plans accordingly. Pre-campaign posters, for example, were booked some months previously and began to appear in the spring. Estimates suggested that by the end of March, Labour had already spent £3 million pounds on posters, and the Conservatives £2 million.[18] The effects of the delay were twofold: the maximum election spending permitted was extended from £15,384,000 to £16,345,500 (based upon a party contesting all 641 British seats) and parties now had to raise further income to cover the extended campaign.

The new PPER Act also created its own tensions. Both the Conservatives and Labour spent at least close to the limit permitted by the Act, but that limit imposed opportunity costs. Thus, if one million was spent on X, then that was one million that could not be spent on Y. Parties had to review their spending to be most effective. Nevertheless, such policies would be complicated by the time of the arrival of income. If money arrives late in the campaign, it is largely ineffective, since most campaign spending requires a lead-time. The exception to this is newspaper advertisements, which can be ordered very quickly, though as we have seen, parties were sceptical of the utility of this campaign technique Thus, 'early money' is better because it provides more choices in terms of spending. As we have seen, the Labour Party had more 'early money' than the Conservatives.

For local parties, indications are that the new legal regulations did cause a few difficulties. Combined with changes to postal voting and rolling registration, local parties faced a heavier workload. With regard to the PPER Act, local parties reported difficulties with recording donations, the question of imprints on leaflets, and generally learning the new legal requirements.[19] Whilst new regulations were welcome, local parties will take time to adapt to them fully.

Conclusion

Despite these difficulties, overall, parties adapted well to the new regulations. There were some uncertainties, notably the status of some forms of donations 'in kind'. Nevertheless, the indications are that the regulations, both in spirit and actuality, were observed. Whether this will occur once parties and donors become fully accustomed with the regulations and possible loopholes remains to be seen. Experience from other democracies suggests that exploitation of loopholes in party finance legislation is commonplace. Yet the British experience with electoral law generally suggests a less pessimistic view. Overall, the PPER Act has had two notable impacts. The transparency of party fundraising has been significantly enhanced. More importantly, it has forced the major parties to be more disciplined financially. The 2001 campaign was marked by a more rigorous evaluation of the efficacy of funded campaign techniques to avoid contravening the rules, together with a desire to avoid large post-election deficits.

Three developments in campaign spending have become apparent. First, the parties are now divided on whether posters are the most effective means of communication. Labour invested heavily in them in the 2001 campaign, whilst the Conservatives cut back. Second, national newspaper advertising is no longer considered good value for money by any of the parties and it has virtually dried up. Rather, if parties do take out advertisements, these are likely to be in local and regional newspapers, usually in target seats. Lastly, expenditure on electronic campaigning continues to be limited, and notwithstanding Labour's innovative use of videos, national campaign expenditure is still concentrated on more conventional activities. However, the sums spent on campaigns provide only a partial picture. All parties designed their campaigns in part for additional 'offspin'. For example, Labour did not spend a great deal on electronic campaigning, but gained a great deal of coverage from it. The Conservatives erected their final campaign poster on only twenty sites, but its contents shaped the final week of the campaign. The regulation of campaign broadcasting to ensure broad equity is therefore essential if the new regulations are to succeed in evening out the impact of electoral spending. In other words, it is pointless limiting what parties can spend, if broadcasters only feature one or two parties.

Justin Fisher

1   J. Fisher, 'Regulating Politics: The Committee on Standards in Public Life' in J. Fisher, D. Denver and J. Benyon (eds), *Central Debates in British Politics*, Harlow: Pearson, 2001.
2   It appears from the graphs that Labour income and expenditure outstripped that of the Conservatives in 1992 and 1997. The reason is that the Conservative financial year runs to the end of March whereas Labour's (and the Liberal Democrats') runs to the end of December. For comparison, therefore, Conservative income and expenditure is classified as being in the year in which the financial year is largely concerned. For example, the FY1996/97 is classified as being 1996, since nine months fell in that year. Thus, much of the income and expenditure of the Conservatives in the run-up to the 1997 election is classified as having taken place in FY1996 and likewise, most of the 1992 income and expenditure is classified as having taken place in FY1991.
3   J. Fisher, 'Economic Performance or Electoral Necessity? Evaluating the System of Voluntary Income to Political Parties', *British Journal of Politics and International Relations*, 2, 1999, pp. 186–7.
4   The Committee on Standards in Public Life, *The Funding of Political Parties in the United Kingdom*, London: TSO, 1998, Cm 4057.
5   The only exception to the recommendations not accepted was the rejection of tax relief on donations of up to £500.
6   http://www.electoralcommission.gov.uk/index.htm.
7   Donations are only allowed from individuals entitled to be registered as UK voters; companies incorporated in the United Kingdom; partnerships based in the United Kingdom or who operate principally in the United Kingdom; registered trade unions and other organisations based in the United Kingdom or those parts of organisations whose principal spheres of operation are based in the United Kingdom.
8   See J. Fisher, 'The Political Parties, Elections and Referendums Act 2000', *Representation*, 38, 2001, p. 15.
9   Two were from existing Labour supporters, Science Minister, Lord Sainsbury and publisher, Paul Hamlyn. The third, however, was from Christopher Ondaatje, a former supporter of the Conservatives.
10 From Stuart Wheeler, chair of a spread betting company.
11 http://news.bbc.co.uk/hi/english/uk_politics/newsid_1295000/1295679.stm 25/04/01.
12 The PPER Act distinguishes between donations made by individuals and those made by collective entities, such as companies and trade unions.
13 J. Fisher, 'Donations to Political Parties', *Parliamentary Affairs*, April 1997.
14 J. Fisher, 'Donations to Political Parties', *Parliamentary Affairs*, April 1997.
15 M. Pinto Duschinsky, 'Financing the British General Election of 1987' in I. Crewe and M. Harrop (eds), *Political Communications: The General Election Campaign of 1987*, Cambridge University Press, 1989, p. 16.
16 Viral marketing is the electronic equivalent of word-of-mouth marketing. It refers to the distribution from one source to many in the form of, for example, forwarding jokes to friends via email.
17 R. Johnston and C. Pattie, 'The Impact of Spending on Party Constituency Campaigns in Recent British General Election', *Party Politics*, 1, 1995; J. Fisher, 'Party Expenditure and Electoral Prospects: A National Level Analysis of Britain', *Electoral Studies*, 18, 1999.
18 http://news.bbc.co.uk/hi/english/uk_politics/newsid_1256000/1256749.stm 02/04/01.
19 These findings are derived from early returns from Denver, Hands and Fisher's analysis of constituency campaigning at the 2001 general election.

ALICE BROWN

Scotland

The 2001 general election in Scotland was another 'first' and historic landmark in the country's contemporary political history. As the first general election held after the establishment of the Scottish Parliament in 1999, many questions were raised in the minds of political, academic and media commentators. Just how significant would this election be for Scottish voters and how would it affect electoral turnout? Also, what would emerge as the key issues in Scotland and how would these differ from other parts of the UK? And to what extent would voters differentiate between Westminster and Scottish elections, and would they judge the political parties by their performance in the Scottish Parliament?

Following the 1997 general election, opinion polls suggested that when Scottish voters went to the polls for the first Scottish elections in 1999 they would behave in line with electors in other countries with decentralised or devolved political systems. Comparison was made in particular with Catalonia, where support for the Nationalists is higher than that for the Socialists in the autonomous elections, but where their relative positions are reversed in elections for the all-Spain Cortes.[1] The results of the Scottish election demonstrated that there was evidence to support this theory and that people in Scotland had used their votes in quite a sophisticated manner, in differentiating between elections for the two parliaments, in operating the different electoral systems, and in splitting their votes between parties.[2] The 2001 general election offered the opportunity to test this theory in a new context.

The 2001 election was a somewhat different event from the 1997 Westminster election when so much was at stake and expectations were high. That contest was seen as critical in delivering a change of government and a programme of far-reaching constitutional reform. In 2001 the contrast was striking. With a Scottish Parliament reaching the end of its second year of operation, the election campaign was not dominated by the constitutional question or the debate that had dictated the past, namely the choice between the status quo, devolution or independence. For this election, that particular issue was settled.

Contrast could also be drawn with the first elections for the Scottish Parliament held in 1999. These elections were conducted on the basis, not of first-past-the-post, but on a more proportional electoral system. The form of Additional Member System adopted for the Scottish Parliamentary elections allowed for a much closer relationship between the votes cast and the seats gained by political parties. Under this system, no single party obtained an overall majority. Seats were distributed between the four main political parties in Scotland (Labour 56 seats, Scottish National Party 35, Conservatives 18 and Liberal Democrats 17). Seats were also won by two of the smaller parties, the Greens and the Scottish Socialists, as well as one independent candidate. Another difference was the emphasis on the representation of women in the Scottish Parliament. As a result of positive action measures taken by the Labour Party and the placing of women high on the party list by the SNP, 48 women were elected from a total of 129 Members of the Scottish Parliament (MSPs), a representation rate of over 37%. These conditions did not apply in the general election in Scotland in 2001.

The campaign: a dull affair?

Reflecting on the campaign, the BBC's political commentator, Brian Taylor, said: 'This time the question was not "did you stay up for Portillo", but "did you stay up at all?".'[3] His remarks echoed the general feelings that the election had been a relatively dull affair and the campaign had failed to capture voters' interest. It was feared that, as in other parts of Britain, a large proportion of the electorate would simply not bother to vote. This situation was not helped by the ongoing speculation over the timing of the election, which started in earnest at the beginning of 2001. It is worth noting that this is another difference from the system in Scotland, where a fixed four-year term operates and the date of the parliamentary election is known. The Prime Minister's decision to postpone the general election from the anticipated May date until June was accepted as appropriate in the wake of the foot-and-mouth crisis, not least because one of the most adversely affected areas was Dumfries and Galloway, but the delay only added to the apparent boredom and the desire to have the election over and done with.

With the opinion polls remaining consistent in the months running up to the election, few changes in the distribution of seats were anticipated. As little was apparently at stake, the media struggled to identify issues that would help bring the campaign to life. One of the ironies was, of course, that the issues of greatest interest to the public in Scotland as in the rest of Britain and which most dominated the campaign—health, education and crime—are all areas that are devolved and fall under the jurisdiction of the Scottish Parliament. The election campaign was also played out on the floor of the Scottish Parliament, with MSPs exploiting opportunities to electioneer. Questions were raised about the activities of some MSPs in their party's general election campaign. In particular, the role of the Labour Minister, Wendy Alexander, in heading Labour's campaign in Scotland was questioned. Nevertheless, the normal work of the Parliament and its committees continued and electioneering on the floor of the house was relatively restrained, partially perhaps because of the warning issued by the Presiding Officer, Sir David Steel.

As in other parts of Britain, the Prescott punch appeared to offer some light relief and did not apparently harm the prospects for the Labour Party. In contrast, the entrance into the campaign of the former Prime Minister, Margaret Thatcher, probably helped remind voters in Scotland of the more negative aspects of previous Conservative administrations and, in particular, their opposition to the establishment of a Scottish Parliament. This was a factor that one of their prominent candidates, Sir Malcolm Rifkind, was only too well-aware of as he sought the support of the electorate in the Edinburgh Pentlands constituency on the grounds of his personal reputation and contribution, rather on the basis of the party card. Another issue which had resonance in Scotland was the relative absence of women from the media coverage of the campaign (see Lovenduski this volume). While the Chancellor, Gordon Brown, caused some hilarity when he responded to a question addressed to Estelle Morris at a press conference south of the border, the Liberal Democrat leader in Scotland, Jim Wallace, also found himself embarrassed at a similar event. Launching their women's day during the campaign, he posed for photographs with a university women's rugby team. When questioned about the number of women candidates put forward by the party in Scotland, however, he confessed rather sheepishly that he did not know the answer.

Although the constitutional question was not a hot issue at this general election, the relative level of Scottish public expenditure and the Barnett Formula hit the headlines yet again. Speculation that the formula for distributing resources to Scotland and other parts of Britain was to be changed followed a story associated with John Prescott, the Deputy Prime Minister. The Prime Minister and the Chancellor were quick to emphasise, and the Secretary of State for Scotland was keen to confirm, that no immediate review of the Barnett Formula was proposed and that in any case the budget for the parliament was fixed under the Comprehensive Spending Review for the period up to 2004. The controversy over funding was fuelled and hit the media headlines when a group of economists made the case for greater fiscal autonomy for Scotland. This was seized upon and supported by the SNP. The proposal had an interesting twist, however, because it was argued that conceding greater fiscal powers to Scotland would strengthen not weaken the union. Ironically this was the same kind of argument that was made in the past by home rulers when making the case for devolution. It is noteworthy also that while the SNP supported greater autonomy especially over fiscal matters, they laid considerably less stress on independence. This was perhaps unsurprising given that the opinion polls conducted since the Scottish Parliament was established have shown a decline in support for the option of independence to around 20%. On the other hand, support for increased powers to the Scottish Parliament has risen.[4]

The parties and the candidates

The political parties entered into uncharted waters at this general election in Scotland, not knowing exactly what to anticipate and how to play the game. As Table 1 illustrates, the last general election resulted in a wipeout for the Conservative Party in terms of seats, even although they received over 17% of the vote. The first-past-the-post electoral system also worked to disadvantage the SNP who gained just six seats despite obtaining over 22% of the vote. With careful targeting of their campaign efforts, the Liberal Democrats obtained ten seats with 13% support from the electorate. As in other recent elections in Scotland, the Labour Party benefited most from the electoral system winning 56 seats (78%) with less than 46% of the vote. But as indicated above, the Scottish Parliamentary elections delivered rather different results under a more proportional system and a closer correlation between votes cast and seats won (see Table 2). It was clear that voters in Scotland were prepared to differentiate between elections for the Scottish and Westminster Parliaments, and also to split their vote between parties when given the opportunity under a different electoral system. Similar patterns are reported in Wales (see Wyn Jones and Trystan this volume), suggesting that split ticket voting may well persist as a general feature of British electoral behaviour.

Most of those who were elected to Westminster in 1997 and then later as members of the Scottish Parliament in 1999, indicated their intention to stand down as MPs.[5] The only exception was Alex Sal-

1. General Election Results in Scotland 1997 and 2001

	1997 Seats N.	1997 Share of the vote %	2001 Seats N	2001 Share of the vote %	1997–2001 Change in the vote %
Labour	56	45.6	56	43.9	−1.7
SNP	6	22.1	5	20.1	−2.0
Conservative	0	17.5	1	15.6	−1.9
Liberal Democrats	10	13.0	10	16.4	+3.4
Others	0	1.9	0	4.0	+2.1
Total	72	100%	72	100%	

2. Scottish Parliamentary Elections, 1999

	Constituency	List	Total seats
Labour	53 (38.8%)	3 (35.4%)	56
SNP	7 (28.8%)	28 (28.7%)	35
Conservative	0 (15.6%)	18 (16.1%)	18
Liberal Democrats	12 (14.1%)	5 (13.0%)	17
Others	1 (2.7%)	2 (6.8%)	3
Total			129

Note: At the Ayr by-election, the Conservatives gained a constituency seat from Labour.

mond, previous leader of the SNP, who decided to stand again for election to Westminster for his seat in Banff and Buchan, and to resign his Scottish parliamentary seat for the area, thus prompting a by-election. In defence of this decision, which raised some questions about Salmond's commitment to the Scottish Parliament, the argument was made that the former leader would provide political weight and experience to the party's representation in the House of Commons. This was especially the case given the relative lack of experience of some of the SNP candidates. In addition, Phil Gallie, the Conservative List MSP for the South of Scotland, was selected as the candidate to fight the Ayr constituency, a seat which the Conservatives had lost in the 1997 general election to Labour. A second by-election for a Scottish Parliamentary seat was triggered by the resignation on health grounds of the Scottish Labour Minister, Sam Galbraith, as an MP and MSP for the Strathkelvin and Bearsden constituency.

Unlike the selection processes for the Scottish Parliament, the selection of the candidates for the general election received little media attention and proved relatively uncontroversial. One contrast with the Scottish elections and the last general election was that none of the political parties operated a mechanism to support more equal representation of men and women. It was predicted that, as a result, the number of women in the House of Commons was likely to fall.[6] An analysis of the candidates fielded by the different parties in Scotland shows that there were 89 female candidates out of a total of 407 (21.9%). With 23 women candidates, the Scottish Socialist Party fielded the largest number (31.9%), followed by the Liberal Democrats with 17 (23.9%), the SNP with 16 (22.2%) and the Labour Party with 15 (20.8%). Of the total 72 Scottish MPs elected, 11 are women. At 15.3% this is significantly lower than the 37.2% in the Scottish Parliament where the 'twinning' mechanism was adopted by the Labour Party and the SNP placed women high on the party lists. It is also lower than the number and percentage of women elected to represent Scottish constituencies at the last general election in 1997.[7] Only two of the parties at Westminster are now represented by women MPs, Labour with ten and the SNP with one woman.[8] The Liberal Democrats failed to select a single woman for their safe seats including the seat held by their only woman MP at the last election, Ray Michie.

For the Labour Party the main challenge was to keep the 56 seats they won in 1997, and hold off a challenge from the SNP, their main political rivals in Scotland. Labour cast itself as the 'natural' party for Scotland and the one still best able to represent Scottish interests at Westminster. They dismissed the SNP as irrelevant in Westminster terms and outlined their 'Ambitions for Britain'. For their part, the SNP claimed 'We stand for Scotland' and prominently featured their new party leader, John Swinney, in their manifesto. Journalists noted the change in tone and strategy in the content and launch of the SNP manifesto. The emphasis was less on independence and more on the positive role that the party had and could play in the Scottish Parliament. In many respects the SNP campaign was an opportunity to raise the profile of their new leader and test out some of their policies in anticipation of the Scottish Parliamentary elections in 2003. The Scottish Parliament also featured in how the Conservatives and Liberal Democrats played the election. In claiming that it was 'Time for Common Sense' the Conservatives sought to build on their reputation in the Scottish Parliament and that of their leader in Scotland, David McLetchie. They hoped to play down their past opposition to a devolved parliament and to stress their role in making the parliament work and in responding to Scottish priorities. Like Labour, their policy on tuition fees and care for the elderly was at odds with the London-based party. The Liberal Democrats found themselves in the position of campaigning against Labour, their coalition partners in the Scottish Parliament. Stressing 'Freedom, Justice, Honesty' they reiterated an argument advanced at the 1997 election in relation to public expenditure and their willingness to raise taxation to improve certain services. In line with the 1997 general election, they continued their targeting of specific seats in Scotland. For the smaller parties, the electoral system meant that they were highly unlikely to win seats. However, they used the opportunity to make their case and raise their profile, more as a means of building their reputations for the Scottish elections in two years' time. The Scottish Socialist Party who offered a left-wing challenge, particularly in Labour strongholds and had gained one seat in the Scottish elections, set a target of winning 100,000 votes at the general election.

The differences between the manifesto promises of the main parties received little media coverage in the campaign with the main focus on the issues which mattered most to the electorate, including health, education and crime. The Labour government was accused of not having achieved enough on these issues in its four years in office at Westminster. As in the past, the manifestos of the British political parties were adapted to reflect conditions in Scotland, with separate publications. An analysis carried out by the Constitution Unit concluded that the parties seemed unaware of the full implications of constitutional change,[9] but to have excluded devolved matters from the manifestos would have been unrealistic and at odds with the fact that devolved and reserved powers are interconnected. In this regard the parties are learning to ride two horses in the political circus at the same time. The fact that there were major differences between the party positions of both the Labour and Conservative parties north and south of the border, most notably over tuition fees for university students and the payment of care for the elderly, appeared to cause less problems for them on the doorstep than had been anticipated.

The main story of the polls in Scotland over the campaign was their

3. Opinion Polls in Scotland (%)

| | System 3 18–21 May 2001 | | ICM 4–5 June 2001 | | |
	All	Certain to vote	All	Certain to vote	Actual result
Labour	50	51	43	44	43.9
SNP	25	24	25	23	20.1
Conservatives	12	12	13	15	15.6
Liberal Democrats	9	8	14	13	16.4
SSP	3	3	4	4	3.0
Others	1	1.5	2	2	1.0

Source: Figures compiled by David McCrone.

remarkable consistency, adding to popular belief that little change was likely to occur in the 2001 general election in Scotland. Compared with the results, Table 3 shows that both System 3 and ICM overestimated the SNP share of the vote and underestimated how well both the Conservatives and the Liberal Democrats would do. System 3 also overestimated Labour's lead.

The results

A very human story was to cause a slight hiccup in the full election results being known in Scotland. A plane chartered to take the ballot boxes from Shetland to be counted in Orkney, instead gave priority to transporting a pregnant woman to hospital in Aberdeen. When all the Scottish votes were counted and the results were finally known, it became clear that there were few surprises. Prior to the election, the main speculation surrounded the likely turnout of the electorate with particular attention focused on the seats deemed to be marginal. Predictions were that, as in other parts of Britain, the turnout was unlikely to exceed 60%, an historic low. The gloomy prognostications were substantiated with an overall turnout of 58.1% being recorded in Scotland. As in other parts of Britain, this was substantially less than the 71.5% at the 1997 general election, however, it was more in line with the 58.8% recorded for the first Scottish Parliament elections in 1999. As in the past, turnout did vary considerably across Scotland. The highest in Eastwood at 70.7% was in a seat held convincingly by Labour at the cost of the Tory chairman in Scotland, Raymond Robertson. This was all the more interesting given that prior to the 1997 general election Eastwood was considered to be a safe Conservative seat. The lowest turnout at 39.7% was recorded in Glasgow Shettleston, a safe Labour seat. Therefore, the Labour vote turned out where it mattered but not where little change was anticipated (see Whiteley this volume).

Prior to the election, the seats which the Conservatives hoped to gain from Labour included the Eastwood seat which required a 3.1% swing, Edinburgh Pentlands which was being contested by Malcolm Rifkind on a mainly person ticket, and Ayr, which the Conservatives had won back from Labour at a Scottish Parliament by-election, giving them their only constituency seat in the chamber. They also held out hopes of winning back Perth from the SNP with a 3.5% swing. The SNP set their objectives on winning Inverness East, Nairn and Lochaber from Labour, which required a 2.5% swing, with a chance of also capturing Dundee East, Dundee West, Aberdeen North and Ochil from Labour. Aberdeen South was the Liberal Democrats most likely opportunity of gaining a seat from Labour requiring a 3.8% swing. As the largest party with 56 seats, the main focus for Labour was to hold their seats. They had some hopes of gaining Tweeddale from their coalition partners, the Liberal Democrats, and included Caithness and Ross, Skye and Inverness on their long list.

In the event, only one seat changed hands from the SNP to the Conservatives in Galloway and Upper Nithsdale (see Table 1). This had not featured as a likely Conservative win but local factors played their part. In an area badly hit by the foot-and-mouth crisis, the 'safe' pair of hands offered by the Conservative candidate, Peter Duncan, carried favour at the expense of the relatively young SNP candidate.

While on the surface, there was minimal change, a closer examination of the results across Scotland show some interesting variations at the constituency level. The distribution of the votes between parties varied considerably and swings in votes not only varied but also did so inconsistently. Sweeping generalisations are, therefore, not possible until more in-depth analysis is available. We can say that, in general terms, the electoral geography of Scotland did not alter significantly and that regional differences in voting still exist. Labour remains dominant in the central belt, especially in Glasgow and surrounding areas. Indeed Labour obtained over 50% of the vote in thirty-three seats. As analysis of the last general election showed, political attitudes vary among the regions too but government action to further social reform commands majority support everywhere. In such a political climate, the Conservative Party remains in a minority in all regions.[10]

The Scottish Socialist Party may have failed to reach their target of 100,000 votes across Scotland, but they came third in two of Glasgow's seats with 9.9% share of the vote in Pollock and 6.8% in Shettleston. They came fourth in Baillieston with 6.7% of the vote and in Maryhill with 7.8%. They also performed well in a number of other seats in Scotland, indicating that their aim of building support in anticipation of the next Scottish parliamentary elections may be paying dividends in parts of the country.

Comparing the 2001 results with the 1997 general election (see Table 1), we can observe that three of the main political parties experienced a fall in their overall share of the vote, with the Liberal Democrats the only one to increase its share of the vote. The SNP suffered a particular disappointment in challenging Labour's domination of the House of Commons, especially under a first-past-the-post electoral system. But there is no room for complacency on Labour's part and assumptions about their performance at the next Scottish elections cannot be drawn from these results. The Conservatives' hopes of rebuilding support on the basis of their Scottish parliamentary performance proved premature in spite of gaining one seat from the SNP. Indeed on the basis of the 2001 results, the Liberal Democrats placed themselves as the third party, ahead of the Conservatives, in the four-party Westminster system in Scotland. While more detailed analysis of the figures and trends are required before definitive conclusions can be reached, it is evident that on the basis of such a low turnout there is a challenge for all the parties to re-engage with the electorate in Scotland.

The unreported seats

Although there were two by-elections being held in Scotland on the same day as the general election — Strathkelvin and Bearsden and Banff and Buchan — reporting of these events was almost entirely absent from the media. This seemed rather extraordinary given the way in which the existence of the Scottish Parliament and the parties' respective roles within it was interlinked with the way in which the general election was fought in Scotland. Yet it was virtually impossible to find out from the media coverage whether the by-elections were indeed going ahead and whether there were any marked differences in the way in which the electorate in the local areas were responding. This reflected the media's preoccupation with the 'national' campaign (both Scottish and British) at the expense of how the general election was being played out in different parts of the country. When the results were finally reported they showed a specific point of interest, namely that more votes were cast for the by-election in the area than for the Westminster seat. In other words, some people had turned up to the polling booth and had voted in the Scottish election rather than the general election. This may have been expected in Strathkelvin and Bearsden, where a local issue very much dominated the campaign. The independent candidate, a doctor, stood in protest against Labour's health policies and proposed changes at a local hospital. While she gained a considerable percentage of the vote it was not enough to deprive Brian Fitzpatrick from winning the seat for Labour. But it also held true in the Banff and Buchan constituency where no such conditions applied.

Conclusion

What is the significance of these results in Scotland? On the basis of the turnout figures we can conclude that the election was only slightly less and no more appealing to voters north of the border than it was to those in England and Wales. Voters were also prepared to turn out in constituencies where their vote could make a difference. They stayed at home where they perceived that their vote was unlikely to have an impact, but also perhaps for other reasons discussed elsewhere in this volume. Similarly, in one sense the issues which mattered most to people varied little between the two electorates, in spite of the fact that responsibility for education, health and crime is devolved to the Scottish Parliament. But this may be because it was not the detail of these policies that was being debated but more fundamental questions about the role of the public and private sectors in delivering crucial services and the links between government funding and provision. Performance, not proposals, was the crux of the debate. This latter point highlights the important differences that were also at play in Scotland where the context of political debate differs from that in other parts of the UK. This is illustrated by the statement made by the Scottish First Minister, Henry McLeish, when he was quick to distance the Labour party in Scotland from the Prime Minister's plans to extend private provision in the health and education sectors. 'Scottish solutions to Scottish problems' is still the main message of the Scottish Labour Party. In taking this route they run the risk of alienating the leadership in Westminster, but failure to do so would leave them exposed to challenges from the other parties in Scotland, especially the SNP and the SSP.

There are competing interpretations of how the parties in Scotland performed in these elections. Clearly the Scottish Labour Party congratulated itself on holding 56 seats, even if the shine was taken off the prize when personally critical remarks about John Reid and Gordon Wilson were not only exchanged between the First Minister and the Secretary of State for Scotland, but also recorded and publicised by a radio station. With such a low turnout, the support enjoyed by the Labour Party should be interpreted less as a wholehearted endorsement of their record and future plans, but more on the grounds that they have been given another chance by the electorate to improve on their performance in key areas. In other words, there is no room for complacency and Labour is only too aware of the challenge posed by the SNP, in spite of that party's disappointing showing in the general election.

Inevitably the SNP played down their poor result, the fact that their share of the vote dropped, and that they not only lost a seat but also held the Perth constituency by just 48 votes. While they were still the main challenger to Labour in Scotland, coming second in a four-party race, there is less clear space than they would wish between them and the Liberal Democrats and the Conservatives. More positively for the party, the next Scottish elections in 2003 are likely to provide their main opportunity to advance. In spite of gaining a seat in Galloway and Upper Nithsdale, even if it was not a seat they thought they were most likely to win, the Conservatives acknowledged their significant defeat in the election, prompting their chairman, Raymond Robertson, to resign and leading figures such as Malcolm Rifkind to call for major reform. For the first time in the party's history in Scotland, the Conservatives came in fourth place behind the Liberal Democrats. As the only larger party to increase their share of the vote, even if this was not translated into a seat gain, the Liberal Democrats had something to celebrate.

The main message seems to be that while very little changed on the surface of Scottish politics with the balance of seats between the parties remaining largely the same, the real stories lie underneath the headline figures. But the results provide little help in predicting what will happen in Scotland in the future, especially as it is becoming clear not only that Scottish and UK parliamentary elections are different but that a significant number of the electorate are also likely to behave differently and to use their vote tactically. This confirms our theory that some people in Scotland, as elsewhere in Europe, are likely to exercise their vote differently in elections for different tiers of government. After the next elections in Scotland it will be possible to test whether they turn out to be more relevant to Scottish voters than UK general elections. They will also come at a time when the Labour government hits its mid-term, a crucial period in the political cycle. In such a scenario, the SNP will be pinning their hopes on performing well at the Holyrood elections, in line with the experience of the Nationalists in Catalonia. Therefore, the next big challenge, and the elections which will provide more spark in electoral competition, are the elections for the Scottish Parliament in May 2003. In the next two years, the parties will be preparing to fight a more hotly contested campaign in an electoral system that provides less comfort and predictability for some of the parties, and more opportunities for others. The 2001 general election was, in some part, a rehearsal for things to come. While in Scotland the Labour Party is still seen as the party most likely to speak for Scotland in Westminster, the question of who speaks for Scotland in Scotland remains open to question.

Alice Brown

1   See A. Brown et al., *The Scottish Electorate: The 1997 General Election and Beyond*, Macmillan, 1999.
2   See L. Paterson et al., *New Scotland, New Politics?*, Polygon at Edinburgh, 2001.
3   Election Specials were organised by the Governance of Scotland Forum and were held at the University of Edinburgh, 30 May and 12 June 2001.
4   See D. McCrone, 'The Opinion Polls in Scotland', *Scottish Affairs*, 2001.
5   In addition to Sam Galbraith, the MPs who stood down from their Westminster seats are Malcolm Chisholm, John McAllion, Henry McLeish and John Home Robertson (Labour); Roseanna Cunningham, Margaret Ewing, Alasdair Morgan, John Swinney and Andrew Welsh (SNP); and Jim Wallace (Liberal Democrats).
6   See chapter by Joni Lovenduski in this volume.
7   At the 1997 general election in Scotland 12 women were elected to represent Scottish constituencies (16.6%) — 9 Labour, 2 SNP and 1 Liberal Democrat.
8   Data collated by Femscot (femscot-admin@quine.org.uk).
9   A. Trench, 'Devolution Literacy' and the Manifestos. See also A. Trench, *Devolution Commitments of the Major Parties*. Both of these documents are available from the Constitution Unit website at http://www.ucl.ac.uk/constitution-unit/.
10 See Brown et al., ibid.

RICHARD WYN JONES AND DAFYDD TRYSTAN

Wales

Wales was the site of the single most memorable visual image of the general election campaign. Video footage of Deputy Prime Minister John Prescott's brief, tawdry brawl with north Wales farm-worker, Craig Evans, on a visit to the decaying seaside resort of Rhyl was subsequently endlessly repeated by television producers eager to inject an element of sensation into a campaign in which the main characters not only seemed to talk past each other (as in a Pinter play), but also, it seems, past large sections of their electoral audience. But while liberals blanched and right-wing commentators seized on the event as some kind of tortured metaphor for the Labour government's relationship with the general public, its overall effect seems to have been negligible. This certainly was the case in Wales where the outcome of the election saw no net change in parliamentary representation since the 1997 general election.

When the last count in Wales was declared for Monmouth, Labour had retained their dominant position with 34 out of the 40 Welsh MPs. Conversely the Tories had repeated their disastrous showing of 1997 by failing to secure a single seat in Wales. Of the six remaining seats, four were won by Plaid Cymru MPs, and two by Liberal Democrats. True these bald figures do hide some changes. Two seats in Wales changed hands, with Labour gaining Ynys Môn from Plaid Cymru, and the nationalists gaining their revenge in Carmarthen East and Dinefwr. But, on the surface at least, the election results in Wales, as elsewhere in Britain, seem to represent remarkably little change.

1. General Election and Assembly Election Results in Wales (%)

	Vote GE 1997	Assembly constituency vote 1999	Assembly regional vote 1999	Vote GE 2001	GE change 1997–2001
Labour	54.7	37.6	35.4	48.6	−6.1
Conservatives	19.6	15.8	16.5	21.0	+1.4
Plaid Cymru	9.9	28.4	30.5	14.3	+4.3
Liberal Democrats	12.4	13.5	12.5	13.8	+1.4
Others	3.4	4.7	5.1	2.3	−1.1

Sources: British Parliamentary Constituencies, 1992–2001; Institute of Welsh Politics — National Assembly Election Results.

The particular significance of the Welsh results lies precisely in the fact that since the 1997 general election the country has witnessed a profoundly significant transformation in its system of governance with the establishment of the devolved National Assembly for Wales. Moreover, at the first election to this devolved body, the electorate delivered an unprecedented rebuff to Labour, and equally striking gains for Plaid Cymru. Analysis of the 2001 general election must, therefore, take cognisance of the impact of devolution on the Welsh political landscape. While the absence of overall change in the pattern of parliamentary representation may suggest that this impact has been minimal at the Westminster level, the following analysis will caution against such a conclusion. Our argument is rather that while Labour has indeed retained its dominant position, the results also represent a definite, if limited advance for Plaid Cymru. For the Conservatives and Liberal Democrats, by contrast, the 2001 general election provides further confirmation of their relative weakness in Wales; weakness that devolution has done little to assuage.

Our analysis will proceed by:

(i)   Outlining what might be termed the 'conventional wisdom' concerning the significance 2001 general election result in Wales, a view profoundly influenced by the changes wrought by devolution to the Welsh political landscape;
(ii) Providing an overview of some of the salient features of the pre-campaign phase of the general election in Wales;
(iii) Describing the nature of the campaigns of each of the four main parties; and,
(iv) Briefly assessing the implications of the results for the future development of post-devolution politics in Wales.

Devolution and the new political landscape

The establishment of the National Assembly represents what is arguably the most fundamental institutional development in Welsh politics since the Acts of Union between England and Wales of 1536 and 1542.[1] Devolution was triggered by a referendum held in the aftermath of Labour's May Day victory in 1997. Following a low turnout poll on the 18 September 1997, a night of high theatre saw the Welsh electorate approve Labour's plans for an Assembly by the most grudging of margins, the majority in favour of 6,721 corresponding to only 0.3% of the potential electorate.[2]

The subsequent election of members to the National Assembly held on the 5 May 1999, again characterised by a relatively low turnout, saw Labour's previously hegemonic position in Wales challenged by a very strong showing by Plaid Cymru (1: General Election and Assembly Election Results).[3] The largely unexpected surge in support for the nationalists, coupled to the more proportional electoral system inscribed in the devolution legislation, left Labour without an overall majority. Most humiliatingly of all, Labour candidates were defeated by their Plaid rivals in three constituencies of key symbolic importance: Llanelli, former seat of Jim Griffiths, who, along with Aneurin Bevan, is credited by Labour as one of the key architects of the postwar welfare state; Rhondda, a constituency whose very name serves to conjure up some of the most iconic images in British labour history; and Islwyn, which was the power-base of the virulently anti-devolution former Labour leader Neil Kinnock.

The effect of these defeats has been to ensure that the first two years of devolved government were uncomfortable ones for Labour. The party has been rocked by continuing instability and internal bickering, while its leadership of the Assembly has been characterised by many as lacking in vision or direction. Having initially decided to form a minority administration, a palace *coup* in February 2000 saw the opposition parties join together with a large section of the Labour group to oust Tony Blair's choice as Assembly First Secretary, Alun Michael. He was replaced by the defiantly, indeed self-consciously, 'off-message' Rhodri Morgan. Subsequently, in October 2000, Labour formed a coalition administration with the Liberal Democrats along the lines — indeed, on the basis of — the agreement forged between both parties in the Scottish Parliament. But while this development has given greater coherence to the activity of the National Assembly, it has done little to assuage tension within Labour ranks, with malcontents shifting their attention to undermining the credibility of the coalition.[4]

It is against the background of the 1999 Assembly election result, and Labour's subsequent difficulties, that the results of the 2001 UK general election have been interpreted by the Welsh political class. Labour politicians and activists have reacted with undisguised glee. Not for them the self-conscious lack of exuberance on display at Millbank. Rather Labour's repetition of its 1997 triumph coupled with Plaid Cymru's apparent lack of progress has been seized upon, as evidence that the 1999 National Assembly election results was simply an unfortunate 'one off'. 'Wales,' it has been claimed *ad nauseam*, 'has come home to Labour.' In Plaid Cymru ranks, where the triumphs of 1999 had generated high expectations, the results have been the cause of disappointment. (There are clear parallels here to the reaction among Scottish nationalists to the 2001 general election results, discussed in another contribution to this volume.) Welsh Liberal Democrats have also been downbeat following their failure to emulate the strong showing of their party elsewhere. Among Welsh Conservatives, the 2001 election has been viewed as an unmitigated disaster that has prompted a major debate about their party's profile and structure. Such are the party's perceptions. As we shall seek to argue, some may well prove to be misplaced.

The pre-campaign phase

In elections, Wales has traditionally been a land of safe seats, large Labour majorities, and MPs who enjoy long periods tenure as parliamentary representatives. Turnover of elected representatives has been minimal from one election to next. The 2001 election promised a change in this pattern with five MPs retiring (four Labour and one Liberal Democrat) and five others standing down to focus their attention on their Assembly seats (three Labour and two Plaid Cymru). The latter group included Rhodri Morgan, Ron Davies and Dafydd Wigley, three of Wales' most prominent parliamentarians in recent times. The importance of the selection contests for these seats was underscored by their status (with one possible exception) as safe seats. Indeed, it is plausible to argue that the selection process was at least as important as the popular vote itself in deciding the nature of the representation these constituencies were to enjoy.

One key question was whether the political parties would seek to follow the example set at the Assembly election by selecting a number of women candidates, or whether there would be a reversion to type, and a reconfirmation of Wales' lamentable record of female parliamentary representation?[5] Following a series of acrimonious selection conferences (one held in a men-only club), ten men were selected for the soon to be vacated seats. Nowhere was the selection process more acrimonious than in Plaid Cymru-held Ynys Môn where the wounds opened during the candidate selection continued to fester up to — and beyond — the general election.

The evidence from the opinion polls during the eighteen months prior to the general election suggested minimal change (see Table 2). The one movement of note was growth in support for Plaid Cymru from 10% in June 1997 to around 15%. But these ratings did not suggest a repeat of Plaid's Assembly election performance. Nevertheless, in the run up to the election Labour clearly remained fearful that the nationalists might prove a threat in a few specific constituencies, particularly those where Plaid Cymru had triumphed in 1999. This fear was evident in the attention lavished by the Labour Party on constituencies like the Rhondda in the pre-campaign phase — constituencies where towering majorities had meant very little campaigning in previous elections.

2. Opinion Polls in the Pre-Campaign Phase (%)					
	Jan 2000	March 2000	May 2000	July 2000	Nov 2000	March 2001
Con	21	20	23	25	25	22
Lab	56	50	47	51	45	52
LibDems	8	12	12	9	13	10
Plaid Cymru	13	16	15	16	15	14
Others	3	2	2	2	2	2

Source: HTV/NOP Opinion Polls.

The campaign

The establishment of the National Assembly meant that, approaching the general election, parties had to deal not only with a new pattern of party competition, but also with a new policy context. A particular challenge was how to approach issues over which responsibility has been devolved. This is no simple matter, given that the 'executive devolution' model upon which the Assembly is based has been subjected to almost universal opprobrium among constitutional experts, in part on the grounds that the division of powers instituted between Cardiff and London is opaque and illogical.[6]

All four main parties published Wales-specific general election manifestos. This is not a new departure for the three main 'British parties', but for Labour and the Conservatives these have usually been thin documents containing little of substance beyond an attempt to add a little local colour to the party's wider commitments. Much the same pattern was repeated for the 2001 election.[7] An assessment of the 'devolution literacy' of manifestos found the Liberal Democrats 'best aware of the effects of devolution', followed by Plaid Cymru. Labour's documents, however, demonstrated only 'a limited awareness of what [devolution] means', while the Conservatives were 'least aware'.[8]

One reason was that the policy-making capacities of the four parties in Wales remains weak. Moreover, the parties were clearly also engaged in preliminary manoeuvring for the 2003 Assembly election. Thus clarity and coherence were readily sacrificed in order to trumpet achievements — or highlight deficiencies — for the battle ahead. Given that a crucial challenge for all the parties in Wales is to reorient their campaigning from a focus on the general election cycle to an electoral cycle characterised by three major elections in every five-year period, we might expect such a 'blurring of the lines' to be a common feature of political communication in Wales in the coming years.

THE LABOUR CAMPAIGN: Even in the context of its long-standing domination of the Welsh political landscape, Labour's performance in Wales in 1997 was particularly impressive. It took eight (notional) seats from the Conservatives, gaining constituencies such as Monmouth and Cardiff North that had only previously been represented by Labour members following the 1966 general election. Given this context, Labour's strategic aims in Wales for the 2001 election were almost entirely defensive — the party sought to hold the eight seats won from the Conservatives in 1997, and also to retain the five constituencies lost at the Assembly election (four to Plaid Cymru and one to the Liberal Democrats).

Labour campaign utilised a mixture of electoral tactics in targeting its key seats, using telephone canvassing, sophisticated voter identification, individual direct mailing along with more traditional door-to-door canvassing and the delivery of leaflets. Secretary of State Paul Murphy fronted the campaign jointly with Rhodri Morgan, this despite the fact that the latter was not, of course, a candidate. His prominent role reflected the fact that Labour has learnt its lesson from 1999 and is now acutely conscious of the First Minister's widespread electoral appeal—and the price that might be paid if that appeal is not brought into play.[9] Labour's campaign in Wales was typically thorough targeting different messages to different audiences, not all of which, it might be argued, were completely consistent with each other. Thus, on the one hand, the frequent reiteration of the mantra of 'stability' so familiar from the campaign on the UK level; and on the other, Rhodri Morgan's deliberately promiscuous use of the 's' word (socialism) in a party political broadcast aimed squarely at the electorate in those Valleys constituencies that deserted Labour in 1999. Here was evidence of 'catch all' politics writ large. Particular interesting in this regard was how the party in Wales dealt with the UK Labour Party's pledge to make greater use of the private sector to 'support public endeavour'. This pledge—however vaguely phrased—was always likely to be controversial in the Welsh context, particularly so among voters in traditional Labour heartlands. And indeed, during the campaign, party spokespersons such as Labour Assembly Health Minister Jane Hutt, implied that the private sector was unlikely to play a prominent role in the provision of public services in Wales. Briefings from figures close to Rhodri Morgan even suggested that the pledge to bring in private sector expertise had been 'toned down' in Labour's Welsh manifesto. This in fact was not the case.[10] In remains to be seen how far this aspect of the UK government's plans to 'modernise' public services will impact Wales.

Though the campaign itself was relatively low-key, with the exception of the Prescott events in Rhyl, the result was another strong performance by Labour. For only the second time since the advent of the universal franchise, the Conservatives were deprived of even a single MP in Wales. While Labour's vote did fall across the south Wales valleys the nationalist threat was largely repelled. The danger now for Labour is complacency; to assume that the Welsh votes have 'come home to Labour', and that the Assembly election was an aberration that has been successfully reversed by a change of leadership in Wales. The evidence suggests, however, that this is not the case and Labour is likely to face a much sterner test in 2003. Of particular concern to more hardheaded party strategists will be the possible consequences of depressed voter turnout for Labour's future prospects. Low turnout in the 2001 general election, explored in depth elsewhere in this volume, followed on from low participation rates in the referendum and Assembly election. With regards the latter, analysis has demonstrated a significant differential effect, with Plaid Cymru supporters significantly more likely to vote than supporters of the other parties, and Labour supporters least likely to vote.[11] Should turnout at the 2001 election herald a further reduction in participation, including at the next Assembly election, a similar pattern of differential turnout could be extremely damaging for Labour.

THE PLAID CYMRU CAMPAIGN: While Labour activists were delighted by the 2001 results, the disappointment amongst Plaid Cymru officials and party workers at their performance has been palpable. This is despite the fact that the party succeeded in achieving its best ever result at a UK general election, both in terms of the share of the vote and (despite the low turnout) actual votes cast. The gloom is a result of the failure to the make the expected inroads into Labour's hegemony in the south Wales valleys. Disappointment has been compounded by the unexpected loss of Ynys Môn.

Plaid Cymru's campaign concentrated on two key sets of issues. Its main focus was Labour's alleged lack of commitment to social justice as highlighted by its parsimonious approach to the welfare state. Plaid's intention was clearly to raise its banner on political territory left of Labour. The party sought to reinforce this message by stressing the continuity between perceived excesses of Thatcherism and new Labour policies. The Blair government, it was repeatedly claimed had 'turned its back' on Wales and the traditional values of Welsh Labour supporters. A subsidiary but nevertheless consistent theme of Plaid's campaign was the need for further constitutional reform, and in particular the establishment of a Welsh Parliament on the same constitutional basis as the Scottish Parliament.

In organisational terms the party's campaign was far better resourced than has previously been the case. It utilised a telephone canvassing system similar to one that had proven successful in 1999. In addition, it sought to benefit from the profile of its relatively new Assembly Members and MEPs by giving them prominent campaigning roles in key constituencies. These were the nine constituencies won by the party at the Assembly election. Plaid Cymru's aim was to ensure that the momentum generated in 1999 was continued in 2001 thus providing an effective springboard for 2003. The headline grabbing loss of Ynys Môn and their failure seriously to challenge the large Labour majorities in the valleys have served to create a general perception that, at best, this momentum has been lost. While this is clearly a plausible interpretation — and perceptions, of course, have a tendency to create their own reality — the reality may be more complex.

Plaid Cymru's performance is placed in a somewhat different light by comparing the party's vote in the five most Welsh-speaking constituencies in the north and west — an area that has come to be known by the Welsh-language term *Y Fro Gymraeg* — with its vote in the rest of Wales. Figure 1 charts Plaid Cymru vote in the two parts of Wales since 1966. Here we find a complex pattern of relationships. From the end of

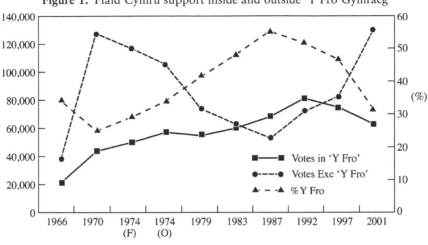

Figure 1. Plaid Cymru support inside and outside 'Y Fro Gymraeg'

Note: 'Y Fro Gymraeg' is defined as the five Welsh constituencies where more than half of the electorate speak Welsh: Ynys Mon, Caernarfon, Meirionnydd Nant Conwy, Ceredigion and Carmarthen East and Dinefwr. Source: Calculations from data in A. James and J.E. Thomas, 1981, *Wales at Westminster: A History of Parliamentary Representation of Wales 1800–1979*, Gomer Press, Llandysul; D. Balsom (ed.), 2001, *The Wales Yearbook 2001*, HTV Wales, Cardiff.

the 1970s onwards Plaid Cymru strengthened its position in Welsh-speaking areas, while its support declined dramatically across the bulk of the country. The trend reversed in the 1990s. The 2001 election demonstrates further considerable growth in Plaid Cymru support in English-speaking Wales, along with a small decline in support in *Y Fro Gymraeg*. The changing distribution of Plaid Cymru support may be read two ways. On the one hand it may be argued that Plaid Cymru's support base in its traditional Welsh-speaking heartlands is being eroded without the party accruing enough votes in the rest of Wales to become a serious challenger to Labour. Another, in our view more plausible, interpretation is that Plaid Cymru is continuing to reach out beyond its heartlands (which, by their very nature, can only provide a limited political base) and is gradually consolidating its position as a serious political force throughout Wales. This shift in support for Plaid Cymru may well, therefore, provide a basis for the consolidation and, indeed, further expansion in its support at the Assembly level.

THE CONSERVATIVE CAMPAIGN: The Conservatives were faced with the challenge of fighting a general election without a single MP in Wales for the first time since 1910. In the event William Hague chose the Swansea-born Nigel Evans, MP for Ribble Valley and Conservative Commons spokesperson on Wales, to lead the Welsh campaign. What-ever the public shows of unity, this choice clearly rankled with the members of the Conservative group in the Assembly. Quite apart from the symbolism of deploying a candidate for a English seat to lead the party's Welsh campaign, Evans's often very thinly veiled hostility to devolution has grated with those members of the party eager to develop a more Welsh image and identity. The party's difficulties were further compounded by the chaotic launch of its Welsh manifesto, an event that threatened to descend into farce when it emerged that the Welsh-language version of the document had been withdrawn at the last moment after a casual perusal by Ffion Hague uncovered a plethora of basic errors.

The Conservative campaign in Wales lacked focus and has subsequently been heavily criticised by members of the party's Assembly group. Campaign themes largely aped those at the UK level. A few more specifically Welsh themes were also raised. In the main these related largely symbolic concerns, such as the possibility of a bank holiday to celebrate St David's Day and the decriminalisation of the Welsh dragon on vehicle number plates. Most enthusiasm was reserved for condemnation of the alleged extravagance of plans to build a debating chamber for the National Assembly.

The future of the Assembly was a key point of interest in the Conservative's election platform. On the evidence of its Welsh manifesto (the UK manifesto makes no mention of the subject), the Conservatives still retain a deeply ambivalent attitude to Welsh devolution. In a vague and studiously non-committal passage on the future of the Assembly, the Tories pledged to establish an independent commission to inquire into the workings of the devolved body. It is unclear from the text whether a recommendation to abolish the Assembly would have been within the commission's remit.[12] Matters were hardly clarified during the manifesto launch. When questioned on the remit of the proposed commission, Nigel Evans stated that neither abolition of the Assembly, nor the extension of its powers, would be on its agenda — thus raising the question of what exactly this proposed commission was meant to achieve. Four years on from the devolution referendum, and two years since the Assembly's assumption of powers, it is hard to avoid the conclusion that the Conservatives have still hardly begun the task of adjusting to the new realities of Welsh politics.

Following their general election result in Wales, Conservatives have reacted with shock bordering on despair. Strong individual performances in Brecon and Radnorshire and in Preseli Pembrokeshire (both constituencies that the Tories will undoubtedly target at the next Assembly election) cannot disguise the fact that the party is in deep trouble. The problems that beset the UK party as a whole are compounded in Wales by a historic and seemingly intractable weakness. It is little wonder therefore that, since the election, prominent Welsh Conservatives have been vocal in calling for radical reorganisation of the party's structure to give the Welsh party more 'autonomy'. Their belief is that the Conservatives must develop a more positively Welsh profile and platform if it is to hope to become a serious political force in contemporary Wales.

THE LIBERAL DEMOCRAT CAMPAIGN: Welsh Liberal Democrats approached the election from the position of being simultaneously Tony Blair's 'constructive opposition' at Westminster and forming part of a coalition administration with Labour in the National Assembly. The party firmly refuted suggestions that opposing at one level of government while cooperating at another placed them in an uncomfortable or contradictory situation, pointing out that such situations are common in states with elected tiers of regional government. However, in the British context, this—along with the parallel Scottish case—does represent a new departure. And in Wales, in particular, continuing hostility towards the coalition among voluble sections of the Labour Party clearly heightened sensitivities. Even without these, tensions would almost certainly have surfaced between the coalition partners given the fact that the Liberal Democrats' one serious target seat was Cardiff Central, a constituency that the party had wrested from Labour during the Assembly election. Liberal Democrats hoped to repeat this feat in 2001 by unseating Labour's Jon Owen Jones. Apart from this constituency, upon which a large proportion of the party's resources were focused, the Liberal Democrats' aim was to improve their position in Ceredigion and Conwy while developing their organisation in a number of largely urban constituency with a view to the next Assembly election.

In the main, the Liberal Democrats' campaign in Wales concentrated on reiterating UK themes in a Welsh context. While the party's manifesto laid great stress on the party's plans for a Welsh Parliament (a 'Senedd'), this featured far less prominently in the party's campaign in Wales. This may reflect a realisation that Liberal Democrat voters are much less enthused by devolution than party activists. But almost certainly more important was need the need to bolster the party's vote by targeting particular messages at key seats—thus the stress on addressing the crisis in the rural economy so cruelly exacerbated by the ravages of the foot and mouth disease outbreak, and the focus on student funding (Cardiff Central playing host to a large student population).

In the event, the results proved a disappointment to Welsh Liberal Democrats, especially given the contrast with their party's success elsewhere in the UK. For despite making significant inroads into Labour's majority in Cardiff Central, it failed to gain this or any other new seats. Moreover, it came within a few hundred votes of losing Brecon and Radnorshire to the Conservatives. The party also fell behind Plaid Cymru in terms of the all-Wales share of the vote. A close analysis of the results of individual constituencies further suggests that difficulties may lie ahead for the Welsh Liberal Democrats in 2003. Should

Liberal supporters in its traditional mid-Wales bastions baulk at their party's involvement in the coalition administration, the prospects for the Welsh Liberal Democrats would be grim indeed.

The implications for the future

Absent of robust individual level survey data, it is clearly difficult to provide an authoritative account of voting behaviour in Wales at the 2001 UK general election, while speculation about the implications of these results for the future is rendered an even more hazardous exercise. Nonetheless, we can tease out some of the possible consequences of the vote for Welsh politics in this post-devolutionary era.

The party reaction to the outcome of the election is largely premised on the assumption that these results are broadly indicative of what is likely to occur in the 2003 Assembly election: hence the jubilation in the Labour camp and the gloom among nationalists. Among Labour politicians and activists in Wales, there is clearly a widely held belief that 7 June has shown that the 1999 Assembly election was indeed an aberration, and that the Labour Party in Wales will now resume its hegemonic position at all levels of Welsh politics. Conversely, Plaid Cymru activists fear that their 'forward march' has been halted almost before it had started. But while the UK and Assembly levels are clearly linked, the evidence does not support such a simplistic reading of the relationship between them.

Political scientists have offered numerous, competing accounts of the interaction between state-level elections and elections to significant regional-level legislatures such as the National Assembly. It is beyond the purview of this analysis to offer an explanation and evaluation here. Nevertheless, a valid generalisation is that none of the best-known paradigms support an argument to the effect that the result of the next Assembly election can simply be 'read off' the result of the UK general election. If, following Reif and Schmitt, the devolved poll is regarded as a 'Second Order' event, then we might expect the governing party in the primary arena, that is Westminster, to lose support (especially at midterm) and for opposition parties to gain support, in particular smaller parties, such as Plaid Cymru, for whom a vote in the 'First Order' election may be regarded as wasted.[13] Theories of 'mid-term loss' would also lead us to expect the relationship between the state and substate levels to be one in which the governing party in the former arena is punished by voters in the latter.[14] Some commentators, including the present authors, have expressed reservations concerning the adequacy of either of these approaches to understanding inter-level dynamics in the context of the devolved UK, arguing instead that 'multi-level voting' provides a more useful conceptual framework. This suggests that determinants of voting behaviour may be distinct at different levels, and that in particular, Wales-specific (or Scotland-specific) factors may play an important role in elections at the devolved level.[15]

Again, this would suggest that the responses of both Labour and Plaid Cymru activists to the significance of the 2001 election for the future are misplaced.

More direct evidence in support of this argument is provided by the Welsh Assembly Election Survey (WAES) conducted in the immediate aftermath of 1999 vote.[16] When asked how they would have voted in a UK general election held on the same day as the Assembly election, survey respondents suggested an outcome remarkably similar to the final results attained by the parties at the 2001 general election. Had a general election been held on the 6 May 1999 WAES suggests that Labour would have received 52.8% of the votes in Wales (compared to the 48.6% achieved in 2001), the Conservatives 18.6% (compared to the 21% achieved), Plaid Cymru 14% (compared to 14.3% in 2001) and the Liberal Democrats 12.6% (compared to 13.8% in 2001). Thus a significant proportion of those Labour identifiers choosing to vote for Plaid Cymru candidates in the Assembly election were already indicating that this would not impact upon their choice at the Westminster level. All of which strongly suggests that an important section of the Welsh electorate are using different criteria upon which to base their partisan choice in the two arenas. While the Welsh electorate may have 'come home' to Labour in 2001 general election, the party would be most unwise to assume that this will be repeated in the 2003 National Assembly election.

Post-devolution politics is a complex and as yet poorly understood business. Just as the institutional relationship between the National Assembly for Wales and the Westminster–Whitehall nexus is still in the process of 'bedding down', and is likely to be the subject of further change and adjustment in coming years, so are the dynamics of party competition in post-devolution Wales still in a state of flux. The fact that the outcome of the 2001 general election in Wales was no overall change should not be allowed to obscure this reality.

Richard Wyn Jones and Dafydd Trystan

1   See L. Paterson and R. Wyn Jones, 'Does Civil Society Drive Constitutional Change? The Cases of Scotland and Wales' in B. Taylor and K. Thomson (eds), *Scotland and Wales: Nations Again?*, University of Wales Press, 1999, pp. 169–97.
2   See R. Wyn Jones and D. Trystan, 'The Welsh Devolution Referendum' in B. Taylor and K. Thomson (eds), *Scotland and Wales: Nations Again?*, University of Wales Press, 1999, pp. 65–93.
3   See R. Wyn Jones and D. Trystan, 'Turnout, Participation and Legitimacy in the Politics of Post-Devolution Wales' in P. Chaney, T. Hall and A. Pithouse (eds), *New Governance: New Democracy?*, University of Wales Press, 2001, pp. 18–47.
4   On 5 July 2001 the Labour-Liberal Democrat coalition suffered a severe blow when the Liberal Democrat leader in the Assembly, Mike German, was forced to resign from his post as Deputy First Minister, following the announcement of a police inquiry into his former business dealing. Prominent Labour councillors in Wales had been at the forefront of demands for such an investigation.
5   From 1918–97, out of the 225 MPs elected from Wales, only seven had been women.
6   See, inter alia, R. Rawlings, 'The New Model Wales', 25 *Journal of Law and Society* 4, pp. 461–509,

and 'Quasi-Legislative Devolution: Powers and Principles', 52 *Northern Ireland Legal Quarterly* 1, pp. 54–81.

7   A. Trench, *'Devolution Literacy' and the Manifestos*. See also A. Trench, *Devolution Commitments of the Major Parties*. Both of these documents are available from the Constitution Unit website at http://www.ucl.ac.uk/constitution-unit/.

8   A. Trench, *'Devolution Literacy' and the Manifestos*, p. 16.

9   Rhodri Morgan chose the announcement of the coalition deal with the Liberal Democrats to retitle his post. So the First Secretary became First Minister. At the same time Cabinet Secretaries became known Cabinet Ministers. This move, which has little basis in the 1998 Government of Wales Act, was an attempt to enhance of the National Assembly by bringing the nomenclature into line with that used in Scotland and Northern Ireland.

10   This is confirmed by a close comparison of the following key sections: *Ambitions for Wales: Labour's Manifesto 2001*, pp. 17–23, and *Ambitions for Britain: Labour's Manifesto 2001*, pp. 17–23.

11   R. Wyn Jones and D. Trystan, 'Turnout, Participation and Legitimacy', op. cit.

12   *Time for Common Sense in Wales*, Conservative Party Welsh Manifesto, 2001, p. 45.

13   K. Reif and H. Schmitt, 'Nine Second-Order National Elections: A Conceptual Framework', 8 *European Journal of Political Research* 1, 1980, pp. 3–44. Also C. van der Eijk and M. Franklin (eds), *Choosing Europe? The European Electorate and National Politics in the Face of the Union*, University of Michigan Press, 1996.

14   For a sampling of the literature see R.S. Erikson, 'The Puzzle of Mid-Term Loss', 50 *Journal of Politics* 4, 1988, pp. 1011–29.

15   See L. Paterson et al., 'May 6 1999: An Election in Scotland or a Scottish Election?' in *New Scotland: New Politics?*, Edinburgh University Press, 2001, pp. 27–45. Also C. Jeffery and D. Hough, 'The Electoral Cycle and Multi-Level Voting in Germany', 10 *German Politics* 2, 2001.

16   More details can be found in R. Wyn Jones and D. Trystan, 'Turnout, Participation and Legitimacy in the Politics of Post-Devolution Wales' in P. Chaney, T. Hall and A. Pithouse (eds), *New Governance: New Democracy?*, University of Wales Press, 2001, pp. 18–47.

PAUL MITCHELL, BRENDAN O'LEARY AND GEOFFREY EVANS

Northern Ireland: Flanking Extremists Bite the Moderates and Emerge in Their Clothes

After signing the 1985 Anglo-Irish Agreement it was the considered policy of the sovereign governments to isolate what they called the 'political extremes' in Northern Ireland and build up what they called the 'moderate centre-ground', from which a power-sharing government could be constructed. The policy did not work, at least not quickly and not as intended, but the Agreement did generate the environment from which came a peace process and a political settlement. The peace process, initially reluctantly welcomed by the sovereign governments, but eventually embraced, first by the Reynolds government, then sceptically by the Major government, and then more enthusiastically by the Blair government, turned the original logic on its head.[1] The extremes were to be integrated, if they wanted to be. John Hume, the leader of the SDLP, kick-started the public side of the process by talking with Gerry Adams of Sinn Féin in 1988 and again in the early 1990s; and that eventually led to everyone (except some in Ian Paisley's DUP) talking with Adams and his colleagues. In short, the paramilitary cessations of violence, and later the historic compromise, the Belfast Agreement of Good Friday 10 April 1998, were achieved by enticing political hardliners into a political and institutional settlement in which they have a stake.

Politics is transformative of identities, as well as a mechanism for their expression and defence, and what was most fascinating about the 2001 Westminster general election in Northern Ireland was the metamorphosis of both Sinn Féin and the DUP. Despite misleading rhetoric to the contrary, both 'extreme' parties moderated their platforms, and may continue to do so, and this softening of their positions partly explains their electoral successes. An era of full anti-system politics which had seen the abstention and exclusion of Sinn Féin, and the frequent self-exclusion ('Ulster just says "no"') of the DUP, is being succeeded by an era of active negotiations, legislative and committee-room politics. These parties, for the time being, have become stake-holders in the panoply of institutions established by the Belfast Agreement — the Northern Ireland Assembly and its novel Executive, the North-South Ministerial Council, the British-Irish Council, the British-Irish intergovernmental conference, the British-Irish inter-parlia-mentary body. The creation of these institutions, to put it mildly, were neither Sinn Féin's nor the DUP's first preference, but their consocia-tional and confederal logics[2] have given both sufficient incentives to participate in styles that are less overtly anti-system than their historic credentials would have suggested.

The absolute — if ultimately futile — opposition of the DUP to the Anglo-Irish Agreement of 1985, and its more nuanced opposition to the Belfast Agreement — working within (most of) its institutions, including its executive, but criticising Sinn Féin — led to subtle shifts in the DUP's position as the elections approached. Far from calling for the Belfast Agreement to be scrapped, the DUP called for its renegotiation. The DUP's best-known rallying cries ('No Surrender') and absolute opposi-tion to any 'Dublin interference' in Northern Ireland had morphed by 2001 into a demand that any North-South institutional relationships be rendered more palatable by requiring that they be made more fully accountable to the devolved administration in Belfast. Such changes in its positioning, ably directed by DUP deputy leader and campaign manager Peter Robinson MP, repositioned the party more competi-tively, especially in relation to the disaffected supporters of an openly fractious Ulster Unionist Party (UUP). The DUP had a long history as a party that favoured devolution, and neither the party nor many of its potential supporters wanted to bring down the new Assembly, they just wanted it run in a different manner, without Sinn Féin in government.[3]

More obviously, Sinn Féin has also progressively moderated its position (notwithstanding current difficulties over decommissioning by the IRA). Since 1996 the party has been the principal electoral benefi-ciary of an end to active war. The IRA's cessation of its armed campaign, Sinn Féin's *de facto* acceptance of the consent principle (i.e. that Irish unification requires the consent of majorities in both parts of Ireland) and its enthusiastic participation in all of the Agreement's institutions have rendered the party more acceptable to others and more relevant to nationalist voters. While the peace process was the hand-maiden of Sinn Féin's electoral 'second coming',[4] the incorporation of Sinn Féin into 'ordinary politics' has undermined the distinctiveness of the SDLP's own strategic position faster than anticipated. Especially for younger nationalist voters, the question increasingly arises: why not vote for the fresher and more assertive brand? For them the SDLP looked aged, and some of its Europeanist and 'post-national' talk cut little ice with voters focused on local issues and quarrels. While it is hard to imagine that the peace process could have been sustained without some electoral rewards for Sinn Féin, few expected the pace of its gains since 1994, and especially its breakout performance in 2001.

Overview of the results

Let us first overview the most dramatic findings of the 2001 Westminster elections. We can do this, first by reviewing the electoral map of Northern Ireland, with that of 1997 (see Figure 1), and then by means of a graphic 'profit and loss account' (in absolute votes; see Figure 2). The upper map shows Northern Ireland's eighteen constituencies. The middle and lower maps confirm the significance of the 2001 result. Nationalists went from holding five to seven of Northern Ireland's eighteen seats. The constituencies which border Ireland are now entirely nationalist: southern and western Northern Ireland have nationalist MPs running in a swathe from Foyle, through West Tyrone, Fermanagh and South Tyrone, and South Armagh, to South Down. The west has been 'deep greened', with three adjacent Sinn Féin constituencies (West Tyrone, Mid-Ulster and Fermanagh-South Tyrone); and in the future South Armagh and possibly Foyle may fall to Sinn Féin with the eventual retirement of the prominent SDLP incumbents, party leader John Hume MP, MEP, and the Deputy First Minister Seamus Mallon MP. Sinn Féin's two best-known leaders, Adams and Martin Mc-Guinness, hold the two nationalist seats away from the border, in mid-Ulster and West Belfast.

The map also confirms that unionists' demographic grip on Northern Ireland is slipping — they are retreating into their heartlands of North Armagh, North Down, Antrim and East Londonderry. A ring of DUP seats now flanks this heartland. Belfast, the distinctive epicentre of conflict, is becoming increasingly greener: the local government results held on the same day as the Westminster elections confirmed that Sinn Féin is the largest party in the city. But in 2001 unionists took three of its four Westminster (DUP: 2, UUP: 1). In the long run, with changing demography and with this electoral system,[5] it seems feasible that South Belfast may go to the SDLP and North Belfast to Sinn Féin.

The DUP had its best ever Westminster election, in seats and vote-share, and Sinn Féin for the fifth consecutive election had by far its strongest result. The much-touted moderate ground, and the centre of 'others', of Northern Ireland politics appears to be sinking (see Figure 2). The fact that the DUP and Sinn Féin have partly achieved such gains by stealing the moderates' positions is likely to be of limited comfort to the UUP and SDLP, the formerly pre-eminent parties in the unionist and nationalist blocs respectively, who are now left, if not naked, at least partially disrobed.

Context and campaign

It was the first Westminster election since the Belfast Agreement had been signed, and partially implemented. The referendum to ratify the

Figure 1. Electoral Map of Northern Ireland, 1997 and 2001

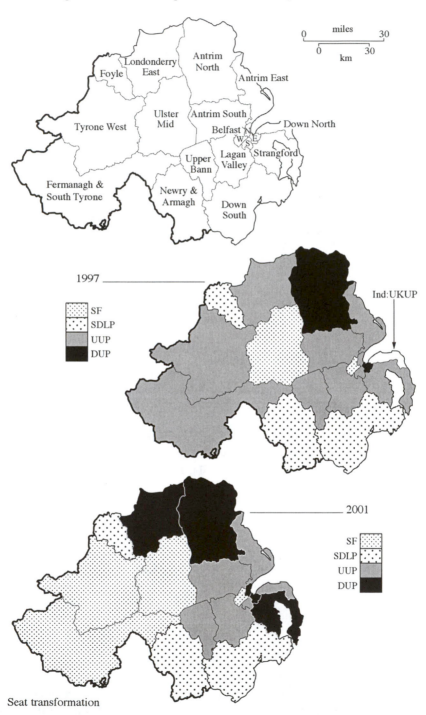

Seat transformation

Figure 2. Profit and Loss Account of Westminster Votes in 2001

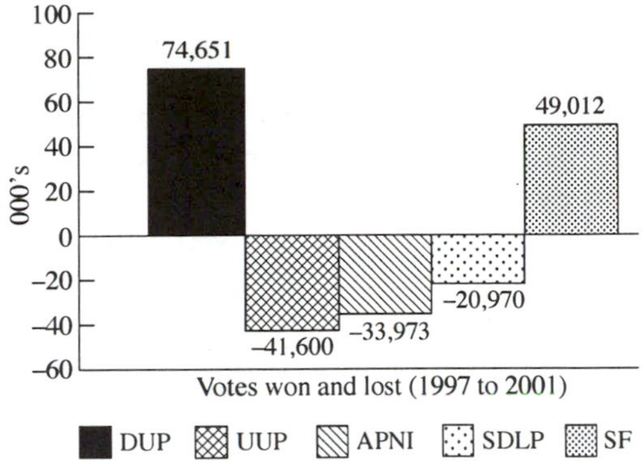

Source: Calculated by the authors from electoral returns.

Agreement in May 1998 led to almost unanimous endorsement by nationalists, North and South. By contrast, it split unionists evenly into 'Yes' and 'No' camps, and their parties likewise: the UUP was for the Agreement, as were the small loyalist parties, the PUP and the UDP; the DUP was against, as was the small UKUP. The pro-Agreement UUP was itself deeply divided. A majority of its Westminster MPs opposed the Agreement, isolating its party leader David Trimble, though as the First Minister of the Assembly he had much stronger support amongst his Assembly members (MLAs).

The general election was called during a local crisis. Though the Agreement's institutions were functioning, deep fissures had erupted within the UUP and rendered Trimble very vulnerable. To compel Sinn Féin to coerce the IRA to start decommissioning its weapons he had embarked on a series of political sanctions. First, he blocked the two Sinn Féin ministers in the power-sharing executive from participating in the North-South Ministerial Council. The Sinn Féin Ministers and the SDLP Deputy First Minister,[6] Seamus Mallon, promptly took Trimble to court, and won, but Justice Kerr ruled his action 'unlawful' in January 2001. Trimble immediately appealed the decision—pending at the time of composition, but likely to go against him. Then just before the UK general election began, Trimble repeated the tactic he had deployed in 2000; he wrote a post-dated resignation letter, effective on July 1 2001, which he declared he would make effective if the IRA failed to move on decommissioning. His long-run calculation was that if his resignation became effective then the UK government would have to choose between suspending the Agreement's institutions (Trimble's preferred default), or leaving the Assembly to trigger fresh elections, because of its failure to replace the First and Deputy First Ministers within six weeks (12 August 2001). His short-run calculation appears to have been that the resignation threat would immunise him, and his party's candidates, from criticism from other unionists over their willingness to share government with Sinn Féin in the absence of IRA decommissioning. Neither calculation was especially shrewd.

Nationalists had spent much of the year before the election trying to redress the UK government's failures to live up to its public promises faithfully to implement the Patten Report on policing, in letter and in spirit, as mandated by the Agreement. These failures were in turn used within the nationalist community to justify the IRA's failure to put its weapons verifiably beyond use, though it had twice supervised international inspections of its arms-dumps as a confidence-building measure, and organised one of these just before the general election. The SDLP had done considerable work at Westminster to amend what became the Police (Northern Ireland) Act 2000, but neither the Act nor the published implementation plans delivered the full Patten, only 'Patten lite'. Sinn Féin and the SDLP therefore made police reform and the full Patten report one of the central planks in their election campaigns — taking stances at odds with both the UUP and the DUP. Feedback from constituencies in unionist safe seats suggested that the UUP lost support to the DUP because of the scale of police reform, while the SDLP lost support to Sinn Féin amongst young nationalists because of the insufficiency of police reform, and because the SDLP appeared more pliant.

The campaign was conducted according to the logic of a dual party system, with competition within the unionist and nationalist blocs being much more important than competition across the blocs.[7] Unlike all other elections in Northern Ireland — local government, Assembly and European — the Westminster election is held under single-constituency plurality rule. One might therefore have expected to see some tacit agreement within the blocs to support a leading candidate in each constituency, to prevent the other bloc from winning a seat. That logic used to operate, especially within the unionist bloc where the imperative to keep out nationalists had restrained the DUP from campaigning against vulnerable UUP incumbents in 1997. Yet within the nationalist bloc, this logic has not operated at all in recent times, because the SDLP had not been prepared to organise pacts with a party associated with support for violence.

One might also have expected the fact that local government elections were being held on the same day, under the single-transferable vote (STV) system of proportional representation, to have restrained rhetorical criticism of rival parties within each bloc. There was no such spillover effect amongst party strategies. The parties fought each system separately, seeking to win under plurality rule at Westminster, while trying to maximise first preference and lower-order STV transfers in the local government ballots.

Competition within the unionist bloc, with the exception of Fermanagh and South Tyrone,[8] was unrestrained. The DUP did not stand in

North Down in order to give anti-Agreement Robert McCartney (UK Unionist Party) a chance of holding his seat. The DUP personally targeted Trimble as a vacillating traitor. Its cartoons lampooned him as a bent-over old man with a long flowing white beard and a resignation letter stuck in his pocket with the caption 'Trust me. I will not wait indefinitely for IRA decommissioning'; its website mocked him as the IRA's delivery boy; it declared 'trust' in politicians was its central concern. For the local government elections the DUP advised its voters to give their lower-order preferences to 'like-minded', that is anti-Agreement, unionists. The DUP's combination of hard-hitting attacks on Trimble, and its offer not to cause chaos, merely to renegotiate the Agreement, paid handsome dividends. Though it did not run candidates in four constituencies it came within a hair's breadth of becoming the largest unionist party in vote-share and seat-share in a Westminster general election. The party's one significant setback was to lose the seat it had gained in a by-election from the UUP, the Reverend William McCrea losing to David Burnside of the UUP.

The UUP leader managed to get all his party's candidates to stand uncomfortably behind a common pro-Agreement platform, albeit one that heavily emphasised the need to achieve IRA decommissioning. This fooled no one, as many of his incumbent MPs (especially William Ross, William Thompson, and the Reverend Martin Smyth) were known to be anti-Agreement, and they tried to stave off criticism from the DUP by emphasising their anti-Agreement credentials. This, of course, merely added to the party's public disarray, aggravated when one of its elderly incumbent MPs, Cecil Walker, put in an embarrassing television performance that threw away the North Belfast seat to the DUP's Nigel Dodds MLA. The UUP's solitary success in nomination strategy was to run a new pro-Agreement candidate, Lady Sylvia Hermon, in North Down, where she toppled McCartney. In the local government elections Trimble advised that voters should 'primarily consider pro-Union candidates after the UUP', rather than other pro-Agreement candidates (BBC website, 26 May), the line taken by the SDLP. This advice made it less likely that small numbers of pro-Agreement Catholics would vote tactically for pro-Agreement UUP candidates.

Within the nationalist bloc Sinn Féin fought an energetic, disciplined, and well-funded campaign. The party's coffers are now swelled by legitimate fund-raising in both parts of Ireland and the USA, and it probably has more activists than any other party in Northern Ireland. It sought to increase its vote share (standing candidates in every one of the 18 constituencies), its seat-share, and to get the nationalist electorate's endorsement for the Agreement, and its stances on policing, demilitarisation and decommissioning. In the republican priority list, the latter was usually last amongst the matters needing to be implemented to fulfil everyone's obligations under the Agreement. Sinn Féin's success in achieving extraordinarily high turnouts, both in its safe and its target seats, is detailed below. Its vote-share rose in every constituency in Northern Ireland, except South Belfast, where it made no tactical sense to vote for the party's candidate. Sinn Féin appear to have won most of the new young nationalist voters, who endorsed the party even in locations where there was an SDLP incumbent, or where the SDLP candidate appeared to have the better chance of winning. Sinn Féin expected to win West Tyrone, where an even nationalist split in the vote had allowed William Thompson of the UUP victory in 1997; but it did not expect its candidate Michelle Gildernew to be so successful in Fermanagh and South Tyrone.

The SDLP's strategy was to portray itself as the key pro-Agreement party, one that had made the peace process and the Agreement possible, and one with a wider social democratic and good governance agenda. It trumpeted its successes in bringing together a programme of government out of the four parties in the Executive. It resisted appeals by the Alliance Party to form a pro-Agreement pact on seats, as did the UUP. The SDLP hoped to hold and slightly expand its vote-share, and to take one additional seat. In fact its total vote fell, but not by that much, in comparison with 1997 — only approximately 20,000 across Northern Ireland. It targeted West Tyrone, withdrawing precious resources from Belfast, to support its high profile and Executive Minister for Agriculture Brid Rogers against the Sinn Féin Vice President Pat Doherty, to no avail.

The inter-ethnic or non-ethnic 'Others', principally the Alliance Party, were crushed in 2001. By comparison with previous elections, not only did the flanking parties take huge chunks from the moderates within their own blocs, but the moderates appear to have eroded the support of the Others, who also made tactical decisions to sacrifice their own prospects. The Alliance's proposals to make pro-Agreement candidate arrangements were firmly rebuffed by the UUP and SDLP, who were determined to maximise their share of the vote (*Irish News*, 3.4.01, 10.3.01).

The campaign once again highlighted the unreliability of polls in Northern Ireland, at least insofar as voters' intentions are concerned: they consistently understate the intensity of their political preferences. If the public had been anywhere near as moderate as they have generally represented themselves to pollsters during the last three decades there would not have been a Northern Ireland question. A *Belfast Telegraph/ Irish Independent* poll conducted by Irish Marketing Services published on 22 May suggested that the UUP, with 25% of respondents likely to vote for it, was 11 percentage points ahead of the DUP (14%), and that the SDLP (25%), was 9 percentage points ahead of Sinn Fein (16%). The poll did pick up two significant pointers: the young unionists are the most anti-Agreement, and in the 18–24 cohorts, Sinn Fein is the most popular party with 24% (compared with 15% for the UUP, 14% for the DUP and 13% for the SDLP, a portent of things to come).

Analysis of the results

The 2001 Westminster elections were the most exciting and dramatic that have ever occurred in Northern Ireland. While political scientists and journalists are fond of saying that a particular election was 'dull', Westminster elections in Northern Ireland have often seemed like a contest of the moribund. With only a small number of seats available, incumbents generally well 'dug in', little partisan change and few floating voters in an ethnic party system, change has appeared glacial.[9] This is not to say that alignments have been frozen and that nothing interesting ever happened, but dramatic gains and losses have been rare by any standards. For example, if we compare the change in vote shares of the five main parties in Northern Ireland (UUP, DUP, SDLP, SF and APNI) in Westminster elections, the volatility index at successive elections was 7% in 1987, 5.2% in 1992, 7.2% in 1997, but then doubled in 2001 to 14.5%.[10] To put this in perspective, the average aggregate volatility for nineteen European countries in the 1980s and 1990s was 9.2% and 11.5% respectively (for the UK alone, 3.3% and 9.3% in the same periods).[11] Similarly, seats very rarely changed hands between parties,[12] whereas in 2001 seven seats changed partisan control and three incumbents survived by narrow margins. In short, in 2001 Northern Ireland had a genuinely competitive and perhaps a watershed election.

Bloc performance

Before considering the performance of parties in detail, let us take stock of the overall bloc changes. In *Britain Votes 1997*, two of the present authors began with what they called a bold and falsifiable prediction. This was that the 1997 Westminster election would likely be the last in which the Unionist (with a capital 'U') bloc would win an overall majority of the votes cast in Northern Ireland.[13] At the 1997 general election the total U bloc (the UUP, DUP, UKUP, PUP, UDP and Conservatives) had managed just 50.5% of the total vote, compared with 40.2% for the Nationalist bloc, comprising the SDLP and Sinn Féin. Although the small Alliance Party of Northern Ireland (APNI) supports the Union, it is usually not defined as part of the U bloc because of its moderate, bi-confessional and inter-ethnic position. In 2001 the prediction was falsified, although the logic behind the prediction is likely to prove accurate about future trends. In 2001 the U bloc actually improved its position to 52.1%, though the nationalist bloc grew by even more to 42.7% (see Table 1 and Figure 3). The interesting question is: why did the U bloc not only hold its own but even manage a modest improvement?

Especially since 1996, unionist politicians and commentators have often explained unionists' less than optimal performances as due to differential abstentionism. In the absence of a full-scale election study

1. The Results of the 2001 Westminster General Elections in Northern Ireland

Party	Votes % 2001	Votes Change 1997–2001	Seats N 2001	Seats Change 1997–2001	Seats % 2001	S-V % 2001
UUP	26.8	−5.9	6	−4	33.3	6.5
DUP	22.5	8.9	5	3	27.8	5.3
UKUP	1.7	0.1	0	−1	–	−1.7
PUP	0.6	−0.8	0	–	–	−0.6
Conservatives	0.3	−0.9	0	–	–	−0.3
NI Unionist	0.2	–	0	–	–	−0.2
Total U bloc	52.1	1.6	11	−2	61.1	9
Sinn Féin	21.7	5.6	4	2	22.2	0.5
SDLP	21	−3.1	3	–	16.7	−4.3
Total N bloc	42.7	2.5	7	2	38.9	−3.8
APNI	3.6	−4.4	0	–	–	−3.6
NIWC	0.4	–	0	–	–	−0.4
WP	0.3	–	0	–	–	−0.3
Others	0.9	−0.1	0	–	–	–
Disproportionality in 2001			7.3			
Mean disproportionality (1981–97)			18.7			

Notes: (1) The measure of disproportionality used is the least squares index (LSq) devised by Michael Gallagher (1991). Disproportionality $\sqrt{1/2\Sigma(Vi-Si)^2}$. Lijphart regards the least squares method as 'the most sensitive and faithful reflection of the disproportionality of election results' (1994: 62). 'Others' and independents have been excluded from the calculations. The 'others' (0.9%) are excluded since they are not a unified bargaining actor. However, their inclusion would make only a marginal difference. (2) The UKUP vote can no longer be considered a 'party vote' – it is effectively a one-person party. All of the UKUP's 13,509 Westminster votes were for Bob McCartney. In the District Council elections the UKUP's eleven candidates managed only 0.6% of the total vote (4,763 votes). Source: Calculated from election returns. Table format based on Table 4.4 in P. Mitchell, 'The Party System and Party Competition' in P. Mitchell and R. Wilford (eds), *Politics in Northern Ireland*, Westview, 1999.

(estimating which individual voters actually went to the polls) we have no direct information on the differential turnout of the unionist and nationalist blocs. An indirect analysis confirms that turnout does appear

Figure 3. The Ever-Growing Nationalist Vote-Share in Northern Ireland, 1979–2001

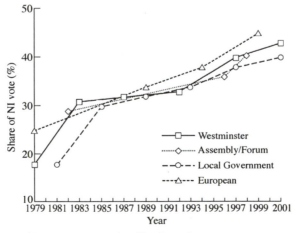

Source: O'Leary and Evans op. cit., updated by the authors.

2. The Turnout Wars

	'Unionist'	'Nationalist'	'Balanced'	N Lead
Number	10	6	2	–
Average turnout in 1998 Assembly election (%)	64.6	74.9	72.5	10.3
Average turnout in 2001 Wesminster election (%)	63.6	74.3	70.9	10.7

Notes: The table shows average turnout by constituency type. 'Unionist' constituencies are those in which at least four of the elected assembly members in 1998 self-identified as unionists in the Assembly (UUP, DUP, PUP, UKUP or independent unionist). Similarly 'nationalist' constituencies are those in which at least four of the elected members belonged to either the SDLP or Sinn Féin. This leaves two 'balanced' constituencies: Fermanagh South-Tyrone elected three nationalists (2 SF, 1 SDLP) and three unionists (2 UUP, 1 DUP); Belfast South elected three unionists (2 UUP, 1 DUP), two nationalists (2 SDLP) and one 'other' (NIWC). The comparison is possible because the constituencies have not changed geographically (the Assembly election involved selecting six members from each Westminster constituency), though of course we are comparing across electoral systems. Source: Adapted and updated from P. Mitchell, 'Transcending an Ethnic Party System? The Impact of Consociational Governance on Electoral Dynamics and the Party System' in R. Wilford (ed.), *Aspects of the Belfast Agreement*, Oxford University Press, 2001.

to be lower in unionist strongholds.[14] As explained in the note to Table 2, the 18 Westminster constituencies (which in the 1998 Assembly elections served as multi-member constituencies, returning six members each) can be delineated into predominantly 'unionist', nationalist and 'balanced' constituencies on the basis of the 1998 results. For example, a predominantly 'unionist constituency' for the purposes of Table 2 is one in which at least four of the members returned to the 1998 Assembly self-identified as unionist.[15] The results in 1998 were clear and quite dramatic: the average turnout in 'unionist constituencies' was 64.6%, just over 10% *lower* than in 'nationalist constituencies'. Differential turnout is, of course, an important competitive dynamic in ethnic party systems, and these results may suggest that the unionist vote had been depressed by a lower willingness of unionists to turn out and vote, partly because there has often been a safe incumbent and no-intra-unionist competition. Thus, a plausible explanation of the U bloc's improved position in 2001 is that the unionist parties were more successful in mobilising some of their more apathetic partisans in the context of a Westminster election that everyone believed would be the most competitive ever. After all, fear of losing seats to ethnic rivals is one of the classic motivators in such segmented party systems. But plausible as this proposition may seem, Table 2 indicates that it is incorrect. In 2001, as in previous elections, nationalists won the turnout wars: indeed the N bloc was even further ahead of the U bloc on this occasion (a lead of 10.7%).

So how did the U bloc vote stay above 50%? The simplest explanation is much more prosaic than complex considerations of differential constituency turnout. Quite simply the U bloc in 2001 had one significant competitor missing: the Alliance party deployed candidates in only ten constituencies, seven fewer than in 1997, in effect sacrificing itself. The Alliance party, in attempting to maximise the chances of the leading pro-Agreement candidate in several constituencies, paid the price of seeing its own percentage vote cut in half (see Table 3). In several

3. Constituency Electoral Dynamics by Bloc Marginality: Order of Party Placement and Share of Vote (%)

Order	1st		2nd		3rd		4th		5th	
'Safe' unionist seats										
North Down	UUP	56.0	UKUP	36.3	SDLP	3.4	Con	2.2	SF	0.8
Strangford	DUP	42.8	UUP	40.3	APNI	6.7	SDLP	6.1	SF	2.2
East Antrim	UUP	36.4	DUP	36.0	APNI	12.5	SDLP	7.3	Ind	3.0
South Antrim	UUP	37.1	DUP	34.8	SDLP	12.1	SF	9.4	APNI	4.5
North Antrim	DUP	49.9	UUP	21.0	SDLP	16.8	SF	9.8	APNI	2.6
Lagan Valley	UUP	56.5	APNI	16.6	DUP	13.4	SDLP	7.5	SF	5.9
East Belfast	DUP	42.5	UUP	23.2	APNI	15.8	PUP	10.0	SF	3.4
Upper Bann	UUP	33.5	DUP	29.5	SF	21.1	SDLP	14.9	WP	1.0
East Londonderry	DUP	32.1	UUP	27.4	SDLP	20.8	SF	15.6	APNI	4.1
'Safe' nationalist seats										
West Belfast	SF	66.1	SDLP	18.9	DUP	6.4	UUP	6.2	WP	1.8
Foyle	SDLP	50.2	SF	26.6	DUP	15.2	UUP	6.9	APNI	1.2
West Tyrone	SF	40.8	UUP	28.7	SDLP	28.7	–		–	–
Newry and Armagh	SDLP	37.4	SF	30.9	DUP	19.4	UUP	12.3	–	–
Mid Ulster	SF	51.1	DUP	31.1	SDLP	16.8	WP	1.0	–	–
South Down	SDLP	46.3	SF	19.7	UUP	17.6	DUP	15.0	APNI	1.3
Marginals										
North Belfast	DUP	40.8	SF	25.2	SDLP	21.0	UUP	12.0	WP	0.6
South Belfast	UUP	44.8	SDLP	30.6	NIWC	7.8	SF	7.6	APNI	5.4
Fermanagh S.T.	SF	34.1	UUP	34.0	SDLP	18.7	Ind U	13.2	–	–

Note: Within each category (e.g. 'Safe' unionist seats) the constituencies are listed in descending order from 'most safe' to 'most marginal' by ethno-national bloc. For example, West Belfast is the safest nationalist seat given that the combined Sinn Féin and SDLP vote is 85%. 'Marginal' constituencies are cases in which there is less than a 10% difference between the blocs (and of course 10% swings are certainly attainable in plurality elections, even if more difficult in ethnic party systems). For example, in the most marginal seat, Fermanagh and South Tyrone, the N bloc managed 52.1% to the U bloc's 47.2%. Of course, nomination strategies often determine who actually wins. For example, if a second unionist candidate had not been present in Fermanagh (the independent unionist anti-Agreement candidate, Jim Dixon) the UUP would have won this seat. Attenuating U bloc competition by fielding a single unionist candidate is precisely the method by which unionists have managed to win in majority nationalist constituencies such as Fermanagh in previous elections. For similar tables of earlier Westminster seat distributions see O'Leary and Evans, op. cit., for 1997 and Mitchell (1995) for the 1983, 1987 and 1992 elections.

constituencies the UUP was a major beneficiary. Indeed, if most of Alliance's 7,553 votes in 1997 in North Down, historically the Alliance's strongest constituency, transferred to the UUP candidate in 2001 to defeat the anti-Agreement incumbent, as was the APNI's intention, then this 'gift' alone constitutes two-thirds of the U bloc's entire gains in 2001.[16]

The results in 2001 were a triumph for the DUP and Sinn Féin; but big winners also beget big losers. The biggest of the losers was the UUP, now merely a front-runner compared with its former hegemonic domination of Northern Ireland politics. While 2001 certainly constituted the UUP's worst-ever Westminster election, in which for the first time in the modern party system it plummeted significantly below the 30% barrier to only 26.8%, it can be seen from Figure 4 that this is just the latest dip in a long-term decline.[17] By contrast, the trend line for the other big loser in 2001 — the SDLP — had been a gentle but steady incline, benefiting from a growing Catholic population and a progressively more nationalist electorate. While the SDLP vote continued to

Figure 4. Vote Share in Northern Ireland Westminster Elections (%)

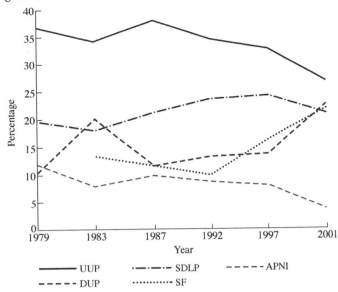

Source: The authors.

rise, its rate of growth slowed appreciably as the 'peace process' continued, with most nationalist gains going to Sinn Féin. For example (see Figure 2), the SDLP vote in 1997 was only a very modest 0.6% increase on its 1992 Westminster performance. Over the same time period Sinn Féin's vote jumped by 6.1% to a total of 16.1% in 1997 (a growth rate ten times higher than the SDLP!). Sinn Féin's accelerated growth continued in 2001 with a further gain of 5.6% to a new total of 21.7% (a 35% increase on its 1997 vote), thus capturing the long sought symbolic prize of becoming the largest nationalist party. Sinn Féin has gone from being an abstentionist party, as it was before 1982, to being the largest nationalist party today and probably the party with the greatest share of young voters, in less than 20 years. The answer to the question 'Who has benefited electorally from the peace process and Belfast Agreement?' could not be clearer.

Attempts to resolve protracted ethno-national conflicts tend not to be universally popular — if they were that would constitute proof that the conflict was not 'deep' or 'protracted'. Thus, while Sinn Féin has captured most of the electoral gains from nationalist enthusiasm for a long overdue process of institutional and policy change, the DUP appears to have ridden the tiger of opposition to these same changes. 'Just saying no' to compromises with one's inter-ethnic rivals has always been a successful strategy in such polarised party systems, but the DUP on this occasion cleverly combined its oppositional stance with partial cooperation with the new devolved governing arrangements, which are

Figure 5a. Intra-Unionist Bloc Competition, 1982–2001

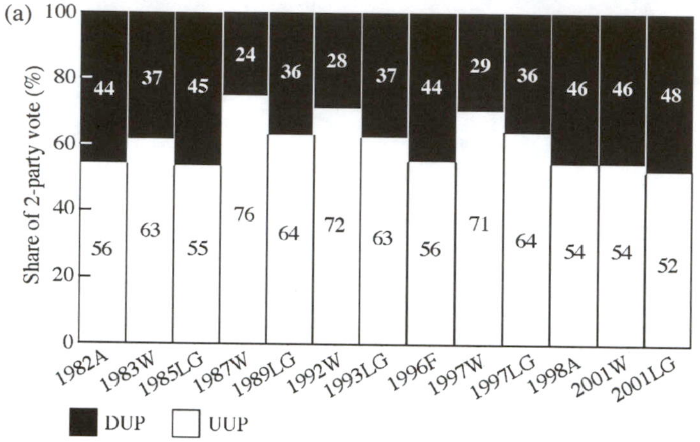

Source: The authors.

locally popular. With the UUP virtually as divided over the Agreement as the UK Conservative party under John Major was over European integration, many UUP voters decamped to the DUP. Nevertheless, the DUP's leap of 8.9% (a 65% increase in on its 1997 vote) was much further than optimistic DUP members could have hoped for.

It has long been noted that Northern Ireland has a dual party system. It is only a mild exaggeration to say that each community holds its own election to decide who will be its pre-eminent tribunes. Winning seats from the other communal bloc, which rarely happens, is a bonus; the more serious party competition usually takes place within each segmented community. Party politics in such systems tends to be characterised by ethnic outbidding among rival parties within each bloc. Figure 5 provides a graphic representation of the changing fortunes of the principal combatants in both halves of the dual party system. It is quite clear that opposition to the peace process has been a powerful electoral weapon for the DUP, which has now almost managed to draw level with the UUP, even in Westminster elections.

As Figure 5 demonstrates a rough ratio of 60:40 in favour of the SDLP in 1996/97 has now been replaced by Sinn Féin emerging as marginally the largest nationalist party in both of the elections held on the same day in 2001. The local government elections, held as usual by single transferable vote, resulted in broadly similar but of course more proportional results (Table 1).[18] The aggregate patterns are very similar — but as yet we cannot analyse the data on 'transfers' as the official tabulations have yet to be published — and so we cannot tell whether there was any significant evidence of cross-ethnic voting in lower-order preferences.

While winning the percentage battle for votes is undoubtedly very

Figure 5b. Intra-Nationalist Bloc Competition, 1982–2001

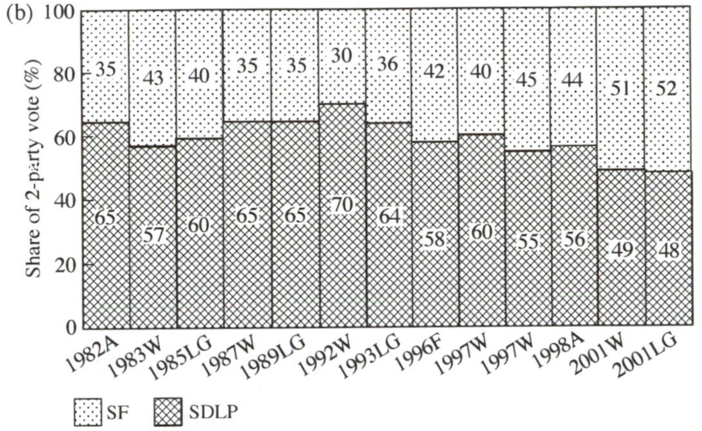

Source: The authors.

important, the seats of course are the actual jobs at stake. Northern Ireland voters, long accustomed to seeing about 17 of their 18 MPs returned in an election, struck a blow for a change in 2001, though their desired changes were often diametrically different. The net result however was that seven seats changed partisan control, and several other MPs survived narrowly. The UUP was the only major party to lose seats (the UKUP lost its single seat; this became the UUP's sole gain).[19] The UUP lost five seats (net four); of these three were lost to the DUP (Strangford, East Londonderry and North Belfast) and two to Sinn Féin (West Tyrone and Fermanagh and South Tyrone). Thus, the DUP gained three seats, Sinn Féin gained two, and the SDLP held its existing three seats. Thus the final seat total was UUP (6), DUP (5), Sinn Féin (4) and SDLP (3). In 2001 three of the new MPs are women (17%). While hardly reaching Scandinavian levels of gender representation this is novel for Northern Ireland. No woman had been elected at any Northern Ireland Westminster election since Bernadette Devlin was returned in 1970.

If the 1998 Assembly results, held under STV (PR), are taken as a reasonably faithful reflection of overall ethno-national bloc divisions then the 2001 Westminster seat allocations were a much more faithful reflection of overall bloc divisions than was the previous Westminster contest in 1997. In other words, the 'appropriate' bloc won all of the seats in 2001, whereas in 1997 two 'nationalist constituencies' returned UUP MPs (Fermanagh and South Tyrone and West Tyrone). The other four seats that changed hands in 2001 were simply changes in the balance of power *within* the unionist bloc (three UUP losses to the DUP, marginally compensated by one UUP gain from the UKUP). In other words the 2001 Westminster results were more proportional with respect to parties *and* ethnic blocs than 1997. Indeed, it is worth highlighting (see Table 1) that the disproportionality figure of 7.3 (on the least squares index) is by a massive margin the most proportional outcome of a Westminster election in Northern Ireland (the average for 1983–97 is 18.7). The decline of the UUP (and hence fall in its average seat bonus from a massive 23% in 1997 to only 6.5% in 2001) is the largest contributory factor.[20] This is not a commercial for the Westminster electoral system, which is highly inappropriate for the genuine multi-party system in Northern Ireland.

Conclusion and prospects

The election did not deliver David Trimble's desires. The IRA did not move on decommissioning and Trimble resigned as First Minister, though not as UUP party leader on 1 July. This provoked the sovereign governments into convening negotiations between pro-Agreement parties and themselves at Weston Park, Shropshire. A blame or blame-avoidance game began.

Observers agreed that two parties and one government shared most of the blame for the impasses implementing the Belfast Agreement and stabilising its institutions: Sinn Fein, the UUP and the UK government.

The IRA had initiated decommissioning of its weapons, if one counts international inspections of its arms dumps, but it had not moved to implement its pledge of 2000 to put its weapons completely and verifiably beyond use. None of its complaints about the UK government's failures to deliver on its pledges absolved Sinn Fein from its obligations to build confidence amongst its governmental partners that they were not sharing power with a party with a private army, and nothing in the Agreement warranted the republican line that actual decommissioning must be the very last act of implementation. Prevarication merely maximised distrust about the IRA's long-run intentions.

The UUP had broken several of its obligations under the Agreement, while demanding that others deliver on their promises ahead of time. It blocked rapid executive formation. It rejected the Patten report on policing, though it met the Agreement's terms of reference. The First Minister blocked Sinn Fein ministers' legitimate participation in the North-South Ministerial Council. He has twice threatened resignation, and the collapse or suspension of the Agreement's institutions, to force Sinn Fein to deliver the IRA to his deadlines. He encouraged the UK government to make the first formal break with the Agreement, and international law, by-passing the Suspension Actin 2000, which Secretary of State Peter Mandelson used, and Trimble has continued to press for its use.

The UK government so far has dishonoured its pledge of May 2000, repeated in March 2001, to produce legislation and implementation plans fully reflecting the letter and the spirit of the Patten report on policing—which had flowed squarely from the Agreement. None of its excuses exonerate it in nationalist eyes, and it also has work to do to fulfil its obligations on demilitarisation, the review of the administration of justice and the protection of human rights.

At Weston Park the two governments sought to put together a package deal linking police reform, demilitarisation, decommissioning, and securing the Agreement's institutions. The talks were not successful in producing agreement, though they were not fruitless. The governments have currently agreed to organise and implement their own package. They will then have three choices: to leave further negotiation to the parties; to suspend the Agreement's institutions; or to have fresh Assembly elections. The first does not seem likely to work. The second option must be rejected by the Irish government, which regards the Suspension Act as a unilateral breach of a treaty. There is speculation about a variation on this option, viz. suspension for a day, followed by another six weeks for renewed negotiations before elections would have to occur. This option is unlikely to endear itself to nationalists and republicans. The third option is to have fresh Assembly elections, consequent upon the failure to re-elect successors to David Trimble and Seamus Mallon. The argument against elections is that they will help the DUP and Sinn Fein. Perhaps that possibility will act as an incentive for the UUP to compromise. But our analysis suggests that in any fresh Assembly elections the DUP and Sinn Fein would do best on moderated platforms. We might anticipate IRA initiatives on arms, and DUP 'renegotiation' briefings. And the emergence of both parties as the clear majority within their blocs would create a fascinating if dangerous spectacle. The two parties would have to choose: accept their respective nominees for the posts of First and Deputy First Ministers, accept moderate SDLP and UUP nominees for these posts, or have fresh elections. That is, they would have to choose between stealing their opponents' clothes and wearing them, or showing that they remain wolves in sheep's clothing.

Paul Mitchell, Brendan O'Leary and Geoffrey Evans

* The authors would like to thank Leigh Somerville, Gitta Frank and Simone Lewis for research assistance, and Jane Pugh of LSE's drawing office. Brendan O'Leary's visits to Northern Ireland were supported by the United States Institute of Peace and by Ulster Television News.

1   See, inter alia, D. McKittrick, *The Nervous Peace*, Blackstaff Press, 1996; B. O'Leary, 'The Conservative Stewardship of Northern Ireland 1979–97: Sound-Bottomed Contradictions or Slow Learning?', 45 *Political Studies* 4, 1997; B. O'Leary, 'The Belfast Agreement and the Labour Government: How to Handle and Mishandle History's Hand' in A. Seldon (ed.), *The Blair Effect: The Blair Government, 1997–2001*, Little Brown, 2001.

2   See P. Mitchell, 'Transcending an Ethnic Party System? The Impact of Consociational Governance on Electoral Dynamics and the Party System' by R. Wilford (ed.), Oxford University Press, 2001, and B. O'Leary 'The Nature of the Agreement', 22 *Fordham Journal of International Law* 4, 1999, or 'The Nature of the British-Irish Agreement', *New Left Review* 233, January–February.

3   It is tempting to say that the DUP has gone from being 'Ulster Says No', to 'Ulster says No to this, maybe yes to that, but don't tell anyone'!

4   See B. O'Leary and G. Evans, 'Northern Ireland: La Fin de Siècle, The Twilight of the Second Protestant Ascendancy and Sinn Féin's Second Coming', *Parliamentary Affairs*, October 1997.

5   For arguments favouring proportional electoral systems for Northern Ireland for Westminster elections
     see B. O'Leary, 'The Protection of Human Rights under the Belfast Agreement', 72 *Political Quarterly*
     3, July–September 2001; B. O'Leary 'The Implications for Political Accommodation in Northern
     Ireland of Reforming the Electoral System for the Westminster Parliament', 35 *Representation* 2–3,
     1999.
6   The First and Deputy First Ministers are equal in powers and functions, and differ solely in their titles.
     They are elected jointly by a concurrent majority of registered nationalists and unionists in the
     Assembly – and the death or resignation of one immediately triggers the other's loss of office, and fresh
     elections within six weeks.
7   P. Mitchell, 'Conflict Regulation and Party Competition in Northern Ireland', 20 *European Journal of
     Political Research* 1, 1991; P. Mitchell, 'Party Competition in an Ethnic Dual Party System', 18 *Ethnic
     and Racial Studies* 4, 1995.
8   Here the DUP decided not to stand for fear of fragmenting the unionist vote – instead it backed and
     campaigned for a local anti-Agreement candidate, Mr Jim Dixon.
9   See P. Mitchell, 'The Party System and Party Competition' in P. Mitchell and R. Wilford (eds), *Politics
     in Northern Ireland*, Westview, 1999.
10   The figures are a slight adjustment to the well-known Pederson volatility index. Although often all
     parties are included in the count, this can lead to a distorted impression of partisan change if there is a
     high frequency of small party emergence, splits and fusions. Since small 'parties' are frequent vehicles
     in Northern Ireland they have been excluded in these calculations. We thus have a comparison from
     1987–2001 of aggregate partisan vote change among the five main parties. These are the only parties
     with even a remote chance of winning a Westminster seat (leaving aside the unusual case of North
     Down which has elected – effectively – independent members). Also among them these five parties
     accounted for 95.6% of the votes cast in 2001.
11   The European figures are M. Gallagher, M. Laver and P. Mair, *Representative Government in Modern
     Europe*, McGraw Hill, 2001, p. 263.
12   In 1987 only two seats changed partisan control, in 1992 one seat, and in 1997 two.
13   O'Leary and Evans, op. cit.
14   P. Mitchell, 'Transcending an Ethnic Party System? The Impact of Consociational Governance on
     Electoral Dynamics and the Party System' in R. Wilford (ed.), *Aspects of the Belfast Agreement*.
     Oxford University Press, 2001.
15   The only purpose of Table 2 is to provide an approximate guide to differential turnout in the absence
     of more direct information. No other assertions are being made here. In total, sixteen of the eighteen
     constituencies can easily be distinguished on this basis.
16   The combined APNI vote in 1997 in the seven constituencies *not* contested in 2001 was 16,073. If this
     had been repeated in 2001 it would have constituted 1.985 of the total votes cast. It cannot be assumed
     that all of these potential Alliance votes were cast for the U bloc instead, but most of these 'missing
     Alliance' party votes were accumulated in three predominantly unionist constituencies in 1997 (North
     Down, 7,553; North Belfast, 2,221; and Upper Bann, 3,017, which incidentally is much more than
     David Trimble's margin of victory in 2001). Exactly 80% of these 'missing Alliance' votes were cast in
     1997 in these three constituencies. Assuming that a small simulation can be excused (purely for fun): if
     Alliance had fielded candidates in these three constituencies in 2001 and achieved its 1997 level of
     support and if, as seems likely, these votes would have been 'reclaimed' from the U bloc, they would
     have constituted exactly 1.58% of the total vote in 2001. And recall that the U bloc's improved
     position in 2001 was a gain of 1.6%. Thus, the suggestion is that with Alliance party competition in
     2001 the total vote of the U bloc would have been approximately 50.5%, i.e. unchanged from 1997.
17   It should be noted that the recent growth of the much smaller unionist parties (the UKUP, PUP, UDP,
     and Northern Ireland Conservatives) is over. At their high point they had collectively taken 8.3% of
     the vote in the 1998 Assembly elections; in 2001 they managed only 2.8% in the Westminster election
     and 2.6% in the district council elections. Indeed, in an extraordinary example of organisational
     disarray the UDP failed to register in time for the 2001 elections – its leaders could stand only as
     independents.
18   For a good account of the 2001 local elections see K. Totten, ' "Two Elections, One Day. Simple but
     Important": The Northern Ireland District Council Elections 2001', *Irish Political Studies*, 16,
     forthcoming.
19   David Burnside's victory over William McCrea of the DUP in South Antrim was a second UUP victory,
     though it did not count as a gain in relation to 1997. This former UUP seat had been won by McCrea
     in a by-election.
20   Sinn Féin's modest 0.5% seat bonus is the first ever positive figure for the party across all elections
     types and systems. For example, their average Westminster 'bonus' (1983–97 is –7%).

JONI LOVENDUSKI

Women and Politics: Minority Representation or Critical Mass?

The result of the 2001 British general election saw the appointment of the first full-time paid Minister for Women, the inclusion of record numbers of women in Cabinet, and high priority given to the issues of health and education, matters of great concern to women. Early indicators are that, maybe after all women will be beneficiaries of New Labour's second landslide. If so, it is unexpected. Prior to the election women's advocates were concerned about fewer women candidates being selected for winnable seats and rumours that the Women's Unit would be downgraded, removed from the Cabinet office, and subsumed into an equalities unit. The near-invisibility of women politicians in the national campaigns of the three main parties added to concerns that the promise of the 1997 'breakthrough' would not be realised.

Overall, the results of the general election of 2001 support both cautious optimism and general concern by those who advocate equality of women's representation. Matters for concern include the failure by major parties to boost the numbers of women in Parliament by expanding the number of women candidates in winnable seats. There was a particularly, and widely remarked, 'masculine' campaign in which the wives/partners of party leaders generally received more national media attention than woman politicians. In terms of policy, all parties appeared reluctant to make gender an explicit dimension of political issues and, in terms of image, the gender coding of the 'job' of politician as male continued. On the other hand a women's lobby, much strengthened since 1997, attempted with some success to draw attention to party neglect of gender politics. The new Blair government immediately honoured its manifesto pledge by including proposals in the Queen's speech to change the laws prohibiting positive action in favour of women candidates. These examples suggest that the feminisation of party and electoral politics continues, but is contested.

Gender and politics: critical mass or minority representation?

A good way to understand the importance of gender to politics is to examine the position of women in political institutions and processes. In such an undertaking, 'gender' is defined as characteristic of both women and men and is expressed in the differences between the sexes that result from the division of labour between the women and men. In public life, gender is normally a hierarchy in which men have more presence and power than women, a syndrome especially apparent in politics. Gender is not a synonym for 'sex', and any examination of gender politics needs to consider both femininity and masculinity. That being said, it is necessary to map the power differentials between women and men to understand how gender affects politics.

Feminist political scientists have used the concept of 'critical mass' as a shorthand-term to describe how the effect of increasing the numbers of women in politics accelerates and makes further increases inevitable. Generally, the figure set for critical mass of women is about 30% of a legislature; for example, that was the threshold set by the United Nations in 1995 as the necessary minimum of women representatives needed for women to be fairly represented. Yet 30% is a rather arbitrary figure and the concept, as applied to politics, remains under-developed. The term 'critical mass' is evocative as it suggests that the size of the minority of women in political office is important, an insight used by Drude Dahlerup in her work on Scandinavian women legislators in the 1980s. Dahlerup argued that, as a minority group, the role of women politicians was better understood by a theory of minority representation. To develop such a theory she used the classification made by Rosabeth Moss Kanter to identify three categories of minority group: the *skewed* group where the minority is no more than 15%, the *tilted* group where the minority is between 15 and 40%, and the *balanced* group where the minority may be around 40%. In 1997 the proportion of women in the House of Commons changed from 9% to 18.9%, that is, from a skewed group to a tilted group. In Kanter's terms, the change was from a token number towards a minority strong enough to affect the nature of the wider group. Members of tilted groups are able to form alliances and act as a coherent force to affect the dominant culture of their institution and in a position to perform the 'critical' acts that Dahlerup argues are necessary to the feminisation of political institutions.[1]

Whilst women did not become a 'critical mass' in the House of Commons in 1997, Labour women became a tilted group. In contrast, Liberal and Conservative women continued to be token women within their parties, dependent on an alliance with women across the benches to make a difference. The overall proportion of women in Parliament after 1997 was toward the lower end of the tilted group range. Yet, expectations of the women MPs were very high and were accelerated by the 1999 elections to the Scottish Parliament and the Welsh Assembly where respectively 36% and 38% of legislators were women. In the 1999 elections to the European Parliament 25% of successful candidates were women and in 2000 women constituted 40% of the newly elected GLA. Applied unmodified to British conditions, Dahlerup's theory of minority representation predicts a steady increase in the proportion of women in all areas except Northern Ireland. Based on this theory, the number of women at Westminster should have risen in 2001.

Observers of British politics, however, were aware long before the election that women's representation in the House of Commons would remain stable or even fall. Their predictions were based on developments in British party and electoral politics. Political parties continue to be the main agents of political recruitment and they have been a powerful obstacle to women's aspirations for representation in Parliament. Strategically British women's advocates are compelled to persuade the main parties to alter their candidate selection methods in order to secure nominations of women in party seats. To obtain such support, feminists inside and outside political parties have made strong claims about women's political values, behaviour and preferences. Inevitably such claims have increased expectations of change once a sufficient number of women are elected. Within this broader theoretical context, to assess the importance of the 2001 election to gender politics, this study reviews major party policies on women's issues; describes the part played by women in the campaigns and examines the politics of selecting women candidates; considers women's voting and the fortunes of women candidates; assesses the entry of women into government; and finally, returns to critical mass theory to address the question whether women politicians make a difference to politics.

Women's issues and party policies

It is useful to distinguish between women's 'issues' and 'perspectives'. Women's *issues* are those that mainly affect women, either for biological reasons (such as breast cancer screening and reproductive rights) or for social reasons (sex equality or child-care policy). Women's *perspectives* are women's views on all political matters. Whilst opinion and attitude data suggest that men and women agree that the same issues are significant, women perceive those issues differently to men. For example, both women and men agree that employment issues are important. However, many surveys have shown that women are more likely to be concerned about work and family life whilst men are more likely to be concerned about pay, career prospects and benefits.[2] When parties court women's votes they have to take both women's issues and women's perspectives into account. In the 2001 campaign the major parties all gave some thought to women's issues but with the exception of Labour's special women's manifesto (see below), none took on the more difficult challenge of addressing women's perspectives.

In the preparations for the Conservative's campaign group, Teresa May MP, the Shadow Secretary of State for Education, devised a set of policies designed to win women's votes including a married couples' tax allowance and child-care package. Their efforts received little campaign emphasis, and were overshadowed by the 'keep the pound' campaign. During the campaign the Conservative Women's National Council accused the Conservatives of ignoring women voters. The Council criticised the Conservative campaign for sidelining women frontbenchers and for ignoring the issues that count most with women voters. Mary-Ann Stephenson, Director of the Fawcett Society, argued that it was a major error for Tories to ignore women when they were, and had always been, their core vote.[3] Conservative women activists repeatedly expressed concern that messages about child care and education had been ignored at the highest levels of the campaign. The main exception was a controversial Conservative broadcast attacking Labour's special early release scheme which sought to blame this policy for two rapes and other crimes. The emphasis on crime sought to draw attention to the implications of Labour's sentencing policies for women's safety and it was a direct attempt to play on the fears of elderly women voters. Curiously, the broadcast was widely criticised as a cynical and irresponsible ploy, but its focus on women attracted little comment.

In contrast to its national media presentation, Labour attempted to address women by producing and distributing a 'women's' version of its manifesto. This 'manifesto lite' as it was termed was entitled 'Your Family' and produced in the format of a mid market women's magazine including a friendly and personally signed 'letter from the editor', a series of self-improvement items (made possible by New Labour) and numerous pictures of happy families gathered around mothers. Its overall 'smile count' (a key statistic for women's magazines) was 125% — some 30 smiles over 24 pages. The cover contained a picture of Tony Blair helping a small child to use a camera and a shot of Valerie Howard to flag her article about returning to her job as a NHS nurse after bringing up her children. According to an unnamed BBC commentator, all 'Your Family' lacked in the mid-market women's magazines stakes was a prize competition.[4] The Labour manifesto *Ambitions for Britain* promised a tax cut for parents of newborn children and pledged to improve public services especially in education and the health service that pre-election surveys showed to be particularly important to women.[5] In addition, in response to campaigns by women's advocates seeking a change in the law on positive action the manifesto contained a pledge to legislate 'to allow each party to make positive moves to increase the representation of women'. A further promise 'to continue to modernise the procedures of the House of Commons so it can effectively fulfil its functions of representation and scrutiny', kept open the possibility that parliamentary modernisation may yet make the Commons more women-friendly.

On 29 May Liberal Democrats belatedly highlighted their promises to women by devoting a day's campaigning to 'women's issues'. They promised more and better quality child care and drew attention to the contribution that their abolition of the 10 pence tax band would make to the reduction of child poverty. Charles Kennedy criticised the invisibility of women in the campaign and pledged that their proposed Equality Bill would include a provision allowing political parties to use positive measures in their candidate selection procedures to recruit more women.

Campaigns

In their national campaigns parties put leading and hence male, politicians in the foreground. The resulting male domination of political news became an issue in the campaign, rebounding on parties perceived to be sidelining their women politicians. In previous electoral campaigns, media and parties have mirrored each other in their male domination. For 2001, however, TV channels increased the number of women presenters in the campaign, a policy designed partly to help overcome audience apathy and partly to provide greater gender balanced coverage of the election. The key anchors were still often men like David Dimbleby, John Snow and Trevor MacDonald, and commentators like Andrew Marr, John Sargeant, and Adam Boulton, but more women featured in campaign coverage, particularly Elinor Goodman. Parties did less well. Prompted by party women, campaign managers knew they needed to win women's votes and to project feminised party images during the campaign. They acknowledged the importance of avoiding presentations of all male line-ups at press conferences. However, it proved to be very difficult for parties to feminise their images in order to attract support. This was particularly evident in their national campaigns where male party leaders paraded their wives, and sometimes their children, to demonstrate their humanity, but forgot to balance their daily press conference and other platforms by including women politicians.

As in 1997 the invisibility of women in the national party campaigns generated considerable comment. In 2001, despite the availability of many more senior women politicians, women were even less visible in national campaigns. Women's organisations criticised all three main parties for turning the election into a 'spectacle of suits shouting at each other'.[6] Their absence was so conspicuous that it became an election story in all of the daily broadsheets. Yet Labour began the campaign with plans to ensure women's presence. Labour's women ministers were dispatched to the provinces. Patricia Hewitt, Estelle Morris, Anne Campbell and Hazel Blears all spearheaded regional campaigns.

Arrangements were made to ensure there would be a balance of men and women at most media events. Somehow, however, the campaign managers did not quite 'get it' and male leaders could not quite make the necessary space for women. When Margaret Beckett appeared alongside Tony Blair, Gordon Brown and Alastair Darling at the first of the campaign press conferences, her only apparent function was to select reporters to ask questions.

Despite an almost uniformly male frontbench, the Conservatives campaign generated a greater media presence for women. The famously silent Ffion Hague, wife of the party leader, produced most of the sightings of women on the election news. Content analysis of campaign news coverage by Loughborough University's Communication Group examined the number of stories about leading figures (see the chapter by Deacon et al.). Frontbench spokesperson on Home Affairs, Anne Widdicombe just made it into the list of the top ten most visible politicians, as did Margaret Thatcher for part of the campaign.[7] The national Liberal Democrat campaign was also very much a male affair, but less coverage for the Liberal Democrats meant that only Charles Kennedy appeared amongst the ten 'most visible' politicians.

By the last week in May, comment about the absence of women in the national campaigns was widespread and embarrassing to campaign managers. Women journalists ensured this would not continue unremarked. Stories about invisible women, almost all written by women, were carried in the *Guardian*, *The Times* and *Independent*. Labour and the Liberal Democrats quickly responded. Suddenly, remarked one observer, 'it was raining women' (*Guardian*, 28.5.01). On May 25 Labour ensured that Chancellor Gordon Brown had two women ministers at his side at the party's early morning press conference, Estelle Morris and Margaret Hodge. During the press conference, *New Statesman* Political Editor Jackie Ashley asked Estelle Morris why it was that Labour's women ministers were never allowed to answer questions at press briefings. Brown interrupted Morris to answer the question that had been put to her, before laughing as he realised how well his behaviour illustrated the point Ashley was trying to make. Later that day on BBC2's Newsnight, Jackie Ashley explained that she had been lucky to put the question at all. She recounted that women journalists had been going around the party press conferences raising questions about the invisibility of women. Labour campaign managers were aware of interventions at other party press conferences, so ignored their requests to ask questions. The support of male journalists was enlisted and all (but one) agreed not to raise their hands to ask a question at the 25 May press conference. The Labour platform had no option but to call on Ashley. This anecdote is indicative not only of the difficulties of feminising party images, but also of the importance of the presence of women in both the press corps and the party leadership to the normalisation of women's representation. The Loughborough campaign media

1. Gender Distributions in Media Coverage by Type of Actor (%)

	Politicians	Politicians' relatives	Celebrities	City/ Business	Media	Other professional	General public	Total
Female	9.8	82.3	46.1	7.9	19.4	17.6	44.6	15.2
Male	90.2	17.7	53.9	92.1	80.6	82.3	55.4	84.8
(Total N)	5949	141	180	191	304	853	513	8131

Notes: Figures are for all media actors coded over the sample period where gender could be reliably identified. Up to five actors could be coded per item. Total number of news items coded = 3022. Source: Communication Research Centre, Department of Social Sciences, Loughborough University, 19 June 2001.

analysis confirmed that in election news, appearances by male politicians outnumbered those by women by a factor of about nine to one. The imbalance is due to campaign management as well as how the news media treat women.

Table 1 shows that during the campaign, men outnumbered women in most categories, a pattern typical of the gender biases of media representations. Although politicians are a male-dominated group, the Labour Party, where woman are one-quarter of its frontbench, could be expected to do better. Moreover, the problem of women's invisibility is also a side effect of the conventions of modern news coverage of political campaigns. The media tends to 'presidentialise' campaigns, focusing on top party leaders, with little coverage of most frontbench politicians (*Guardian*, 28.5.01). If parties are serious about changing their campaign images, it will be necessary for them to include more women in their top leadership.

Candidates and MPs

At dissolution there were 120 women MPs in Parliament: 100 Labour, 14 Conservative, 4 Liberal Democrats and 2 SNP. Several well-known women retired from the House including Mo Mowlam, the popular former Northern Ireland Minister and Betty Boothroyd, the much-admired former Speaker of the House. At the close of nominations on 22 May the tally of women candidates from the main parties was 412.[8] The election returned 118 women to the House of Commons as Labour's contingent of women fell from 102 to 95, the Conservatives' increased from 13 to 14, the Liberal Democrats' rose from 2 to 5 (see Table 2). In Northern Ireland, SNP, Sinn Fein, UDUP and UUP voters elected one woman each. Among women MPs, three Labour (Christine Butler, Fiona Jones and Eileen Gordon) and one Liberal Democrat

2. Women Candidates and MPs, Major Parties, 1987–2001

	Conservative		Labour		Liberal Democrat	
	Candidates	MP	Candidates	MP	Candidates	MP
1987	46	17	92	21	105	2
1992	63	20	138	37	143	2
1997	67	13	159	102	142	3
2001	92	14	146	95	135	5

(Jackie Ballard) lost their seats to Conservative men. Twelve new women MPs were elected, including four Labour members (Vera Baird, Ann McKechin, Ann Picking, Meg Munn), three Liberal Democrats (Sue Doughty, Patsy Carlton, Annette Brook). Angela Watkin won Upminster for the Conservatives, Iris Robinson won Strangford for DUP, Sylvia Herman won North Down for UUP, Michelle Gildernew won Fermanagh and South Tyrone for Sinn Fein and Annabelle Ewing won Perth for SNP. In short, the changes were small, but the pattern of increasing the number of women in Parliament was reversed for the first time since 1979.

In total only 20 seats changed hands. The numbers of women MPs fell because no party used effective positive action measures to place women in winnable seats. During the 1990s Labour was the party that had been most willing to facilitate women but they faltered in selecting candidates for 2001. Women contested only four of the seats where Labour MPs retired. The 'breakthrough' of 1997 was not sustained. Between 1979 and 2000 organised Labour Party women campaigned for increased representation of women in the party and repeatedly intervened in debates about candidate selection processes. By the end of the 1980s quotas of women had been established in all Labour decision-making committees, placing women in key positions and at the same time increasing the pool of politically experienced women interested in standing for election to the House of Commons. Gathering support, women's advocates finally won the introduction of quotas for women in the form of All Women Shortlists in 1993.

The controversial policy was eventually challenged in the courts (*Jepson and Dyas-Elliott* v *Labour Party and Others*). In 1996 the Leeds Industrial Tribunal found all-women shortlists to be in contravention of the Sex Discrimination Act in a decision that, at best, might be regarded as ironic. After the Jepson case an internal Working Party on Women's Representation was convened, chaired by Hilary Armstrong who then chaired the NEC women's committee. This committee reported its recommendations to the candidate's office of the party in the spring of 1997. It endorsed the creation of panels of approved candidates and the radical 'Twinning' proposals for the elections to the new legislatures for Scotland and Wales. 'Twinning' is a system whereby pairs of neighbouring constituencies combine and select one man and one woman candidate, ensuring that women are half of the candidates. For Westminster, however, the committee had been instructed that quotas were not on the agenda, and its subsequent endorsement of equal opportunities selection, based on 50/50 shortlists and fairly constructed approved panels was thought to be the 'least worst option'. The policy of equal numbers of men and woman on each shortlist was adopted over the protests of many feminists in the party who regarded the measure as a set back. Thus the drop in Labour women candidates in 2001 was largely due to its selection procedures which, in contrast to the pre-1997 nomination period, contained only weak measures to facilitate the selection of women. In the context of the Westminster electoral system, the change from positive discrimination (mandatory quotas of women) to positive action (voluntary quotas of women candidates) made it possible for party resistors to reaffirm their preferences for male candidates. Anecdotal evidence suggests that constituency shortlisters in many localities deliberately chose weak women applicants over well-qualified ones in order to fix the selection for a man. Many women seeking selection reported a backlash from men claiming that it was now their turn. Claims that the fall in the number of qualified prospective Labour women candidates is a supply problem (i.e. that few women come forward to pursue political careers) are mistaken and possibly disingenuous.[9]

No women were selected for vacant Conservative-held seats. Given its longstanding base of support among women voters, the Conservatives have been remarkably reluctant to take the measures necessary to field women candidates. After the 1997 general election William Hague proposed a 25% quota of women among Conservative candidates. The party rejected this proposal and the Conservatives did not take even weak action to assist the nomination of women in its winnable seats in 2001. Prominent Conservative women protested as selection meeting after selection meeting nominated men. In April 2001 Angela Browning, then Shadow Leader of the House of Commons, attacked the gender coding of Conservative selection decisions saying that 'those who selected candidates to stand for Parliament were often "prejudiced" and "unprofessional"'. They had no idea how to interview people 'having never interviewed anybody for anything in their lives', harboured outdated views of what would make a good MP and were tougher on women than men. 'The overriding perception of what an MP looks like is usually male, with a nice wife who does a bit of work in the background, and two dear photogenic children' (*Telegraph*, 25.4.01). Browning's comments were made shortly after the party women's council warned Teresa May MP, Conservative Shadow Minister for Education and spokeswoman on women's issues, that the Conservative failure to select women for winnable seats risked alienating voters and prompting a legal challenge under the Human Rights Act. The previous year, Teresa Keswick of the Centre for Policy Studies criticised the Conservative Party for its poor progress in increasing women's political representation. In 1999 three senior Conservative women activists proposed radical reform of party organisation and of candidate selection procedures.[10] Although William Hague repeatedly urged Conservative Party activists to do more to select women for safe seats, such exhortations resulted in little change. Moreover, the reformed party infrastructure did not accommodate women organisationally. The Conservative Women's National Committee does not have a desk in Central

Office, and there is no vice-chair or equivalent level party official with responsibility for women's interests.

Liberal Democrats increased their number of women MPs to five, but in the process lost, in the excellent Jackie Ballard, one of their most talented and popular politicians. The Liberal Democrat record on selecting women candidates is an odd one. No women were selected for vacant Liberal Democrat seats. Despite growing support inside the party, Liberal Democrats stopped short of positive action in the selection of women candidates in all contests except the 1999 European elections when they used 'zipping', that is, they alternated men and women's names on party lists, to ensure women got equal representation to men in their delegation to the European Parliament. However, for the elections to the Scottish Parliament, the Welsh Assembly, and Westminster in 1997 and 2001, action to equalise representation was limited to voluntary measures. The result is that that the Liberal Democrat groups in Westminster and the Scottish Parliament are disproportionately male, although three LD men and three LD women were elected to the Welsh assembly in 1999.

Amongst the other parties the pattern varied. Neither of the Nationalist parties used effective positive action measures; both the SNP women MPs retired and a woman candidate replaced only one retirement. Plaid Cymru, having operated quotas for elections to the Welsh Assembly, selected no women to contest its Westminster retirement seats. Northern Irish voters however returned three women MPs, equal to the previous total of all women MPs from the province. This may have been a result of the response by parties to the challenge of the province's women's party, the Northern Ireland Women's Coalition who nominated candidates (unsuccessfully) for Westminster in 1997 and 2001 and (successfully) for the Northern Ireland Assembly in 1998. In summary, none of the major parties did much to increase the number of women in 2001, with the predictable result that the number of women MPs did not rise. To improve the situation parties had to nominate women for their vacant winnable seats, but that is precisely what they did not do. A total of five women and 70 men were nominated for vacant seats held by their parties produced by the retirements of 65 men and ten women.

Women and voting

At least two dimensions of voting are important to understanding the gender dynamics of electoral choice: how women vote in comparison to men and how voters react to women candidates. The long-standing gender gap whereby women were more likely than men to vote for the Conservative Party appeared to have closed in the 1997 general election, when exit polls indicated the gap had diminished to insignificance. After the election, analysis of the 1997 British Election Study by Pippa Norris demonstrated that differences in men's and women's voting continued and could be understood as a Con–Lab gender-generation gap whereby younger women were more likely than younger men to vote for the Labour Party and older women were more likely than older men to vote for the Conservative Party.[11] With more older women voters in the electorate the gender gap was especially beneficial to the Conservatives. The greater preferences of younger women for Labour, and the turn away by younger men from Labour, were indicators both that gender politics had become less stable and that women voters might be persuaded to vote Labour. Subsequent work by Rosie Campbell indicates that a full explanation also needs to take account of changes in patterns among men, notably that young men are turning away from the Labour Party, voting for other parties, or abstaining (*Guardian*, 5.4.01).

In the aftermath of the 1997 election Norris's analysis was accepted by feminists, who used the notion of a gender gap to influence party strategists interested in courting women's votes. Such advocacy sometimes came from unexpected sources. In spring 2001 *Good Housekeeping* magazine commissioned BMRB International to poll women on their political preferences and voting intentions. The results, published in early May 2001, just before the delayed election was called, were widely reported. The poll suggested that women doubted any political party was particularly interested in them. The majority of the women surveyed said they voted on issues and not on party lines. Only 51% were prepared to state a preference for a political party, some 29% thought Labour best served women's interests, whilst 13% preferred the Conservatives and only 9% the Liberal Democrats. Because of its one-off nature and the wording of its questions, the poll cannot be read in conjunction with standard analyses of voting intentions. However, it does accord with other findings about women's political preferences. The non-partisan feminist campaigning group the Fawcett Society analysed MORI polls conducted throughout 2000 in conjunction with focus groups conducted in October 2000.[12] Their report found that compared with men, women more likely to intend to vote, less likely to express satisfaction with the government, and more likely to be floating voters. In terms of priorities, women were more likely to seek assurances about education, health and pensions, but less concerned about Europe or taxes. Both women and men favoured paid leave for parents of newborn babies and affordable high-quality child care. Higher turnout, greater volatility, and more interest by women in domestic issues are characteristic features of the British gender gap, recurring in some form in every general election. The Fawcett Society used poll evidence to put pressure on politicians, arguing that a new kind of politics was necessary to win women voters. The society published a series of polls on women's representation and gave frequent press conferences on issues of women's representation and used every opportunity to draw attention to the gender gap in women's voting.

3. Estimated Con–Lab Voting Preference by Sex and Age, 2001

| | Men (%) | | Women (%) | | |
	Conservative	Labour	Conservative	Labour	Gender gap
18–24	29	38	24	45	12
25–34	24	52	25	49	−4
35–54	29	43	31	43	2
55+	33	39	40	38	−8

Notes: The gender gap is calculated as Conservative lead over Labour among men minus Conservative lead over Labour among women (% Con men − % Lab men) minus (% Con women − % Lab women). Source: Calculated from MORI General Election Aggregate May–June 2001.

With no demographic information from the exit polls, it is difficult to determine at present if a gender gap was present in 2001. The available evidence from the MORI campaign polls, consolidated to produce a total sample of 18,657 adults interviewed during the election, weighted by vote result and turnout, suggests that among the younger generation (18–24) the Labour lead over Conservatives among women was about 20 points, twice as much as among men. In the 25–34 and 35–54 age groups, however, either there was no gender gap or it was slightly reversed. Among the over 55s women preferred the Conservatives and MORI data describe a traditional gender gap of 8 points (see Table 3).[13]

Most studies agree that British voters do not penalise women candidates. Data from the British Parliamentary Constituency Results database suggests there was no penalty for women candidates in 2001. Indeed for the Labour and Conservative parties there may be a small gender bonus. For Labour candidates, the Labour to Conservative swing between 1997 and 2001 was greater for men (1.41) than women (1.21). For the Conservatives, the Labour to Conservative swing was greater for female (1.46) than male (1.35) candidates.[14]

Cabinet and government

Parliament is not only an institution of representation; it is also training ground for government. The presence of fair proportions of women in successive intakes of MPs is an important element in insuring that future governments are representative of both sexes. The successive increases in the number of women MPs during the 1990s are the basis for the remarkable feminisation of British government. Tony Blair's new government contained 33 women (31%) including seven in the Cabinet and 26 in other government positions. Three women are in charge of major spending departments — Margaret Beckett at the new Ministry of Food and Rural Affairs, Estelle Morris at Education and Skills, and Patricia Hewitt at Trade and Industry, who also has responsibility for women. Tony Blair's former political secretary, Sally Morgan, following an accelerated appointment to the House of Lords, becomes Minister for Women, a full-time paid post. She will be responsible for the women's unit, to be relaunched as the Women's and

Equality Unit, and she will chair the new Ministerial Subcommittee on Equality. Both Hewitt and Morgan are feminists and committed to the success of the women's ministry. Most of the women in Cabinet and government have political track records as women's advocates. Now most of them have the political experience to make a difference.

The inclusion of 33 women in the new Labour government depended mainly upon their entry into Parliament in previous elections, a phenomenon not matched in the other parties. Neither Liberal Democrats nor the Conservatives have a sufficient pool of women MPs on which to draw to form a leadership that is representative of women. This is well-illustrated by the Conservative leadership contest. Following the withdrawal of Anne Widdicombe, there are no women contenders for the Conservative leadership. Few Conservative or Liberal Democrat women MPs have name recognition; hence it is difficult to see how their future women leaders will be recruited.

Will women make a difference?

When the number of women MPs doubled (to 18%) after the 1997 election, much was expected of them. Since 1997 the key question about having more women in politics has been what difference they have made. Sometimes this has been a hostile question; asked by those observers whose distaste for women's presence in this once male bastion is palpable. The new Labour women MPs were frequently criticised in the press as nothing more than lobby-fodder and many were pilloried for adhering to party discipline in the House of Commons, criticism that reached its peak in the first session of Parliament when benefits to single mothers were cut and Labour women voted with their party. Such criticisms were often based on impressionistic evidence and unrealistically high expectations. In fact the available evidence is mixed. As discussed by Cowley elsewhere in this volume, analysis of legislative division's in the last Parliament shows that the new intake Labour women MPs were slightly less likely than their male equivalents to vote against their party.[15]

Although substantial qualitative evidence exists that women politicians work effectively on behalf of other women, raise women's issues and bring in women's perspectives, there are few systematic studies in Britain to confirm this. Realistically, it is probably too soon to know. Fewer than one fifth of MPs are women. Not all are feminists. Nor are all in favour of many of the proposals for parliamentary modernisation. About half of them have served only one term in an institution whose procedures are arcane and complicated.

Although women MPs have neither revolutionised the House of Commons, nor been roll call rebels, there is evidence that women MPs have worked well behind the scenes to secure reforms. For example, Fiona MacTaggart MP has described substantial policy changes that resulted from the interventions of women MPs.[16] Sarah Childs' interviews of Labour women MPs show that the 1997 cohort now contains many experienced women who think of themselves as in some sense, women's representatives. They are supported by many 'new men' who realise it is in their interest to regender politics.[17] An example of the effectiveness of Parliamentary women working together with women's advocates outside of Parliament is the campaign to change the law to allow positive action in favour of prospective women candidates. The Queen's speech setting out the legislative programme of the new Parliament included a pledge to legalise positive action in favour of women candidates. This means parties may, if they wish to, set compulsory quotas of women candidates and establish procedures to implement them. It returns the struggle for equality of women's representation to the political parties. It remains to be seen how the parties will act. The pledge to change the law is the result of a long campaign in which women MPs and ministers, women's advocacy organisations and even the notoriously timid Equal Opportunities Commission pressured for change. Influential pamphlets and reports making the case for change were published by the Fabian Society, the Constitution Unit and the Fawcett Society.[18] Recognising that, in the absence of legal change, the number of women in the next Parliament would fall, immediately after the 1997 election feminists inside and out of Parliament planned and implemented strategies to secure legal change. By the time of the election of 2001 women from the retiring Cabinet had sought and secured the Prime Minister's agreement to include the pledge in Labour's manifesto. However, that pledge is not yet redeemed and women MPs, ministers and lobbyists are continuing the pressure. The measure was included in the Queen's speech only after Harriet Harman, Solicitor General and Hilary Armstrong, Chief Whip insisted in the previous week's Cabinet meeting that delays would make it hard for parties to agree and introduce the required systems in time for the next elections. At the ensuing full Cabinet meeting Patricia Hewitt and Stephen Byers, Secretary for Transport, Local Government and the Regions had to fight for it again and the Prime Minister's intervention was required to guarantee its inclusion.[19]

Just as women's political preferences do not straightforwardly map onto party politics, feminist politics do not map directly onto parliamentary politics. It would be surprising if they did. Government is another matter, however. More than 30% of its members are women, some are in powerful positions. Their action over the law to allow positive action shows they do not intend to pull the ladder up after them.

Conclusion

The theories of critical mass and minority representation highlight the implications of long-term changes in women's representation. To understand and predict changes in a particular political system, however, it is necessary to take account of the methods of political recruitment, and also to consider the part played by advocates of women's representation inside and outside the political parties, Parliament and government. For women to benefit from the proposed measure, political parties will have to change their ways. Well aware of this imperative, feminists in all the main parties have begun mobilisation to ensure new procedures to ensure women's nominations for winnable seats. Labour and the Liberal Democrats are pledged to introduce some form of quota of women candidates, although the situation in the Conservative Party is currently unclear. Only one contender for the Conservative leadership (Michael Portillo) has publicly expressed support for quotas.

Feminist minority representation theory argues that a crucial point in the struggle for sex equality in politics comes when women politicians want to influence policy on behalf of women. Such measures are critical acts, that is, acts that change the position of the minority and lead to further changes. The most important critical acts are those that mobilise governing institutions to improve things for the minority group. If the government enacts the proposed new legislation permitting positive discrimination, then the minority of women politicians, working with the women's movement will have achieved a critical act of some importance. The adoption of quotas by political parties would provide an institutional resource for the future mobilisation of women who will no longer be required to struggle over and over again for political representation. The implementation of the law permitting positive discrimination will be a watershed in British politics, a striking indication of the growing political influence of women.

Joni Lovenduski

1   D. Dahlerup, 'From a Small to a Large Minority: Women in Scandinavian Politics', *Scandinavian Political Studies*, 1988; R.M. Kanter, *Men and Women of the Corporation*, Basic Books, 1977.
2   S. Tibballs, *The Sexual Renaissance*, Women's Communications Centre, 2000; 'Why Women are the Key to the Election', *Good Housekeeping*, May 2001.
3   *Independent Digital*, 5.6.01.
4   www.bbc.co.uk/vote 2001, accessed 21.5.01.
5   B. Gill, *Where is Worcester Woman?*, Fawcett Society, 2001.
6   M.A. Stephenson, Director, Fawcett Society.
7   Compiled by Loughborough University's Communications Group. For more details see Deacon et al. this volume.
8   Other party nominations of women were SNP: 16, PC: 8, Sinn Fein: 3, UDUP: 1, UUP: 2, SDLP: 6.
9   See B. Criddle, *Telegraph*, 9.6.01.
10   T. Keswick, R. Pockley and A. Guillaume, *Conservative Women*, Centre for Policy Studies, 1999.
11   P. Norris, 'Gender: A Gender generation Gap' in G. Evans and P. Norris (eds), *Critical Elections: British Parties and Values in Long-Term Perspective*, Sage, 1999.
12   B. Gill, *Where is Worcester Woman?*
13   MORI General Election Aggregate, 2001, information supplied by Roger Mortimer.
14   British Parliamentary Constituency Database, 1992–2001.
15   P. Cowley, 'An Uncritical Mass: New Labour Women MPs in the House of Commons', PSA Women and Politics Group Conference, Oxford, 17.2.01.
16   F. MacTaggart, Fabian Society Briefing Paper, 2000.

17 S. Childs, 'In Her Own Words: New Labour Women and the Substantive Representation of Women', *British Journal of Politics and International Relations*, June 2001.

18 M. Russell, *Women's Representation in UK Politics: What can be done within the Law*, Constitution Unit, 2000; H. Harman and D. Mattinson, *Winning for Women*, Fabian Society, 2000; B. Gill, *Winning Women: Lessons from Scotland and Wales*, Fawcett Society, 1999; M. Eagle and J. Lovenduski, *High Time or High Tide for Labour Women*, Fabian Society, 1998.

19 A. Perkins, *Guardian*, 21.6.01, p. 7.

SHAMIT SAGGAR

The Race Card, Again

Against expectations, the 2001 general election campaign illustrated the depth of ongoing disputes over race and immigration in British politics. These political differences were as much intra-party as inter-party in their nature and impact. Some six weeks before polling day, a political row erupted over the Commission for Racial Equality's Election Compact. The casual observer of the electoral landscape might have been forgiven for believing that British politics was following the path of the great arguments over race and immigration previously witnessed during the mid- to late 1970s. After more than a generation, the shrillness of those earlier debates could, it appears, be evoked at short notice and with considerable reverberations across the party system. The implication of this picture was serious and potentially alarming. It contained three core elements. Firstly, that political parties continued to assume that a 'race card' existed and might be deployed to sap the support of those caught on the wrong side of populist sentiment on race and immigration. This echoed the historic position that the Labour Party had found itself occupying starting with the Smethwick episode in 1964 and climaxing in its much larger electoral vulnerability on the immigration question during the late 1970s. In 2001, it was surmised, a similar potential lay dormant in voting behaviour and its deployment continued to guide the calculations of party strategists.

Secondly, the 2001 contest reignited, in the most dramatic fashion, long-standing divisions within the Conservative Party on matters of ethnic and cultural pluralism. These divisions had been debated extensively in proxy terms during the 1997 Parliament. At one level, senior figures in the party wished to present this debate as part of the challenge of modernising the party, chiefly in organisational and structural, rather than ideological terms. At another level, the venom that the debate invoked suggested to many that a long-seated, structural fault-line existed in the Conservative Party on race. Navigating these rival interpretations rapidly developed into a core element of party leadership in 2001 and, with it, acted as a useful metaphor for wider evaluation of leadership effectiveness and credibility.

Thirdly, partially as a result of the two earlier points, the major political parties gave fresh attention to the question of the political recruitment and candidacy of blacks and Asians. Labour's record in this area may barely have been questioned, but its difficulties in managing local disputes over 'ethnic entryism' continued to feature prominently. For the Conservatives, the problem of scarce ethnic minorities in winnable seats, was just one element in a wider concern about the party's willingness to promote an inclusive Conservative doctrine. Lady Thatcher's speech on 29 May 2001 in Northampton calling for increased number of Tory black and Asian parliamentary candidates raised the fundamental underlying question of how far the party, especially at local level, wished to welcome such activists to begin with. This in turn amounted to another opportunity to address the matter of Conservative renewal, both philosophical and managerial, on not merely racial questions but also in terms of several other intractable issues such as relations with the EU, personal morality, and criminal justice.

The politics the 'race card' thesis, 2001

The notion that anti-immigrant and anti-ethnic minority sentiment underscores mass electoral behaviour has been a familiar — and often depressing — feature of modern British politics. Indeed, so common has this claim become in the past two generations, it has emerged as something of a dictum among practitioners and analysts of British politics.[1] The 'race card doctrine', as this argument has become known, appears a semi-permanent feature of general elections. This ascendancy is not particularly surprising, given the nature of party competition and strategy over the immigration question in the 1960s and 1970s. The political landscape by the late 1970s was rooted in an assumption that the political interests of ethnic minorities were deeply unpopular among voters at large and, more controversially, that such sentiment was relatively easily turned into electoral spoils for parties wishing to exploit this truth. Debates have persisted on the nature and scale of this type of race card dividend but most commentators suggest that the factor has been an important influence upon Tory and Labour strategy over more than thirty years. The idea of a race card, therefore, is a form of political science and journalistic shorthand that refers generally to the structural advantage enjoyed by one major party over its rivals on the electoral issues of race and immigration. More specifically, in the British context, the thesis concerns the head start that the Conservative Party has had over Labour on this broad issue, not least within the contiguity of electoral unpopularity during the 1970s on other more mainstream issues (e.g. trade union reform and social welfare provision). The head of steam that had developed in the run-up to the 1997 general election surrounding the Conservative position on the race card cannot be understated. Likewise, in 2001, similar expectations existed about the opposition's willingness to exploit electoral populism on this issue.

The assumption spans academic and journalistic commentary and it has been treated in some quarters as an iron law of white antipathy and hostility to non-white immigrants and their offspring. That is to say, this caricature is thought to unite the bulk of white opinion in a near-permanent and fatalistic way. Parties, therefore, might choose to turn their backs on such skewed public opinion and its associated opportunities; however, traditional rational choice considerations suggest that they adopt such a line at their own peril.

There are some implicit suggestions that arise from parties taking the race card as some sort of irresistible force in this way: first, that political parties are both fully cognisant of the structure and character of public opinion, and second, that parties are able to alter their position on issues at short notice and with little cost to themselves. The race card in this sense amounts to a case study in the wider-reputed features of party competition. By testing the limits of the thesis, we can draw some useful conclusions about the underlying dynamics of parties, issues and voters.[2]

The context of the 2001 campaign

The 2001 campaign differs from earlier campaigns in many important areas. To begin with, fairly robust evidence shows that the electoral unpopularity of ethnic minorities and their associated interests, however widespread or otherwise, was no longer singularly associated strongly with the Labour Party. Indeed, this turnaround in comparison with previous era had already taken place in 1997. Colleagues in the 1997 British Election Study (BES) consortium had shown that New Labour had successively jettisoned its earlier mass image as the party especially linked with promoting black and Asian interests.[3] The proportion of whites that felt that Labour was 'very closely' identified with such interests had more than halved between 1987–97, thereby questioning fundamentally one of the main planks of the traditional race card thesis. Secondly, the 1997 Parliament witnessed extensive party and media interest devoted to the issue of asylum and its political management, raising the profile of the topic of immigration to a level far higher than that seen since the very early 1980s. The possibility — probability even — remained that asylum amounted to little more than a reprising of the much older immigration debate. If voters saw few real distinctions between these matters, the most likely outcome would be a tactical attempt to harness public hostility in electoral terms. For this most basic of reasons, both the major parties have broadly adopted a strategy of issue containment, whereby the presumption remains that a powerful electoral penalty would be incurred for ignoring public opinion. Labour's recognition of this constraint can be dated explicitly to the mid-1990s whilst in opposition. Jack Straw, speaking as then Shadow Home Secretary, announced in 1995 that: 'We should not allow so much as a cigarette card to come between the Labour Party and the Tory government on immigration.'[4] On the Conservative side, the approach was built on adaptation of scepticism towards the value of immigration, whether economic or political. Under the watch of Anne Widdecombe in the Shadow Home Affairs portfolio, the strategy was to draw on this background and focus on the alleged lack of managerial credibility of the Labour administration.

Making the implicit connection between the asylum and immigration issues, the debate in the 2001 election begged the question as to how far the electorate's mood continued to be as hostile as it had been a generation earlier. On this point, there have been heated arguments as well, not least surrounding the partly conceptual dimensions of the asylum and immigration issues in the minds of voters. For instance, somewhat surprisingly, the pollster ICM released evidence in the middle of the campaign that questioned fundamentally the popular assumption that tough anti-immigrant public sentiment existed (ICM data quoted in the *Guardian*, 21.5.01). The poll showed that 70% of respondents supported the proposition that 'more people should be allowed to come and live in Britain who have skills that are in short supply here, like teachers, nurses and doctors'. Conversely, three quarters of those in the same poll opposed policies to encourage the entry of those without such short-supply skills. Finally, the ICM poll also confirmed that, beneath the surface, clear racial or colour-led distinctions existed in public attitudes towards the sources of possible increased immigration to meet labour shortages. Some 54% reported that they approved of such migrants settling in their neighbourhood who were drawn from a white South African background. For other non-white nominated groups support was generally much lower: just 23% approved of local settlement by Iraqis, although this figure surged to 47% who approved of more Chinese immigrants in their neighbourhoods.

If evidence of public attitudes such as the ICM data revealed anything, it was that aspects of the popular electoral mood did not chime so clearly with the strategy adopted by the Conservative Party. At one level, the data indicated that the Tories had in effect lost the lead over Labour on the asylum issue. This meant that the traditional race card argument could not be applied to the 2001 general election campaign and such evidence pointed to signs of serious miscalculation by the official opposition. The Conservative's approach appeared to be guided by the logic of the 1992 campaign during which Andrew Lansley had boasted that 'the immigration [issue] had played particularly well in the tabloids and has the potential to hurt'. By 2001 Lansley had become a senior election strategist at Central Office, carrying with him much the same outlook as nine years previously. An editorial in the *Guardian* made the devastating point that this outlook now seemed outdated at best and counterproductive at worst:

Ironically, the public is applying the common sense which William Hague so frequently calls for. It has rightly displayed utter scepticism towards Tory

1. Attitudes Towards Non-White Immigration, 1997 (%)

	White	Indian	Pakist	Bang.	Bl-Af	Bl-Car	Misc.
Very/fairly good	19.5	65.8	65.6	67.2	65.2	63.2	55.2
Neither good nor bad	41.1	23.7	17.9	17.2	22.0	21.1	22.9
Fairly/very bad	36.6	6.8	8.9	3.4	5.5	12.0	17.1
DK/not answered	2.9	3.8	3.7	12.1	7.3	3.6	4.8

Notes: 'Do you believe immigration by blacks and Asians has been good or bad for GB?', weighted data; N = 4,204 BES 1997. Source: S. Saggar, *Race and Representation*, Manchester University Press, 2000.

asylum policy. For good reasons too. [The evidence] turns conventional Westminster wisdom about immigration — the impossibility of opening a door for economic migrants — on its head (*Guardian*, 23.5.01).

Furthermore, evidence gathered earlier by the 1997 BES suggested that a long-run sea change in public attitudes was a distinct possibility. The BES showed, somewhat surprisingly, that public attitudes on the immigration question from the past were not as polarised as many political elites had assumed. As Table 1 below shows, it was striking that clear, anti-immigrant white opinion, even when expressed in such historic terms, amounted to just over a third of the sample. An ample majority were, in other words, either enthusiasts for past immigration or, crucially from the perspective of mobilising voters, they preferred to sit on the fence on the issue. An obvious lesson from such evidence is that party strategists' thinking had tended to exaggerate the scale of the underlying level of public sentiment against past immigration. It was comparatively easy then to take at face value polling evidence during the parliament that indicated a robust and hostile attitude among voters towards the claims of asylum seekers. Voters appeared to see distinctions between the legacy of past New Commonwealth immigration and current rows over asylum. The Conservative opposition saw greater conflation of the two, and may have constructed a much bolder voter strategy than underlying public attitudes could sustain.

Some further issues and paradoxes buried in the 1997 BES data show wider social attitudes on questions of ethnic and cultural pluralism. To begin with, a generational element is found in the 61% of whites who failed to embrace the anti-immigration line: this figure rose to 86% of those below the age of 24. The 1997 BES also reported that 41% of whites accepted that Britain 'had a lot to learn' from other countries rising to 64% below 24. Meanwhile, the 1997–2001 Parliament was punctuated by a number of poll findings in which reasonably robust levels of scepticism and opposition were expressed in relation to asylum seekers. A cross-section of these polls showed that between a half and two-thirds of respondents stated that they were opposed to further immigration in general, with attitudes tightening against the idea of liberalising entry requirements for asylum applicants.[5]

A further twist was the Labour government's steady desire to revisit the question of economic migration. In September 2000, the immigration minister, Barbara Roche, delivered a long awaited speech setting out a strategic vision to encourage greater competition by the UK for the skilled and talented would-be migrants. Labour had historically been reluctant to press such a case in public for fear that its traditional support among white working-class voters may be damaged as a result. This had been the experience of the party in and out of government in the 1960s and 1970s. Political memories of this kind, quite naturally, are slow to fade. The upshot was that the party's psycho-political posture was highly guarded on the issue, even though the policy instincts of senior members of the administration were to re-examine the case for economic immigration. Publication of the report commissioned by the government was delayed by almost six months because of this ongoing dilemma.[6] It was eventually released as a Home Office research document partly to establish some political distance between its recommendations and its original sponsor, the Prime Minister.

The challenge faced by parties in the 2001 general election was to face up to the catch-all assumption that immigration, of whatever kind, was an automatic vote loser. The evidence suggests that it was not, at least in the sense that the question was far from being seen as a one of the key salient issues of the election campaign. Where public attitudes were mobilised it is not certain that anti-immigration sentiment was as one-sided as it had been in the past. Finally, the Labour administration's decision to tackle this potentially damaging issue on the front foot can only have served to water down the electoral penalty it faced. In this regard, the Conservative Party's sudden display of internal dissent over multiculturalism and its own record, permitted the Labour Party to operate with much greater leeway than it had enjoyed in past elections.

Internal Conservative discord on race

The 2001 general election demonstrated the capacity of the issues of race and immigration to dominate the agenda of the campaign at short notice. The principal reason for this was the difficulties experienced by the Conservatives in managing a coherent party line on such issues. In mid-March 2001, the Conservative Party voluntarily participated in a public signing ceremony for the Election Compact, an open statement of intent, sponsored by the Commission for Racial Equality (CRE), to refrain from exploiting racial and ethnic stereotypes in the forthcoming general election. All three main party leaders took part in the event that received only limited media coverage. The Compact had in fact been first used by the CRE in the 1997 election, but by 2001 it sought to raise the profile of the exercise. Whereas in 1997 party leaders had been asked unambiguously to sign on behalf of their MPs and party membership, in spring 2001 this point remain hazy. It was on this technical-procedural matter that a major row erupted when the CRE, in response to press inquiries, publicised the fact that individual MPs had been asked to sign and register their support and that a small number of

Tory MPs had declined to do so. John Townend, MP for Yorkshire East bordering William Hague's own seat, went further and began a media campaign to explain his (in)action alongside his wider views on British multiculturalism and the role of government in failing to build such a society. By mid-April the Conservatives' problems escalated hugely with the intervention of John Taylor, the only black Tory life peer, who had reached prominence in 1991–92 as the party's PPC in Cheltenham. The Cheltenham episode had sparked massive infighting among the Tories on race, some fairly blunt, and had left the party nursing open wounds on the question. Moreover, it had not helped resolve the long-term position of black and Asian party members with ambitions to build political careers at Westminster. Taylor struck out against Townend in an effective battle of 'Two Johns' to try to capture the future direction of party thinking on racial and ethnic integration. The result was little more than a score draw, with both men and their supporters citing elements of victory ('Tightrope walk in search of harmony', *Guardian*, 24.4.01). It was Taylor's challenge that went furthest, however, since his supporters made plain that he would consider defecting from the party unless William Hague successfully reigned in the Townend tendency.

The Conservatives rediscovered that they were a party in which a series of *ad hoc* and opportunistic agreements had evolved on racial issues over many years. These lay beneath the immediate dynamics of an internal race row and were not hard to identify once the argument threatened to go beyond a pre-campaign skirmish. The row quickly reverted media and grassroots attention back to the Conservative's own track record in appealing to ethnic minority voters. The evidence in this arena was far from reassuring.[7] Data on voting behaviour displayed some depressing messages for the Tories. In 1997 BES evidence showed that the party attracted only 11.5% of all votes cast by blacks and Asians. This figure comprised some sharp variations among specific component groups of the minority electorate but nevertheless was a poor record overall. Such evidence rekindled fears expressed within and around the party that minority voters found elements of the Conservative's sub-Powellite rhetoric highly off-putting. Party membership evidence gathered in the mid-1990s estimated that the black and Asian membership of the Tories stood at no more than 1%. The same data reported continuing adherence to uncompromising Conservative attitudes on immigration: some 70% of party members declared their support for the repatriation of immigrants.[8] Again, this tended to reinforce a picture of an unattractive environment for would-be black and Asian party members, one of the core elements of Taylor's attack on the party leadership.[9]

Against this backdrop, the new party leadership after 1997 was undoubtedly keen to make advances in raising the profile of the Tories in the eyes of black and Asian recruits and supporters. One obvious element in this strategy was the advantage thought to accrue from the youthfulness of William Hague. On these grounds, the impression was given that Hague was arguably more at home in a multiethnic, multicultural society. Indeed, his dubious early decision to be photographed 'at home' at the Notting Hill carnival was largely inspired by this perspective. In truth, however, it was a tactic that was first deployed by John Major in the 1990s. Beyond personal leadership, the Conservatives were also pre-occupied in their first spell in opposition with the task of re-engineering the party's membership base and organisational character. The vice-chairmanship of Archie Norman, and later Steven Norris, involved major efforts to widen the membership base. Recruiting and retaining new types of party members was partly spearheaded by a new organisation, Conservative Network, as well as by the Cultural Unit, a small dedicated infrastructure at Central Office. The work of individuals such as Baroness Peta Buscombe in promoting a broader membership, especially among younger women, was cited to back the effort of modernisers. Finally, the party's first period out of office for a generation was also significant in prompting a reasonably sophisticated internal debate over its core values and how these failed or succeeded to be transmitted to ethnic minority potential supporters. For some this debate went too far and smacked of a convenient denunciation of immediate past strengths. For others, it was an admission that the party had missed obvious opportunities and that it had no one to blame for its general image among minority voters. At the party conference in October 2000, one notable right-winger, John Bercow, made a passionate speech in which he conceded that many Conservatives had made a poor job of bringing aspiring blacks and Asians into the Tory fold. The principal reason, he argued, had been an excess of nationalist and isolationist rhetoric in the past, some of which he accepted had been a fall-out from the Thatcherite agenda of the 1980s. The speech was widely caricatured as a *mea culpa* admission of collective guilt, implying that more such admissions may be required before the party stood ready to rebuild, let alone regovern.

Another element of the underlying debate was to do with the basic stance of the Conservative Party toward past and future immigration. On this point, a delicate truce has been in force within ranks of the party for many years. Strong critics of past immigration increasingly recognised that it was difficult for the party to reopen arguments about the legitimacy of South Asian and Caribbean immigration during the 1950s–1970s. Criticism was instead reserved for the long run consequences of that earlier immigration. The social and cultural demands that immigration had brought were thus emphasised sidelining much discussion of the opportunities it may have created as well. Thus, Robin Cook's celebration of 'Chicken Tikka Masala' as Britain's national dish just prior to the formal campaign was designed above all to direct fire at the Tories. This was because the Conservative Party contained a large structural fault line on this core question and Labour strategy held that it could only be electorally productive to target this sensitivity. Perversely, Cook's condemnatory remarks aimed at Anne Widdecombe, Shadow Home Secretary, must have come close to the type of exploitative behaviour that the original CRE Compact was designed to prevent.

The Taylor/Townend row failed to bring the Conservatives any closer to a resolution on this fault line. Following the heavy general election defeat, it is apparent that senior Tories in the leadership race, including Michael Portillo and Kenneth Clarke, have been prepared to cite the tough campaign on the asylum issue as electoral folly.[10] At the very least, these Tory modernisers argued, the issue entrenched the image of the party as an extreme force. It is also equally the case that many other senior figures, led by Iain Duncan Smith, have resisted this charge, thus demonstrating that the old divisions over immigration remain as precarious as ever. Ultimately these doubts over the value of immigration are not just designed to play on public attitudes about past immigration. The stance of the party towards any major recalibratation of the immigration regime in the future is also at stake. This in turn will affect the bipartisan nature of future policy direction. The parallel case of the US Republicans appears to be relevant here. In the 2000 presidential nomination and general election contest, it was striking to note how far the leadership of George W. Bush was prepared to adopt a market liberal-inspired, pro-immigration stance. In August 2000, the *Wall Street Journal* concluded that: 'The Republicans first walked into the immigration cul-de-sac about 15 years ago. They then jumped off the cliff in the early 1990s. Governor Bush has avoided the immigrant-bashing trend. He is now putting his stamp on the national party, with a platform that describes immigrants as wealth-producers, not as drains on the Treasury' ('Republicans meet the world' (editorial), *Wall Street Journal*, 2.8.00). Allowing for obvious differences in policy-making party machinery in US politics, it is not hard to see the kind of prize envisaged by one part of the Conservative Party. The difficulty is that something of the opposite is treasured by another faction within the party. It was therefore no surprise to observe the clash between these competing visions.

The 2001 campaign row may also serve as a useful barometer of Tory attitudes and instincts on a wide variety of policy concerns. These range from the narrow immigration and asylum agenda, through to relations with European Union partners, European integration, globalisation, and collective security arrangements. These are arguably major political debates across the British political landscape but all draw upon each party's underlying orientation towards internationalism versus isolationism. The Conservative Party experienced heavy short-term pressures on all these fronts, questioning the party's true intellectual, cultural and even emotional instincts. These may have become muddled and less coherent in the cold climate of an impossible election campaign.

This may be a charitable interpretation since the party leader had set as his core task the need to provide a clear lead on these matters. In that sense, the Taylor/Townend affair marked an important, late test for the quality of judgment under Hague's leadership. Supporters and critics alike appeared to conclude that he had failed to meet this task, not least by stalling for time on the presumed need to discipline alleged heretics. During the campaign the Labour Party presented this as a challenge that would help to settle the question of Hague's long-term security as party leader. In the event, Hague had previously decided to step down if he did not achieve his minimal electoral goal of gaining 30 seats. The basic point was not lost on party supporters and ex-supporters, however, namely that Hague's position contrasted sharply with Blair's hold over his party. Additionally, it was widely noted that any successful Tory leader would need to be prepared to push through organisational, policy and other changes in order to rejuvenate the Conservative Party. In other words, the challenge to Hague's leadership was not merely to find a way to silence opposing camps on race but rather to develop and implement a plan for a more enduring peace.

Recruiting and electing ethnic minority candidates

It has been fourteen years since the election of the first wave of black and Asian MPs to the Commons in the modern era. All four of these pioneers — Diane Abbott, Paul Boateng, the late Bernie Grant, and Keith Vaz — were elected as Labour MPs. This development served as a watershed in getting the broader issue of political representation of ethnic minorities onto the radar of modern British politics. One of those elected in 1987, Paul Boateng, later drew specific reference to the mandate that black and Asian MPs had, in his words, 'struggled for racial justice'. Moreover, he claimed, the presence of black and brown faces in the Commons went beyond symbolism.

By 2001 pressure had grown to evaluate the wider context of race and political representation and recruitment in British politics. The past decade has seen a small number of high-profile controversies over race, candidate selection, performance (such as the John Taylor episode in Cheltenham) and numerous rows over 'ethnic entryism' in the Labour Party.[11] In the years since 1987, several more black and Asian MPs have entered Parliament.[12] The pioneers here have been Ashok Kumar and Parmjit Dhanda, both of whom have arguably broken through the colour-coded mould elected to represent ethnic minorities. At local government-level, the number of black and Asian elected councillors has swollen in recent elections, reaching near or parity levels in many industrial cities and in several of the capital's boroughs.[13]

Yet this superficial record of progress still belies the difficulties and dilemmas faced by ethnic minority political aspirants in gaining a foot on the ladder to elected office. Many of these tensions are far from new, but increasingly they take place in an atmosphere in which there is renewed interest in race and political representation. The chief bone of contention has been the debate over so-called 'under-representation'. In particular, this debate has asked: how far is it reasonable to caricaturise the established political parties as unresponsive to change? Additionally, against what benchmarks of representative theory should party efforts to advance ethnic minority candidacies be measured?

The 2001 general election saw a record number of ethnic minority PPCs (64 in total) in the colours of the three main parties. This figure was a third higher than in 1997, whilst back in 1979, there had been only five such candidacies. Back in June 1970, David Pitt, Labour's black candidate in the winnable seat of Clapham, suffered a dramatic defeat, and thus underscored the virtual absence of minorities in candidate roles. The received wisdom from his experience was that minority candidates were an electoral liability for parties. The long-term result was a form of imputed discrimination against black and Asian hopefuls, with risk-averse party selectors conceding that such candidates ought to be held back, not because of their prejudices but rather those of the voters.

Of those successfully elected in 2001, the earlier pattern of Labour dominance continues. The newcomers, Parmjit Dhanda and Khalid Mahmood, have served to increase Labour Party's presence to 12 MPs. The third would-be new boy, Shailesh Vara, for the Conservatives, was defeated in Northampton South. Despite this setback, he had attracted enormous attention as the sole Tory hopeful in the 2001 contest. Moreover, as a younger, professional Asian, Vara was widely expected to embody a fresh start in his party's underlying relationship with ethnic minority groups. The genuinely interesting distinction, however, operated not between Labour and Conservative, young and old, or even front and backbench; rather, it lay between the bulk of minority MPs who were returned as representatives of constituencies with large minority populations, and those who are not. The latter in essence includes only Dhanda and the incumbent Kumar. This pattern is described in Table 2.

2. Ethnic Minority MPs, 2001

Candidate	Constituency	1997 Majority (%)
P. Khabra	Ealing Southall	39.2
A. Kumar	Middlesborough South	19.8
K. Vaz	Leicester East	41.5
M. Sawar	Glasgow Govan	9.0
M. Hendrick	Preston	38.9
D. Lammy	Tottenham	53.6
O. King	Bethnal Green and Bow	25.3
P. Boateng	Brent South	57.1
D. Abbott	Hackney North and Stoke Newington	47.6
M. Singh	Bradford West	8.5
K. Mahmood	Birmingham Perry Bar	41.3
P. Dhanda	Gloucester	14.3

Source: *The Times Guide to the House of Commons*.

The nature of Britain's representative democracy can be measured across a number of indicators. John Taylor and others thrust one potential indicator — the representation of ethnic minorities — into the glare of public scrutiny by a series of complaints in the run-up to the 2001 general election. The ability and willingness of political parties and democratic institutions to respond to multicultural diversity has become for some a key test of the representativeness of British political life. For instance, the Parekh Report (based on the Commission on the Future of Multi-Ethnic Britain) reported in 2000 that: 'Each party should publish plans on how it proposes to ensure that more Asian and black candidates are selected for safe and winnable seats. Parties should particularly aim to include Asian and black candidates on shortlists in constituencies where at least 25% of the electorate is Asian or black.'[14] In the eyes of critics of the Report, this approach ran the risk of a form of political ghettoisation. Nevertheless, this conclusion was far from heretical within the growing debate on ethnic minority political representation. It remains too early to speculate as to whether the Dhanda case in 2001 will prove to be part of a longer run trend. At present it appears much of an exception along with Kumar in Middlesborough.

One of the principal reasons behind the pattern of ethnic minority candidate selection has been the widespread notion that former electoral liabilities (as minority hopefuls were universally viewed ten or twenty years ago) may have emerged as effective electoral assets for parties facing constituencies with many ethnic minority voters. For instance, the incumbent Keith Vaz found himself facing an Asian LibDem PPC, while Marsha Singh had to battle with high-profile Asian LibDem and Conservative opponents. Indeed, this was a pattern found among half of the total number of successful black and Asian candidates as shown in Table 2. This in turn was heavily influenced by recent evidence to show that the force of ethnic loyalty could on occasion trump the usual allegiances of party label. After all, the memory of 1997 had not faded by 2001: King in east London and Singh in Bradford both experienced significant negative swings to their Conservative opponents. In both cases, the Tories had fielded candidates drawn more closely from the ethnic character of the local minority electorate than the Labour Party. In 2001 there was a widespread expectation of a further demonstration of the 'pull' of ethnic loyalty in voting behaviour. In the event there was no repeat of the scale witnessed in 1997. However, rows about the manner of selection of a handful of black and Asian PPCs reignited long-standing arguments over 'ethnic entryism' in the Labour Party and, to a lesser degree, among its opponents. Allegations and counter-allegations of malpractice and deceit especially clouded Mahmood late selection (February 2001) in Birmingham. There had been other similar rows in the 1997 Parliament although on a smaller scale than those seen in the selection battles of the previous parliament. The underlying theme of these debates was the charge that elements of Asian community-based political mobilisation threatened the traditional ideological and class basis of Labour's organisational and voting character. At worst it was suggested that specific methods of gathering and deploying party members were improper in that they fed the political ambitions of specific candidates who shared ethnic characteristics rather than others. At best the concern was that Labour might become too closely associated with Asian community politics with the residual risk of a white electoral backlash.

The 2001 election also took place in a mood of greater probing and inquisition about the nature of political representation. The Wakeham Commission on Lords Reform had reported during the parliament and, whatever else, had endorsed the principle of an upper chamber that was a better social reflection of British society. The presence of ethnic minority members of a reformed upper house was singled out as an important marker. Meanwhile, the Electoral Reform Society was engaged in two pertinent reviews, one of which looked at parliamentary scrutiny and the other at candidate selection. Both inquiries served inevitably to raise the salience of issues of ethnic minority political representation. The Labour Party launched in 2000 a new campaigning body, EQ, designed to promote equality themes in the party's policy-making and candidate recruitment arenas. The Conservative's Cultural Unit took on a similar, though lower profile, agenda in the party and was especially active in support and networking roles for Tory black and Asian political hopefuls. The Liberal Democrats, alone among the major parties, launched an Ethnic Minority Mini-Manifesto at the start of the formal campaign. In addition to endorsing the general case for increased ethnic minority political participation and representation, the party placed heavy emphasis on its existing commitment to electoral reform. The document singled out the Jenkins Commission's proposed for AV+ as an acceptable first step to be put a public referendum, but stressed that its preferred STV option would be most effective in making parliament accountable to and reflective of British society. Beyond parties themselves, NGO campaign groups had also raised the profile of selection and representation themes. Operation Black Vote, a cross-party pressure group, successfully pioneered an ethnic minority parliamentary shadowing scheme during the 1997 Parliament. An important outcome of this initiative for OBV was in raising its political credibility on debates over future reforms of parties' candidate selection procedures. A timely opportunity for this arrived just before the election when Baroness Jay, the government's Leader in the House of Lords, signalled her willingness to reopen the legal barriers against all-women shortlists. As expected, this proposal was translated into a formal commitment shortly after Labour's re-election in which a permissive, though not mandatory, legal regime would be introduced into party selection rules (see Lovenduski this volume). The obvious parallel lay in the degree of commitment, if any, to bring about similar concessions for all-minority shortlists. For OBV and its supporters, this development represented a major breakthrough and the basis of a fresh campaign.

Conclusion: Labour in office and racial politics

A decade before Labour's emphatic re-election of 2001, the party's outlook towards issues of race and immigration had been shaped by two principal concerns. First, in 1992 (and previously in the routs of the 1980s), senior party figures had concluded that an excessively close association with black and Asian political interests in the minds of voters had been a powerful factor behind the party's electoral crisis. Ethnic minorities, whether as organised interests, voting groups or representatives of discrete communities, were essentially viewed as an electoral liability. Of course, Labour, along with its rivals, was able to extract short-term advantage in mobilising black and Asian voters, but, overall, the picture gained from the party's links with minorities was depressingly bleak. Above all, the historic legacy of the 'race card', encapsulated in Labour's palpable vulnerability on the immigration issue since the 1960s, meant that the strategic posture of the party was the minimise and offset this negative imagine of the party. Tough, uncompromising rhetoric — and action — on immigration and asylum policy was just one, highly tangible manifestation of this outlook.

The experience of holding office from 1997 onwards partly readjusted this outlook and allowed some, though not all, of the anxieties of the past to melt away. The upshot was a posture during the 2001 election campaign that could scarcely have been imagined a decade previously. For instance, the process of commissioning the Stephen Lawrence Inquiry, and the resultant recommendations of the Macpherson Report, during the parliament had demonstrated to Labour's own leaders and supporters that issues of racial harassment and equality could indeed be prioritised in office. This had been an uneasy experience for Labour in office, not least because elements of the Macpherson conclusion had not commanded the bipartisan support of previous policy initiatives on race and inequality (e.g. the three Race Relations Acts, the Scarman Report, and urban renewal efforts under the Conservatives in the 1980s). The final product of the Labour administration's focus on racial equality was the 2000 Race Relations (Amendment) Act, a major legislative achievement that the party would have habitually vetoed from consideration whilst in opposition.

The 2001 election therefore served to reopen in the Labour Party the hitherto orthodoxy that the party 'was damned if it did, and damned of it did not' to take any sort of policy lead on race and immigration. The first term had witnessed significant initiatives taken in both areas, together with a considerable effort to re-engineer major planks of social policy and welfare provision. These latter two policy domains were closely identified with Labour's over-arching strategy of trying to deliver reforms that were sensitive to black and Asian interests in employment, housing and public services whilst in no way seeking to target explicitly such groups. In terms of political representation and participation the election largely extended trends that had been long established. Labour's historic grip of black and Asian voters and representatives was barely questioned, let alone challenged, in the election. The longer run significance of the 2001 contest, therefore, lay in serving to demonstrate — to the Labour Party as much as others — that its earlier, well-founded phobia of close identification with ethnic minorities no longer drained its electoral competitiveness. The election result is probably an insufficient reason to conclude that the basic calculus of racial and electoral politics has been altered fundamentally. It is, however, a basis for thinking that the equation has been — and is being — revised. Descriptions of the map of British electoral politics will need to take account of this important revision.

Shamit Saggar

1   See for instance: I. Crewe, 'Representation and Ethnic Minorities in Britain' in N. Glazer and K. Young (eds), *Ethnic Pluralism and Public Policy*, Heinemann; S. Saggar, 'Smoking Guns and Magic Bullets: The "Race Card" Debate Revisited in 1997', *Immigrants and Minorities*, 17, 1998, 1–21; Y. Alibhai-Brown, *True Colours: Public Attitudes to Multiculturalism and the Role of Government*, London: Institute for Public Policy Research, 1999.

2   The shift in the policy mood running up the 2001 general election is a point also pursued in the introductory chapter. It is worth stressing the point that the Conservative's overarching strategy appeared to engage a public opinion structure that was insufficiently tuned to 2001, despite several obvious advantages in terms of the saliency of the asylum issue. See also: J. Stimson, *Public Opinion in America: Moods, Cycles and Swings*, Westview, 1991.

3   A. Heath and J. Curtice, 'New Labour, New Voters?', paper presented to 1998 PSA annual conference, Nottingham University.

4   Quoted in K. Amin and R. Richardson, 'Campaigning and Politics for a Multi-Ethnic Good Society' in S. Saggar (ed.), *Race and British Electoral Politics*, UCL Press, 1998.

5   See http://www.telegraph.co.uk/et?ac=000116001100774&rtmo=gj7ngwSu&atmo=gj7ngwSu.

6   *Migration: An Economic and Social Analysis*, PIU/Home Office RDS Occasional Paper 67, 2001.

7   At the time of publication the results of the 2001 General Census were not available. Using 1991 Census data, the UK's population drawn from a black or Asian ethnic origin totalled a little under 2.4 million persons. Estimates based on Labour Force Survey data from the mid- and late 1990s suggest that the black and Asian population may have risen by between 20 and 25% from the official 1991 count. Estimates of voter numbers depend in turn on differential age structures, registration and turnout rates, and these are not as a whole markedly out of line with whites. Ethnic minority electors constituted 5.5% of the population, and the proportion within the electorate would have been a little less than this figure. The 2001 Census figures are likely to update these existing proportions quite considerably. See: S. Saggar, *Race and Representation*, Manchester University Press, 2000, p. 94.

8   P. Whiteley et al., *True Blues: The Politics of Conservative Party Membership*, Clarendon Press, 1994, p. 253.

9   A recent poll of 500 Conservative Party members (including a handful of local chairmen) revealed that grassroots attitudes on issues of multiculturalism have probably hardened, rather than softened. This evidence further extends the picture sketched several years previously by Whiteley et al., (op. cit.) and demonstrates how far the party remains unreconstructed on this and other core attitudinal concerns. See: http://www.YouGov.com.

10 Amanda Platell's notorious campaign video diary claims that Portillo intervened during the campaign to advise that Hague publicly reject Lady Thatcher's sceptical remarks about multiculturalism. Platell reports that the party leader failed to take this advice, at least partly because of the existing tough line on the asylum issue.

11 A. Geddes, 'Race Related Politics and its Representational Consequences' in S. Saggar, K. Thomson

and A. Heath (eds), *Social Change and Minority Ethnic Groups in Britain*, British Academy/Oxford University Press, forthcoming.

12 Dianne Abbott (elected June 1987), Paul Boateng (elected June 1987), Piara Khabra (elected April 1992), Oona King (elected May 1997), Ashok Kumar (elected May 1997; first elected in a by-election in November 1991; defended unsuccessfully in April 1992 and re-election in May 1997), David Lammy (elected July 2000 by-election), Mark Hendrick (elected 2000 by-election), Mohammed Sarwar (elected May 1997), Marsha Singh (elected May 1997), Keith Vaz (elected June 1987); Parmjit Dhanda (elected June 2001); and Khalid Mahmood (elected June 2001).

13 M. Le Lohé, 'Ethnic Minority Participation and Representation in the British Electoral System' in S. Saggar (ed.), *Race and British Electoral Politics*, UCL Press, 1988, p. 94. Both Paul Boateng and Keith Vaz had served in ministerial positions during the 1997 Parliament. The former had occupied junior and middle ranking ministerial roles at Treasury, Health and Home Affairs (returning to Treasury after the 2001 election); the latter had been a DETR minister followed by a spell as the high-profile Minister for Europe at the FCO (he was dropped from the front bench after the election).

14 *The Future of Multi-Ethnic Britain* ('The Parekh Report'), Profile Books/Runnymede Trust, 2000, p. 231.

PAUL WHITELEY, HAROLD CLARKE, DAVID SANDERS AND
MARIANNE STEWART

Turnout

'A low voter turnout is an indication of fewer people going to the polls'
George W. Bush

In many respects the 2001 general election was a rerun of its 1997 predecessor, with the parties obtaining rather similar shares of the votes and seats in the House of Commons. In one very important respect, however, it was a very different election. The turnout of 59% was the lowest in a general election since universal adult franchise was established in Britain in the 1920s. The 2001 election represents an extreme case of declining turnouts that may have occurred in many advanced industrial democracies.[1] The decline is all the more puzzling since the dominant model of political participation in political science — the civic voluntarism model — predicts that as educational opportunities expands and incomes rise, turnouts should increase rather than decline.[2] So the turnout in the 2001 general election has general implications for theoretical models of participation as well as for the wider political system.

There are two rather different theoretical traditions in political science which study turnout. One seeks to explain turnout in terms of sociological variables and attitudinal indicators of various kinds.[3] The civic voluntarism model is in this tradition, although it focuses on political participation defined rather more broadly than just turnout. Some of this work looks at turnout in a comparative context, taking into account the institutional and cultural factors influencing electoral participation across democratic countries.[4] The other tradition, derived from the public choice literature, sees turnout as the product of a rational calculus in which citizens compare the costs of voting with its benefits.[5] While it is clear that 'hard' or narrow rational choice accounts of turnout cannot explain why anyone would vote at all,[6] 'softer' versions which take into account a wider variety of incentives appear to provide an increasingly plausible account of participation.[7]

The precipitous decline in voting in Britain between 1997 and 2001 serves to undermine purely sociological accounts of turnout, since the variables at the centre of such accounts like social class, education, ethnicity and gender do not change enough in four years to provide an adequate explanation of what occurred. In this case, variables such as attitudes and changing incentives to participate take centre stage in any adequate theoretical account.

The purpose of this paper is twofold. Firstly, to describe the variations in turnout in the general election of 2001, looking particularly at aggregate effects attributable to the constituency context in which voters found themselves. Secondly, to test a model of turnout based on individual level survey data from the 2001 British Election Study. The latter should help to throw light on the decline in the turnout since 1997. The results of the survey analysis show that turnout in the 2001 British general election was significantly influenced by four factors in particular: the electorate's evaluation of the party leaders, their perceptions of the government's economic performance, policy discontent with the delivery of public services, and general boredom with the campaign. Before examining the individual-level evidence from the British Election Study (BES) supporting these claims, we begin by examining variations in turnout at constituency level.

Constituency variations in turnout in 2001

The first point to make about the overall turnout in the 2001 election is that it was actually lower than 59.2%, or the official figure. This is because the official turnout is calculated on the basis of the number of valid votes cast as a proportion of the people on the electoral register. It therefore ignores people who for one reason or another are not on the register yet there are a growing number of citizens who do not appear in the official figures. Considerable light was thrown on this point by the Home Affairs Committee report of the House of Commons published in 1997/1998, which stated that:

(T)here may have been around four million people who were totally omitted from the register and therefore unable to vote at the 1997 general election.[8]

If we add people who would be eligible to vote if they were on the register and repeat the calculation, then the turnout was more like 54%. This means that the Labour landslide was based on capturing the votes of 23% of this eligible electorate, or 25% of the registered electorate.

There was considerable variation across the country in the official turnout figures: from 34.1% in Liverpool Riverside to 72.3% in Winchester.[9] The scale of the decline in turnout since the previous election can be gauged from the fact that only two constituencies — Brecon and Radnor and Winchester — had turnouts greater than the average of 71.6% in 1997. Only eleven constituencies had turnouts of 70% or more and no less than 68 constituencies had turnouts of 50% or less. The standard deviation of the turnouts increased in comparison with

1. Turnout by Region, 1997 to 2001

Census regions	2001	1997	Change
South-East	61.3	73.9	–12.5
East Anglia	63.6	74.5	–10.9
Greater London	55.1	67.6	–12.5
South-West	64.8	75.0	–10.2
West Midlands	58.2	70.8	–12.6
East Midlands	60.8	73.4	–12.6
Yorkshire and Humberside	56.5	68.2	–11.8
North West	55.2	69.9	–14.7
North	57.6	69.5	–11.9
Scotland	58.0	71.2	–13.2
Wales	61.6	73.6	–11.9

Source: The British Parliamentary Constituency Database, 1992–2001.

1997, from 5.6% to 6.4%, so the picture is one of both declining turnouts and increasing variation in constituency turnouts over time.

Table 1 shows regional variations patterns with the smallest falls in the South-West and East Anglia, and the largest in Scotland and the North-West. These results are related to the competitiveness of the contests in these regions, since a third of the seats in the South-West and 27% of the seats in East Anglia had majorities under 5% in 1997. In contrast, only 3% of the seats in Scotland and 4% in the North-West were in this category. The relationship between turnout and the marginality of the seat explains much of the regional variations.

Table 2 classifies all British constituencies by their 1997 marginality, and it confirms the relationship between turnout and marginality in 2001, a pattern first identified in the 1970s.[10] Turnouts in the marginal seats were almost 10% higher in 2001 than turnouts in very safe seats. As earlier research shows, there are two rival explanations of this effect. One argues that it derives from the elector's perception that their votes count more in marginal seats than in safe seats, and the other derives from the fact that parties campaign harder in marginals than in safe seats.

As discussed further by Curtice in this volume, the distortions in the relationship between seat shares and vote shares caused by the electoral system continued to operate with a vengeance. The fact that Labour took 40.8% of the UK vote and 62.7% of the seats in the House of Commons was, in part, explained by differential turnout. Table 3 shows the average turnouts in the seats won by the different parties in 2001, with turnouts significantly lower in seats won by Labour than in those

2. Turnout and Marginality

Majorities in 1997	Mean turnout 2001	Number of seats
Very marginal (under 5%)	64.4	68
Fairly marginal (5% up to 10%)	62.0	83
Fairly safe (10 % up to 15%)	62.6	84
Very safe (15% up to 20 %)	62.5	70
Ultra safe (over 20%)	55.4	329

Source: The British Parliamentary Constituency Database, 1992–2001.

3. Turnouts by Winner, 2001

Winner of the seat in 2001	Mean turnout	Number of seats
Labour	56.7	413
Conservatives	63.0	166
Liberal Democrats	63.8	52
Plaid Cymru	64.2	4
Scottish National Party	59.0	5
Independent	70.0	1

Source: The British Parliamentary Constituency Database, 1992–2001.

won by the Conservatives. Labour wins more seats with a given number of votes than the Conservatives, and this, in part, explains their seat advantage.

Prior to the campaign it was suggested that Labour might face a problem of mobilising supporters in its heartland constituencies, arising from discontent with the performance of the government in delivering public services.[11] Clearly if so then turnout should have been depressed, particularly in safe Labour seats. Table 4 shows a multiple regression model where turnout in 2001 is predicted by the vote shares for the two major parties in 1997.

The model shows that turnout declined in Labour seats by a significant amount in 2001, even after controlling for turnout in the previous election. The Conservative vote share in 1997 and Labour incumbency were also taken into account in this model.[12] The larger the Labour vote share in 1997, the bigger the turnout fall, indicating that the problem was worse in Labour's heartland. At the same time, the control for Labour incumbency was not significant, so the effect was not confined to Labour-held seats. Equally, the Conservative vote share in 1997 had no effect on the turnout in 2001, so it was a distinctively Labour problem. Therefore, Labour had a turnout problem in its heartland constituencies, although an aggregate analysis cannot identify if this was due to abstention by Labour supporters or to some other effect.[13]

There is a well-documented relationship between turnout and the social characteristics of constituencies in Britain. The theoretical explanation for this relationship derives from the civic voluntarism model of participation. Parry, Moyser and Day used this theoretical

4. The Effects of Vote Shares in 1997 on Turnout in 2001

	Standardised coefficients	Sig.	T-ratios
Turnout in 1997	0.81	***	46.4
Labour vote share in 1997	−0.20	***	7.6
Conservative vote share in 1997	0.01		0.4
Labour incumbent prior to election	0.01		0.7
R-squared	0.88		

Note:Standardised regression coefficients from OLS models with the percentage turnout in 2001 as the dependent variable. *** = statistically significant at the $p<0.01$ level. Source: The British Parliamentary Constituency Database, 1992–2001.

framework to investigate political participation in Britain in the 1980s, and they explained the mechanism in the following terms:

In looking at the factors that constrain or promote participation, we start with the notion of 'resources'. By 'resources' we mean material wealth, education, and skills and membership of organised groups. These are all resources in the sense that they can be employed to the advantage by those who possess them in any attempts to promote their own interests by some form of political action ... A lack of resources might be expected to make successful participation appear much more of an uphill struggle.[14]

This implies that constituencies with a high proportion of poor, socially deprived and unemployed voters will have significantly lower turnouts than constituencies with many affluent, home-owning white-collar professionals. To examine such relationships we model the effects on turnout of various indicators of the social characteristics of constituencies, using variables from the 1991 census and from Acorn Demographics 2000.

The evidence in Table 5 shows that social resources explain much of the variance in turnout. The strongest effect is associated with the proportion of lone parents in a constituency, which seriously depresses the turnout, perhaps because lone-parent families are generally more deprived than other types of families. The second strongest effect is the number of suburban wealthy achievers in a constituency, which significantly boosts the turnout. The proportion of young voters also depresses turnout, but motivational factors probably play a more important role in explaining this than just resources; although it is also true that young people generally have fewer resources than their older counterparts. The second model in Table 4 incorporates the size of the majority in 1997 as a measure of the marginality of the constituency, and there is a strong negative relationship between this and turnout. This confirms that the relationship between marginality and turnout remained strong, even when the social characteristics of those seats were taken into account.

An examination of the aggregate voting statistics is interesting, but it

5. Turnout and Constituency Characteristics

	Standardised	Coefficients
Council estate residents in greatest hardship	−0.17***	−0.09***
Council estate residents with high unemployment	−0.07**	−0.10***
Census proportion of families with dependent children headed by a lone parent	−0.31***	−0.26***
Census proportion of the population aged 16 to 24	−0.20***	−0.20***
Affluent executives in family areas	0.07***	0.05*
Affluent greys in rural communities	0.19***	0.14***
Wealthy achievers in suburban areas	0.23***	0.18***
Percentage Majority in 1997	−	−0.26***
R-squared	0.71	0.76

Note: All coefficients are statistically significant at the p<0.05 level. Source: British Parliamentary Constituency Database, 1992–2001.

throws little light on the decision-making process at work which motivates citizens to turnout during a general election. To gain insight into this we have to examine individual-level survey data.

A model of individual turnout behaviour

This section examines explanations for the drop in turnout, using individual-level survey data. To construct a model, we hypothesise that individuals participate in response to three kinds of incentives. Firstly, there are those associated with their own *values and beliefs as citizens*, particularly the attention they pay to politics and to the general election campaign, and subjective feelings of efficacy. A second group of incentives arise from *the parties and the party leaders*. If individuals are strongly attached to one or other of the political parties, or if they are satisfied or dissatisfied with the party leaders and the policy achievements of the government, these factors are likely to influence their participation. A third group of incentives are associated with the *context of the general election*. Two ideas will be tested; firstly, if respondents believed that the outcome of the national election was a foregone conclusion for government, with Labour winning another landslide, that might have deterred them from voting. It is analogous to the point made earlier about the relationship between turnout and marginality. If electors perceive the contest to be uncompetitive, either at the national or the constituency level, then they may not participate. A second and related point can be made about the election outcome in the respondent's own constituency. If voters believe that their own preferred candidate cannot win in their constituency, they may vote for another candidate rather than by abstaining. If so, these tactical voters are more likely to turnout than other types of voters.

These ideas are investigated with data from the campaign survey conducted during the four weeks of the official campaign as part of the British Election Study.[15] This part of the study was a rolling cross-section which involved interviewing approximately 150 electors per day by phone. The data can be analysed in a number of different ways but for the purpose of this paper it is cumulated into a file of over 4,800 respondents. It has the advantage of being conducted up to 6 June, the day before polling day. This means that responses are not contaminated by the outcome of the election itself, which is a problem for a post-election survey.

Figure 1 illustrates the distribution of responses to an 11-point scale asking respondents to estimate their likelihood of voting. It can be seen that some 60% of respondents scored themselves 10 on this scale, the 'very likely' to vote category. This was of course very close to the actual turnout in the general election. This will be the dependent variable in the model and it has the advantage of capturing a broader spectrum of turnout intentions than the usual post-election dichotomous variable, which asks people to indicate if they voted or not. The scale distin-

Figure 1. The Likelihood of Voting in the General Election

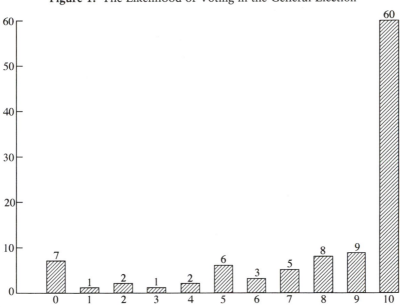

Please think of a scale from 0 to 10, where 10 means very likely and 0 means very unlikely. How likely is it that you will vote in the General Election on June 7th? Source: British Election Study Source: British Election Study campaign study; fieldwork dates 8.5.01 to 6.6.01. N=4,810 See http//www.essex.ac.uk/bes for further information.

guishes between individuals who decided that they were definitely not going to vote, individuals who may have wanted to vote but for one reason or another did not, and those who did actually vote.

Turning to the first group of interest-related measures, three relationships will be examined. Firstly, there is the influence of the individual's level of interest in the general election campaign on vote intentions. It is fairly obvious that high levels of interest in the campaign are likely to stimulate turnout, but the magnitude of the effect is unclear, meriting a further investigation of the question. Moreover, if the campaign data is analysed dynamically across the four weeks of the election, it suggests that the public lost interest during the campaign.[16] The evidence shows that interest in the campaign rallied in the final week, but nonetheless for much of the time the campaign demotivated voters. Overall, just over a quarter of the respondents were very interested in the campaign, and about a third were not interested in the election to any great extent. Clearly, many of these were likely to be non-voters.

Moving from a specific interest in the general election itself to a wider interest in politics, it is possible that some voters were generally interested in politics, but were bored by the election campaign.[17] Accordingly, it is interesting to test if the individual's overall attention to politics influenced their willingness to vote. On an eleven-point scale designed to measure interest in politics, some 58% of the respondents scored themselves above 5, suggesting that there is fairly widespread interest in politics in Britain today. People pay more attention to politics in general than they did to the general election campaign, so this is included as a separate predictor in the turnout model.

A third factor is the extent to which people feel that they can influence politics, that is the extent to which they have a sense of political efficacy. This is a key variable in both the civic voluntarism model and also rational choice models of participation.[18] The distribution of scores on an 11-point efficacy scale suggests that most people believe, quite rationally, that they do not have much influence on politics. Some 35% of respondents gave themselves a score of zero on the scale. However, roughly a quarter of the respondents give themselves a score of five or more, indicating that a significant minority did feel a sense of political efficacy.

Turning to the party-related variables likely to influence turnout, it is possible that affective feelings towards the party leaders play a role in stimulating turnout. Again, respondents were asked to give a score to the party leaders along an 11-point scale, depending on how much they liked or disliked them. The mean scores for the three leaders were 5.7, 5.2 and 3.9 for Blair, Kennedy and Hague respectively. Clearly, the Conservative leader was much less popular than his rivals, although none of the leaders received high scores. High scores can be expected to stimulate turnout. The theoretical reasoning behind this type of effect derives from the political psychology literature, which shows that citizen use a 'likeability' heuristic as a 'short-cut' device for making complex decisions about politics.[19] In making a decision whether or not to vote, individuals can avoid examining the complexities of policy alternatives and past government or opposition performances, and simply decide that they dislike the party leaders. This rule of thumb is easy to apply and allows them to decide with minimal information processing costs.

Another factor which can be used to make judgments about voting is the partisanship heuristic. There is a well-established relationship between the strength of the individual's partisanship and their party choice.[20] But this implies that the strength of their partisanship is clearly a stimulus for them to vote, in comparison with non-partisans. Counting just the 'very' or 'fairly' strong partisans, 37% of the respondents were Labour, 21% Conservative and 7% Liberal Democrat. Thus Labour had almost twice as many very or fairly strong partisans as the Conservatives.

The aggregate analysis showed that turnouts were well down in the Labour heartland constituencies. One plausible explanation for this phenomenon is that many supporters were disappointed by Labour's performance in government, particularly in relation to the public services, such as the National Health Service and education. If at the same time people believed that no other party could do any better, then they might well abstain from voting altogether rather than switch parties.

The BES asked people to give the government a score out of ten for its performance in handling crime, the National Health Service, taxation and education. There appeared to be quite a lot of policy discontent with the government on these issues; some 31% of the respondents gave the government scores below five for the National Health Service and crime, 25% did this for taxation and 22% for education. Clearly, if policy discontent weakened the motivation of some voters, then low scores on these performance scales should be associated with non-voting. One complication is that the performance scales were highly correlated with each other, and so in order to be able to estimate effects they were combined into a single scale using a principal components analysis.[21]

Again, in relation to policy discontent, the BES asked an open-ended question about which issue in the election was the single most important one for each respondent. This was followed by a question asking which party was best at handling this issue. If policy discontent inhibits participation, then respondents who thought that no party could handle their most important issue should be less likely to vote than people who did not take this view. Altogether, 6% of respondents thought that no party could handle their most important issue, so the variable is included in the model to test effects.[22]

Government performance in relation to the public services was not the only policy issue in the election. In particular, as Sanders discusses elsewhere in this volume, the state of the economy has long been an important factor in influencing the voters in British general elections.[23] It has been shown that pessimists about their own economic futures are likely to punish the incumbent party and to support the main opposition party. On the other hand, optimists are likely to support the government, on the grounds that they want economic prosperity to continue. The effect of economic optimism or pessimism on turnout has not been investigated, however, and it is possible that pessimists will not vote at all, particularly if they think that the opposition party is no better than the incumbent. Voters were asked the question: '*How do you think the financial situation of your household will change over the next 12 months?*'.[24] Although the optimists outnumbered the pessimists, there were enough of the latter to test the hypothesis.

The third category of variables related to the general election context, and two measures are included. Firstly, some speculated that Labour's large lead in the polls in the run-up to the election would inhibit participation by those who saw the election as a foregone conclusion. People were asked to indicate which party they thought was going to win the general election and 87% stated that they thought this would be Labour. If the hypothesis is correct then individuals who thought that Labour was going to win should be less inclined to vote than individuals who took a different view. So the variable is included in the model to test this hypothesis.[25]

Finally, another election-related issue involves tactical voting. This was measured using the following question: 'People give different reasons why they vote for one party rather than another. Which of the following best describes your reasons for deciding to vote for . . .' Respondents were then given three alternatives: 'It has the best policies', 'it has the best leader', 'I really prefer another party but it stands no chance of winning in my constituency'. The real purpose of this question was to measure the size of the third group, the tactical voters, and altogether 9% of respondents chose this alternative. Tactical voters are expected to be more likely to turnout than individuals who are not. Accordingly, this variable is included in the model.[26]

Table 6 includes the estimates of the turnout model, using the three classes of predictors to estimate effects. The model also includes controls for education, employment, gender, age and social class. The coefficients are standardised and so directly comparable to each other, and it can be seen that almost all of the variables in the model have a statistically significant effect on turnout. The strongest effects are associated with the first group of interest-related variables. Perhaps not surprisingly, interest in the campaign has the strongest effect of all in the model, although attention to politics has a significant additional effect too. One interesting finding is the efficacy measure, has no effect on the probability of voting once these other measures have been taken into account.

The party-related variables are also important in influencing turnout. Affective feelings for the party leaders stimulate turnout, although the

6. The Turnout Model

	Standardised coefficients	T-statistics
Interest in the general election campaign	0.38***	23.3
Attention to politics	0.09***	5.1
Influence on politics	0.01	0.9
Government performance on policies	0.03*	1.7
No party can handle most important issue	−0.05***	3.9
Economic expectations over the next year	0.02*	1.6
Very or fairly strong Labour	0.12***	6.5
Very or fairly strong Conservative	0.17***	9.4
Very of fairly strong Liberal Democrat	0.04***	3.0
Feelings about Blair	0.06***	2.9
Feelings about Hague	0.03*	1.7
Feelings about Kennedy	0.08***	5.6
Tactical Voter	0.03**	2.1
Expects Labour to win election nationally	0.03**	2.3
Education	−0.02	1.5
Unemployed (1/0)	−0.02*	1.8
Gender (Male 1/Female 2)	0.07***	5.1
Age (years)	0.03**	1.7
Social Class	−0.03*	1.7
R-squared	0.31	
F ratio	94.00***	

Note: Regression models with likelihood of voting as the dependent variable. Education is the age the respondent completed full-time education; social class is the standard market research scale of A, B, C1, C2, D and E. Source: British Election Study, 2001.

effect associated with William Hague is significantly weaker than the effects associated with Tony Blair and Charles Kennedy. Not surprisingly, partisanship stimulates turnout, with the strongest effect being associated with Conservative partisanship followed by Labour and Liberal Democrat partisanship. The hypothesis that policy discontent demobilised voters is strongly confirmed. If an individual believed that no party could handle their most important issue they were significantly less likely to vote. In addition the government policy performance index influenced turnout, as did economic optimism. Individuals disillusioned with the government's delivery of key services like education and health care, or individuals who were pessimistic about their own economic prospects were less likely to vote. Clearly, policy performance was one of the key factors which help to explain the declining turnout.

Finally, the hypothesis that tactical voters are more likely to turnout than others is also confirmed, although interestingly enough the perception that the election was going to be won by Labour did not reduce turnout, but rather stimulated it. Clearly, the belief that the election was a foregone conclusion, though widely held in the electorate, did not appear to demobilise the voters. This suggests that the aggregate relationship between marginality and turnout observed earlier was not driven by the perception that Labour was going to win the election. Unfortunately, we are unable to test the rival hypothesis that variations in turnout depend upon local campaigning by the political parties, since there were no indicators of such campaigning in this particular survey.[27]

Conclusion

In the absence of exactly comparable data from the 1997 general election, conclusions about the decline in turnout must remain tentative, and a fuller analysis will be possible when the 2001 BES post-election survey is available. But returning to the key question of why the turnout fell in the election, four points stand out as important.

Firstly, there is the *continuing decline in partisanship* in the electorate. In 1997, 30% of the electorate identified with the Conservatives, 46% with Labour and 13% with the Liberal Democrats.[28] By 2001 this had changed to 27% identifying with the Conservatives, 45% with Labour and 10% with the Liberal Democrats. The percentage of the electorate not identifying with any party at all increased from 7% to 10% during this period. None of these changes are very large, but they confirm that the secular trend in declining partisanship, which has occurred over many years, is continuing. Given that the strength of partisanship is an important predictor of turnout, then dealignment should produce falling turnouts.

Secondly, a *reduction in leadership popularity* will have reduced turnout, given the relationships observed in Table 6. In June 1997 82% of the electorate were satisfied with Tony Blair's performance as Prime Minister, but by December 2000 this had fallen to 49%.[29] Moreover, the relative unpopularity of the Conservative leader and to a lesser extent, Charles Kennedy, compared with their predecessors reinforced this process. William Hague was markedly less popular than previous Conservative leaders of the Opposition,[30] and Charles Kennedy consistently failed to reach the levels of popularity of Paddy Ashdown during his period of leadership of the Liberal Democrats.[31]

A third factor is *policy discontent*, which played a major role in turning off the electorate. It is important to note that the 1997 election study also showed much discontent with the performance of John Major's government. At that time, 75% of electors thought that standards had fallen in the National Health Service, 59% thought the same about education, and 79% thought that crime had increased during the Conservative years. Moreover, large majorities of the voters blamed the Conservative government for these developments. This fact meant that abstention rather than party switching became a much more attractive option for voters discontented with Labour's performance on these core issues in 2001. The record of the Conservative government would not encourage them to switch parties if they wanted better public services.

A final factor, which may be the most important of all given the effects in Table 6, is that *levels of interest in the general election campaign* appear to have declined significantly. In the 1997 post-election study survey 76% of respondents said that they 'cared a great deal which party won' the election and only 24% 'did not care very much'. Only 27% of electors were 'very interested' in the campaign in 2001. Even though the questions are not directly comparable with each other, they do suggest a large increase in voter apathy. If this is true, we know from Table 6 that it was not due to the widespread assumption that Labour would win the election.

These developments link to the demobilisation of the electorate during the campaign. This may be partly due to the fact that the campaign was unusually long, because the expected May election date was postponed until June. But it is also plausible that the micro-management of campaigns by the party professionals and spin-doctors robs them of any spontaneity, and as a result they become boring and predictable. It is noteworthy that the punch thrown by the deputy Prime Minister on the campaign trail was generally well received, because it appeared to be the first exciting and spontaneous event to occur in the Labour campaign. Clearly, this is a topic for further research. More than five million fewer people voted in the 2001 election than did so in 1997, which itself had a lower turnout than its predecessor in 1992. The word crisis is often abused in contemporary accounts of politics. But if this is not a crisis of democratic politics in Britain, then it is hard to know what would be.

Paul Whiteley, Harold Clarke, David Sanders and Marianne Stewart

1   See R.J. Dalton and M.P. Wattenberg, *Parties without Partisans: Political Change in Advanced Industrial Democracies*, Oxford University Press, 2000, pp. 71–6.

2   See S. Verba, K.L. Schlozman and H.E. Brady, *Voice and Equality*, Harvard University Press, 1995; and G. Parry, G. Moyser and N. Day, *Political Participation and Democracy in Britain*, Cambridge University Press, 1992.

3   For example, R. Wolfinger and S. Rosenstone, *Who Votes?*, Yale University Press, 1980; A. Heath, R.M. Jowell and J. Curtice, *The Rise of New Labour*, Oxford University Press, 2001.

4   C. van der Eijk and M. Franklin, *Choosing Europe? The European Electorate and National Politics in the Face of Union*, University of Michigan Press, 1996.

5   The starting point of this was A. Downs, *An Economic Theory of Democracy*, Harper and Row, 1957. But other examples of this include W. Riker and P. Ordeshook, 'A Theory of the Calculus of Voting', *American Political Science Review*, 1968; and J.A. Ferejohn and M. Fiorina, 'The Paradox of Non-Voting: A Decision Theoretic Analysis', *American Political Science Review*, 1974.

6   See D.P. Green and I. Shapiro, *Pathologies of Rational Choice Theory*, Yale University Press, 1994; B. Grofman, 'Is Turnout the Paradox that Ate Rational Choice Theory?' in B. Grofman(ed.), *Information, Participation and Choice*, University of Michigan Press, 1995.

7   G. Brennan and L. Lomasky, *Democracy and Decision*, Cambridge University Press, 1993; A. Blais, *To Vote or Not to Vote*, University of Pittsburgh Press, 2000; P. Whiteley and P. Seyd, *High Intensity Participation: The Dynamics of Party Activism in Britain*, University of Michigan Press, 2002.

8   See http://www.publications.parliament.uk/pa/cm199798/cmselect/cmhaff/768/76805.htm,p. 2.

9   All the aggregate data comes from the British Parliamentary Constituency Database 1992–2001.

10 D. Denver and G. Hands, 'Marginality and Turnout in British General Elections', *British Journal of Political Science*, 1974.

11 P. Whiteley, 'Vote Tote', *Guardian* (2.6.00).

12 The correlation between the Labour and Conservative vote shares in 1997 was −0.67, so there is a risk of multi-collinearity in this model. Accordingly, the variance inflation factors (VIF) were calculated for each variable and the largest one associated with the Labour vote share variable was 3.6. The rule of thumb accepted by econometricians is that a VIF of 5 or above indicates a problem, so this model can be interpreted with confidence (see A.H. Studenmund, *Using Econometrics*, Addison-Wesley, 1997). Note if the Liberal Democrat vote share is included in the model, then multi-collinearity does become a serious problem.

13 Assuming that the effect was due to differential abstention by Labour supporters would be to commit the ecological fallacy, since it could equally well be due to vote switching.

14 G. Parry, G. Moyser and N. Day, op. cit., 1992, p. 64.

15 The British Election Study was funded by the Economic and Social Research Council and was co-directed by David Sanders and Paul Whiteley from the University of Essex, and Harold Clarke and Marianne Stewart from the University of Texas at Dallas.

16 See http://www.essex.ac.uk/bes.

17 This is a point developed in the report on attitudes to voting derived from surveys conducted by MORI during the election campaign. See: www.MORI.ac.uk, http://www.mori.com/polls/2001/elec_comm_rep.shtml.

18 See J.H. Aldrich, 'Rational Choice and Turnout', *American Journal of Political Science*, 1993.

19 This is discussed extensively in P. Sniderman, R.A. Brody and P.E. Tetlock, *Reasoning and Choice, Explorations in Political Psychology*, Cambridge University Press, 1991.

20 See H. Clarke, M. Stewart and P.F. Whiteley, 'New Models For New Labour: The Political Economy of Labour Party Support, January 1992–April 1997', *American Political Science Review*, 1998.

21 The first principal component explained 72% of the variance in the data and had an eigenvalue of 2.9. All the factor loadings exceeded 0.80. The use of this principal component in the regression model avoids problems of multi-collinearity referred to in n. 12.

22 On this variable, respondents who thought that no party could handle their most important issue score one, and respondents who do not think this score zero.

23 See P. Whiteley, *Political Control of the Macroeconomy*, Sage, 1986; H. Norpoth, *Confidence Regained: Economics, Mrs Thatcher and the British Voter*, University of Michigan Press, 1992.

24 Responses were 'get a lot better' (7.9%); 'get a little better' (28.2%); 'stay the same' (47.2%); 'get a little worse' (11.8%); 'get a lot worse' (4.9%).

25 Respondents who thought Labour would win scored one, and respondents who felt otherwise scored zero.

26 This is a dummy variable, so that respondents who chose the tactical option score one and all others score zero.

27 The post-election survey contains such measures, so in due course it will be possible to test this hypothesis. At the time of writing this survey was still in the field.

28 See G. Evans and P. Norris, *Critical Elections*, Sage, 1999, p. 67.
29 See A. King, R.J. Wybrow and A. Gallup, *British Political Opinion 1937–2000*, Politico's, 2001, pp. 107–8.
30 See A. King et al., op. cit., p. 208.
31 See A. King et al., op. cit., p. 228.

DAVID SANDERS, HAROLD CLARKE, MARIANNE STEWART
AND PAUL WHITELEY

The Economy and Voting

There has been a long-running controversy as to how far economic performance and voters' economic perceptions affect the electoral fortunes of incumbent governments. At its simplest, the 'economic voting' model suggests that voters support the ruling party (or coalition) if the economy is going well and transfer that support to the opposition if the economy is going badly.[1] The British general elections of 1992 and 1997 at first sight seem to contradict these claims. In 1992, John Major's Conservative government was re-elected in spite of the fact that the UK economy had just experienced its worst recession since the 1930s. In 1997, economic growth was strong and unemployment and inflation were both falling—yet the incumbent Conservatives were defeated humiliatingly by New Labour.

The balance of evidence, however, suggests that, even in 1992 and 1997, voters' economic perceptions played a significant role in their judgments about the major parties.[2] In 1992, notwithstanding the length and depth of the 1990–91 recession, a clear majority of voters still believed that the Conservatives were the party best able to handle the economy if it ran into difficulties. Labour, quite simply, was not trusted to provide competent macroeconomic management. The turning point of UK party politics was the September 1992 Exchange Rate Mechanism crisis. The fundamental reversal of the government's approach to economic policy that the crisis engendered severely damaged the Conservatives' reputation for economic management competence. New Labour's political triumph under Tony Blair and Gordon Brown after 1994 was to convince voters that Labour was now the party of fiscal responsibility and competent macroeconomic management. Their success in this regard seriously impaired the Conservatives' ability to benefit electorally from the rising sense of economic optimism among voters that the Chancellor delivered in the 18 months or so prior to the 1997 election.[3]

Having been elected, in part, on the promise of providing competent macroeconomic management, it was crucial to New Labour's project that its reputation for fiscal responsibility and economic competence was maintained. The government's determination in this regard was

1. Comparison of Major and Blair Governments' Performance on the Leading Macroeconomic Indicators, 1992–2001

		Segment A: Conservative performance			
	Unemployed (%)	Inflation	Interest rate	Tax index	Gross domestic product
May 1992	9.5	4.3	10.0	−0.8	90.7
April 1997	5.6	2.4	6.0	−0.9	105.7
Change 1992–97	−3.9	−1.9	−4.0	+0.1	+15

		Segment B: Labour performance			
	Unemployed (%)	Inflation	Interest rate	Tax index	Gross domestic product
May 1997	5.4	2.6	6.25	−0.9	105.7
May 2001	3.2	2.3	5.5	−0.2	116.4
Change 1997–2001	−2.2	−0.3	−0.75	+0.7	10.7

Notes: Unemployment is measured as the seasonally adjusted Great Britain rate. Inflation is the Change in Price Index. Interest Rate is selected banks minimum lending rate. The Tax Index is obtained by subtracting inflation (the Change in Price Index) from the government's monthly Change in Tax and Price Index. Gross Domestic Product is measured quarterly rather than monthly. The figures reported are for 1992Q1, 1997Q2 and 2001Q1. The annual average change in the GDP index for the Conservatives was 10/5 = 3 points per year. The equivalent figure for Labour was 10.7/4 = 2.7 points per year. Source: Office for National Statistics, *Monthly Digest of Statistics* and *Financial Statistics*.

signalled by its decision not to exceed the spending plans of the previous Conservative administration for the first two years of the 1997 Parliament. The government's awareness of the need to reinforce the electorate's perception of Labour as the party of fiscal responsibility was illustrated in the repeated references to economic competence made at successive annual party conferences, Commons debates, media interviews, and in the 2001 election manifesto.

This study examines the extent to which New Labour's economic performance, and voters' perceptions of that performance, affected the outcome of the 2001 general election. Section 1 summarises the 'objective' performance of the economy and compares it with the performance of the previous Conservative government. The evidence reported suggests that 'objective' macroeconomic conditions do not explain New Labour's success in 2001. Section 2 uses aggregate-level data in order to show that voters' economic perceptions exerted a continuing influence on the pattern of party support during the 1997 Parliament. Section 3 uses individual-level data, based on the 2001 British Election Study, to assess the relative importance of economic perceptions as determinants of voters' electoral preferences. The results provide strong support for the conclusions arrived at in Section 2. Controlling for other factors that are known to influence voting, voters' economic perceptions play a significant role in determining their electoral choices.

Labour's 'objective' macroeconomic performance, 1997–2001

Labour's campaign for re-election in 2001 made considerably play of the government's strong economic record. As Segment B of Table 1 shows, between 1997 and 2001, all of the leading macroeconomic indicators moved in the right direction. Unemployment fell by 2.2

percentage points to a near historic low of 3.2%. Inflation remained low; at 2.3% in May 2001, it was 0.3 points lower than when Labour took office. Interest rates fell by 0.75 points to 5.5%. The overall tax burden on the average voter did not change significantly. And the official index of Gross Domestic Product (GDP) rose from 105.7 points in 1997Q2 to 116.4 in 2001Q1.

On the face of it, these figures look impressive. They would appear to offer at least a partial explanation of Labour's electoral success in June 2001: Labour delivered sound economic progress over the course of the 1997 Parliament and was accordingly rewarded with continued support by a grateful electorate. However, comparison with the record of the previous Conservative government suggests that such a straight-forward interpretation may not be appropriate. Segment A of Table 1 reports the equivalent figures for the 1992–97 Major government. The Tories reduced unemployment (admittedly from a higher base) by almost 4 percentage points between May 1992 and April 1997. They reduced inflation by almost 2% and interest rates by 4% in the same period. The tax burden on the average voter barely changed at all. And the GDP index rose by 15 points, an average annual increase of 3 points compared with Labour's annual rate of increase of 2.7 points. The Tories macroeconomic record, in short, was not noticeably worse than Labour's, and in respect of GDP growth was, if anything, better.

Figures 1–5 provide more detailed evidence to support the view that Labour's economic performance between 1997 and 2001 was not markedly different from the Conservatives' performance between 1992 and 1997. GDP (Figure 1) shows a consistent trend increase for both governments. Unemployment (Figure 2), after its peak in December 1992, shows a clear trend decline. Inflation (Figure 3) varies during both periods but remains low throughout. Interest rates (Figure 4), once

Figure 1. Changes in Index of Gross Domestic Product, 1992–2001

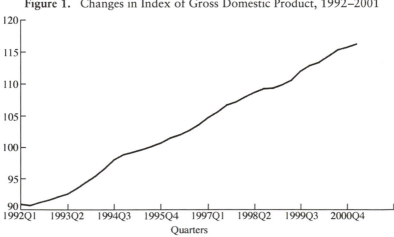

Quarters

Figure 2. Changes in Unemployment, 1992–2001

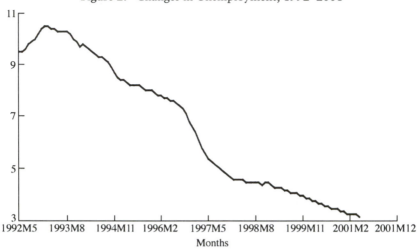

they had been brought down in the autumn of 1992, remained fairly stable — and at historically low levels — until 2001. And although the tax index (Figure 5) was higher at the end of New Labour's first term than it had been in 1997, it remained very much within the upper and lower bounds set by the previous Conservative administration.

This lack of a connection between objective macroeconomic performance and electoral outcome is reinforced by the findings shown in Table 2. Unemployment is the only major macroeconomic indicator that can be broken down by region. If changes in unemployment affected support for the incumbent government, we might expect to find that

Figure 3. Changes in Inflation, 1992–2001

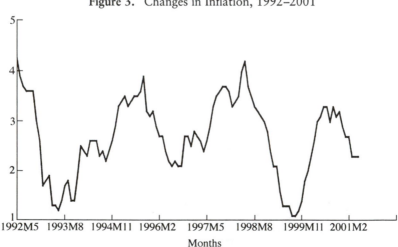

Figure 4. Changes in Interest Rates, 1992–2001

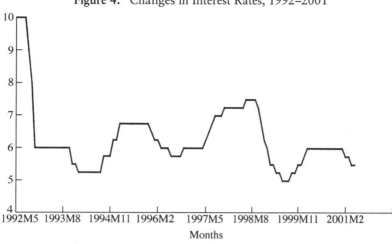

Months

regions which experienced relatively large falls in unemployment
between 1997 and 2001 remained most loyal to Labour in the 2001
election. As the Table shows, however, this was simply not the case.
Regions in which unemployment fell most were no more likely to
remain loyal to Labour than regions in which it fell least. Indeed, there
was no correlation between the change in unemployment and the
change in the vote share of any of the major parties.

All of this suggests a straightforward conclusion. There was no simple
equation in the 1992–2001 period, in which the Conservatives were
punished for *poor* macroeconomic performance between 1992 and
1997 by electoral *defeat*, whereas Labour was rewarded for *sound*
macroeconomic performance between 1997 and 2001 by electoral

Figure 5. Changes in Tax Index, 1992–2001

Months

2. Changes in Unemployment, Vote Share and Turnout, 1997–2001

Region	Unemployed	Change in (%)			
		Labour vote	Cons vote	LibDem vote	Turnout
North East	−0.6	−4.7	+1.6	+3.8	−12.1
North West	−0.3	−2.9	+1.7	+2.3	−14.3
Yorks/Humb	−1.0	−3.3	+2.3	+1.1	−11.6
East Mid	−0.5	−2.7	+2.3	+1.9	−12.4
West Mid	−0.2	−2.1	+1.2	+0.9	−12.4
East	−1.0	−1.8	+2.3	+0.4	−12.2
London	−0.5	−2.1	−0.7	+2.9	−12.3
South East	−0.6	+0.2	+1.0	+0.4	−12.0
South West	−0.8	−0.2	+1.8	−0.1	−10.1
Wales	−0.5	−6.2	+1.5	+1.5	−12.0
Scotland	−0.7	−2.3	−1.9	+3.4	−13.2
Correlation*		−0.16	−0.17	0.28	−0.50
		(0.31)	(0.30)	(0.20)	(0.06)

* Correlation with change in unemployment (significance level in parentheses). Source: Office for National Statistics, *Monthly Digest of Statistics*.

victory. The objective economic performance was remarkably similar in both cases — yet the electoral outcomes for the two incumbent governments were markedly different.

The connections between economic perceptions and party support: aggregate-level evidence

But if *objective* macroeconomic circumstances fail to provide a compelling explanation of the varying fortunes of the Major and Blair governments, does this mean that economic considerations were unimportant in either 1997 or 2001? It does not. On the contrary, the available evidence indicates that voters' *subjective economic perceptions* played a decisive role in both elections.

Figure 6 shows how voters' perceptions of the relative economic management competencies of the Conservative and Labour parties varied between 1992 and 2001. The data are taken from responses to the following regular, monthly Gallup question: '*With Britain in economic difficulties, which party do you think could handle the situation best — Labour or the Conservatives?*' The graph shows the percentage that prefer the Conservatives minus the percentage that prefer Labour. When the graph is above the zero line, the Conservatives are preferred; when it is below, Labour is preferred. The results demonstrate that, in the wake of the 1992 ERM crisis, the Conservatives lost a crucial electoral resource: their reputation for economic competence. It also shows that New Labour, having acquired the mantle of economic competence in advance of its election in 1997, successfully maintained it thereafter; the only brief exception being during the short-lived fuel crisis of September 2000.

Voters' changing perceptions of the two main parties' relative economic competencies help to explain why similar macroeconomic conditions in 1992–97 and 1997–2001 produced such contrasting

Figure 6. Conservative vs. Labour Economic Competence, 1992–2001

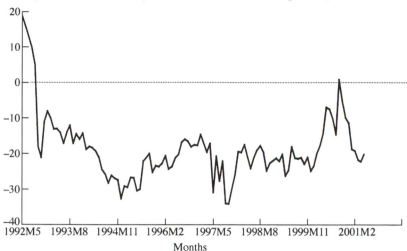

Months

outcomes for the incumbent governments. It seems likely that the crucial difference between the two situations was voters' *prior* expectations about the respective governments' economic management competence.

John Major had been re-elected in 1992 by voters confident about the Conservatives' ability to manage the economy. The 1992 ERM crisis led to a rapid revision of that perception, a reversal from which the Conservatives under Major never recovered. At the same time, New Labour was very much an unknown quantity. The Labour governments of the 1960s and 1970s had been renowned for their lack of economic management skills. The Callaghan government, in particular, had been conspicuously unable to handle the succession of inflation-driven crises that its macroeconomic policies had seemed to engender. This had left a legacy of mistrust among voters about Labour's macroeconomic management skills. When New Labour's stewardship of the economy from June 1997 continued to deliver falling unemployment, inflation and interest rates, rising GDP, and no huge rises in taxation, many voters found their initial mistrust dissipating. Here was a Labour government that could manage the economy effectively. Even if its objective record was no better that that of its Tory predecessor, its economic performance had not disappointed the majority of voters who had supported it in 1997. In a situation where the Conservatives still seemed hopelessly out of touch with the majority of voters, New Labour's relatively modest macroeconomic record represented an important resource that predisposed many voters to continue to support it.

Economic competence, however, is not the only economic perception that has traditionally affected the fortunes of British governments.

Figure 7. Aggregate Personal Economic Expectations, 1992–2001

Much evidence has shown that voters' personal economic expectations are strongly correlated with patterns of party support.[4] The more optimistic voters are about the economic future of their own households, the more likely they are to support the incumbent government. A simple rational choice mechanism underpins this relationship. If I am optimistic about the economic future, then I am more likely to wish to preserve the political *status quo* that has created my optimism; if I am pessimistic, I am more likely to want to change it.[5] Figure 7 shows how 'aggregate personal economic expectations' — sometimes described as 'the feel-good factor' — varied between 1992 and 2001. The index is calculated as the percentage of voters who expect their own financial position to improve over the next 12 months minus the percentage who think it will get worse. Governments typically try to ensure that expectations are on an upward trend as an election approaches, in order to maximise the chances that the feel-good factor will translate into votes for them.

As Figure 7 indicates, both the Major and Blair governments achieved a rising trend in expectations as the election approached. For Major, however, both expectations and Conservative popularity had fallen so low in the aftermath of the ERM crisis that the increase in expectations was insufficient to give the Conservatives any chance of an electoral victory. Nonetheless, the evidence suggests that the Conservatives' defeat in 1997 would have been even worse had it not been for the recovery in expectations that took place.[6] As far as New Labour was concerned, expectations were maintained at relatively high levels throughout the 1997 Parliament — and they increased progressively in the year or so before the election was called.

3. Model of Labour Party Support, May 1997 to May 2001

Independent Variable	Coeff	St Error	Sig.
Labour support (t–1)	+0.15	0.07	0.03
Aggregate personal economic expectations	+0.15	0.04	0.01
Costs of ruling (time)	−0.22	0.03	0.01
Blair 'honeymoon'	+2.73	0.09	0.01
September 2001 fuel crisis	−9.38	1.51	0.01
Corrected R^2	0.90	–	–
Durbin-Watson	1.81	–	–
LM serial correlation	17.34	–	0.14
RESET	0.008	–	0.97

Note: The dependent variable is monthly Labour support as measured by the Poll of Polls, supplied by Peter Kellner. Aggregate expectations data supplied by Gallup.

A simple statistical model demonstrates that aggregate expectations were indeed an important source of the continued support that New Labour enjoyed throughout its first term. Table 3 reports the results of a parsimonious model of Labour support from May 1997 to May 2001. The model has four explanatory components. The first, following the logic outlined immediately above, is aggregate personal economic expectations: support for New Labour is expected to rise (fall) as expectations rise (fall). The second explanatory component of the model is a measure of how long the government has been in office. Nannestad and Paldam[7] have shown that governments in all democratic countries are subject to a 'cost of ruling'. Generally speaking, the longer they remain in office, their support tends to seep away. On average, net of all other effects, democratic governments tend to lose around three percentage points during the lifetime of a typical parliament. There is some debate as to the precise mechanism involved in this process. But it is generally believed to be the consequence of the fact that governments, unlike oppositions, can be held responsible for almost anything that goes wrong in the country while they are in office. This generalised attribution of blame gradually eats into the government's support — unless it can counter the phenomenon by conspicuously performing well in other ways, such as creating a huge economic boom or winning a war abroad. The 'costs of ruling' in the model outlined in Table 3 are measured by the simple passage of time, which is expected to have a negative effect on Labour support.

The third and fourth components of the model involve two terms that seek to measure the effects of unusual events. The first seeks to capture the fairly prolonged 'honeymoon' effect that the Blair government enjoyed for its first few months in office. The term (a dummy variable that takes the value of unity for June–October 1997 and zero otherwise) assumes that this effect built up for the first six months of the New Labour government. The second term is a dummy variable for the fuel crisis that briefly caused Labour's support to waver in September 2000. The specification assumes that both of these effects decayed fairly rapidly after their respective initial impacts.

4. Vote Intention and Personal Economic Expectations, May–June 2001 (%)

| | 'Financial situation of the respondent's household over the next year will . . .' | | |
	Get worse	Stay the same	Get better
Conservative	57	30	20
Labour	17	46	64
Liberal Democrat	18	20	13
Other	7	4	3
	100%	100%	100%

Notes: Numbers may not sum to 100 because of rounding errors. N = 4646. Chi-squared = 542, significant at 0.0001. Source: BES 2001 Campaign Study.

The results reported in Table 3 show that the model is well-determined and passes the standard battery of diagnostic tests. All the coefficients are significant at conventional levels and have the predicted signs. Economic expectations exerted a positive and significant effect on Labour support. The significant negative coefficient for the 'costs of ruling' term (b = −0.22) indicates that, net of all other effects, Labour lost 0.22 of a percentage point from its popularity for each month that it held office. The key intuition underlying these two effects is that, on the one hand, as expectations rose, Labour support increased (and *vice versa*). On the other hand, however, as time passed the government lost support because of the 'cost of ruling'. Over the course of the 1997 Parliament, these two processes were roughly in balance. As a result, controlling for the 'honeymoon' and 'fuel crisis' effects, which produced temporary deviations from the general trend pattern, Labour's support remained at broadly a constant level throughout the 1997–2001 period.[8] In short, economic expectations did influence party support levels during the 1997 Parliament, and rising expectations in the run-up to the 2001 election contributed significantly to Labour's victory.

The connections between economic perceptions and party support: individual-level evidence

The aggregate-level evidence reported above is certainly consistent with the idea that economic perceptions were a significant influence on party preferences during the 1997–2001 period. Yet the case for a continued role for economic perceptions would be considerably strengthened if similar results were obtained using individual-level data. Tables 4 and 5 respectively show the simple bivariate relationships between party preference and personal economic expectations and perceptions of economic management competence. These individual-level results clearly support the idea that economic perceptions are strongly related to partisan preferences. As Table 4 shows, fully two-thirds of voters who thought that their economic circumstances would improve over the next year voted Labour. Of those who thought that their economic situation would worsen, over half voted Conservative. A similar, and even stronger pattern is observed in Table 5. Here, three-quarters of voters who thought that Labour was best at handling Britain's economic

5. Vote Intention and Perceived Economic Management Competence, May–June 2001 (%)

'If Britain were in economic difficulties, which party could handle the situation best . . .'

	Labour best	Conservative best	Neither/Don't Know
Conservative	3	76	22
Labour	74	9	30
Liberal Democrat	18	12	34
Other	4	3	14
	100%	100%	100%

Notes: Numbers may not sum to 100 because of rounding errors. N = 4678. Chi-squared = 2871, significant at 0.0001. Source: BES 2001 Campaign Study.

difficulties voted Labour. A similar proportion of those who thought the Conservatives were best voted Conservative.

Simple bivariate relationships, however, can be misleading if the appropriate statistical controls are not applied. Table 6 reports the results of estimating logistic regression models of the Labour, Conservative and Liberal Democrat vote in 2001. The data are taken from the British Election Study Campaign Survey, which interviewed over 4,800 respondents during the course of the four-week campaign. The dependent variable in each model is whether or not the respondent intended to vote for the party in question. The models shown in Table 6 control for a wide range of variables that previous research has shown to be associated with vote preference.[9] These include: perceptions of the party

6. Models of Labour, Conservative and Liberal Democrat Support, May–June 2001

	Labour vote/not		
	Coeff	Significance	Exp(B)
Personal economic optimism (3-point scale)	0.38	0.000	1.46
Labour best at economic management/not	1.72	0.000	5.56
Nagelkerke pseudo R2	0.62		
Percent correct	84		

	Conservative vote/not		
	Coeff	Significance	Exp(B)
Personal economic optimism (3-point scale)	0.05	0.493	1.05
Labour best at economic management/not	−2.43	0.000	0.09
Nagelkerke pseudo R2	0.69		
Percent correct	89		

	LibDem vote/not		
	Coeff	Significance	Exp(B)
Personal economic optimism (3-point scale)	−0.16	0.025	0.85
Labour best at economic management/not	0.20	0.10	1.22
Nagelkerke pseudo R2	0.36		
Percent correct	86		

Notes: Logistic Regression Models of Labour, Conservative and Liberal Democrat Support, May–June 2001; effects of Personal Economic Expectations and Perceptions of Labour's Economic Management Competence. The models estimated here apply statistical controls for the following: perceptions of the party leaders; party identification; attention to politics; evaluations and salience of the government's performance on the NHS, education, taxes and crime; attitude towards the EU and the single currency; evaluation of the government's handling of the foot and mouth crisis; class, gender, home ownership, region; tactical voter/ not. Full results available from the authors on request. Source: British Election Study, 2001.

leaders; party identification; attention to politics; evaluations and salience of the government's performance on the NHS, education, taxes and crime; attitude towards the EU and the single currency; evaluation of the government's handling of the foot and mouth disease crisis; class, gender, education and region.

The results in Table 6 strongly confirm the notion that, net of all other measured effects, economic perceptions exerted powerful effects on voters' electoral choices in the 2001 election. The terms relating to perceptions of Labour's economic management competence are highly significant in both the Labour and Conservative equations. The Exp(B) figure of 5.56 in the Labour equation, for example, indicates that, net of all other effects, the 'average' respondent who believed that Labour was best at handling the economy was over five times more likely to vote Labour than a respondent who was identical in all other respects, except s/he believed that Labour was not best in this regard. Similarly, personal expectations show a positive and highly significant effect on Labour voting. The Exp(b) of 1.46 indicates, for example, that the 'average' respondent who was also financially optimistic was almost one-and-a-half times more likely to vote Labour than equivalent respondents who believed that their economic situation was likely to 'stay the same'. Although the personal expectations term in the Conservative equation is non-significant, it is highly-significant and negatively signed in the Liberal Democrat equation. This result suggest that while it was Labour that benefited from rising financial optimism in the run-up to the election, it was the Liberal Democrats, rather than the Conservatives, who benefited most from the residual economic pessimism that persisted among some voters.

Conclusion

Much of the discourse surrounding the 2001 general election focused on the images of the major party leaders and on Labour's performance in the provision of public services — particularly in health and education. As viewed from Millbank, one important danger for New Labour was that many voters might forget its fiscal prudence and competent stewardship of the economy. With inflation and unemployment both low and apparently unlikely to rise significantly in the medium-term, voters might cease to prioritise macroeconomic performance in their voting calculations. Economic success, in short, might fail to elicit an appropriate electoral reward for the government.

Labour's 'objective' macroeconomic achievements between 1997 and 2001 were perhaps not quite as remarkable as many commentators appear to have assumed. Indeed, comparison with the second Major administration suggests that Labour's economic performance, though undoubtedly competent, was no more impressive than that of its predecessor. Where Labour scored was in terms of *prior expectations* about its performance. Voters in 1997 certainly believed that Labour better able to manage the economy than (what were perceived to be) the divided and sleaze-ridden Tories. But, given the record of failure of previous Labour administrations, they remained suspicious of New Labour's ability to deliver on its promises of sound economic management.

The fact that New Labour's economic record was objectively no better than the Tories had been between 1992 and 1997 was not as important as the fact that New Labour did not make any dramatic mistakes. There was no currency crisis; no flight of capital; no balance of payments crisis; no recession; no failure to control either public spending or inflation. In these circumstances, modest objective performance was sufficient to secure Labour's continuing reputation for macroeconomic management competence. That continuing reputation in turn made it possible for Labour to benefit electorally from the rising tide of economic optimism that the Chancellor was able to engineer in the run-up to the 2001 general election. The irony was that this was exactly the approach that successive Conservative chancellors had successfully deployed between 1979 and 1997. The objective economy appeared to have almost no effect on New Labour's victory in 2001. But the subjective economy — the calculations about economic competence and about the economic future that voters make inside their heads — continued to exert a very powerful influence on voters' electoral preferences.

David Sanders, Harold Clarke, Marianne Stewart and Paul Whiteley

1   See, for example, M. Lewis-Beck, *Economics and Elections: The Major Western Democracies*, University of Michigan Press, 1988; C. Anderson, *Blaming the Government: Citizens and the Economy in Five European Democracies*, M.E. Sharpe, 1995.

2   D. Sanders, 'Government Popularity and the Next General Election', 62 *Political Quarterly*, 1991, 235–61; D. Sanders, 'Economic Performance, Management Competence and the Outcome of the Next General Election', 44 *Political Studies*, 1996, 203–31.

3   D. Sanders, 'Conservative Incompetence, Labour Responsibility and the Feel-Good Factor: Why the Economy Failed to Save the Conservatives in 1997', 18 *Electoral Studies*, 1999, 251–70.

4   H. Clarke, W. Mishler and P. Whiteley, 'Recapturing the Falklands: Models of Conservative Popularity, 1979–83', 20 *British Journal of Political Science*, 1990, 63–82; H. Clarke, M. Stewart and P. Whiteley, 'Tory Trends: Party Identification and the Dynamics of Conservative Support Since 1992', 27 *British Journal of Political Science*, 1997, 299–319; D. Sanders, H. Ward and D. Marsh, 'Government Popularity and the Falklands War', 17 *British Journal of Political Science*, 1987, 281–313; D. Sanders, 'The Real Economy and the Perceived Economy in Popularity Functions: How Much Do Voters Need to Know? A Study of British Data, 1974–97', 19 *Electoral Studies*, 2000, 275–94.

5   D. Sanders, 'Government Popularity and the Next General Election', 62 *Political Quarterly*, 1991, 235–61.

6   D. Sanders, 'Conservative Incompetence', op. cit.

7   P. Nannestad and M. Paldam, 'The VP-Function: A Survey of the Literature on Vote and Popularity Functions after 25 Years', 79 *Public Choice*, 1994, 213–45; P. Nannestad and M. Paldam, 'Its the Government's Fault! A Cross-Section Study of Economic Voting in Denmark, 1990–93', 28 *European Journal of Political Research*, 1995, 33–62; P. Nannestad and M. Paldam, 'Into Pandora's Box of Economic Evaluations: A Study of Danish Macro VP-Functions, 1986–97', 19 *Electoral Studies*, 2000, 123–40.

8 Although it is not reported here, a 'mirror-image' model of Conservative support for the 1997–2001 period produces similar results.

9 A. Heath, R. Jowell and J. Curtice, *How Britain Votes*, Pergamon, 1985; A. Heath, R. Jowell, J. Curtice et al., *Understanding Political Change*, Pergamon, 1991; A. Heath, R. Jowell and J. Curtice (eds), *Labour's Last Chance? The 1992 Election and Beyond*, Dartmouth, 1994; G. Evans and P. Norris (eds), *Critical Elections*, Sage, 1999; M. Fiorina, *Retrospective Voting in American National Elections*, Yale University Press, 1981.

JOHN CURTICE

The Electoral System: Biased to Blair?

The 2001 election result has been widely described as a second landslide Labour victory. This is hardly surprising. After all, Labour won just six seats fewer than their record tally of 419 in 1997. The party's overall majority of 167 is greater than that enjoyed by any British government between 1945 and 1997. Yet if we look at the outcome of the 2001 election in terms of votes, Labour's performance looks much less impressive. At 42.0%, the party's share of the vote in Great Britain was lower than that enjoyed by any postwar British government apart from the two administrations formed by Harold Wilson after the elections in February and October 1974. Equally, at 9.3%, Labour's lead over the Conservatives was less than that enjoyed by Clement Attlee in 1945 and by Margaret Thatcher in both 1983 and 1987. Yet none of those contests produced as large a majority for the winner as that enjoyed by Tony Blair.

But perhaps the most telling comparison is with the outcome of the 1992 general election. At 42.8%, John Major's share of the vote at that election was actually a little higher than that secured by Tony Blair in 2001. And at 7.6%, Mr Major's lead over Neil Kinnock was only just over one-and-a-half points less than Tony Blair's lead over William Hague. The Liberal Democrats' share of the vote in 1992 was only 0.5% different from their 18.8% score in 2001 too. Yet in stark contrast to Mr Blair John Major secured nothing like a landslide. Instead he obtained a majority of just 21, a figure that actually proved to be too low to withstand the impact of by-election losses and defections over the course of the 1992–97 Parliament. So Labour's second landslide victory raises significant questions about the operation of Britain's electoral system. It appears to have treated Tony Blair in an unprecedentedly favourable manner. Why was this so? And what are the implications of our findings for the debate about electoral reform in Britain? These are the two questions that this study seeks to address.

The British electoral system

Elections to the House of Commons are conducted using the single-member plurality electoral system. Under this system the United Kingdom is divided into 659 separate constituencies. Within each constituency voters are invited to place a single cross against the name of one candidate, and the winner in each constituency is simply the candidate who receives most votes. Votes cast in one constituency have no impact on who is elected in any other constituency and there is, therefore, no formal mechanism that ensures that there is a guaranteed or predictable relationship between seats won and votes cast across the country as a whole.

Despite the absence of any such formal mechanism, however, it is often argued that the single-member plurality system does exhibit two reasonably regular and predictable characteristics. First, it gives little reward to third parties.[1] Second, it gives a 'bonus' to the winning party such that it will usually have an overall majority of the seats even if it wins considerably less than 50% of the vote.[2]

These two alleged characteristics have made it possible to construct an important normative defence of Britain's electoral system.[3] By discriminating against third parties and giving the winner a bonus, it ensures that elections are a contest between two alternative governments. As a result, it is voters who determine who runs the country rather than backroom deals between politicians in post-election coalition bargaining. Meanwhile, because governments are formed by a single party and can easily lose their overall majority at a subsequent election, they are clearly accountable to the electorate for their actions. And, it is argued, these benefits — giving voters a direct say in who runs government and ensuring that governments are accountable — are much more important than ensuring 'fairness' between seats won and votes cast. But the validity of this normative defence clearly rests on just how 'reasonably regular and predictable' the two key characteristics of the single-member plurality system actually are. In fact over the last twenty years or so doubts have been expressed about whether this has proven to be the case in Britain.

First, the electoral system appeared to be less effective at keeping third parties out of the House of Commons. On average there were just ten such MPs elected in the seven contests held between 1950 and 1970. But at the four subsequent elections held between 1974 and 1983, the figure rose to 34.

Second, the electoral system appeared less likely to produce a 'winner's bonus'.[4] Curtice and Steed argued that changes in the distribution of geography of party support meant that since 1970 there had been significantly fewer seats that were marginal between Labour and the Conservatives. This had the effect of reducing the size of the winner's bonus. Thus, whereas on a number of occasions between 1950 and 1970 the electoral system had granted the winning party an overall majority even though its lead in votes over the second party was little more than two or three points, after 1970 this could no longer be relied upon to happen. Indeed in October 1974 Labour's failed to secure an overall majority in even though it enjoyed a 3.5-point lead in the popular vote.

Curtice and Steed argued these two developments indicated that the alleged key characteristics of the single-member plurality system were not in fact 'reasonably regular and predictable'. Rather both were contingent on the geography of party support. The system did not discriminate against third parties if their support was geographically concentrated (as it was, for example, in the case of the Welsh Nationalists). And it did not produce a winner's bonus if too many seats were either safely Conservative or safely Labour — as had become the case in Britain thanks to an increasing concentration of Labour's vote in northern and urban constituencies and that of the Conservatives in southern and rural seats.

But the one argument Curtice and Steed did not raise, and indeed was the subject of relatively little discussion anywhere in the literature,[5] was that the system was significantly and consistently biased in its treatment of the two main parties in any way. It might have lost some of its ability to turn small leads in votes into large leads in seats, but this was something that made it harder for both Labour and the Conservatives to win elections rather than making it more difficult for one of them rather than the other. If any such bias were to arise, it would present a severe challenge to the traditional normative defence of the single-member plurality electoral system. Whatever the size of the winner's bonus, that defence can only be valid if the winner's bonus does actually go to the party with the most votes. Equally, the two largest parties must have an equal chance of securing a safe overall majority. If in fact one of the two largest parties is treated more favourably than the other, such that it might secure more seats even when it has fewer votes, then it can no longer be claimed that the single-member plurality system ensures that it is the choices made by voters that determine who runs the government.

That the single-member plurality can produce biased outcomes is evident from what happened in two elections in the postwar era. In both 1951 and in February 1974 the party that secured most seats was not the party that won most votes. In 1951 the Conservatives won 0.8% less of the UK-wide popular vote than Labour yet emerged with an overall majority of 16. In February 1974 Labour was behind the Conservatives by a similar amount, yet emerged with four more seats than their principal opponents. True, in 1951 it could be argued that the outcome in votes was distorted by the failure of the Conservatives to fight some seats while themselves being unopposed in four seats in Northern Ireland. And at least the system did not actually give Labour an overall majority in February 1974. Even so, neither result fits easily with the traditional defence of Britain's electoral system.

In any event, we now clearly have an important question to ask about Labour's landslide majority in 2001. Is it in fact an indication that the arguments put forward by Curtice and Steed are no longer valid? Are there now more marginal seats once again, with the consequence that the electoral system is now more than capable of giving the winning party a bonus? If so, then the outcome of the 2001 election represents an endorsement of the traditional argument in favour of the existing electoral system. Or in contrast, does the result indicate that the system is significantly biased in Labour's favour? Would the Conservatives in fact not have been treated so generously if they had enjoyed a nine-point lead, much as John Major was apparently ill-served by the electoral system in 1992? If this is indeed the case then the 2001 election will have served to further undermine the case for retaining the existing electoral system.

Illustrating bias

In fact it is relatively easy to demonstrate that Labour won so many seats in 2001 because the system was biased in its favour rather than because the winner's bonus has returned to its traditional size. This demonstration is executed in Table 1 which shows what the outcome in seats would be as a result of some key swings in votes from Labour to the Conservatives. Thus, for example, in the second row of the Table we show what would happen if there were a 4.7% swing from Conservative to Labour compared with the 2001 result, which is the swing that would be required for the Conservatives to draw level with Labour in terms of votes. In calculating what this swing would mean in terms of seats we assume that the Conservative share of the vote would increase by 4.7 percentage points in each and every constituency in Great Britain, that Labour's share would fall by the same amount, while in all other respects, such as the electorate, turnout and the votes cast for the Liberal Democrats and other parties the position would be exactly as it was in 2001. Note that we make these assumptions not in order to claim that this is what would happen in the event of a 4.7% swing at the next election but rather to illustrate how the spatial distribution of party support that pertained at the 2001 election affected the two main parties' ability to win seats.

1. How the Electoral System is Biased

Swing to Con	Con lead	% Votes (GB)				Seats (UK)			
		Con	Lab	LD	Other	Con	Lab	LD	Other
0%	−9.3	32.7	42.0	18.8	6.5	166	**413**	52	28
4.7%	0.0	37.4	37.4	18.8	6.5	224	**364**	43	28
6.5%	3.7	39.2	35.5	18.8	6.5	263	**329**	39	28
8.8%	8.3	41.5	33.2	18.8	6.5	297	297	38	27
9.3%	9.3	42.0	32.7	18.8	6.5	305	290	37	27
10.4%	11.5	43.1	31.6	18.8	6.5	330	269	35	25

Notes: This Table shows the outcome in votes (in Great Britain) and in seats (across the United Kingdom as a whole) in the event that the swing specified in the first column should occur in each and every constituency, while in all other respects the outcome was the same as it was at the 2001 election. Figures in bold indicate party with an overall majority. Source: Calculated from BBC Election Results database.

If the electoral system were unbiased in its treatment of the two main parties, this exercise should produce two key results. First, when the Conservatives and Labour have the same share of the overall vote they should also have the same number of seats. And second, those two parties should require exactly the same lead in votes in order to obtain an overall majority. However, neither of those characteristics is in evidence in Table 1. For example, when the Conservatives and Labour have the same share of the vote then far from the two parties having the same number of seats, Labour still have 140 more MPs than the Conservatives. In fact Labour have to be no less than 3.7 points behind the Conservatives before they lose their overall majority and as much as 8.3 points behind before the Conservatives overtake them in seats. Moreover the Conservatives have to be no less than 11.5 points ahead of Labour before they secure an overall majority. A 9.3-point lead such as obtained by Labour in 2001 would still leave the Conservatives 25 seats short of an overall majority.

So, Labour won a landslide majority in 2001 not because the single-member plurality electoral system was working in the manner claimed for it by its advocates, that is by providing the winner with a bonus. Rather it did so because the system is now significantly biased in its favour. Indeed the bias is so strong that there now appears to be a significant chance that Britain's electoral system could produce the wrong winner. Labour could be one, two or even three points behind the Conservatives in votes yet still have an overall majority.

In fact this bias is not a new phenomenon.[6] Rather the 2001 election was the third in a row at which the electoral system has displayed a significant and indeed growing bias in Labour's favour. After the 1992 election the equivalent calculations to those in Table 1 showed that Labour would have 38 more seats than the Conservatives if the two parties were had the same share of the overall vote.[7] In 1997 that figure grew to 80 seats.[8] Now, as we have seen, it is now no less than 140.

So as well as being substantial the electoral bias displayed by the electoral system in 2001 can also not simply be dismissed as a one-off event. Rather it appears to be becoming a permanent feature of our electoral politics. Moreover, by denying John Major the substantial majority that he might reasonably have expected to win in 1992 it has already had significant political consequences. No longer is the single-member plurality electoral system simply 'unfair' in terms of the arguments put forward by the proponents of proportional representation. Rather it now appears to be 'unfair' too in terms of what the system is supposed to deliver according to its advocates.

Explaining the bias

How is it possible for the single-member plurality system to display a bias that appears to be so much at variance with the claims of its advocates? There are two main reasons why this can happen.[9] The first is that one of the two main parties concentrates its vote more in seats that are smaller in size. The second is that one party's vote is more efficiently distributed than that of the other, that is that it wins more seats by small majorities and fewer seats by big majorities than does its opponent. In other words, just as the existence of winner's bonus depends in practice on how parties' votes are distributed geographically across the map of constituencies, so also is it the case that the presence or absence of bias also depends on the spatial pattern of party support.

Under current legislation, parliamentary constituency boundaries are reviewed in Britain every eight to twelve years. In addition the boundary commissions are charged with the task of ensuring that the boundaries they create are as equal 'as is practicable'. So in theory the legislative framework ensures that there is little chance of serious electoral bias arising as a result of unequally sized constituencies. In reality, however, the legislative framework is inadequate. One reason is that throughout the postwar period it has ensured that constituencies in both Scotland and Wales have a lower electorate than do those in England. And as Wales has always been an area of Labour strength while Scotland has gradually become one, this means that Labour is nowadays the clear beneficiary of the over-representation of these two parts of the United Kingdom.

But this is far from being the only problem. When the boundary commissions set about their task, they aim to ensure that the electorates of constituencies are as equal as possible at the date when they commence their review. What they do not do is to take into account projections of future population growth. As a result their proposals are out-of-date even when they are first implemented, let alone by the time that the next review is completed. Thus the current constituency boundaries, used in both the 1997 and 2001 elections, were drawn up on the basis of 1991 electorates in England and 1992 electorates in Scotland and Wales. In other words the 2001 election was fought on the basis of constituencies that were ten years out-of-date.

Moreover, as it happens the pattern of population change in Britain has consistently been correlated with the distribution of party strength. Britain's population has persistently been growing more rapidly in suburban and rural areas than it has in the inner cities. Equally the population has also become increasingly concentrated in the southern half of England rather than in the northern half (or indeed Scotland and Wales). As Labour is generally the stronger party in Britain's inner cities and in the northern half of the country, this means that as constituency boundaries age so an increasing gap opens up between the size of the typical Labour held seat and that of its Conservative counterpart.

Thus, even by the time that the existing boundaries were first used in 1997, the average seat won by Labour at that election contained 65,387 electors while the average seat won by the Conservatives included no less than 70,626, a gap of over 5,200 voters. Meanwhile, by the time of the 2001 election that gap widened even further to nearly 6,400 as the average Conservative seat gained an extra 1,514 voters in the intervening four years while the average Labour one added only 361.[10]

But ensuring that constituency boundaries were more up-to-date would not be enough to ensure that the first source of electoral bias did not occur. For what matters for the presence or absence of electoral bias is not the average number of electors in seats won by each party but rather the average number of voters. The latter, of course, reflects not only differences in the sizes of constituencies but also in the propensity of electors to turnout and vote. If the turnout is systematically lower in seats won by one of the main parties then the electoral system will exhibit a bias in its favour. And indeed one of the striking characteristics of both the 1992 and the 1997 elections was that what was already a tendency for turnout to be somewhat lower in seats won by Labour became even more pronounced.[11] As a result the average turnout in seats won by Labour in 1997 was, at 69.7%, nearly five points lower than the average turnout in seats won by the Conservatives (74.4%).

In 2001 that gap widened yet further. The turnout in the average seat that Labour was defending fell by 12.9% to 56.8% while that in the average Conservative seat dropped by 11.1% to 63.2%. Moreover, because this gap in turnout occurred around a much lower overall level of turnout in 2001 than in previous elections, this meant it was relatively more important. One indication of the increased impact of the gap is to note that whereas in 1997 62.6% of the all the votes cast in Great Britain were cast in seats won by Labour at that election, in 2001 that figure fell to 61.2%.[12]

So we can see that the first potential source of bias, already evident to some degree at the 1997 election despite the implementation of a new set of boundaries, was even more apparent in 2001 thanks to both widening differences in constituency size and the level of turnout. But this was not all that happened. Having already profited to a significant degree from it in 1997, Labour also proceeded in 2001 to benefit even more from the second potential source of bias, that is from winning more votes where it most counted.

In 1997 the Conservatives lost most votes, and Labour gained most votes, in those seats that the Conservatives were defending against Labour, that is where it would make most difference to the outcome. The Conservatives were the victim of declining support in their middle-class 'heartlands', while Labour's performance in these seats was much enhanced by tactical switching by Liberal Democrat supporters to Labour designed to defeat the incumbent Conservative.[13]

Clearly one thing that might have happened in the 2001 election is that some of this tendency might have reversed. But for the most part there was little sign of that. Instead the key pattern was a striking difference between the swing in those seats that Labour was defending by small majorities and what happened in virtually every other kind of seat in the country. Across the country as a whole the average swing to the Conservatives recorded in the 638 seats fought by both parties in 1997 and 2001 was 1.4%. But in fact in the 57 seats that Labour won in 1997 with a majority over the Conservatives of less than 10%, on average the swing was actually to Labour — by 1.3%. Indeed, but for the fact that in some one-third of these seats the swing did follow the national trend in the Conservatives' direction, Labour would not have lost any seats to its principal opponents at all. In the event five Labour seats did switch to the Conservative column, though one of these was counterbalanced by a Labour gain. Even so, this was far smaller haul than the 13 seats that would have switched if the average national swing of 1.4% to the Conservatives had occurred in these crucial marginal constituencies.

Why did Labour do relatively well in these seats? One reason was that Labour MPs who were defending a seat for the first time, many in marginal seats, did better than their counterparts. This reflects the fact that many of them will have been able to use the four years since they were first elected to develop a reputation as good local MP and win some electoral support accordingly. Equally Labour also seems to have profited from some of the targeting of resources into its key 'battle-ground' seats (see also the contribution by Patrick Seyd in this volume). Yet neither of these patterns proved the decisive factor in explaining the swing to Labour in its most marginal seats. For Labour did better in its most marginal seats than in less marginal ones where a new Labour MP was defending for the first time or which were 'battleground' target seats. Rather, what appears to have been decisive in these most marginal seats was a squeeze on the Liberal Democrat vote.[14]

Thus, Labour's share of the vote in the 57 seats where it was most vulnerable to a Conservative challenge was up on average by 1.8%, very different from the 1.9% drop that occurred on average across the country as a whole. Meanwhile, the Liberal Democrat vote fell on average by 1.1%, in contrast to the 1.5-point average increase across the country as whole. However, the average Conservative performance in these seats (+0.5%) was only a little down on their national average figure (+0.8%). This suggests that the decisive factor that enabled Labour to hold so many seats against the national tide was that in some of Labour's marginals even more Liberal Democrat voters made a tactical switch to Labour than had already done so in 1997.[15]

At the same time that Labour was performing particularly well in marginal seats, it also lost ground most heavily in those seats where it has previously been strongest. Thus, in seats where the party started off with more than 50% of the vote in 1997, its share of the vote fell by 3.7%, nearly twice the national average. Between them the two patterns meant that Labour's vote was clearly even more efficiently spread than

2. Measures of Electoral Bias at Recent British Elections

	Mean-overall	Con % of two-party vote Mean-median	Median-overall
1992	−1.2	−0.0	−1.2
1997	−0.3	−1.3	−1.6
2001	−1.4	−1.6	−3.0

Note: Two-party vote: Votes cast for Conservative and Labour combined. Figures based on all seats in Great Britain. Northern Ireland is excluded.

it was in 1997, with fewer votes being wasted on piling up small majorities and more being expended at holding on to small ones.

So the electoral system was so heavily biased in Labour's favour in 2001 because the party benefited significantly from both potential sources of bias. One way of summarising this story is illustrated in Table 2 which contains two key statistics.[16] The first is the difference between the Conservatives' average share of the vote cast for the Conservatives and Labour only (the two-party vote) in each of the 640 constituencies they both contested and the Conservatives' share of the two-party vote across Britain as a whole. This difference reflects the impact of differences in the number of people voting in the typical Conservative and the typical Labour held constituency. A positive figure indicates a bias to the Conservatives, a negative one a bias to Labour.

The second figure in Table 2 is the difference between the Conservatives' share of the two-party vote in the median constituency and their average share in each of the 640 constituencies. This difference reflects the impact of the relative efficiency of the distribution of the two parties' votes. If this figure is negative it means that the Conservatives would win less than half the seats even if they had half the votes.

As we would anticipate from the discussion so far both statistics now indicate the existence of a similarly sized bias in Labour's favour. Indeed they appear to be more or less of equal importance, though it is the first source of bias that increased the most between 1997 and 2001. Their combined effect is indicated in the third column of Table 2, which shows the difference between the median Conservative share of the two-party vote and their overall share across the country as a whole. Comparison of this final statistic with that for all previous postwar elections reveals that never before have the two sources of bias together operated so strongly to one party's advantage.

The winner's bonus and the others

But what can we say about Curtice and Steed's original critique of the electoral system, viz. the absence of a winner's bonus and its apparent increasing failure to deny representation to third parties? So far as the latter is concerned, the electoral system once again clearly failed to live up to the expectations of its proponents. In 1997, 75 MPs were elected from parties other than the Conservatives and Labour, the highest total since 1923. In 2001 however the total rose yet further to no less than 80 or 12% of the Commons total membership.

In particular, Britain's principal third party, the Liberal Democrats managed to add a net total of six seats to the 46 that they won in 1997. But perhaps of even greater importance is the fact that a higher proportion of Liberal Democrat seats now appear to be safe. Whereas after the 1997 election nearly one in three Liberal Democrat MPs had a majority of less than 5%, now less than one in four do so. As in the case of newly elected Labour MPs, many Liberal Democrat MPs who were elected for the first time in 1997 appear to have established a personal vote over the intervening four years, thereby helping to entrench themselves in their constituency. While, as Table 1 shows, the party is still vulnerable to any revival of Conservative fortunes, reversing the rise in the number of Liberal Democrat MPs has now become more difficult.

Meanwhile, relatively little happened in 2001 to the size of the winner's bonus. As we indicated earlier the size of that bonus depends on the number of seats that are marginal between the Conservatives and Labour. After the 1997 election there were 114 such constituencies, defined as those seats where the Conservative share of the two-party vote would lie between 45% and 55% in the event of a uniform shift of votes such that the two main parties had the same share of the vote across the country as a whole.[17] This figure was higher than the low point of 80 reached in 1983, following Labour's success at recent elections in regaining ground in the southern half of Britain, but still well below the figures of 149 and above that pertained in 1970 and earlier. In 2001 the number of marginal seats remained exactly unchanged at 114.

Conclusion

The outcome of the 2001 election poses a serious challenge to the traditional arguments commonly used in defence of the use of single-member plurality elections to the House of Commons. It demonstrated that the system is capable of exhibiting significant and growing bias in favour of one of the main parties rather than the other. The result casts doubt upon the continued ability to keep third parties from securing representation in the House of Commons. Meanwhile, the winner's bonus remains much lower than it was in the immediate postwar period. The claim that the system enables voters to choose between alternative governments and then hold those governments accountable has never looked weaker.

True, there is reason to believe that some of the electoral bias that occurred in 2001 will be reversed by the time of the next election. Immediately after the election the Parliamentary Boundary Commission for Scotland embarked upon a review of parliamentary constituencies that, under the terms of the Scotland Act 1998, will end Scotland's over-representation at Westminster, at least for the time being.[18] Meanwhile, a review of constituencies in England is already well under way based on 2000 electorates. So some of the current inequalities in the size of Conservative and Labour constituencies are in the course of being removed.

But as we have seen, even if completed in time for the next election, this process will touch upon only part of the reason for the electoral bias that occurred in 2001. If turnout remains low in Labour held seats or if Labour's vote remains more efficiently distributed than that of the Conservatives, there will still be significant electoral bias at the next election, a bias that, in a closer contest than 2001, contains the potential to result in the party that comes first in votes failing to do so in terms of seats. Indeed the current pro-Labour bias has already unfairly denied the Conservatives a safe overall majority on one occasion (1992). Doubtless none of this will do anything to encourage Labour to revive its 1997 promise to hold a referendum on electoral reform. But in truth the need to re-examine the merits of the single-member plurality system has never been greater.

John Curtice

1   A. Lijphart, *Electoral Systems and Party Systems: A Study of Twenty-Seven Democracies, 1945–90*, Oxford University Press, 1994, p. 20.
2   D. Butler, 'An Examination of the Results' in H. Nicholas, *The British General Election of 1950*, Macmillan, 1951; M. Kendall and A. Stuart, 'The Law of Cubic Proportions in Election Results', *British Journal of Sociology*, 1951; R. Taggepera and M. Shugart, *Seats and Votes: The Effects and Determinants of Electoral Systems*, Yale University Press, 1989.
3   For a longer version of this argument see J. Curtice, 'The British Electoral System: Fixture without Foundation' in D. Kavanagh (ed.), *Electoral Politics*, Clarendon Press, 1992.
4   J. Curtice and M. Steed, 'Electoral Choice and the Production of Government: The Changing Operation of the Electoral System in the United Kingdom since 1955', *British Journal of Political Science*, 1982; J. Curtice and M. Steed, 'Proportionality and Exaggeration in the British Electoral System', *Electoral Studies*, 1986.
5   But see D. Butler, *The British General Election of 1951*, Macmillan, 1952; D. Butler, *The Electoral System in Britain*, Oxford University Press, 1963; G. Gudgin and P. Taylor, *Seats, Votes and the Spatial Organisation of Elections*, Pion, 1979.
6   J. Curtice and M. Steed, 'Neither Representative nor Accountable: First-Past-the-Post in Britain' (Paper presented at the Annual Workshops of the European Consortium for Political Research, 1998); D. Rossiter, R. Johnston, C. Pattie, D. Dorling, I. MacAllister and H. Tunstall, 'Changing Biases in the Operation of the UK's Electoral System, 1950–97', *British Journal of Politics and International Relations*, June 1999.
7   J. Curtice, 'The Hidden Surprise: The British Electoral System in 1992', *Parliamentary Affairs*, October 1992.
8   J. Curtice and M. Steed, 'The Results Analysed' in D. Butler and D. Kavanagh, *The British General Election of 1997*, Macmillan, 1997.
9   R. Johnston, *Political, Electoral and Spatial Systems*, Clarendon Press, 1979.
10 Yet the gap widened less between 1997 and 2001 than it did between 1992 and 1997, when the average Conservative seat gained 1,961 electors while the average Labour one lost 265. The difference is greater than can be accounted for by the shorter time period between 1997 and 2001 and may be an indication the pattern of population movement may now be generating somewhat less bias to Labour than in the past.
11 J. Curtice and M. Steed, 'The Results Analysed' in D. Butler and D. Kavanagh, *The British General Election of 1992*, Macmillan, 1992; J. Curtice and M. Steed, 1997, op. cit.

12 Strictly speaking what determines the level of bias is not the difference in the total number of votes cast in Conservative and Labour won seats, but rather the total number of votes cast for those two parties alone. And the pro-Labour impact of the changes in electorate size and turnout discussed in the main text were further exaggerated by the fact that the share of the vote cast for third party candidates fell between 1997 and 2001 from 28.3% to 25.3% in seats won by the Conservatives while it rose from 18.5% to 21.0% in seats won by Labour, a pattern that further reduced the effective size of Labour held seats.

13 J. Curtice and M. Steed, 1997, op. cit.

14 For further details see J. Curtice and M. Steed, 'The Results Analysed' in D. Butler and D. Kavanagh, *The British General Election of 2001*, Macmillan, 2001.

15 G. Evans, J. Curtice and P. Norris, 'New Labour, New Tactical Voting?' in D. Denver, J. Fisher, P. Cowley and C. Pattie (eds), *British Elections and Parties Review Volume 8*, Frank Cass, 1998.

16 C. Soper and J. Rydon, 'Under-Representation and Electoral Prediction', *Australian Journal of Politics and History*, 1958.

17 J. Curtice and M. Steed, 1997, op. cit.; J. Curtice and M. Steed, 1998, op. cit.

18 J. Curtice, 'Reinventing the Yo-Yo? A Comment on the Electoral Provisions of the Scotland Bill', *Scottish Affairs*, 23, 1998.

PHILIP COWLEY

The Commons:
Mr Blair's Lapdog?

One of the prime functions of the Commons is to determine which party will enter government, and then to maintain that administration in power. Bagehot thus described the Commons as 'the assembly that chooses our president'.[1] But once it has done this, the Commons—like most legislatures—remains important, for both substantive and symbolic reasons.

Substantively, any government has to get its legislation through both Houses of Parliament. Despite coming to power promising to modernise Parliament, the most frequent complaint from the media, Opposition politicians, and even some Labour backbenchers has been that the independent role for Parliament in scrutinising the government's legislative programme became yet further marginalised under Blair. One Conservative MP even claimed that the 1997 Parliament would go down in history as the 'abused Parliament' (HC Debs, 27 February 2001, c. 726). A common criticism was that Labour's MPs have become excessively loyal and deferential lapdogs, unquestioningly trooping through the division lobbies in support of the government. If these complaints are fair, it suggests that Westminster has lost one of its prime functions in criticising, counterbalancing and checking the excesses of executive power. But are the gripes about the deference and acquiescence of Labour MPs actually valid? And has the project to modernise Parliament made it a more effective and efficient body?

Moreover, Parliament also matters symbolically. As the debating chamber of the nation, it can be argued that *who* MPs are can be just as important as *what* they do. Even if the link between the social characteristics of legislators and their behaviour proves only partial and sporadic, those social characteristics still matter for symbolic representation. The 1997 election saw some small changes in the composition of the Commons, most obviously a sizeable increase in the number of women elected. But in line with most legislatures, the British House of Commons has long been overwhelmingly white, male, middle-aged and middle-class. So what difference will the new MPs elected in 2001 make to its composition? And what are the prospects for the new Parliament?

Modernisation

Labour's 1997 manifesto trailed three reforms of the Commons: 'modernisation' of the Commons; improvement to the process by which the Commons scrutinised European business; and modifications to Prime Minister's Questions (PMQs) to make it 'more effective'.

Changes to PMQs were announced on 9 May 1997. They involved moving from two 15-minute slots on a Tuesday and Thursday, to one half-hour slot on a Wednesday. In opposition, Blair had thought the amount of preparation required twice a week a 'ridiculous use of a Prime Minister's time'.[2] But the new half-hour sessions allowed greater persistence in questioning, something William Hague — frequently at his best in the Commons — often used to his advantage. As a result, Blair — frequently at his worst in the Commons — had some sticky moments. The change itself was disputed by many MPs, and a proposal to return to twice-weekly PMQs was contained in the Conservative manifesto in 2001. What proved most controversial was the way the reform was introduced: by diktat, rather than by consultation and agreement.

The main vehicle for the modernisation of the Commons, and the means by which procedures for dealing with European business were reformed, was the Select Committee on the Modernisation of the House, established in June 1997. The Committee produced 15 substantive reports, covering a wide range of subjects. The House accepted most of its recommendations. By November 1999 the Committee was able to note with pride that '[o]f the 56 recommendations we have made, 47 have been approved by the House and implemented either in full or in part' (HC 865, 1998–99, para. 1).

Despite this, the Committee's work was much criticised. The first strand of complaint — predominantly from Conservative MPs but also from some more traditionalist Labour MPs — was that its proposals went too far. Members reserved especial scorn for the newly-created parallel debating chamber (known as 'Westminster Hall'). There was also criticism of the practice of deferred divisions, where some less significant votes (that would normally be taken after 10pm) are deferred to the following Wednesday, where MPs fill in ballot papers rather than use the division lobbies. But Members were also critical of many, if not most, of the other changes. This was not solely because of parliamentary conservatism, but also because they believed that some of the proposals detracted from the ability of the Commons to hold the government to account, such as changing the parliamentary timetable to make the House more 'family friendly'. One Labour MP complained:

I was sent here to do a job, and it has been put to me that in many ways, the proposals will make my job easier. But I was not elected to have an easy job; I was elected to scrutinise legislation (HC Debs, 7 November 2000, c. 176).

The second criticism—predominantly from Labour MPs, especially newer Labour MPs—was the exact opposite: that the committee did not go far enough. For the most part, the Committee's recommendations were neither radical nor novel. For example, most recommendations on reforms to the legislative process contained in its first report (HC 190, 1997) had long been advocated. The proposals on ways to improve the scrutiny of European business in the seventh report (HC 791, 1998) were almost identical to those suggested by the Select Committee on European Legislation in 1996. The more imaginative ideas were the exception rather than the rule. Those who expected modernisation to bring about radical change were disappointed. Moreover, Members were often critical of the pace of reform. The Committee attempted, not always successfully, to generate cross-party consensus for its proposals. Many Labour MPs—again, especially the newer ones—felt that this gave undue power to the very MPs who would rather have seen no change at all, creating a sense of frustration with the Committee.

The third critique was that the Committee's recommendations lacked coherence. Its terms of reference were broad: 'to consider how the practices and procedures of the House should be modernised, and to make recommendations thereon'. But as Philip Norton noted, the term modernisation is all-encompassing: 'it covers everything and consequently means nothing'.[3] The Modernisation Committee was able to roam widely—and it did. Some of its proposals—such as removing the requirement to wear a hat when making a point of order during a vote—were useful and sensible. Some of the ideas—such as Westminster Hall—might have done some little good (or little harm). But few of its proposals had the potential to enhance the scrutinising role of the Commons. Of its 15 substantive reports, only two—the first (on the Legislative Process) and the seventh (on the Scrutiny of European Business)—helped enhance the power of the Commons in relation to the Executive. The others were designed for cosmetic or tidying-up purposes, or for the convenience of Members. As one observer argued, although many of the changes introduced by the committee were desirable in themselves, '[t]he basic questions of scrutiny and accountability—of power—have not been addressed'.[4] When changes were proposed to enhance the power of the Commons—such as in the report by the Liaison Committee entitled *Shifting The Balance* (HC 300, 1999–2000) that proposed enhancing select committees—the government gave them short shrift.

Marginalisation

If the Commons has been 'abused'—as the Conservative MP cited at the beginning of this chapter claimed—then this has three separate components.

First, there were Labour's reforms to the House of Lords, where the government was frequently defeated by the votes of hereditary peers. The first stage of the government's reform was the removal of precisely these troublesome hereditary peers, leading to the charge that it was emasculating the second chamber, weakening the one last significant check on its behaviour within Parliament. As John Redwood complained:

The House of Lords has the ability to inflict defeats upon the Labour Government's programme. It has the capacity for people to make speeches critical of the Labour Government's intentions . . . None of these sit comfortably with the Labour modernisers' belief that the government is always right.[5]

Second, in the House of Commons, the massed ranks of 418 Labour MPs — 'it's like that scene from Zulu', said one Conservative MP when he first saw them assembled — meant that the government enjoyed the largest majority of any single party since 1935, and Labour's largest ever. This part of the marginalisation thesis was perhaps inevitable — the power of Parliament to influence the executive varies with the size of the government's majority, and because the Blair government enjoyed an enormous majority, Parliament's influence was therefore limited. But the problem was exacerbated by two factors. There was the contrast between the Blair government and its predecessor. For much of the 1992 Parliament the Conservatives had a majority that was in single figures or non-existent. For five years before May 1997, therefore, the outcome of parliamentary votes was not always known before they took place and things were (almost) exciting. For the four years after 1997, by contrast, they were terribly predictable. And to make matters worse, there were complaints that too many Labour MPs gave unquestioning support to the government. The new methods of whipping implemented just before the 1997 election — including tighter standing orders and the use of electronic message pagers to keep MPs informed of the party line — led to criticism that Labour MPs were too slavishly following the party line. The use of phrases such as 'Daleks', 'clones', and 'spineless' was common. Especially criticised were the new women MPs elected in 1997, who were disproportionately less likely to vote against the party line.[6] Nor did such criticisms come solely from the opposition: one long-serving Labour backbencher claimed that most of his colleagues were a 'model army of programmed zombies' who displayed 'an instinctive bovine loyalty'.

Because of this large, apparently compliant, majority, and the personality of the individuals concerned, a third criticism emerged: that Labour ministers were arrogant and dismissive of Parliament. The changes to PMQs were announced to the House as a fait accompli, even before the Modernisation Committee had been established. Labour ministers were repeatedly accused of releasing information to the media before informing the Commons, provoking several complaints from the Speaker, including a formal complaint to both the Cabinet Secretary and the Leader of the House. The Prime Minister was an infrequent participant in the Commons: Blair led his government in fewer debates and participated in fewer divisions than any recent Prime Minister.[7] Even when the Prime Minister or other Ministers were in the Commons, the complaint was that Labour backbenchers colluded with the government. Three Labour MPs were suspended from the House for leaking Select Committee reports.[8] Others were accused of asking patsy questions to ministers. As one Labour backbencher, Andrew Mackinlay, complained in a now famous question:

Does the Prime Minister recall that, when we were in opposition, we used to groan at the fawning, obsequious, softball, well-rehearsed and planted questions asked by Conservative Members . . .? Will [he] distinguish his period in office by discouraging such practices — which diminish Prime Minister's Question Time — during this Parliament? (HC Debs, 3 June 1998, cc. 358–359).

Concern about the marginalisation of the Commons was thus not solely the product of Opposition politicians. Labour's former Chief Whip Derek Foster even complained that the Commons had become the Prime Minister's 'poodle'.

Yet if that is the case for the prosecution, then it does not take Perry Mason to construct the case for the defence. The first problem with most of the criticisms is not that they are necessarily wrong (because many of them are not) but that they pretend to be describing something that is somehow new. Most of the analysis was profoundly, and depressingly, a-historic. Tony Blair did attend parliament infrequently, but the fall in prime ministerial participation in the business of the Commons is nothing new, having been declining since the mid-nineteenth century. There were particularly steep drops in the 1980s and 1990s, under the Conservative premierships of Margaret Thatcher and John Major.[9] Labour backbenchers did frequently ask sycophantic questions to ministers, but it is a trick they perfected after years of watching Conservative MPs do the same.[10] Nor is the Blair government the first to prefer to announce policy outside of the House of Commons. An earlier Speaker, Bernard Weatherill frequently had to persuade a very reluctant Margaret Thatcher to come to the Commons to report on policy decisions. She used to complain that it was 'such a nuisance'.

The second problem with many of the criticisms is that they misunderstand or misrepresent what is currently taking place. This is particularly true of complaints about the reform of the House of Lords. Far from removing an independent check on the government, the Lord's reforms (perhaps unwittingly) have created a more assertive and confident body. The change is as much qualitative as quantitative (not so much more defeats, but more significant defeats), but the end result has been an upper chamber that has become increasingly prepared to take on and challenge the Commons.[11] It is also true of the criticisms of the cohesion of Labour MPs. As discussed in more detail below, the real reasons for the high levels of cohesion seen on the Labour benches are far more complicated than any instinctive bovine loyalty.

The third problem with the orthodox criticism of the Commons is that it focuses on peripheral matters, whilst overlooking the deeper, and more profound, challenges to Parliament.[12] Most other institutions have, for example, come to terms better with Britain's integration into mainland Europe than Parliament. Parliament today also faces a judiciary that is increasingly assertive, and — because of the Human Rights Act — increasingly empowered. Moreover, changes to the structure of government have undermined most of the traditional notions of accountability and created alternative centres of power, such as the development of agencies and regulatory authorities and devolution. Changes in the mass media have meant that increasingly little attention is paid to Parliament. To cap it all, globalisation, and rise of anti-politics (a la Seattle), has challenged both what Parliament could, and should, be doing. In short, Parliament is being 'squeezed out of the political debate'. Some of these problems may have been exacerbated by the actions or inaction of the Blair government, but most existed long before 1997. They are shifts in the tectonic plates of political life, and they have little to do with, and are more important than, whether Tony Blair turns up once or twice-a-week to answer questions.

Parliamentary voting

There was a delicious historical irony in the complaints that the Parliamentary Labour Party (PLP) was too supportive of the government. Their record in the past was one of a rebellious, fractious, and troublesome body, having regularly given Labour's Party managers sleepless nights. Even with his enormous majority, Blair could not afford to be blasé about the behaviour of his MPs. Governments with large majorities are not always immune to defeat — as Mrs Thatcher discovered to her cost on several occasions — and even rebellions that do not result in defeat have the potential both to influence policy and to be an embarrassment.

Yet the PLP elected in May 1997 proved the most cohesive for a generation.[13] There were fewer revolts by government MPs between 1997 and 2001 than in any full-length Parliament since the 1950s. And Blair's was the first government since that of 1966 not to be defeated at least once by its own backbenchers.[14] As we have seen, reaction to this high level of parliamentary cohesion was not entirely positive. Whereas Labour leaders always used to be criticised for not being in charge of their MPs, Blair was criticised for being too much in control. When Labour MPs used to rebel, they were labelled as divided and split; when they rebelled less frequently, they were labelled as spineless and acquiescent.

Most of the criticism was misplaced. For one thing, high levels of cohesion did not mean absolute cohesion. Many Labour MPs were

1. Large Labour Rebellions, 1997–2001

Issue	Total number of MPs to vote against their whip (excluding abstentions)
Acess to Justice Bill (1999)	21
Child Support, Pensions and Social Security Bill (2000)	41
Competition Bill (1998)	25
Criminal Justice (Mode of Trial) Bill (2000)	37
Criminal Justice (Terrorism and Conspiracy) Bill (1998)	37
Freedom of Information Bill (2000)	41
House of Lords Bill (1999)	35
Iraq (1998)	22
Social Security Bill (1997)	47
Teaching and Higher Education Bill (1998)	34
Transport Bill (2000)	65
Welfare Reform and Pensions Bill (1999)	74

Note:The table shows all rebellions in which 20 or more Labour MPs voted against their party whips. In cases where there were multiple revolts on an issue, the total number of rebels may be larger than the largest single revolt on that issue. Source: University of Hull, Centre for Legislative Studies.

prepared to vote against the government. A third of the PLP—that is, around half of all backbenchers—voted against the government at least once. Moreover, the average (mean) size of rebellions under the Blair government was the third highest of any Parliament since 1945. Labour MPs may not have rebelled very often, but when they did, they rebelled in numbers and across a wide range of issues (with the larger rebellions listed in Table 1). Although there were some remarkably sycophantic Labour backbenchers (as there had previously been some remarkably sycophantic Conservative backbenchers), these MPs tended to attract disproportionate media coverage thus masking the three real reasons for the low levels of cohesion.

First, there was a high level of self-discipline by Labour MPs. The legacy of 18 years in opposition created a widespread desire to avoid being seen as divided, almost at any cost. As one MP said: 'If it's a choice between being seen as clones or being seen as disunited . . . then I'd choose the clones any day.' This applied right across the political spectrum: the Campaign Group, the one organised left-wing grouping in the PLP, took a self-denying ordinance that they would only rebel if they believed the public would understand the reasons for any revolt.

Many Labour MPs were also keen to stress that they were prepared to rebel against the government but that they rarely felt the need to, because they usually agreed with the government's policies. In part, this was because of a notable rightward shift in the attitudes of the PLP, especially the newer, younger, MPs.[15] But even on the left there was a reasonable level of satisfaction with the government's actions. As one member of the Campaign Group said: the government was 'doing most of the things that we want it to do. It might not be doing them quite at the speed some of us want, but lots of good things are happening nonetheless'.

The third reason—and the one most often overlooked—is that,

despite its reputation as autocratic, the government was usually willing to negotiate with its backbench critics. Even some of those who rebelled argued that the government listened to their concerns as much as might be expected, particularly after the scale of the lone-parent revolt in December 1997 made the government realise that coercion alone would not suffice in preventing rebellions. Where genuine consultation did not take place, or where the government adopted a macho stance—as with lone-parent benefit or disability benefit—rebellions were noticeable, but where it adopted a more consultative approach, being prepared to sugar the legislative pill, rebellions were muted or non-existent. A good example came in the second session of the Parliament, with the government's plans for dealing with asylum seekers. Some 61 Labour MPs signed an Early Day Motion opposing the proposals, and *The Times* (10 June 1999) claimed that the government faced potential defeat. Yet after concessions granted by Jack Straw, the Home Secretary, just seven Labour MPs voted against the bill.[16]

Seen in this light, the lack of rebellions is rather more positive. Rather than being a Bad Thing—caused by MPs who are too scared to defy their leaders—it is a Good Thing, the result of agreement and consultation as much as of coercion. When the government was not able to placate its critics, there were sizeable rebellions. For sheep—one of the most common phrases used to describe Labour MPs—they could bark loudly when provoked.

More old faces than new

The 'abused Parliament' (if that is what it was) was one of compositional change. It is being followed by a Parliament of compositional continuity. The electorate's rejection of the Conservatives in May 1997 led to the largest turnover in the composition of the Commons since 1945. The scale of the victory was such that when Nick Brown, then Labour's Chief Whip, first addressed the new PLP he began by saying: 'Normally I would ask "How are you?" But this time, I should ask, "Who are you?" '.[17] By contrast, the election of 2001 saw 560 sitting MPs re-elected. Seventy-eight MPs retired and just 21 went down to defeat. Eighty-five percent of the House was therefore exactly the same after the election as it had been before—the lowest turnover at the end of any full-length Parliament since 1945.[18]

The retirements from the Commons prior to the 2001 election included the usual combination of familiar faces and obscure backbenchers. The former included eleven ex-Cabinet ministers—two of them Prime Ministers (Edward Heath and John Major)—as well as four ex- or current opposition party leaders (Paddy Ashdown, John Swinney, Ieuan Wyn Jones and Dafydd Wigley). The Commons is without a former Prime Minister for the first time since the early months of 1945.

Devolution was responsible for higher than usual levels of retirement from the Commons in both Scotland and Wales, as those with dual mandate (that is, elected to both Westminster and a devolved body) left to concentrate on devolved politics. There is no legal bar on dual mandate, but the five Welsh MPs with dual mandate all retired from the Commons, as did eleven Scottish MPs. The latter included five of the SNP's MPs, with the sixth, Alex Salmond, resigning his Holyrood seat instead. Also retiring from Westminster was Ken Livingstone, the first directly-elected Mayor of London. By contrast, in Northern Ireland dual mandate appears to be almost *de rigueur*: almost all the Northern Irish MPs are also Members of the Northern Ireland Legislative Assembly (MLAs).

A late rash of Labour retirements, facilitating the parachuting in of central party apparatchiks on NEC-composed short-lists, now appears to have become a feature of general elections, with those retiring frequently being given peerages. Twelve retiring Labour MPs, including many who decided late in the day, were elevated to the Lords in the pre-election honours lists, including David Clark (South Shields) and Tom Pendry (Stalybridge and Hyde). The former seat went to David Miliband, the latter to James Purnell, both from the Downing Street Policy Unit. The most high profile case, though, was one where the retiring MP did not get rewarded with a peerage (although this was rumoured simply to be because it would look too obvious): Gerry Bermingham stepped down after 18 years as the MP for St Helens South, allowing Shaun Woodward — unsuccessfully searching for a seat since his defection from the Conservatives — to win the nomination, albeit only after the local council leader had been excluded from the short-list.

The average (median) retiree had served almost twenty years in the Commons (having been first elected in 1983), although five of the retiring MPs had parliamentary careers dating back to the 1950s. Tam Dalyell (first elected in 1962) became the new Father of the House — the MP with the longest uninterrupted service. The number of MPs retiring after brief parliamentary careers was distorted somewhat by the departure of those with dual mandate, but even so there were some prematurely early departures. Of the 1997 intake, Jenny Jones and Tess Kingham both retired after just four years in the job, making scathing criticisms of the Commons as they left.

The Class of 2001 numbered 99, including seven former MPs (so-called 're-treads'), all Conservatives who had lost their seats in the first Blair landslide of 1997. Following the government's reforms to the House of Lords, Viscount (John) Thurso became the first hereditary peer elected to the Commons. The new intake also included three former MEPs. The law required amendment to allow David Cairns (a Roman Catholic priest until 1994) to enter the Commons as MP for Greenock and Inverclyde. Less problematic — at least in legal terms — were Chris Bryant, the former curate of All Saints, High Wycombe, who won Rhondda for Labour (although, as a public school-educated

2. Experience of MPs in the New Parliament, by First Election

Date of first election	%
Pre-1970	1
1970–73	3
1974–78	3
1979–82	3
1983–86	10
1987–91	13
1992–96	16
1997–2000	36
2001	14
Total (%)	100
N.	659

Source: *Dod's Parliamentary Companion.*

gay English former-Conservative standing in a heartland Labour seat, he faced other problems that it wasn't possible simply to legislate away) and Paul Goodman (a former novice monk) who held Wycombe for the Conservatives. Iris Robinson, the wife of Peter Robinson, the MP for Belfast East, won Strangford for the DUP, creating the fifth husband and wife team in the Commons.

Each election reduces the number of MPs who were active in the era of consensus politics. Perhaps more remarkably the majority of the Commons has never experienced any Parliament other than that under Blair, and as Table 2 shows, two-thirds of the Commons have under a decade's experience.

MPs might appear to be becoming younger, but this is (I'm afraid) just because you are getting older. The 2001 election brought in one MP under the age of 30 (Parmjit Dhanda, b. September 1971), but the youngest MPs in the new House are the same as in the old House: Chris Leslie, Claire Ward and David Lammy (all b. 1972). The oldest of the new entrants is the Independent, Dr Richard Taylor (b. 1934), the oldest from any of the main parties is Angela Watkinson (b. 1941), but the oldest MP of all remains Piara Khabra (b. 1924). As Table 3 shows, the vast majority of MPs fall well between these extremes: between 65% and 77% of the MPs of all three parties are aged between 40 and 60. The median age of a Labour MP rose from 48 in 1997 to

3. Age of MPs in the New Parliament, by Party

Years old	Conservative (%)	Labour (%)	LibDems (%)
Up to 39	14	10	29
40–49	40	35	27
50–59	32	41	40
60–69	13	12	4
70+	1	2	0
%	100	100	100
N.	166	412	52

Source: *Dod's Parliamentary Companion.*

50 in 2001 (while that of a Conservative fell from 50 to 49): the Commons continues to suffer from serious middle-aged spread.

The new intake contained a dozen women, including three from Northern Ireland (the first time the Province has had any women MPs since 1974). They were outnumbered by those women leaving, either through retirements (10) or defeat (4). As a result, for the first time since 1979, the total number of women in the Commons fell (see Lovenduski this volume). The general problem — as always (save for in 1997 when Labour were operating a policy of all-women short-lists) was the parties' inability or unwillingness to select women candidates in winnable seats. But because so few seats changed hands, the more specific problem in 2001 was that few women were selected for 'inheritor' seats, that is, those that the party already held where the incumbent was retiring. Of the 78 retirements, just five women were selected to replace the retiring MPs. As the party with the most women MPs — and the most MPs in general — most of the criticism about this focussed on Labour. In fact, although Labour's record was not good, it was better than either of the other two main parties. The Conservatives and the Liberal Democrats chose not a single woman in any of the seats that they held. As discussed by Saggar in this volume, the number of MPs from ethnic minorities rose again very slightly, for the fourth consecutive election. Khalid Mahmood won Birmingham, Perry Barr, Parmjit Dhanda won Gloucester, and all the incumbents held their seats, bringing the number of Black or Asian MPs to 12 (all Labour).

The controversial cases of (usually London-based) Labour candidates being parachuted into (usually Northern heartland) seats drew attention away from the extent to which many Labour candidates had local connections. It is difficult to be precise about the number of MPs with 'local' roots, not least because candidates frequently stress even the most tenuous of constituency links, in order to ingratiate themselves with both the selectorate and electorate. But even so, around half of Labour's candidates had clear local connections, and around two-thirds had prior experience in local government, frequently in the same area. For every David Miliband or James Purnell, there were three or four like Iain Luke (Dundee East), John MacDougall (Fife Central), Meg Munn (Sheffield Heeley), or Dave Wright (Telford). Successful Liberal Democrat candidates commonly had local roots and/or council experience, but Conservatives were far less likely to have either: under half the successful Conservative candidates had experience in local government, and a bare handful had community roots. Those like Andrew Rossindell, the Essex-born and bred victor in Romford, were few and far between. Whereas Labour and Liberal Democrat MPs are becoming — just like in The League of Gentlemen — local candidates for local people, as in previous general elections, Conservative candidates are still more likely to come carrying a carpet-bag.

Just as it is difficult to define 'local', so it is often problematic neatly to classify MPs' occupational backgrounds. Many had multiple jobs before entering the Commons — sometimes involving upward social mobility — and their most recent job may not always be the one that best defines their background. How, for example, does one classify Rob Marris, the new Labour MP for Wolverhampton South West, who worked as a firefighter, a labourer, a trucker and a bus driver before becoming a solicitor? But the overall trends are clear. Both parliamentary parties consist largely of professionals, but very different types. The new Conservative MPs are drawn predominantly from private sector occupations, either from the professions (especially the law) or from business (often banking), topped up by a few landowners, farmers and journalists. Only one new Conservative MP has a public sector job — Angela Watkinson (Upminster), a local government officer. The remainder have made a living out of being political advisers, or are from the armed forces. Conversely, the bulk of Labour's new intake consists largely of those from teaching, the law, local government and union officials — the last category accounting for the single largest grouping amongst the new intake. Just six of the new Labour intake could broadly be classified as manual workers, but few had come straight from the tools, often having been full-time councillors or union officials long before their entry into the Commons. But, unlike the Conservatives, Labour MPs are often first-generation middle-class, the children of working-class parents.

Prospects for the new Parliament

In compositional terms, then, the 2001 Parliament is almost identical to the 1997 Parliament, and indeed reflects patterns long familiar from earlier elections. In behavioural terms, though, there is greater possibility of change.

The growing perception that Parliament is being sidelined has created increasing pressure for reform. This has, bizarrely, been strengthened by the low turnout in 2001 generating the perception that the public is disaffected with the institutions of representative democracy (as if strengthening select committees, say, will make people in Liverpool Riverside troop out to vote). The Conservative Party's 'Commission to Strengthen Parliament', chaired by Philip Norton, published its report in July 2000. And shortly after the election, the Hansard Society's 'Commission on Parliamentary Scrutiny', chaired by Tony Newton, published its final report, *The Challenge for Parliament: Making Government Accountable*. Both were well-received by commentators and practitioners. There has also been a potentially significant change in personnel. Robin Cook's predecessor as Leader of the House, Margaret Beckett, was executive-minded, and largely uninterested in parliamentary reform, except insofar as it could expedite the government's programme. Not only is Cook temperamentally more parliament-minded, he also has the chance to enjoy a political Indian summer in the post. His early actions — including his appointment of reformist Special Advisers — are at least positive signs for those who want reform.

There is also the possibility that Labour's backbenchers will prove less cohesive in the coming Parliament. As shown above, Labour MPs cohesion in the 1997 Parliament resulted not from any lack of back-bone, but from a general sense of agreement, self-discipline, and an ability to influence government behind-the-scenes. Labour MPs were willing to rebel — and rebel in numbers — when they did not agree and where they could not influence government. The largest revolts were on social security reform and initiatives that involved private finance of public services, and the second term is likely to involve plenty of both. Labour MPs began the new Parliament at a hostile PMQs on 4 July 2001 by making clear their opposition to reforms to incapacity benefit. Moreover, the second Blair government cannot rely on as much defer-ence. There were signs even in the last Parliament of self-discipline beginning to weaken, as the third session saw more revolts than the first two put together. And the early votes of the new Parliament saw more than 100 Labour MPs defy the government over the composition of two deparmental select committees. The government will therefore be forced to negotiate; otherwise the second Blair Parliament could see some sizeable backbench revolts. The people in Parliament may largely be the same, but their behaviour may well be very different.

Philip Cowley

* This article draws on research into the voting behaviour of Labour MPs funded by the Leverhulme Trust. Mark Stuart did all the hard work. All unattributed quotations are taken from interviews with MPs carried out as part of that research.

1   W. Bagehot, *The English Constitution*, [1867] Fontana, 1963, pp. 150, 157.
2   D. Draper, *Blair's 100 Days*, Faber, 1997, p. 36.
3   P. Norton, 'Parliament' in A. Seldon, *The Blair Effect*, Little Brown, 2001, p. 47. Similarly, as Richard Rose noted, the term 'shows a preference for what is new rather than what is old, and for change as against the status quo. But it does not identify what direction change should take'. See R. Rose, *The Prime Minister in a Shrinking World*, Polity Press, 2001, p. 228.
4   P. Riddell, *Parliament Under Blair*, Politico's, 2000, p. 248.
5   J. Redwood, *The Death of Britain*, Macmillan, 1999, pp. 68–9.
6   The newly-elected Labour women were half as likely to have voted against the party line as other Labour MPs. Differences remained significant even after controlling for length of parliamentary career, method of selection, electoral environment, political background, age, values and attitudes, and role perceptions. See P. Cowley 'An Uncritical Critical Mass? New Labour Women MPs in the House of Commons', unpublished paper given at the PSA Women and Politics Specialist Group Conference, February 2001.
7   A. Tyrie, *Mr Blair's Poodle*, Centre for Policy Studies, 2000, p. 31.
8   Ernie Ross (Dundee West), Don Touhig (Iswyn) and Kali Mountford (Colne Valley).
9   P. Dunleavy and G.W. Jones, 'Leaders, Politics and Institutional Change: The Decline of Prime Ministerial Accountability in the House of Commons, 1968–90', *British Journal of Political Science*, 1993.
10   One study found that little difference between the behaviour of Labour MPs in 1997 and those of Conservative MPs in 1992. See R.C.V. Nash, 'New Labour and the Marginalisation of Parliament', unpublished dissertation, University of Hull, 2000.

11 See P. Cowley and M. Stuart, 'Parliament: A Few Headaches and a Dose of Modernisation', *Parliamentary Affairs*, 2001.

12 This is, essentially, the convincing case made by Peter Riddell, op. cit.

13 This section summarises the findings of P. Cowley, *Daleks and Deviants: Parliamentary Voting Under Blair*, Politico's, forthcoming.

14 See P. Norton, 'Parliamentary Behaviour since 1945', *Talking Politics*, 1996.

15 See P. Norris 'New Labour, New Politicians? Changes in the Political Attitudes of Labour MPs, 1992–97' in A. Dobson and J. Stanyer (eds), *Contemporary Political Studies 1998*, Political Studies Association, 1998.

16 See other examples given in Cowley and Stuart, op. cit.

17 Draper, *Blair's 100 Days*, op. cit., p. 31.

18 That is, excluding 1950–51 and February–October 1974.

INDEX